A CHALLENGE
TO DEMOCRACY

A CHALLENGE TO DEMOCRACY

MILITANT CATHOLICISM
IN MODERN IRELAND

MAURICE CURTIS

The
History
Press
Ireland

First published 2010

The History Press Ireland
119 Lower Baggot Street
Dublin 2, Ireland
www.thehistorypress.ie

British Library Cataloguing in Publication Data.
A catalogue record for this book is available from the British Library.

ISBN 978 1 84588 969 2

Typesetting and origination by The History Press
Printed in Great Britain
Manufacturing managed by Jellyfish Print Solutions Ltd

CONTENTS

Acknowledgements   6

Introduction   8

I   The Diverse Roots of Militant Catholicism   11

II   Independence, Emancipation and the Search
        for Irish Identity – the Drive to Organise   42

III   Influence, Control and Censorship   78

IV   The Collapse of Capitalism –
        Hallmarking the 1937 Irish Constitution   103

V   The Economy at the Crossroads   137

VI   The Flight from Statism and the Quest for Political Power   155

VII   Reaction and Change: The State, the Family
        and the Constitution   181

        Conclusion   203

        Epilogue   214

        Endnotes   216

        Index   253

ACKNOWLEDGEMENTS

Particular thanks must go to Professor Mary Daly of the School of History at the National University of Ireland/UCD. She was instrumental in seeing this book to its conclusion. Without her guidance, advice and inspiration, and endless patience, this work would not have come to fruition. Dr David Doyle of the American History Department was a beacon of light for his strong encouragement. The School of History in UCD has over the years been of much help, stimulation and encouragement and for this I am grateful.

Professor Oliver Rafferty SJ steered me on certain issues. Professor Dermot Keogh of UCC first mooted the idea of the need for research in this area and thanks also to Dr Andrew McCarthy, also of UCC, for his suggestions to publish.

Special thanks to the former archivist of the Jesuit Archives, Fr Stephen Redmond. The Dublin Diocesan Archives gave me access to the records of so many Catholic organisations operating in Ireland. The National Archives were indispensable for details on censorship in Ireland and the relations between the Irish Government and the Catholic Truth Society of Ireland (CTSI). Other institutions were of great help, including the Central Catholic Library, the National Library of Ireland, Dublin City Libraries, RTÉ Archives, and the Irish Film Institute Archives. Thanks also to those responsible for the archives of the Society of St Vincent de Paul, the Legion of Mary, the Catholic Protection and Rescue Society of Ireland (now Cúnamh), St Joseph's Young Priests' Society, Muintir na Tíre, CTSI, the Apostolic Work Society, and the Holy Ghost Archives.

Tom Sheridan, Director of the of the Catholic Young Men's Society (CYMS), provided me with free and unfettered access to the archives of his organisation and was consequently indispensable in furthering my research.

Revd Dr Michael O'Carroll of Blackrock College was unique in his reminiscences on Archbishop John Charles MacQuaid of Dublin, on Professor Alfred

O'Rahilly, one of the leaders and foremost exponent of militant Catholicism in Ireland, and on Frank Duff, founder of the Legion of Mary.

Patrick Waldron, a son of one of the founders of An Rioghacht, was helpful with his memories on growing up against the background of the zealous study of Catholic social principles and their application to Ireland's problems in the 1930s and '40s.

Thanks also to individuals such as local historian Eamon MacThomáis, politicians from across the political divide, trade unionists, ecclesiastics, and most noteworthy, the activists in many of those voluntary organisations who provided me with memories of their times and much else.

Dublin's second-hand bookshops were indispensable in sourcing long-lost pamphlets and forgotten reports. To Eoin Campbell of XMLW, to Patricia of the Business Depot and to Maeve Convery of The History Press – many thanks!

And finally, this book is dedicated to Mercedes, Leesha and my mother, Josephine, for their infinite patience and tolerance.

INTRODUCTION

The primary purpose of this book is to examine the need, the role, the activities and the influence of Catholic lay organisations which were established or developed in Ireland during the first half of the twentieth century. The call to 'Catholic Action' by the Catholic Church, to protect and bolster its position, gave lay Catholic organisations their militancy and crusading spirit, their 'Militant Catholicism'.

The Catholic Church in Ireland had recognised the value and usefulness of lay organisations for the defence and promotion of its interests and to consolidate its social, cultural and political ambitions. The intention of the new Catholic Action movement, then, was to secure the new State for the Church and to reinforce the Catholic Irish identity.

In Ireland, the principal question facing the Catholic Church in the post-independence years was: what would Irish Catholics do with their inherited Catholicism now that they had their land and their power? In the 1920s, the Church was living in a new context that would demand imaginative adaptation.

The Catholic Church was, in fact, deeply insecure about its role in the new state, which had been borne out of violence – a violence, moreover, which had revealed how unstable and volatile its flock could be. The Civil War, with its ruthlessness and cruelty, had appalled Churchmen, and the Catholic Church's support for the new government aroused hostility from a large minority of republicans. The depth of this hostility, with its potential for anti-clericalism, shocked many in the clergy and the hierarchy. In the years after the Civil War, the bishops' pastorals were full of gloomy, doom-laden pronouncements about the inherited sinfulness of the people and the need for constant vigilance against threatening influences.

The picture of a triumphalist Catholic Church in post-independence Ireland has often been set in stone, but this triumphalism was deceptive. In a real sense, the establishment of the Irish Free State was not the beginning of Irish Catholic Nationalism; it was its apotheosis, its final act. Catholicism had served the Irish; it had helped them regain political and economic control. It was time to move on. However, the Catholic Church, while recognising new realities, still behaved as if its influence, inconveniently interrupted by the Reformation, had been re-established. To ensure that this influence would be maintained, it found an ally in the new militant crusading movement called Catholic Action.

Militant Catholicism at work through the Catholic Action movement may be seen in a pamphlet published by the Catholic Truth Society of Ireland (CTSI) in 1933, in which it advocates the 'necessary movement of lay Catholics into the front line trenches of the fight between Christianity and paganism. To be effective in this fight they must be trained, organised, and disciplined as efficiently as the forces which are arrayed against them.'

In a 1934 pamphlet, also published by the CTSI, called *The Serried Ranks of Catholic Action*, the author, again utilising military semantics, reviews the 'existing troops of Catholic Action':

> Our main army of advance will consist of the formative and constructive societies. The general staff will be the CTSI. The centre or main strength of the Catholic Action army will be the CYMS with its core of seasoned veterans. On the right, our eager new levies, the Knights of St Columbanus. On the left will flutter the banners of the Legion of Mary. Many other units will be gladdened by the spectacle of our Irish army of Catholic Action marching in serried ranks to battle and to victory.

In the newly independent Ireland then, Catholic lay organisations played a crucial role in asserting the Catholic Church's influence on both politics and society.

This is a neglected aspect of Irish social and political history. While its heyday may have been from the 1920s to the 1950s, against the backdrop of the First World War, changing social mores, the Great Depression, the Blueshirts and the rise of Fascism, the Spanish Civil War, and the fear of the spread of communism, it continued to be influential until well into the 1960s – and up until the early years of the twenty-first century. It had an influence on censorship, on social legislation, on the framing of the 1937 Constitution of Ireland and on the policies of the main political parties in Ireland, as its strident propaganda against socialism, communism, atheism, and social behaviour had an impact on public opinion. Although widely recognised, the Catholic Action movement's real influence is rarely acknowledged. It was pivotal in helping to shape and consolidate public opinion, in copper-fastening the Catholic-Irish identity, and in helping to enshrine the moral code in Irish law. Moreover, its influence can be seen in the growth of democracy and the political party system in Ireland, in the ideologies embraced by Fine Gael, Fianna Fáil and Clann na Poblachta, and consequently on governments' social and economic policies.

These were benighted times in Ireland, for the hopes, whatever they were, of the outcome for Irish independence were not achieved. Poverty persisted, emigration continued, agriculture (let alone industry) remained underdeveloped. There is much that the leaders of those days, in all parties, might be blamed for.

Indeed it is only since the retirement of the Civil-War generation, so to speak, and the advent of Seán Lemass to the leadership of his party and the country in 1959 that things began to really change for the better.

We must remember that before the Second World War the threat to the stability of Ireland from both left and right, from the communists and republicans on one hand, and those over-influenced by Action Francaise/Catholic Action and Mussolini on the other hand, threatened to tear the country apart. The 'vocationalism' of the Irish Constitution, some have thought, owes as much to the ideals of European authoritarianism such as Fascism as to the Church. There were even those, let us recall, who talked of the need to abolish political parties and suggested 'a national government'. That democracy survived here is down more to the good sense of the people than the wisdom of some of their leaders.

What, then, did the Catholic Action movement leave behind? Are the militantly Catholic organisations we see today canvassing to either protect or amend the Irish Constitution the inheritors of the ideology of Catholic Action?

I

THE DIVERSE ROOTS OF MILITANT CATHOLICISM

THE QUESTION OF CATHOLIC ORGANISATION

The need for Catholic organisation, i.e. the grouping of lay Catholics into Catholic societies, was a primary concern of the Church in Europe towards the end of the nineteenth century. The French Revolution and the Industrial Revolution had brought tremendous disruption to the life of Europe. The Catholic Church's response was to identify with the parties of order and authority. Every conceivable form of liberalism was condemned, culminating in the 1864 *Syllabus of Errors* and the 1870 doctrine of Papal Infallibility. Not only that but the Pope was landless, a prisoner in the Vatican. A few sensitive Catholics like Frederick Ozanam (founder of the Society of St Vincent de Paul in 1835), saw the need for a new approach, but were dismissed as impractical visionaries. In the 1860s and 1870s, Bishop Von Ketteler in Germany had slightly more success in his campaign to alert the Catholic Church to the gravity of the situation.[1]

Philosophers such as Marx and Nietzsche, however, did much to question settled beliefs and to create new ideas and attitudes.[2] These new secular philosophies were grounded in the cult of science and liberalism, in politics and economics, and increasingly, they became the accepted ideology. The Catholic Church replied to the changing social fabric in a rather *ad hoc* fashion – there developed teachings and attitudes which were reactions to particular sets of historical circumstances, and led to a renaissance, a realignment, and a mobilisation of Catholic forces under a new guise.[3]

The concern of the Catholic Church had reverberations in Ireland. The successful implantation of the devotional revolution coincided with the new stirrings in Irish nationalism. By the beginning of the twentieth century, ambition and grievance were major factors in drawing Irish Catholics into specifically Catholic organisations such as the Catholic Association and the Catholic Defence Society.[4] But wider Catholic Church concern at independent lay initiative saw the issue of clerical approval, both in mainland Europe and Ireland, becoming of crucial importance for the success of any campaign involving Catholic lay organisations.[5] In Ireland, Catholics had their own Irish Parliamentary Party so there was no scope for political Catholicism. Organisations developed that had a narrow focus and concentrated more on Catholic vigilance and charitable activities rather than on activities which might have a political dimension.

At the same time, and of vital significance for the future direction of Catholic organisations in Ireland, the modernist crisis reached a climax under the new Pope, Pius X (1903-1914). He was determined to 'unmask' the rot of liberalism which he saw everywhere in Catholic intellectual life[6] and consequently in Ireland, organisations sprang up which reflected this new era. The Catholic Truth Society of Ireland, the Irish Vigilance Association, and the Catholic Protection and Rescue Society of Ireland, all reflected the narrower focus that concentrated on vigilance activities on behalf of the Catholic Church.

DEVELOPMENTS IN EUROPE

By the end of the nineteenth century, in many areas of the continent, Catholics had established a network of organisations with a social purpose: co-operatives, farmers' organisations, youth movements, trade unions and friendly societies. This development had political, social and economic motivations.[7] It was also in response to Catholic workers and farmers, who were afraid of falling into the hands of socialists.

However, the new organisations were also a generous response by many Catholics to the social evils of the day. The extent and success of the movement varied also. In much of southern and eastern Europe it was weak. In the Catholic parts of Germany and Switzerland, in Austria, France and parts of Italy, it was powerful. It was also particularly strong in Belgium and the Netherlands. Taking Europe as a whole, the rise of the movement was one of the most important developments among Catholics in late nineteenth and early twentieth centuries.[8]

Intellectually, the movement was underpinned by a growing number of study circles, specialist periodicals, and congresses, which started in France and were soon imitated everywhere, including Ireland (the first CTSI Congress was held in 1903). The ideas propounded and discussed were summed up and ratified by Pope Leo XIII in his encyclical on the social question, *Rerum Novarum*, in 1891.[9] The document was a cautious encyclical, which left a wide range of social and economic policies open to Catholics. As against socialism, it asserted the right to private property. As against individualism, it asserted the State's right to intervene against bad working conditions. In place of the class warfare of the socialist, and the unrestricted competition of the individualist, it proposed an ideal of class harmony as the goal towards which Christians should aim. It provided ample opportunities for Catholic social activists to elaborate the doctrine and to apply it to particular circumstances in the various countries. For example, in Belgium and northern Italy, 'Catholic' trade unions were formed. Also in Belgium, the Boerenbond, a union of peasant farmers, became a very powerful and successful Catholic co-operative.[10] In Germany, Bishop Von Ketteler established the Volksverein to campaign for Christian reform in the face of increasing industrialisation. Apathetic German Catholics were stirred into vigorous action on a wide variety of social problems. In 1870, the German Centre Party was formed under the leadership of a prominent lay Catholic activist, Windhorst, to oppose Bismarck's Kulturkampf, and the promotion of a Catholic social programme became a central item in its policy.[11] France witnessed the development of Catholic Workingmen's Clubs, a Catholic Liberal Party, Catholic Social Weeks, and many Catholic publications devoted to the social question. In Switzerland after 1885, Fribourg became a centre for meetings of socially minded Catholics from all over Europe, known as the Union of Fribourg. From these meetings there emerged, in the 1880s, a Catholic sociology offering an alternative to the major ideologies of the day – economic liberalism and Marxian socialism. Belgium followed suit when the University of Louvain became the first university to create a Chair of Social Studies.[12]

Amongst English Catholics, it was not until 1909 and the foundation of the Catholic Social Guild at Oxford, that a definite movement started to take shape.[13] Cardinal Manning's intervention in the London dock strike of 1889 was a small step in that direction, but little had developed since. Fr Charles Plater, a prominent activist in the CSG, wrote his book *The Priest and Social Action* (1914) as a result of what he had seen on the continent, and how Catholic social principles had shown a marked influence on social legislation and public opinion.[14] He was firmly convinced that the future direction for the Catholic Church was in shaping this public opinion, since the old paths of influence were being worn away. The spread of the Catholic social movement had shown that organisations of lay Catholics could exert influence.[15]

Another factor that greatly facilitated the organisation of Catholics was the strategy of ultramontanism, i.e. national churches acknowledging Vatican authority, down to details of ecclesiastical administration. This, combined with the pastoral strategy of promoting sacramental practice in organised parishes and bringing popular devotions under clerical control, provided a religious basis for group identity. The *Rerum Novarum* was a document of the ultramontane Church. Priests, rather than the laity, were urged to take leadership of the workers' cause. Pope Leo XIII expected ordinary Catholics to participate through the developing Catholic organisations, but such organisations would be under clerical control. He regularly warned against independent lay action, but it was his successor, Pius X, who took particular action to ensure that there would be no misunderstanding on the issue.[16]

The *Rerum Novarum* had laid down the principle of social action, but did not suggest how its ends were to be achieved. Consequently, within the movement, and particularly in Italy, there developed a radical left-wing tendency that alarmed the Catholic Church, which was endeavouring to avoid political confrontation at all costs. The result of the move to separate a possible alliance of Social Catholicism from a political movement was the 1901 encyclical *Graves de Communi*, which expressed anxiety at the ambiguous attitude adopted by some organisations.[17] The encyclical rejected both Christian socialism and Christian democracy, terms newly coined by the Italian Catholic lay organisation Opera dei Congressi.[18] These terms were interpreted by the Church as dangerous because of their political and social overtones. By accident rather than design, this 'Catholic Action' (the preference of the Catholic Church for charitable action instead) came into official use as the accepted description and alternative for Christian democracy. Shortly after Pius X became Pope in 1903, he issued a decree which stated that, 'much that is useful and beneficial may be obtained when the laity and their Congresses and their action, are rightly directed and disciplined'.[19] Two years later in 1905, further clarification of the relationship between the clergy and laity was given in the landmark encyclical *Il Fermo Proposito*.[20] Although touching upon the social question, this document did not have the ideological strength of purpose or commitment of *Rerum Novarum*. Instead it laid down guidelines and criteria for the role of the laity in the organisations as recommended by Pius X's predecessor. Directed charity, rather than fighting for justice, was the new Pope's approach, and with this stance he laid down the course that lay organisations were to take for the next thirty years. The term 'Catholic Action' was now used more frequently, appearing in *Il Fermo Proposito* to refer to the many works undertaken for the welfare of the Catholic Church. There was to be no rocking the status quo of existing political structures. Any increased activity in this domain had to take place with 'respectful submission to authority',[21] both political and ecclesiastical. The encyclical may be considered the charter of Catholic Action. Pius X spoke of those 'select Catholic troops who intend to combine all their forces to fight anti-Catholic civilisation'. During his pontificate (1903-1914), lay movements were founded or gained strength. Most importantly, his pontificate indicated a radically different agenda to that of his predecessor.[22]

Pius X had an undeviating devotion to absolute ultramontanism, combined with a strong distrust of modern society.[23] The relatively open atmosphere of Leo XIII's pontificate, which had seen the encouragement of Social Catholicism engaging with the problems of modern society and seeking solutions in social policies, did not appeal to Pius X. His pontificate witnessed a definite retreat from the strategies mapped out by his predecessor. While passionately believing in an active laity as the key to the success of the Catholic Church's mission in society, he was deeply suspicious of lay activity without unquestioning obedience to clerical direction. He insisted therefore that all organisations must submit themselves to 'the advice and superior direction of ecclesiastical authority'.[24]

Encouraged by the freer atmosphere of Leo XIII's pontificate, Catholic theologians and philosophers had tried to adapt Catholic thought to a new age. But under Pius X these new Catholic intellectual trends were ruthlessly crushed. Deeply hostile to intellectualism of every kind, the Pope and his advisers detected, in every attempt at the liberalisation of Catholic theology and social thought, nothing but heresy and betrayal.[25] In 1907, Pius issued a decree, *Lamentabili*, against the modernist 'heresy', and two months later, the encyclical *Pascendi Gregis*, which gathered a variety of new ideas together under the blanket term 'modernism' and characterised these new ways of thinking as 'a compendium of all heresies'.[26] The encyclical was also characterised by extreme violence in language. 'Modernism' was seen as 'the meeting place of all heresies'.[27] It was regarded as a coherent, organised movement with the intentionally concealed purpose of overthrowing Catholic orthodoxy from the inside. *Pascendi Gregis*, together with the 1910 decree *Sacrorum*, prescribed draconian measures for removing modernism from the Church. Vigilance committees, extensive and intensive censorship, the encouragement of spying and informing that guaranteed anonymity – these were to be the new order of things. Not only that – new priests had to take an oath against modernism.[28]

The trouble lay in the undiscriminating character of the condemnation, its unfocused severity, and its reactionary nature. The encyclical was simply the opening shot in what rapidly became nothing less than a witch-hunt.[29] The Pope's denunciation, not merely of ideas but of motives, unleashed a flood of suspicion and reprisal, which soon had reverberations in Ireland, and the consequences would have far-reaching effects on the Catholic Action movement and its agenda. In Europe, liberal Catholic newspapers and periodicals were suppressed; seminary teachers and academics suspected of tolerating new ideas were disgraced and dismissed from their posts. A secret organisation designed to root out suspects, the Society of St Pius V, was encouraged by the Pope.[30] No one was safe, and distinguished bishops and theologians found their every action and word watched and reported. A new intransigence became the required mark of a 'good' Catholic. 'Real' Catholics were 'integralists', accepting everything the Pope taught, not picking and choosing. In September 1910, the general atmosphere of suspicion was institutionalised when a lengthy oath was devised to impose a straitjacket of othodoxy on suspects, and taking the oath became a routine and repeated part of the progress of every cleric's career.[31] The impact of the modernist crisis on Catholic intellectual life was catastrophic, and persisted till the latter part of the twentieth century. The Anti-Modernist Oath remained in force into the 1960s, a feature of the intellectual formation of every Catholic priest, creating a stifling ethos of unjust and suspicious orthodoxy, and discouraging all originality. Obedience, not enquiry, became the badge of Catholic thought. The canonisation of Pius X in 1950 demonstrated that he had set a pattern of papal behaviour that went on influencing his successors.

COMPARISONS BETWEEN IRELAND AND EUROPE

In Ireland, Catholicism linked itself to the political question, whether the Home Rule movement or the land struggle, but only insofar as those activities coincided or advanced the position and influence of the Church.[32] The last decades of the nineteenth century and the first of the twentieth century, saw land and education at the top of the agendas of both the Church authorities and the elected representatives. In Europe, however, the Catholic Church was rapidly losing its influence, particularly because of the political and economic revolutions. In Ireland, on the other hand, Catholicism and political initiative were inextricably linked, and mutually inter-dependent. In Europe, Catholicism suffered at the hands of the French Revolution and the rise of the new, liberal, Enlightenment ethos. The previously dominant Catholic vision of the world was rejected by the new political and economic elite. Social Catholicism was therefore seen as the Church's hope in the facing of competing ideologies. Irish Catholicism had never achieved the luxury of being influential politically and then having that omnipotence threatened, as was the case in Europe. While European Catholicism was losing ground, in Ireland the reverse was happening. Catholicism was nurturing politics to develop, enhance and protect its growing stature and vital interests. Not only that, but the British government, unlike the French, German and Italian, was not intent on restricting the Church in managing its own affairs.[33]

The commitment of the Irish Catholic Church to politics generally differed from Europe. There was no 'Catholic' political party, and no 'Catholic' trade unions developed. There were also differences in the extent of the involvement of the Catholic clergy. They were involved to an exceptional degree in Ireland – mainly because they were better educated than most of the Irish people. Daniel O'Connell built his Catholic Association thanks to their organising skills.[34] And since most of the priests came from farming families, they had little interest or understanding of the plight of city dwellers suffering from the excesses of industrial exploitation. They had shown particular suspicion at the very rudimentary attempts at the unionisation of the rural workers, and this did not augur too well for a dynamic Catholic social movement in Ireland.[35]

Writing in 1930, Fr Edward Cahill SJ, one of the leading figures in the Catholic Action movement, argued that a Catholic social movement along European lines was practically impossible in Ireland because of the 'land struggle, the fight for educational freedom, the national contest, the work of the church building and religious organisation' which had 'engaged the energies of the priests and people during the nineteenth and first quarter of the twentieth centuries'.[36] Germany, France, Belgium and Holland, where the social movement was strongest, did not have the issue of national independence. Similarly, they had no such social problem as the land issue, which was not finally settled until the Wyndham Land Act of 1903. They had no need to build such basic institutions as churches, schools and charitable institutions.

Despite the efforts of individual priests and religious, the social record of Irish Catholicism was unremarkable.[37] In fact, the Jesuit priest Fr Lambert McKenna was to remark in 1913 that Ireland lagged behind the continent by between thirty and forty years in the area of Catholic social work.[38] Sir Horace Plunkett, the pioneer of the rural co-operative in Ireland at the turn of the century, noted that the record of the Irish clergy compared unfavourably with that of their counterparts in Europe.[39] He did receive some support from the Irish clergy with his movement but it was of minor significance.

Discontent at the ambiguous attitude and the apparent aloofness of the clergy was reflected in the anti-clerical writing that began to appear at the turn of the century. M.S.F. McCarthy in his book *Five Years in Ireland, 1895-1900*,[40] criticised what he saw as the 'baneful influence of the Catholic Church in Ireland in temporal affairs', which he felt made the 'Catholic Irish layman despised by every man who considers their position'. He concluded that it was the power they exercise over the mass of poverty, ignorance and suffering, which gives the priests the position of importance which they claim, and which so many persons concede to them.[41] Patrick McGill in *Children of the Dead End* (1914), was equally critical,[42] as was Gerald O'Donovan, author of *Father Ralph* (1913).[43] These works were a bitter social comment and highlighted the fact that although the land question was being solved through the various Acts, it was the tenant farmers who benefited, not the real poor. The huge tide of emigration was criticised by the Catholic Church but only in terms of the effects on the faith and morals of the emigrants, as is indicated in the booklets of the Catholic Truth Society of Ireland on the subject.

Horace Plunkett, in his *Ireland in the New Century* (1904), indicted the economic influence of the Catholic religion as interpreted by the Irish clergy as being 'non-economic if not actually anti-economic'.[44] Plunkett was active in the growing co-operative movement of the late 1890s and the early twentieth century. In 1907, we obtain an outsider's view of Ireland with L. Paul-Dubois's *Contemporary Ireland*.[45] He was a social analyst who observed that, 'no one can visit Ireland without being impressed by the intensity of Catholic belief there'.[46]

One of the prominent socially minded priests was the Jesuit Fr Finlay, who was vice-president of the Irish Agricultural Organisation Society. By 1913 this society had a membership of 985 affiliated organisations. To a considerable degree, the rural revival movement was inspired by the advanced state of agricultural co-operation in Denmark – Ireland's principal competitor in the British market. Organisational models were derived from other countries also, notably France and Germany.[47] Fr Peter Coffey was another like-minded priest with a strong social conscience. Of Meath farming stock, he was appointed Professor of Philosophy in Maynooth in 1902. Four years later, in 1906, the CTSI published his pamphlet *The Church and the Working Classes*, in which he pulled few punches.[48] For Coffey, the right to strike was necessary if provoked by a 'cruel and heartless employer'. He expressed some approval for 'Christian Socialism', which had already been condemned by the Church, and this aroused opposition against him in influential clerical circles. He was discouraged from writing on social and related issues. The crucial factor here was that social modernism was as equally suspect at this time as was doctrinal modernism.

Any hint of democracy or any mention of equal participation in the government of the Church was opposed to Catholic social teaching. Central to this teaching was the emphasis on obedience to external authority, whether political or ecclesiastical, and in a framework of relations of subordination.[49] The ideal of social equality that Irish social activists aspired to was seen by the Irish Catholic Church as a chimera, and a socialist one at that. Workers must be taught to know their place. To oppose this basic tenet was to ignore the Natural Law as interpreted by the Church, and hence to undermine the social hierarchy, doctrine of private property, and any semblance of social order. The notion of a trade union prepared to strike, even as a last resort, was morally intolerable and a question mark therefore hung over the motives of Irish trade unionists, who had been becoming better organised since the 1890s.

Catholic social teaching, with its inherent inertia and impotence, explains the frustration of a priest like Fr Gerald O'Donovan, who was particularly active in the west of Ireland. Other social activists included the prominent Sinn Féin supporter Fr Michael O'Flanagan, who always remained on the fringes of clerical circles, such were the suspicions levelled against him.[50] Fr Lambert McKenna is also worth mentioning, as he made some effort to grapple with the appalling social conditions in Dublin.[51] But for the most part, under the new Pope, Pius X, clerics were becoming more conservative (in contrast to earlier activities in the land campaign). This is visible in the increasingly integralist climate that was permeating Catholic social teaching. Clergy who had become involved in social reform were inevitably ostracised. The official response was evident in some of the speeches given at the Maynooth Union meetings, in which the same moral principles were preached to both employers and employees.[52] The tendency was to fight shy of positive and concrete suggestions and solutions.

CATHOLIC CHURCH CONCERNS AND THE FULFILLMENT OF THE
IRISH–IRELAND IDEAL

In mid-1902, the Dominican publication the *Irish Rosary*, in an article, 'The Question of Catholic Organisation', voiced the rumblings of discontent that it noticed amongst Catholic professional and business groups.[53] While the ambitions of educated Catholics in the professions and the civil service grew, and were encouraged by a university-educated Catholic elite,[54] so too did their belief that opportunities at the highest levels in professional and social life were closed to them.[55] Crucially, this cocktail of ambition and grievance was soon to pass beyond rhetoric and into action. David Patrick Moran, the editor of the new periodical *The Leader* (1900), had argued vehemently that, 'it was about time that organisation was met with organisation' if 'organised foreignism' was to be defeated.[56]

The contention that the well-to-do Catholic was the exception rather than the rule was argued by Moran in July 1901.[57] He highlighted anti-Catholic discrimination by Protestant employers.[58] According to Patrick Maume, Moran's central project 'was the synergic linking of cultural revivalism, Catholic pride and an enterprise mentality'.[59] He was particularly influential in setting in motion a series of Catholic defence associations in the first decade of the twentieth century. David Miller interpreted the United Irish League's revival and the Church's readjustment to the evolving political situation as of long-term significance.[60] Not only were the clergy actively involved in promoting the UIL, but simultaneously they were controlling the expansion of two new Gaelic movements, the Gaelic Athletic Association and Conradh na Gaelige (Gaelic League), founded in 1884 and 1893 respectively. These two organisations give an indication of the growing mood for a return to and an appreciation of things Irish – in other words, a Celtic revival. D.P. Moran was to be a very significant figure and catalyst in this new movement.

He expounded his Irish–Ireland philosophy for the first time in the *New Ireland Review* in 1898, when he proposed that de-anglicisation was the only way forward for Ireland.[61] His argument 'The Battle of Two Civilisations' appeared in the same publication in 1900. For Moran, anglicisation had to be fought incessantly. Among the symptoms of 'West Britonism' that he attacked in the columns of *The Leader* were 'gutter' literature and imported amusements offered in Dublin theatres and music-halls.[62] Such concerns coincided with the preoccupations of the clergy. Moran saw as synonymous the Gaelic and Catholic identities of Ireland. He believed that Ireland was about to blossom with the demise of the landlords and that a new Ireland would develop on Gaelic and Catholic lines. The Catholic University Graduates Association took to heart this outlook, and became prominent contributors to *The Leader*.[63] Its outspoken Catholicism quickly attracted a clerical audience who, argued Paul-Dubois, partly saw the new revival as 'a moral antiseptic'.[64] Daniel Corkery, writing in the periodical in May 1906 similarly argued that 'Catholicism is an integral part of Irish Nationality'.[65]

The strength and vehemence of Moran's vitriol can also be understood when one considers that according to the 1901 Census figures more than three quarters of the population of the country were Catholic.[66] Observers from every point of view were struck by the piety of the people, including Paul-Dubois and Plunkett.[67] The Catholic Church had a unique grip in that it largely controlled education and social welfare. At the same time, since the 1840s, the Catholic Church had boosted the increasingly conscious and growing Catholic middle classes.

It was amongst these middle classes that the first specifically 'Catholic' organisation had been established in 1881 – the Catholic Commercial Club – for the express purpose of advancing the interests of Catholic businessmen.[68] Supported by Archbishop Walsh of Dublin, who opened their new headquarters in Dublin's Sackville (now O'Connell) Street in 1890, the club flourished. Walsh hoped it would 'protect Catholic interests in Dublin'. Members included T.D. Harrington and Thomas Sexton of the Irish Parliamentary Party, H.J. Gill of the famous publishing house, John Power of the distillery, and Edward Dwyer, MP and owner of the *Freeman's Journal*. The establishment of this association signalled a drive for the organisation of well-placed Catholics in business, cultural and civic life. Moreover, the decision to flaunt the catholicity of the organisation and its members highlights the growing tendency for influential Catholics to lead their fields in the name of their religion.[69]

The establishment of a number of Catholic school unions heralded an era of expansion of Catholic societies.[70] In 1889, Blackrock College was the first of the elite Catholic schools to establish a past-pupils' and teachers' society. The Clongowes Union followed in 1897. Castleknock College established its union in 1902 and Belvedere College followed four years later. Similar efforts were made to establish unions in Christian Brothers' schools in 1901. The PPUs helped pave the way for the further organisation of educated and influential Catholic men. The *Castleknock Chronicle* typically argued in 1903 that 'cohesion among Catholics is a grave need in the present time'.[71]

The Catholic Truth Society of Ireland, established in 1899, to some extent owed its pedigree to the influences of the Anglo-Irish literary renaissance.[72] Already, in 1892, Douglas Hyde had argued for the necessity for de-anglicising Ireland.[73] His main argument was that books and periodicals should be abandoned as people's reading, particularly if that reading was coming from England. He strongly believed in the need for protection against English influences. Without this protection Ireland would become a nation of imitators, he argued.[74] The most important of D.P. Moran's essays was called '*The Battle of Two Civilisations*'.[75] In it, he argued that 'you cannot effectively reach the proper public through the existing newspapers'.[76] He also referred to the 'thousands filing into the circulating libraries and the penny novelette shops for reams of twaddle about Guy and Belinda … and literary clubs discussing the ideas of English literary men'.[77]

In this climate, the Catholic Church was not slow to respond. Bishops' pastorals in the late 1890s contained many warnings against 'pernicious' reading. At this time technological advances had made it possible to print more cheaply than ever before. The flood of inexpensive literature into Ireland was led by the first halfpenny newspaper, the *Daily Mail*, in 1896. This was followed by the 'penny dreadfuls' – cheap novelettes. English weeklies and dailies now found a much wider circulation.

At the 1898 Maynooth Union meeting, Fr Michael O'Hickey, Professor of Irish at St Patrick's College, Maynooth, prominent Gaelic League activist and its vice-president until 1903, sounded the alarm bells in his paper 'The Old Order Changeth'. He saw the rapid spread of the reading of periodical literature of various kinds as 'one of the most noteworthy and remarkable developments of our time'.[78] One class of literature that worried O'Hickey was the 'gutter literature', the chief fruits of which were, he said, 'noxious dreams, a plethora of air-built castles, and hysteria in abundance'. His solution was, 'to arrest the circulation of objectionable periodicals on the one hand; and on the other hand, to apply some antidote for the mischief they are calculated to cause'.[79]

Not long afterwards O'Hickey gave a public lecture on the theme of 'The True National Idea', which was later published as the first of the Gaelic League pamphlets.[80] For him, 'an iron had entered the Irish people's souls, and they had become almost completely anglicised. The process of national decadence goes merrily on, and the moral tone of the nation is being lowered, national distinctiveness is passing away. I for one feel strongly, fiercely, savagely...'

Not only that, but as far as he was concerned, the writers of the imported publications were ignorant of the 'most elementary principles of Christian dogma, of Christian philosophy, of Christian ethics, of Christian economics'. The problem then was not just the lack of a Catholic University, although he recognised that it played a part, but that there was no Catholic laity competent and ready to fight on the platform or in the press for the recognition of Catholic principles in public, social and intellectual life. He had, however, met such people at the Catholic Truth Society and Catholic Young Men's Society Congresses in England and amongst other Catholic organisations elsewhere. According to O'Hickey, a similar need was felt in Ireland. Within a year of giving these two lectures, an organisation was founded which aspired to implement his two hopes for an organised Catholic laity and a movement to fight against 'gutter literature'.

Other countries in Europe in the nineteenth century, especially in Germany, had provided cheap and popular Catholic reading. Even in Ireland such attempts had not been altogether lacking, as there were societies engaged in such work earlier in the century, including The Catholic Society of Ireland for Promoting the Dissemination of Moral and Religious Books among the Humbler Classes of Catholics, which was responsible for some very solid publications in the 1840s when proselytism was a major worry for the clergy. Towards the end of the century the publications of the English Catholic Truth Society (CTS) were in circulation in Ireland. In addition, in the closing years of the century, a diocesan CTS had been formed by Bishop Henry of Down and Connor. In Limerick, Fr Edward O'Dwyer (later bishop) established the Catholic Literature Crusade, as, according to a colleague, 'he was most anxious about pure literature'.[81]

In 1899, exactly one year after Fr O'Hickey's speech, another Limerick priest, Fr Michael O'Riordan, addressed the Maynooth Union.[82] His paper, 'A Catholic Truth Society for Ireland', argued that despite doing excellent work, the English CTS did not meet special Irish needs. O'Riordan believed that Ireland's surest defence against what he saw as 'current paganism', lay in a livelier realisation of her Catholic heritage. Irish biography, history, religious traditions, presented in a popular, imaginative way, were needed in addition to the more general publications of the CTS.

During the animated discussions that followed O'Riordan's paper, definite proposals were made for establishing the new society. Bishop Sheehan of Waterford urged that it would not be just another branch of the English CTS, but should be distinctively Irish. Undoubtedly, O'Hickey had an influence on the proceedings because even before O'Riordan's speech, plans were being made for some kind of organisation among Maynooth students. On the evening of O'Riordan's lecture, a provisional committee met to establish the society. On 12 October 1899, the specifically 'Irish' Catholic Truth Society of Ireland was established. The new organisation aimed to promote 'cheap' Catholic literature by publishing penny pamphlets. This was regarded as being one of the solutions to the problem of imported English literature.[83] On 6 June 1900, the first twenty-five titles were put on sale at the new depot in Lower Abbey Street, Dublin. By 22 September, 250,000 copies had been distributed. A notice on 24 November in *The Irish Catholic* newspaper (established 1888) read, 'the first exports have been decided upon'.[84] On 15 June 1901, there was a reference to the establishment of 800 branches attached to parishes throughout the country, which were responsible for the distribution of pamphlets. By this date sales had risen to 650,000.[85] By 1903, 164 new titles had been issued. The bestsellers over the following years were the cheap devotional booklets, such as Fr O'Loughlin's *Penny Prayer Book*, which had sold 1.4 million copies by 1914. Other topics included Catholic doctrine, fiction and literature, history and biography, philosophy and sociology, economics, education, culture and art. The first booklet in the Society's series was one by Bishop Edward O'Dwyer of Limerick, covering the vital issue of *A University for Catholics in Relation to the Material Interests of Ireland*.[86] In the area of fiction, several hundred titles were published, and included, particularly in the early years, stories aimed at fostering temperance or at discouraging emigration. These were major social issues and concerns in Ireland at the turn of the century. Titles on the latter issue included: *The Irish Emigrant's Orphans* (1901); *The Evils of Emigration* (1902); *Life in New York, an Irish Emigrant's Experience* (1905).[87] All of these titles emphasised the dangers facing emigrants.[88]

The early annual conferences of the CTSI also reflected the current concerns of the Irish Catholic Church. These conferences were inspired by the effectiveness of the Catholic Congresses (particularly in Germany) in developing Catholic opinion. The Katholikentag began around 1848, and revolved around about half a dozen papers. Revd Professor Walter MacDonald of Maynooth saw the CTSI and the conferences as opportunities for lay Catholics to make themselves heard, although, according to his estimation:

...it must be confessed that, either because they are apathetic or because they are
not invited to come forward, the CTSI is also in some danger of being worked in
the interests of the clergy; such interest, that is, as is not always identical with that
of religion and the Church.[89]

His honest and prophetic tone did not endear him to his fellow clergymen.

The first conference was held in Dublin's Mansion House in October, 1903.
The Congresses of the European Catholic Social Movement not only inspired
the organisation of the conferences, but the speakers repeatedly referred to the
happenings on the continent. John Horgan, the author of the CTSI publication *Great Catholic Laymen* (1905), in his address to the 1906 meeting, spoke
of his positive impressions of the work of the Catholic laity in Germany,
America, Belgium and Italy.[90] He called for a network of Catholic lay organisations throughout the country to advance the Society's work. Every conference
expressed sentiments similar to Horgan's, calling for a 'trooping of the Catholic
colours as in other countries'. Fr O'Riordan published a book in 1906 called
Catholicity and Progress in Ireland,[91] which challenged Horace Plunkett's ideas
as expressed in the latter's book *Ireland in the New Century* (1904), in which
Plunkett seemed to imply that the Catholic Church was in some way responsible for the backwardness of Irish farming. O'Riordan argued that the Irish
clergy were prominent in many projects of a social nature and had played
an important part in social developments, such as the rural co-operatives.[92]
O'Riordan was applauded at the conferences for his work. Another conference speaker bemoaned that the Irish people were still hewers of wood and
drawers of water, three quarters of a century after O'Connell had marshalled
the Catholics of Ireland. The speaker called on his listeners to do 'what the
Germans did in the days of the Kulturkampf', and he argued that the organisation of the German Catholics in the Centre Party and in the Volksverein
'was what Ireland needed'. He hoped that 'Catholic organisation' would then
become the controlling force in social, political and civil activity.[93]

This mood was widespread among the panel of lecturers at the CTSI conferences, which were becoming less heavily clerical, as the number of lay activists
grew. Many of these speakers were drawn from the Catholic, and later, the
National University. The Society was gradually being seen as a sounding board
and as a directive force for Catholic thought and action in Ireland.

Pope Pius X's encyclicals of 1903 and 1905 on Catholic Action doubtlessly
gave an added stimulus to the forward movement for a more organised Catholic
laity in Ireland. It was no coincidence that in 1905 the CTSI published John
Horgan's book on *Great Catholic Laymen*. Horgan included among his subjects Daniel O'Connell, Windthorst (the German 'Liberator'), and Frederick
Ozanam, the founder of the Society of St Vincent de Paul.[94]

In Dublin, the new Catholic magazine *The Irish Rosary* had taken up *The
Leader*'s themes and began to promote through its pages the idea of exclusive

dealings by Catholics in retaliation for alleged discrimination.[95] Compared to *The Leader*, *The Irish Rosary* was aimed at a far wider readership, both lay and clerical. It had been established in 1896 and this publication first suggested the idea of a national Catholic Association.[96] Bishop Henry of Down and Connor, had already established the Belfast Catholic Association in 1896, representing 70,000 Belfast Catholics, to petition Parliament for adequate municipal representation.[97]

In November 1902, a movement was inaugurated at St Saviour's Priory in Dominick Street, Dublin, which was chaired by Edward Martyn, a supporter of the Gaelic League and an influential figure in the Irish literary revival.[98] Martyn, who was president of Sinn Féin from 1905-1908, was in the peculiar position of having a large private means, and he was involved in almost every phase of the Irish Revival.[99] He aided the Catholic cause through his endowment of the Palestrina Choir in Dublin's Pro-Cathedral. With Sarah Purser and Harry Clarke, he helped to create a stained-glass enterprise that became famous on both sides of the Atlantic – An Túr Gloine.[100]

Also in attendance at the first meeting of the Catholic Association were William Dennehy, editor of *The Irish Catholic*, D.P. Moran, businessman Arthur Clery, and Fr Finlay, activist in the growing co-operative movement. *The Handbook of the Catholic Association* (1902) indicated the intent of the new organisation, 'We must fight with all our might until we have laid our hands on as much of the power, place and position of this country as our numbers, our ability, and our unabated historical claims entitle us to demand'.[101]

Consequently the primary thrust of the movement was to promote exclusive dealings by Catholics for Catholics. The clarion call went out to campaign to establish Catholic leadership of Irish social and cultural life. Once more the Catholic Association's *Handbook* pointed out what they had in mind:

> To build up the Catholic social structure upon every side is what we urgently need. It is a work of pressing importance, too, since we cannot too early begin to make a society of our own. The ideal which sees supreme, social responsibility only outside the Catholic circle will have to go.[102]

It was no coincidence that the Past Pupils' Unions Movement was particularly developing its organisational structure at this stage. The Catholic Association secured affiliation with the St James Catholic Association in Dublin, the CYMS, various temperance associations (including the recently formed Pioneer Total Abstinence Association in 1899), and the Belfast Catholic Association. One of the Catholic Association's chief aims was to encourage Catholics to meet and establish informal business and social contacts which would aid Catholic enterprises and expose the 'greedy extremes' to which Protestants descended to 'keep good jobs in their own hands'.[103] The organisation formed a small committee which sought interviews with company directors and boards suspected of discriminating against Catholics. The initial focus was on the employment practices in the railways, and the hardwood and ironmongery trades. Informal links soon developed into an organised campaign, whose aim was to encourage Catholic patronage of Catholic businesses. Bishop Edward O'Dwyer became a strong supporter of the organisation.

Despite its high profile and sweeping aims, the Catholic Association soon faced criticism.[104] Infighting and reckless calls for exclusive trading led to its censure by Dublin's Archbishop William Walsh. Walsh was concerned about the University Question and he did not want to alienate support from the establishment. Similarly, Pope Pius X's fears about independent lay initiative would have been noted by Walsh. In August 1903, *The Irish Catholic* reported his denunciation of the organisation's failure to secure immediate clerical approval as a 'grave error'.[105] Walsh refused to meet a delegation from the organisation. This led to its collapse, as several key members resigned. Edward Martyn was the first to go. William Martin Murphy, who had backed the association through the *Irish Independent*, withdrew his support. The rapid dilution of support was further evident at the Maynooth Union gathering in late 1903.[106] The Union had been formed in 1895 by Walter MacDonald, Professor of Theology, and its papers over the years reflected current clerical thinking and concerns. Whilst Fr Gerald O'Donovan, an Irish language and co-operative enthusiast, applauded the Catholic Association as a means of establishing equality in the country's economic life, and as a means of fostering an 'educated Catholic lay opinion', many of the respondents to his address expressed concern about lay independence from clerical authority.[107]

In January 1904, Archbishop Walsh condemned the Catholic Association in a pastoral letter and described it as being unequivocally detrimental to Catholic interests.[108] His pastoral was endorsed by Bishop Foley of Kildare and Leighlin on 22 February in another pastoral. The organisation was described as a body to which the bishops 'had never committed themselves and from which they had formally disassociated themselves'.[109] Cardinal Logue, a firm supporter of the organisation, agreed that without Walsh's backing it should wind down. He proposed, however, that things be allowed to 'quiet down for the present and later we will reform ourselves as a purely defence association'.[110]

The establishment of the Catholic Association signified both Catholic hostility to social and economic impediments, and Catholic confidence and determination to band together to win social and professional gains. However, it was made particularly clear by the Catholic hierarchy that no organisation with the word Catholic in its title could develop without the approval of the clergy. Lay Catholics soon fell into step with clerical demands and a crucial organising principle was firmly established. Another organisation, the Catholic Laymen's Committee, which had been formed in 1902 to present evidence to the commission on University Education in Ireland, paid the price of dissenting from clerical opinion. Its involvement in the university debate earned condemnation from Walsh, whose support for the new Catholic Defence Society was partly due to his determination to counter the work of the Catholic Layman's Committee.

Despite its demise, we can appreciate the Catholic Association's significance on a broader scale. Its terms of reference placed it in the vanguard of the European Catholic social movement, particularly because of its insistence on the necessity for 'Catholic' organisation. The European influence is indeed interesting, since Geraldine Grogan in her work *Daniel O'Connell and the German Catholic Movement*, shows that the German movement was itself inspired by the successes of the Irish organisation established by O'Connell.[111] The 'Introduction' to the *Handbook of the Catholic Association* pointed to the Volksverein as an example of successful lay organisation.[112]

A lecture delivered to the Maynooth Union gathering of 1904 on 'The Place of Laymen in the Catholic Church' was followed by another on 'The Attitude of Protestants towards their Catholic Countrymen'.[113] The second paper emphasised the issue of Catholic under-representation in public bodies and positions. The two papers were linked. The former had called for the organisation of Catholics for 'defence and furtherance of Catholic interests',[114] whilst the second examined the 'aggressive spirit of Irish Protestantism and its strangle-hold in the Government; its monopoly of judicial and administrative offices and of higher education and the public departments'.[115]

The 'apathy of Catholics and their indifference to their civil rights' was criticised. It was argued that a special organisation of Catholic 'forces' was necessary, but not along the lines of insulting Protestants or exclusive dealing among Catholics.

In August 1905, the call was taken up with the establishment of the Catholic Defence Society in Dublin. The Catholic hierarchy's need for strict episcopal control and approval necessitated the drafting of a 'Constitution and Rules', which were submitted to the hierarchy by the remnants of the old Catholic Association.[116] The organisation's aims complemented that of the bishops who approved the constitution, 'cordial approval of the proposal to establish an organisation to defend the rights of Catholics and to secure approval for them'.[117] Again the organisation took as its frame of reference the Catholic movements in Germany and America.[118] Its span of life, 1905-1914, saw it campaigning against indecent literature, co-operating with past-pupils' societies, exposing discrimination against Catholic men, urging Catholic lawyers to organise themselves into professional cells, and protesting against obscene theatre.[119] The change of name from Association to Defence Society reveals the growing militance of Catholic organisations, and also the siege atmospherics which would be a dominating feature of successive Catholic organisations in the ensuing years.

The Irish Rosary commented in 1907 that the Catholic Defence Society had already 'wrought considerable good', for example in securing places for Catholics in the Veterinary Council, in the Fire and Life Insurance Company, and in the Pharmaceutical Company.[120] The establishment of open competitive examinations for banks and railways, which followed the organisation's activities, was claimed as a remarkable advance, as much for the important principle it enshrined as for the availability of employment for Catholics that it made possible.[121] The CDS organised large-scale entertainment for its members, including annual dances and banquets held in Dublin's Gresham Hotel. It also pursued a policy of protecting Catholics from social and professional bigotry, a campaign in which Archbishop Walsh played a prominent part. Its major ambition was to end Anglo-Irish domination, and it became, within a few years, the crucial Dublin nucleus of the embryonic organisation, the Knights of St Columbanus.

FROM DEFENCE TO VIGILANCE: THE ANTI-MODERNIST CAMPAIGN

The level of public discourse on the discrimination experienced by Catholics signalled both the expansion in the number of Catholics qualified to take employment in professional and other fields, and their increasing militancy. Though Ireland in the new century promised opportunity, diversity and prosperity, vigilance became the watchword for many ambitious Catholics.

On another front, with the domestic priorities of the Catholic hierarchy being eased with a solution to the University Question in 1908, their latent suspicion at the behaviour of Irish political representatives at Westminster started to come to the fore.[122] The liberal alliance had concerned the bishops, and in particular the liberal sponsorship of secular education for the English schools. Clerical uneasiness partly stemmed from their apprehension that Ireland's representatives were gradually becoming contaminated and corrupted by liberalism.[123] There were real fears that the legislative programme of the new liberalism would affect their interests prejudicially, for example it was felt that if the liberals extended the public services, provision for education would suffer. Not only that, but Home Rule for Ireland would be no nearer.[124] Irish efforts were being undermined by the Lord's veto and all that was on offer was the meager Irish Council Bill, which fell far short of people's aspirations. From 1906 to 1909, the House of Commons was particularly influenced by nonconformist opinion which regarded Home Rule as 'Rome Rule'. The Irish politicians at Westminster, in order to allay the fears in the Commons in this regard, tried to portray themselves as a National rather than a strictly 'Catholic' party. David Miller, in his work *Church, State and Nation*, came to the conclusion that, 'in the absence of the imminent prospect of Home Rule, there was no further reason for the Church to be indulgent of the Liberal alliance'.[125]

Yet we must look to Rome for an even wider framework. A hint of alarm on the part of the Irish Catholic Church with regard to developments on the continent appeared in the Lenten pastorals of 1907. Many of them dealt with the difficulties facing the Catholic Church in France. Cardinal Logue interpreted the newly enacted Separation Law as 'a weapon to crush Christianity itself'.[126] Similar difficulties for the Catholic Church in Spain and Portugal compounded

the fears of the Irish Catholic hierarchy. Then, a few months later, the loom-
ing modernist crisis came to a head with the publication of the Vatican decree
Lamentabili Sane, which condemned a great number of the 'modern errors'.[127] In
September 1907, Pope Pius X issued an encyclical, *Pascendi Gregis*, condemning
these 'errors of modernism'.[128] These documents would have had a wide readership amongst the Irish Catholic clergy, since they were published in the *Irish
Ecclesiastical Record* and given prominent attention in the *Irish Catholic Directory*.
In the papal condemnation the modernist movement was seen as a complex of
clearly defined heresies.[129] Of long-term significance to a Catholic social movement in Ireland was the fact that the term was applied without distinction to all
who refused to adopt a strictly conservative standpoint. In one respect, it heralded
the end of a possible Catholic social movement in Ireland on the radical lines of
some European countries. Thenceforth the lay movement, albeit still in the adolescent phase, would be pruned to take a different direction from the necessary
socio-economic one.

The decree had enumerated sixty-five of the propositions of the Catholic
modernists as a latter-day *Syllabus of Errors*. The encyclical went further and
specified penalties for those refusing obedience to ecclesiastical authority and
for those interested in 'novelty'. It set forth a number of measures for 'combating' modernism, with which the Irish clergy was soon familiar.[130] The principal
stipulations were as follows:

1. There was to be definite emphasis on the fundamental importance of scholastic philosophy and theology in the seminaries and Catholic universities.

2. Modernists were to be removed from their positions and from teaching.

3. The bishops were to ensure that their clergy and laity had nothing
   to do with the modernist press. This meant any kind of press which
   sprang from the modernist culture. The English Liberal culture would
   have been viewed as being part of that mould and this partly explains
   the Irish bishops' growing dislike for the liberal alliance. Not only
   that but there was a strong modernist movement in England under
   the Anglo-Irish Jesuit George Tyrell, which had links with European
   developments. The English language facilitated the spread of these
   ideas in Ireland through English religious journals and periodicals.

4. A council of censors was to be established in each Diocese for the scrutiny and revision of every Catholic publication.

5. A Vigilance Council was to be established in each Diocese to prevent
   the diffusion of modernist errors.[131]

From this time the word 'vigilance' cropped up frequently in the clergy's vocabulary and in their preaching. It was to embrace the whole nature and function of Catholic Action organisations also.

The encyclical *Pascendi Gregis* (1907) regarded modernism as the 'synthesis of all heresies'. Bishops were exhorted to 'drive out' of their Dioceses 'any pernicious books' that may have been in circulation. Booksellers were instructed 'not to engage in the evil trade'. Reading matter in seminaries was to be strictly supervised, as was that of the Catholic laity. The result was the stepping up of the campaign against what was described as 'evil' literature, and which by 1911 saw a widespread 'vigilance' campaign in Ireland.

At the distribution of prizes in Maynooth College in October, 1909, Cardinal Logue warned the students to prepare themselves to meet the 'crisis' that faced the Catholic Church.[132] He referred to the link between modernism and immoral literature. He was concerned about the power of the Protestant press and reminded his listeners, 'that dangers were already creeping in, and two or three papers published in Dublin by Catholics ... a priest had sent him extracts which were not only not Catholic, but anti-Christian'.[133]

The case of Revd Professor Walter MacDonald is one indicator of the draconian measures which the Irish Catholic Church was intent on taking in order to suppress intellectual debate and to ensure a conforming and compliant clergy. MacDonald was an influential Maynooth academic, but he was distrusted by the Catholic hierarchy (in the anti-modernist backlash) for many of his ideas.[134] His book *Reminiscences of a Maynooth Professor* (published posthumously in 1925) described the difficulties in trying to get anything published – he had not the least chance of being published in Dublin and if he was somehow published elsewhere, the book would be immediately sent to Rome and 'would be quickly condemned there'.[135] He was always aware of 'the watch-dogs of orthodoxy sniffing and asking what new heresy is this?', or if there was any attempt to depart from the well-trodden path. His four volumes of theology were banned even though he went out of his way to avoid errors at all costs. He wrote ruefully:

> And yet the pen I am not allowed to use at the service of my mistress, would perhaps, be welcomed heartily and rewarded handsomely by her enemies. So that one has at least the consolation of reflecting sometimes on the sacrifice which one is privileged to make, if not in her service, then for her sake.[136]

He saw his whole life as 'one long protest'. Even the highly respected Maynooth Union, which he had founded in 1896, was subject to the same scrutiny, and he found it difficult to fix on a subject that would have been safe enough to discuss. The proceedings of the meetings were reported widely in the newspapers, and the ecclesiastical censors requested that any paper to be delivered by a prospective speaker would henceforth have to be submitted for censorship or revision no matter how harmless the subject.

In 1906, Professor MacDonald and other Maynooth academics launched the *Irish Theological Quarterly*, though according to MacDonald, 'the suspicion with which our project was regarded manifested itself soon'.[137] He overheard Cardinal Logue warning that the review would have to be carefully watched. Logue later drew his attention to a forgotten college statute that bound Professors to publish nothing without first submitting it to the President of the College and obtaining his permission. MacDonald refused to seek this approval, although he was aware of the positive disapproval of others in the Catholic hierarchy. He went ahead and published with 'an uncomfortable feeling that we were under suspicion and disliked', and that his writings were under observation. The *ITQ* eventually folded in 1922. The fears of the hierarchy were not altogether unfounded, as an article in the first issue was not unsympathetic to the writings of Loisy, one of the chief modernists.[138]

That suspicion should fall on one of their own illustrates the near witch-hunt attitude that the Irish ecclesiastical authorities undertook to rid the country of any hint of heresy. No one would become immune from the search. Not only that, but the suppression initiated by the encyclical *Pascendi Gregis* was followed by an even harsher measure when, in 1909, all clergy were required to take the 'anti-modernist oath'.[139] The clergy as a whole submitted without much outward resistance. There were only forty exceptions. One of those was Fr Gerald O'Donovan, the well-known Loughrea priest, who refused to take the oath and resigned from the priesthood.[140] He recounted his views in a semi-autobiographical book, published in 1913, called *Father Ralph*, which became a best-seller.[141] He was described by Seán Ó Faoláin years later, in 1945, as 'a Modernist', and O'Faolain hoped that his name would inspire in the battle being waged for a more liberal, tolerant and pluralist Ireland.[142] *Father Ralph* shows O'Donovan's growing disillusionment with the priesthood. His book depicts the growing internal crisis facing O'Donovan in the light of the anti-modernist reaction that had become more evident in Ireland. He abhorred the response of the Catholic hierarchy and clergy in Ireland to the strictures from Rome:

> ...there is a rush already to toe the line. Cardinals and Bishops who coquetted with Modernism when it seemed a growing movement are falling over each other in their profession of loyalty. No words are strong enough to express their abhorrence of the views they held a month ago, or fulsome enough to express their admiration for the wisdom of the Pope.[143]

O'Donovan believed that the Irish clergy were reduced to sycophants by the system. His book captures the reaction of the Catholic Church in Ireland to the modernist crisis and similarly draws a useful portrait of the Irish Catholic laity. He speaks through the words of a lay editor of a magazine:

> There are worse forms of torture than the rack. The Church has reduced social torture to a fine art. Why, even a layman like me can only escape it by burying

himself somewhere. Do you think I could live in Dublin or anywhere in Ireland, once the Church had definitely attacked me? I have already experienced innuendoes, secret accusations, efforts to prevent me getting work, defamation and calumny, persistent, continuous.[144]

O'Donovan's dismal conclusion was that the great majority of priests in Ireland accepted the Pope's decree on the anti-modernist oath from sheer cowardice, as otherwise they would have to leave the priesthood and face the ensuing scandal, as he himself had done.

The integralist reaction to modernism reached its climax during 1912-13, a period that coincided with a similar movement in Ireland.[145] The reaction in Ireland ranged over the years 1907-1913, from the time the encyclical on modernism was issued to the high point of the vigilance campaign in 1913.[146] There was no doubt that Maynooth was petrified at the idea being contaminated. The Irish Bishops' pastorals of 1908-1909 clearly reflected this concern. Archbishop Walsh said that the movement was spreading from England, and 'sympathies in Ireland savoured strongly of the symptoms'.[147] The Irish Rosary was vehement in its denunciation, with the heading, 'Smashing Up Modernism', and it expressed its concern about the 'enemies concealed within' and the 'lover of doubts and theories and speculations'.[148] According to one contributor, these would have to 'submit' or be 'cut off, be he lay or anointed – the axe is ready for the rotten branches'. Again in 1910, The Irish Rosary set the tone for vigilance when in a number of articles it recommended that 'effective remedies' were needed to control what it described as 'filthy periodicals'.[149] The demands of D.P. Moran and others in the Irish Revival were coalescing with the anti-modernist campaign to outlaw the usurpation of the Catholic neo-scholastic tradition by practically any kind of English publication. Both movements overlapped and were at times synonymous. In 1910, The Irish Rosary wrote in terms of what it regarded as a 'state of intellectual warfare'.[150]

The Catholic Truth Society of Ireland played its part in this new campaign. In 1907, in response to the new anti-modernist encyclical, it published pamphlets extolling the virtues of the scholastics, such as University Life in the Middle Ages.[151] In 1909 it published The Value of Scholastic Philosophy[152] and The Intellectual Claims of the Catholic Church.[153] All three were issued to encourage the laity into the area of vigilance activity. The 1909 annual conference of the CTSI focused on three main issues: the importance of the medieval philosophers; the urgent need for greater Catholic organisation; the attitude Catholics should adopt towards the press. All three were linked, and reflected the hierarchy's fears over the encroachment of modernist ideas. Dr Joseph McGrath praised the speech of Dr Windle, President of UCC for his defence of the scholastic philosophers, and particularly for his sounding a 'note of warning'. Dr McGrath, of the National University, called on the conference to be 'up and doing' and said that they 'must equip themselves for the fight'.

The conference concluded with an agreement on the utmost urgency for the immediate organisation of the laity of Ireland'.[154]

It was Bishop O'Dwyer who heeded the conference's call. He was founder of the Catholic Literature Institute in Limerick and writer of a pamphlet defending Cardinal Newman against the modernists.[155] In 1908, he was personally thanked by Pope Pius X for vindicating, in his pamphlet, the orthodoxy of Cardinal Newman against the inferences of the modernists. In a letter to O'Dwyer, the Pope declared that the Bishop had 'not only exposed the contumacy of the modernists, but their artifice as well'.[156] Under O'Dwyer, the Limerick Men's Confraternity at the Redemptorist church had grown to be the largest in the world, with an average annual membership of 7,000. This figure remained constant for many years after his death until the 1940s.[157] It was from this confraternity that the first members of the Irish Vigilance Association were drawn.

O'Dwyer was not reluctant to openly criticise the Irish Party and their alliance with the liberals, using words such as 'contamination' and 'subservience'.[158] In the 1910 elections, in only one Munster constituency, East Limerick, was there an organised, clerically led revolt against the party. His sympathies in the First World War were with the Catholic Empire of Austria and the 60 million Catholics in Central Europe, against the infidelity and Protestantism as represented by the Allies.[159]

The founding of the Catholic Literature Institute reflected his concern for 'pure literature'. In his Lenten pastoral of 1910, Bishop O'Dwyer spoke of the danger coming from too close a union of Ireland and England. He saw England's literature, whether periodical or newspaper, as, 'steadily drifting away from revealed religion and at best it is Protestant and bitterly anti-Catholic and at its worst it is agnostic and impartial in its hostility to all religion'.[160]

The difference between the CTSI movement initiated ten years previously and O'Dwyer's statement was that in the intervening period the Catholic Church had been rocked to its very foundations by the modernist crisis. The CTSI's mandate involved it in a propaganda and defensive campaign, whereas O'Dwyer intended to go beyond this. He questioned the effects of English reading material on Irish minds.

Immediately after his Lenten pastoral was issued, the first practical steps were taken in Limerick to combat the sale and distribution of English popular literature. Acting on the exhortations of O'Dwyer and his clergy, a number of citizens established a Vigilance Committee to prevent the sale of English Sunday newspapers and immoral literature. The Redemptorists, who were known for their fiery missions, enlisted the aid of numerous members of the Limerick Confraternity of the Holy Family.[161] As a result of the combined efforts, twenty-two local newsagents pledged themselves to sell no newspaper which the committee found objectionable. The poet Austin Clarke, who was then a student in Mungret College, recalls that, 'even at that time the wicked English Sunday newspapers were burned occasionally in the streets of Limerick, and these acts of piety were praised in our national press'.[162] Writing in the *Daily Irish Independent* shortly afterwards, the Vigilance Committee spelt out their aim:

> We appeal to the people of Ireland to help us in our crusade. The movement we have instituted against vile literature has spread rapidly to many places in Ireland. We are anxious that the workers in this campaign should be formed into an Irish National Society for the suppression of evil literature.[163]

But there was to be no national co-ordinated organisation. Sporadic and temporary organisations sprang up in different parts of the country with divergent approaches. The Tuam Vigilance Committee, in a letter to the *Freeman's Journal* in late 1910, declared that the only practical approach was to provide an ample supply of safe and otherwise readable books, to meet the needs of every class of the community.[164] *The Irish Catholic* echoed this view a few months later when it suggested that, 'one of the first things necessary to be done by the Crusade is to provide an anti-dote, especially by improving and diffusing existing periodicals so that they may come to replace those which are so rightly banned'.[165]

The *Industrial Journal* also considered the deleterious effects of the flow of 'bad' literature. For them it was not really a moral question as 'it also effects the industry, the vigour of the intellect, of a race'. It saw people being gradually 'weaned away' from informative reading, and many young boys and girls 'being brought up on halfpenny novelettes'.[166]

The high point in the campaign came in 1911, ably assisted by a combination of bishops' pastorals, the establishment of Vigilance Committees, and widespread support from sections of the media. Doubtlessly, some of the Irish newspapers recognised the monetary rewards that would come their way if English newspapers were discouraged.

An important landmark in the new movement was the publication of Fr Timothy Hurley, a priest of the Diocese of Elphin. *Legislation of the Catholic Church on the Production and Distribution of Literature*, published in 1911, covered such areas as the prohibition of books, censorship of the press, 'the Rules of the Index', the flood of 'pernicious literature', the worry of 'Socialistic literature in the Press', and the 'poison of immorality and unbelief', which he saw as springing largely from the unbridled licence of the press.[167] All this echoed the decree and encyclical recently issued by Pope Pius X. Two years later Hurley brought out a large booklet, *The National Crusade against Evil Literature*, showing the progress of the campaign in Ireland.[168] Both publications were circulated widely amongst the clergy and laity, and they indicate that Ireland was responding vigorously to the internal modernist crisis within the Catholic Church.

The movement was greatly enhanced with the establishment of the Dublin Vigilance Committee on 5 November 1911 at a meeting in the Iona Hall, Glasnevin, Dublin, that was held under the auspices of the CYMS. This society, originally an anti-proselytism organisation, had already been active in 1907 against 'evil literature', in response to the calls of *The Irish Rosary*. Indeed, the CYMS had secured convictions against several people engaged in the sale of indecent postcards.[169] The society had strong links with the Dominican Order, the publishers of *The Irish Rosary*. Members of the CYMS were active in the Confraternity in Dominick Street and Aughrim Street parishes. The Dominicans initiated the meeting in Iona Hall, a CYMS venue, and they used *The Irish Rosary* as a vehicle for the movement's ideas and activities. The February 1913 editorial pointed out that:

> Vigilance committees have been established and are carrying out the fight with determination and perseverance. They have not secured the total banishment of these papers that are condemned as bad, but they have materially lessened their circulation, and they have awakened a sound, healthy public opinion on the question.[170]

These groups who sought stricter control over imported literature appear to have represented a large body of opinion within the country. Undoubtedly, their motives varied from moral grounds and fears about unbelief and modernism, to nationalistic and separatist concerns. Fr Myles Ronan saw the Dublin Vigilance Committee as the best means 'to defend our people against the insidious attempts of modern journalism to corrupt them', and he called on people 'to proclaim the war from the rooftops'.[171] *The Leader* reported that, 'great things have been accomplished in a short time in seriously crippling the movements of the reptile Press; but we have scorched the snake, not killed it'.[172] The fundamental problem was organisation, since there was no central executive linking the many local organisations and giving them a united plan of action. This task would eventually fall to the CTSI, which for many years after the campaign had waned was still reminding the public of the need to 'undo the work of the British mind with its Kantian and Modernist outlook as expressed in its publications which flooded Ireland'.[173] Fr Walter MacDonald's book *Reminiscences of a Maynooth Professor* was to echo through the decades after his death in 1920. The conscience of independent Ireland was being shaped during those crucial formative years prior to 1921, and was to find expression in the CTSI censorship legislation campaign of the 1920s.

THE CHALLENGES OF SOCIALISM AND PROSELYTISM

Much of the Catholic clergy seemed to have scant understanding of the real miseries of so many of the city and town labourers in the first decade of the new century. Among the clergy there was certainly a real, and not well-informed fear of 'socialism'.[174] The troubled events from 1910-1913 were to show how wide the gap between priest and people could be. The clergy saw the labour troubles in Dublin and elsewhere as a syndicalist revolutionary plot, and in their fear they did not exactly cover themselves with glory in a display of social concern.[175]

In stark contrast to the art and symbolism of the literary revival was the reality of life in the slums of Dublin. Housing conditions were atrocious, with 36.6 per cent of families occupying a single room.[176] There were some industries, but much casual employment and much unemployment. The skilled craft workers of Dublin had an established tradition of unionisation. Trouble arose with the unionisation of the unskilled and casual workers.

In 1906, the CTSI published a pamphlet, *The Church and the Working Classes*, written by Fr Peter Coffey, Professor of Philosophy in Maynooth, which showed that he had a strong social conscience.[177] For a priest of farming stock he pulled no punches. The degrading Poor Law and private philanthropy were no answer to the reality of poverty. While he condemned 'an un-provoked or unnecessary or unjustifiable strike', he declared that it was the employer's 'great and principal duty' to give his workers a fair wage. The legitimate object of a trade union was to secure by fair and lawful means that just and equitable treatment that would lead to social peace.

Perhaps it was the fact that Coffey spoke with approval of 'Christian socialism', which had been recently rejected by Pope Pius X in favour of 'Catholic Action', that roused opposition. Certainly thereafter Coffey and his social conscience were consigned to the temperance movement.[178] Fears of socialism were widespread and many clergy were uncertain as to what socialism actually was, except that it threatened the established order, religion included. The clerical response was to stick to general recommendations, and priests preached the same moral principles to workers and employers, and stayed clear of any positive suggestions.

The labour leader, James Connolly, tried to wean the Irish worker away from blind acceptance of their miserable status quo.[179] In his *Labour, Nationality and Religion* (1910), Connolly replied to criticism of socialism by Fr Kane SJ of Gardiner Street church.[180] Another labour leader, Jim Larkin, was not slow to castigate the Catholic Church for its attitude to social problems.[181] In 1908 he founded the Irish Transport and General Workers' Union. Within a short time the Dublin Trades' Council was dominated by members of the Socialist Party and the Larkinites. The years 1911–1913 saw a wave of strikes sweep over Britain and this quickly spread to Ireland. When Larkin challenged the Dublin United Tramways company the problems for the Dublin workers worsened.

On 20 July 1911, Monsignor Curran, Archbishop Walsh's secretary, advised him that 'the mania for strikes is spreading'.[182] Fr Kane, giving his Lenten lecture in Gardiner Street church, referred to Larkin's 'secret hostility to Christianity' and his commitment to the subversive overthrow of the existing order.[183] 'Larkinism' was used by many clergy as a synonym for socialism, anarchy and unreasonable behaviour.[184] At the 1912 CTSI annual conference, Archbishop Healy warned his audience to be prepared to meet the 'difficulty'.[185] Other speakers referred to the 'spirit of unrest' or the 'unscrupulous revolutionaries' who had got their hands on trade unions.[186] Cardinal Logue put the blame squarely on the workers themselves. He said that they should have ignored the 'counsels of those who preached irreligion and atheism'.[187]

Such concern led to the establishment by the CTSI of a subcommittee which became known as the Leo Guild, taking its name from Pope Leo XIII, author of the encyclical *Rerum Noyarum*. The new organisation's main objective was to 'determine means to counteract anti-Christian movements'.[188] This was to be achieved by promoting a 'practical knowledge' of the papal encyclicals on social questions.[189] It proposed to establish sections of the Leo Guild in parochial halls and workingmen's clubs. Revd Professor Corcoran SJ of the National University, was to act as Director of Studies. It was 'educated Catholic laymen' who were, in the main, the early students of Corcoran. It was hoped that they would eventually form a body of informed Catholic opinion, able to counteract anti-Catholic social doctrines, and also to propose a constructive policy of reform.

The CTSI was inspired by developments on the continent. Inspiration also came from the recently established Catholic Social Guild in England. The founder of the Catholic Social Guild, Fr Plater SJ, after a visit to Dublin, had recommended a similar organisation for the city. The CTSI published his reflections in a pamphlet in 1912, entitled *The Priest and Social Action*.[190]

William Martin Murphy's newspaper, the *Freeman's Journal*, hailed the new organisation in an article headed 'The Church and Democracy'.[191] There was some initial enthusiasm among the Catholic laity for organised social study and the ideals of the Leo Guild. In 1914, John Hughes, one of its members, carried out a detailed investigation of poverty in Dublin and came to the conclusion that a considerable proportion of Dublin citizens 'are habitually without the essentials of decent living'.[192] Dublin, for Hughes was the happy hunting ground of social reforms. There was no lack of reports, official and unofficial, on its health and sanitary conditions, the condition of its housing and its slums, and the exploitation of labour. He called the statistics of infant mortality, 'the massacre of the innocents', because of the excessively high rate. Hughes was also critical of the divine dictum which he had heard so many times from Church people, 'the poor you will always have with you', i.e. the Catholic Church viewed poverty in Dublin as being deplorable but yet unavoidable.[193]

In 1913, Fr Lambert McKenna SJ wrote, 'Of Catholic social work properly so-called, there is little, very little indeed, in Catholic Ireland'.[194] His sympathies lay with James Connolly, and Connolly's efforts to right those injustices.[195] However the official Church seemed to resort to the language of authority, which was no substitute for empathy.

The practical aspect of the labour difficulties that impinged most strongly on Catholic Church authorities was the problem of 'waifs and strays'. This had been highlighted at the CTSI 1910 annual conference.[196] Fr Glynn SJ described them as the 'flotsam and jetsam' of the city and he appealed to the Catholic laity to 'rescue' them before they became involved in vice.[197] But Glynn's real concern was that Dublin's poor children would be swept into institutions and brought up as 'Protestant O'Neills, O'Donnells, and Ryans'. Interestingly, Protestants at this time feared the reverse for their poor. These fears on the part of the Catholic Church were not new, as Desmond Bowen has shown in his study of nineteenth-century souperism.[198] The CYMS had been founded in 1849 with the express purpose of counteracting this ploy.[199] Such was the concern of the Irish Catholic Church with the issue of proselytism, that all Synods of Irish Bishops until and including the 1927 Synod of Maynooth, referred to it in strong terms. So it was not surprising that proselytism became a burning issue in 1913.[200] The Traynor case received considerable publicity in the newspapers at the time.[201] It involved a legal tug-of-war wrangle over the religion in which three orphaned youngsters should be brought up.

In October 1913, Archbishop Walsh wrote to the daily papers about the plight of the children of the strikes.[202] He was incensed by what he saw as an 'organised endeavour to deport large numbers of poor children' when English trade unionists offered to help families for the duration of the strike. Vigilance parties got wind of the situation and rushed to Westland Row station,[203] to the North Wall and to Kingstown (Dún Laoghaire) to block the departure of the children.[204] The atmosphere in Dublin was marked by public hysteria and there were a number of quayside incidents involving Catholic clergy.[205]

The Ancient Order of Hibernians, a Catholic organisation established in 1838, viewed the rise of the working classes under Jim Larkin as a threat to the Irish Parliamentary Party.[206] The *Irish Worker* of 8 November, in a front page article, 'The AOH, The Childer, and The Faith', castigated the 'lying crying of proselytism', and suggested that the 'real villain' of the affair was T.P. Nugent, 'the gallant secretary of the Hibernians'. According to this article, the entire opposition to the children's holiday scheme had been orchestrated by the 'Ancient Order of Hypocrites'. It also criticised the Dublin newspapers which by 'half-truths and whole lies' had made many people believe that the men of the Transport Union represented 'a revolutionary movement of ignorant, unscrupulous men'.[207]

At the end of October a circular was sent to all the parish priests in Dublin spelling out the problem, 'As usual, in times of distress, the proselytisers are energetically active. If they are to be effectively combatted, it must be a combined effort'.[208]

The 'combined effort' necessitated the active involvement of the Catholic laity. William Martin Murphy, of the recently formed Employers' Association, and late of the 1902 Catholic Association, became one of the founding members of the Catholic Protection and Rescue Society of Ireland which was established in Dublin in late 1913.[209] The new organisation's objective was to protect the religion of Catholics from proselytising influences, and to rescue

Catholics who had already fallen under them. The society felt that the only way to counteract what it saw as 'systematic and energetic warfare' against Catholics was through the power of Catholic organisation. They hoped to do this by establishing branches all over the country, which would 'keep vigilance on all the proselytising activities'.[210]

The publications of the CTSI for the period reflected these concerns. Two in particular sold well – *Souperism* and *Rescued*, and *Miss Patience Hope Discovers the Soupers*.[211] The Society hoped that the 'apathy' it saw in Dublin towards proselytism would be erased by the work of the CPRSI and that the 'Catholic community would be aroused to their responsibilities'.[212] One person who took the call very seriously indeed was a civil servant and member of the Society of St Vincent de Paul, Frank Duff. For six years he placed pickets on a 'mission' in Whitefriars Street, Dublin, where free meals were dispensed with the proviso that the beneficiaries attend Protestant services. A few years later he went on to found the Legion of Mary Society and applied his 'vigilance' training to new issues. The mould was beginning to set already with the 'organisation' of the Catholic laity being seen as increasingly vital to the Catholic Church.[213]

The concern of the clergy with socialism started to fizzle out in early 1914, with the gradual return to work of the strikers. The Irish Bishops' joint Lenten pastoral of 1914 quoted parts of *Rerum Novarum*, in order to 'save men from following the will-o-the-wisp into the quagmire of socialism'.[214] By January 1915, membership of the ITGWU had fallen to 3,500.[215] The outbreak of the European conflict saw thousands of men join the armed services, a factor which lessened the sour after-effects of defeated strikers.

Some of the CTSI's publications related to the social question, such as *The Workingman's Champion: A Sketch of the Life and Teachings of Bishop Von Ketteler*[216] and *The Problem of Poverty in Ireland and Its Remedies*.[217] The sentiments expressed were far removed from the actual lives of a huge proportion of Dublin's poor and unemployed. Another pamphlet of 1913, *A Plea for Social-Work*, recommended organisation as a solution to the problems. But it was not organisation along trade union lines. Rather, the publication spelt out that, 'Catholic Social Action is the Best Antidote Against Socialism'.[218] This involved organisation along the lines of the Leo Guild, the CTSI or the CPRSI. These organisations would have catered for the educated middle classes and not for those who bore the brunt of harsh working conditions. Only the penny pamphlets of the CTSI would have percolated down.

Like the CTSI, the Jesuit-run *Irish Messenger* office brought out a series of *Social Action* pamphlets in 1913-1914, responding to the crisis facing the Catholic Church. This series, in contrast to the CTSI pamphlets, recognised the need to prevent destitution, to organise labour, and to provide economic security for the workers. They also recognised the need for some form of social re-adjustment and for the Catholic Church to be in the forefront of the movement.[219] This series of pamphlets remained in print until the heady days of vocationalism in the 1930s, and had a significant impact on Catholic Actionists in that decade. It was at this time also, that the young Edward Coyne (later Fr Coyne SJ), then a student in Belvedere College and an activist with the Belvedere Newsboys' Club, won an award for an essay on the social question. Thirty years later he presented the government with the 'Report of the Commission on Vocational Organisation'.

Fr Connolly, in the introductory booklet to the *Irish Messenger* office's *Social Action* series, *The Social Question and a Programme of Social Pamphlets*, referred to the changing social and political circumstances, 'We have to lay the foundations of a new social order in Ireland.'[220] He was conscious that new political and social frameworks could create a different Ireland, with new groups such as Sinn Féin or the Connolly–Larkin movement challenging both the Home Rulers and the Catholic Church.

There was no concerted action, however, to promote change. It developed instead in a very haphazard manner. The membership of the St Vincent de Paul Society increased in response to the plea for organisation among Catholics.[221] In 1904, there were 183 conferences (branches) in Ireland of which 25 were in Dublin. By 1919 this had increased to 258 branches and 56 in Dublin. According to the 'Report of the Council of Ireland of the Society of St Vincent de Paul', the ruling body of the society, there were 4,000 members in 1921, an increase of nearly 1,500 on the 1900 figures, and up 1,000 on the 1910 figures.[222] A new social consciousness was also in evidence since 1910, as the society embarked on a variety of new schemes, ranging from free legal advice to the establishment of the City Labour Yard.[223] In 1911, the society published the *Handbook for Catholic Social Workers in Dublin*, which was aimed at organised lay Catholics.[224] This was followed in 1920 by a new edition, containing twenty-five pages devoted to the social legislation which had been enacted by the British government.[225] Thus an awareness of the charitable dimension to Catholic social principles was being inculcated into an increasingly organised Catholic laity.

In Belfast, Canon James O'Neill took up Pope Pius X's call for Catholic Action. He was based in a slum parish within hostile Protestant surroundings, which presented all the drab appendages of industrialisation at its worst. He circulated copies of the Pope's regulations for Catholic Action among branches of the St Vincent de Paul Society.[226] In 1912, he established another branch, the St Anthony's University Graduates' Conference. He also contacted the Catholic Centre Party in Germany requesting books and pamphlets explaining its methods for dealing with current social problems. Canon O'Neill directed a prominent Belfast solicitor, James B. Kerr, to compile a manual of social action and this was later published as *A Catechism of Catholic Social Principles*. For Kerr, the dangers to the Catholic religion came from a combination of Orange ascendancy and British socialism. Like his Dublin counterparts, he believed that the challenge had to be met by organised Catholic Action.[227] O'Neill and Kerr both agreed that Catholic Action in Ireland lacked a consolidated and structured organisation. In a letter to Cardinal Logue in early 1915, Kerr and a group of laymen from the St Anthony's University Graduates' Conference pointed out the urgent need to develop 'leaders of opinion'.[228] Catholic social principles were threatened by one weakness – scattered and unorganised opinion. Only by intelligent combination could they secure fair play for Catholics. The result of his deliberations was the formation of a new organisation – the Knights of St Columbanus.[229] The name came from a comparable society in the USA, the Knights of Columbus, in which the American Catholic laity was becoming increasingly active and vocal on matters affecting their interests. Like their American counterparts, the Irish organisation derived its inspiration from the 1903 and 1905 encyclicals of Pope Pius X on the need for an organised Catholic laity. By the end of 1916, branches had been established throughout the Diocese of Down and Connor. By June 1917, after negotiations with members of the Catholic Defence Society, the first Dublin branch was established. A branch was founded in Cork in January 1919.[230]

Professor Alfred O'Rahilly of UCC was angry at the injustices and poverty in Cork City and he tried to radicalise the local St Vincent de Paul Society. He became so frustrated with his failed attempts, that he soon resigned from the organisation. At the CTSI annual conference in 1916 he hit out at the Cork Catholic employers for the 'sweating which flourished unabashed and unashamed'.[231] He argued that since public opinion was uneducated and incompetent, Catholic employers were not 'forced' to act as Catholics in business life and consequently workers were neglected. The solution for O'Rahilly was the setting up of societies 'to regenerate and infuse vital breath into the dry bones around us'.[232] The following year he was instrumental in founding the Catholic Social League in Cork.[233] Both he and Professor Smiddy, also of UCC, became pioneers in their native city in the investigation of social problems. The sheer determination of people like O'Rahilly, as was the case with James Kerr, lent focus and urgency to the issue of Catholic organisation and its possibilities for influence and change. Both individuals were to have a major influence on the direction of independent Ireland, partly because of their recognition of the influence that Catholic organisations could have on attitudes and policy.

Not long after the establishment of the Catholic Social League, O'Rahilly brought out the University and Labour Series of pamphlets.[234] The aim of the series was to bring UCC into closer contact with social workers and working-men. He also published the Guide to Books for Social Students and Workers, which included Fr McSweeney's Poverty in Cork. Writing in the Jesuit periodical the Irish Monthly in 1917, O'Rahilly stressed that the primary function of the Catholic Social League was to empower the social workers and workingmen of Cork through the 'diffusion of Catholic social publications'.[235] The Catholic Social League also organised social study clubs.

The changing political and social situation in the second decade of the twentieth century greatly alarmed the Catholic hierarchy in Ireland. Consequently,

they encouraged the greater involvement of the laity in Catholic organisations. This was certainly the message given by the prominent Jesuit Fr Richard
Devane when he addressed the 1917 CTSI annual conference, which had as its
theme, 'The Need for Catholic Social Organisation in Ireland'.[236] Devane was
concerned at a recent speech given by Mr McPartlin in his presidential address
at the Trade Union Congress in Derry, in which he referred to the 'real opening
of the class war' with the advent of the Irish Parliament. Devane also recognised that with the dramatic success of Sinn Féin in the elections of 1917, new
political divisions and parties would arise. He envisaged Catholic lay organisation as being essential in order to neutralise any potential social revolutionary
movement.[237] Devane's views found an echo at the subsequent CTSI annual
conferences from 1918 to 1920. The society decided on a radical overhaul of its
organisational structure throughout the country.[238] In 1920, a major report was
presented to the Catholic hierarchy, which indicated that the 're-organisation
scheme' would provide for the 'Society's improved working in every parish
in Ireland'; it would co-ordinate the positive (propaganda) and negative (vigilance) sides of its work; and would make the Society more truly representative
of Catholic Ireland.[239] On the eve of Irish political independence, the Catholic
Church was anticipating a new understanding for its position in the country. It
decided that Catholic lay organisations would have an important part to play in
securing and stabilising the influence of the Catholic Church.

The CTSI would have a significant role in the new scheme of things. The
small initial beginnings in 1899 were enormously helped by the increased
outpourings of pamphlets from the printing presses of the CTSI and the *Irish
Messenger* office. The roots of Catholic Action, laid in the crucial first two decades of the twentieth century, were an outgrowth of both changing national
circumstances and European Catholic developments. The European Catholic
Social Movement played a part, as did Pope Pius X's call to Catholic Action in
1903 and 1905. The modernist crisis shook the Catholic Church to its foundations and was to have major long-term effects on Ireland. In Ireland itself, the
Celtic Revival in its many and varied manifestations also greatly stimulated and
facilitated Catholic Action and its diverse programmes. Vigilantism and nationalism were not strange bed-fellows; both sought a certain kind of purification.
It came as no surprise that both Church and Nation should share the same
platform at the 1923 CTSI annual conference to discuss the future direction of
independent Ireland.

II

INDEPENDENCE, EMANCIPATION AND THE SEARCH FOR IRISH IDENTITY – THE DRIVE TO ORGANISE

Catholic Action was a term used to designate both a concept and an organisation of laity. It refers specifically to such actions of lay groups as have been so defined and mandated by the local bishop. This factor is crucial in understanding the clergy–laity relationship in Ireland during the first decades of Irish independence. In this sense, the term denoted a tightly structured organisation that served as an arm of the hierarchy in lay life. The mandate was essential. The ambiguity of concept became apparent in clashes at different times between the Legion of Mary, the CTSI, the Catholic Girl Guides and Dublin's Archbishop Byrne. In the late 1930s, the Jesuits and the Catholic hierarchy drew up separate reports on Catholic Action in Ireland to try and put some order into a disparate movement. Even as late as 1958, Fr Jeremiah Newman of Limerick wrote a book on the issue, entitled *What is Catholic Action?* Throughout the period of our survey, it is obvious that there was a certain uneasiness among the hierarchy with the precise meaning and connotation of the term.

As we saw in Chapter I, Pius X was the first pope to use the term, stressing its importance in several encyclicals. It was Pius XI (often known as 'The Pope of Catholic Action'), however, who gave to it its classical definition as 'the participation of the laity in the apostolate of the Church's hierarchy'. The concept was implicit in his first encyclical, *Ubi Arcano Dei* (1922). Pius XI gave Catholic Action a charter, a spirit, and an apocalyptic urgency. He tended to restrict the term to: 1. action or work of the laity which was, 2. organised, 3. apostolic, and 4. done under the special mandate of the bishop.

A spate of manuals and handbooks developed these points and one in particular, *A Manual of Catholic Action* (1935) by Luigi Civardi, became the veritable bible for Catholic Actionists. The organisations at work in Ireland had varied forms. The Legion of Mary (1921) and An Rioghacht (1926) were perhaps polar types, the former with popular and widespread appeal, whereas the latter was more elitist and intellectual. The Legion was more of an evangelising arm of the Catholic

Church, concentrating on reviving Catholic practice among the negligent, whereas the latter, on the other hand, was more concerned with Christianising economic and social institutions. The CTSI concentrated on disseminating Catholic literature, working for censorship legislation, and helping to organise the 1929 Catholic Emancipation Centenary celebrations and the 1932 Eucharistic Congress. The Society of St Vincent de Paul continued its charitable activities and in the 1930s established Sunshine House to give holidays by the sea to thousands of Dublin's deprived children. The revived CYMS (1927) with a mainly working-class membership, found a *raison d'être* in vigilance and militant anti-communist activities. The Knights of St Columbanus, who regarded themselves as the 'cream of Catholic Action' with a very secretive strategy, directed their energies in the 1920s mainly towards the organisation of branches but increasingly to enhancing Catholic social and business interests. There were a number of other Catholic organisations with particular concerns that sprang up in Ireland during these years and these will be considered in the course of the narrative.

In this chapter, we will look at how the movement developed at a crucial juncture in Irish history, with the signing of the 1921 Anglo-Irish Treaty and the establishment of the Irish Free State. With the national question nearly resolved there was a need to consider the state of Irish society and its future direction.

If the sodalities and the confraternities were some of the great shaping and binding forces in the second half of the nineteenth century, then the Catholic Action organisations can be said to have had a similar impact on Irish mores and attitudes during the first half of the twentieth century.

DEFINING CATHOLIC ACTION – DEFINING THE IRISH FREE STATE

After the First World War, perceptions on lax morality, and the rise of fascist and communistic totalitarianism, became the inspiration for the new Pope's (Pius XI) first encyclical, *Ubi Arcano Dei – Concerning Catholic Action* (1922), which was devoted specifically to calling the Catholic laity to join Catholic organisations. Pius XI gave Catholic Action a new centralised and hierarchical structure, with emphasis on the crucial role of lay organisations. These organisations would act as a Christianising influence in a society which appeared to be becoming more secularised. He defined Catholic Action as 'The Participation of the Organised Laity in the Hierarchical Apostolate of the Church'. The encyclical expressed alarm that, 'people of every social category are restless and embittered; insubordination and idleness are almost the fashion. The frivolity of women and girls has gone beyond the bounds of moral decency, in dress, and in dancing especially.'[2]

The remedies he proposed were 'the varied and excellent movements for the proper development of religious culture'. In essence the 'good fight', the 'battle to be undertaken on many sides', was to be henceforth undertaken by lay organisations under the overall name of Catholic Action.[3] Pius XI also warned against 'social modernism', which he saw manifest in 'party agitation and such unbridled ideas and perverse views'.[4] He similarly warned against 'a certain kind of modernism in morals, and in matters touching authority and social order'.[5]

The significance of the 1922 encyclical lies in its giving existing and new Catholic Action organisations a definite 'mandate'. Because of the exigencies of post–War Europe, as well as the decline in vocations, the Catholic Church was quickly awakened to the fact that it possessed a valuable resource in an educated and politically aware membership, and one, once harnessed, well able to promote and defend Catholic interests.[6]

Catholic Action, then, was part of that Catholic Church strategy for cultural control and influence. It was an aspect of a many-pronged model, organised through parallel Catholic structures, schools, hospitals, political parties, and lay organisations, that intervened at strategic points in the new social complex. Catholic education, of course, played a crucial role in this strategic model. But in the new order of things, control was now also to be mediated and indirect – through Catholic Action. From being on the defensive, the Catholic Church was now going on the offensive. This confidence was to be a feature of Catholic life in Europe and America for the next few decades. It created a unique situation where Catholicism became respected and influential in the wider culture.

That, combined with the recent achievement of Irish political independence, helped to create a potent mixture for the new rulers, ecclesiastical and political, in the early decades of independence in Ireland. This new vision helped the Irish Catholic hierarchy to reach an accommodation with the new masters of the Irish Free State and it guaranteed that their previous influence would not be diluted. We will see this strategy working in the first decade of independence.

IRELAND: RELIGION OF THE KNEE JOINT

The maintenance of the socio-hierarchical order was also much emphasised in the encyclical *Ubi Arcano Dei*, as it was of paramount significance in the Catholic Church's conception of the right ordering of society. The laity's 'mandate' only came from the Catholic Church. This accepted understanding between priest and people was a crucial dynamic in the intention of the Catholic Church to mobilise the laity into battalions of organisations. It was greatly facilitated by the fact that the institution of the Catholic Church was overwhelmingly, not to say suffocatingly, vested in the aura of divine mystery. The sense of sacredness and mystery was concentrated in the Catholic hierarchy. The priest himself was seen as 'a man apart', whereas the laity was seen as profane and unmysterious.[7] The Catholic Church's essence identified with its hierarchical element. In this respect, the 1918 Code of Canon Law was an almost mathematically constructed impeccable system of legislation.

Above all else, however, was the fact that the Irish Catholic Church overwhelmingly controlled the minds and hearts of the people through the education system. This situation had gone from strength to strength, particularly since the 1850 Synod of Thurles, which had laid down the structures and strategies for the governance and development of Irish Catholicism from the mid-nineteenth century onwards. Of particular importance also were the devotional structures such as those embryonic organisational infrastructures existing in every parish, namely the sodalities and confraternities, at which attendance on the part of the laity was deemed obligatory. These were pious religious groupings or guilds whose main activities were devotional and processional. They were, as we saw earlier with the Irish Vigilance Association of 1911, essential recruiting grounds. In Limerick, the Archconfraternity of the Holy Family was a particularly powerful one, and it was reported in 1923 that, 'seven thousand Limerick men, members of the Archconfraternity, marched today through their native streets'.[8]

A year later, Archdeacon Fallon PP, addressing the Sacred Heart Sodality in Castlebar, expressed his belief that they had, 'in sodalities, forces strong enough not only to oppose those dangers [of pagan literature] but any other dangers that might turn up, provided that their forces were organised'.[9]

In 1925, in Ardee, Co. Louth, Archbishop O'Donnell, addressing 3,000 members of the Sacred Heart Confraternity, said that, 'an active confraternity could do much to exclude evil literature, discourage the pernicious habit of betting, and confine amusements'.[10]

Lenten pastorals for these years similarly expressed this pessimistic outlook and also emphasised the need for organisation. Bishop O'Doherty of Galway called for a 'campaign' to be started, 'to clear the rotten shops of Galway of this foul stuff'[11] (referring to imported literature). Archbishop Byrne of Dublin, in his pastoral, also saw the need for 'a strong Catholic opinion', which would be helped by the growth of lay organisations.[12]

THE CATHOLIC TRUTH SOCIETY OF IRELAND ANNUAL CONFERENCES

Ever since the early 1900s the Catholic hierarchy had been quick to make use of the CTSI's annual conferences for the widespread dissemination of their views on important matters of the day. Cardinal Logue addressed the 1921 conference in Dublin's Mansion House and he advised his audience that when Ireland was safely through its troubles, 'a forward Catholic movement would be undertaken'.[13] As part of this strategy, in 1920 a major 'Re-Organisation Plan' had been drawn up by the CTSI on the instructions of the Catholic hierarchy.[14] This plan envisaged the establishment of vibrant branches of the Society in every parish in the country, with the express aim of promoting a strong Catholic public opinion. For the next three decades the CTSI worked on this design and its annual conferences became the forge in which the Catholic identity of the Irish Free State was hammered out and its moral and social values articulated.

In particular, the conferences tended to focus on the need to 'catholicise' the new State. At both the 1922 and 1923 conferences, Catholics were urged to give their loyalty to the Free State and they were reminded in strong terms that the Catholic hierarchy accepted the legitimacy of the new order of things.[15] Some of the later conferences helped to expound this Catholic nationalist identity. The 1928 meeting had as its particular theme, 'The Catholic Nation', and the various papers explored the topic in depth, for example, 'Its Governing Authority and Functions', 'A Catholic Nation: Its Laws and Its Citizens', and 'A Catholic Nation and the Catholic Church'.[16] The following year's conference, which incorporated the national emancipation centenary celebrations, explored the 'Struggle for Faith', the Penal Laws, and the Elizabethan and Cromwellian persecutions.[17]

These conferences and others helped to shape the Catholic nationalist identity of the Irish Free State with their emphasis on the historic struggles of Irish Catholics in previous centuries for religious freedom. The fact that the CTSI were the foremost organisers with the government of both the 1929 emancipation celebrations and the 1932 Eucharistic Congress also illustrated the bond between Church and State. 'The Soldier's Song' might have been the national anthem sung at both events but 'Faith of Our Fathers' struck the appropriate twin cords of nationalism and Catholicism.

It was the 1922 annual conference that hallmarked the direction of this relationship.[18] The theme was 'Catholics and Citizenship' and Irish citizens were informed of the duties expected of them towards the new government and State. Bishop O'Doherty pointed out that, 'We have rulers now whom we cannot but regard as lawful and we must learn to cultivate towards them that spirit of reverence and honour'.[19]

This was echoed by *The Irish Catholic* newspaper in its report of the conference when it declared that, 'it is the duty of the citizen to show respect for and yield obedience to the Government which is now the people's Government and not one set up by a foreign nation, as was the case until recently'.[20] It was made quite clear at the 1923 conference that the new Irish Free State would certainly be strongly Catholic in both its outlook and its legislation.

The 1923 conference was of particular significance, with Civil-War tensions still high in Ireland. There were difficulties outside the Mansion House as republican demonstrators heckled and jostled prominent clergymen as they made their entrance. Members of the CYMS and the AOH were on hand, however, to provide protection, having been forewarned to anticipate trouble. It was agreed by the organisers that the conference should afford Irish Catholics, 'an opportunity of considering steps to be taken individually and collectively in order that the problems of the day as they relate to Ireland may be solved'.[21]

They also planned a special reception for the Governor General and the President of the Executive Council during the conference, and in discussing the protocol, decided that they would join a procession; the Governor General with Cardinal Logue and the President with the Archbishop of Dublin.[22] The 1923 conference arrangements represented plans for a symbolic unification of Church and State, as equals, in the new order of things. Kevin O'Higgins, TD and Minister of Justice, the principal speaker, would give support, sustenance and credence to this hope and belief.

On another level, the organisational drive of the CTSI was to be given its greatest kick-start. Already taking their cue from the 1922 encyclical on Catholic Action, *Ubi Arcano Dei*, they had published for Ireland a number of English pamphlets on the subject. They also published a booklet called *Catholic Organisation in Holland – A Lesson for Ireland*.[23] One of the strongest themes running through the conference was the potential role of the Catholic laity in Ireland. Representatives from Church and State called on the Catholic laity to be 'up and doing'. Sir Joseph Glynn, a prominent Catholic layman, president of the St Vincent de Paul Society and vice-president of the CTSI, stressed the need to build the state along Catholic lines and he called on Catholics to 'restore to their public life the Catholic atmosphere it once possessed' and to build a state, 'in keeping with Catholic traditions and polity'.[24] In doing so, he deplored the poor level of organisation among the Catholic laity of Ireland in contrast with continental countries.

In his opening address, Cardinal Logue showed clearly that the Irish Catholic Church was taking seriously the warnings and advice as regards the changes facing the post-War Europe which were included in *Ubi Arcano Dei*. The encyclical and its sentiments were forcibly expressed by the Cardinal and he emphasised his commitment to 'make Ireland what she ought to be – a good, sound, solid, Catholic nation'.[25] He interpreted any forms of objectionable morality as being 'an outcrop of the corruption of the age'. In an article on 'Religion and Identity', Margaret O'Callaghan suggests that the context of Cardinal Logue's remarks, and the ensuing moral zeal and puritanical vigour in the Catholic Church in the 1920s, 'must be viewed not merely as an intensification of a Jansenist streak in Irish Catholicism, but as a reaction to the demands they believed Irish independence made upon the people's moral calibre'.[26]

We must, however, add to these dimensions the internal Catholic Church dimension; crucially the fact that the Church was still living and reeling in the shadow of the early-twentieth-century modernist threat, an issue which Pope Pius XI pointedly referred to in his encyclical.

THE ADDRESS OF KEVIN O'HIGGINS

Of particular significance was the keynote address of Kevin O'Higgins.[27] He was as anxious as the Catholic hierarchy to preserve traditional values and this was most evident in his paper 'The Catholic Layman in Public Life'.[28] He stressed the importance of the Catholic laity participating more fully in public life. He spoke of 'the Catholic laity breathing powerful life into the nostrils of democracy'. He argued strongly that, 'Now is the time for the Catholic layman to break away from both fanaticism and Machiavellianism and to revert to Catholic social doctrine which on examination is seen to be the highest and most distinctive creed ever published.'[29]

He also questioned the social principles and convictions behind Irish democracy, 'they are not Catholic in the measure to be expected – rather an admixture of feudalism and brigandage in one quarter and a deplorable amount of grabber and gombeen morality generally'.

His conclusion emphasised that 'it is time to be up and doing', working together constructively to create the new Ireland. The expression 'up and doing' thenceforth came to be associated with the Catholic Action movement over the years, and became a catchphrase – a clarion call – for the movement. O'Higgins speech was published in booklet form by the CTSI and was widely distributed to coincide with the launch of their major organisational drive in the mid-1920s.[30]

An examination of the papers of the CTSI conferences shows that prominent members of the Catholic laity played an important role as speakers and contributors. But much of what they had to say was in support of, rather than independent of, the priests and bishops. When W.G. Fallon addressed the 1928 conference, he described the role of the Catholic intelligentsia as interpreters of Church teaching rather than initiators, thus indicating an acceptance of the subservient role for the Catholic laity.[31] This attitude reinforced and reflected the widespread unquestioning passive stance of Irish Catholics. As we shall see in the case of the CTSI itself and particularly with regard to the Legion of Mary, initiative was indeed frowned upon and strongly discouraged.

Despite this, the CTSI had no difficulties in attracting establishment figures to grace their conference platforms. Businessmen, politicians, academics, educationalists, and representatives of the legal profession were always on the platform and had no difficulty in participating in that process, which asserted Catholicism as the indispensable lever, link, and bond, in the forging of an emerging independent but shaky Irish identity.

THE SCOPE OF CTSI ORGANISATIONAL SUCCESS IN THE MID-1920S

As well as their very successful annual conferences, the Society was engaging in a nationwide organisational drive.[32] Particular impetus had been given in 1923 by Kevin O'Higgins's call for Catholics to be 'up and doing'. In 1924, Missionary Orders, and in particular, the Redemptorists, were recruited to help the Society's campaign.[33] The Parish Mission was hugely influential in securing publicity and membership for the Society. The Missioners were exhorted by the CTSI to build upon the 1923 conference theme, with the express view 'of bonding all Catholics in one great organisation for the defence of Catholic principles and truth'.[34] According to the CTSI circular, the immediate need for branches was because 'the working classes are flooded with the most pernicious books, pamphlets and papers on industrial questions which are anti-Catholic – and contain the poison of Communism'.[35] The circular also indicated that in the area of politics, a CTSI branch 'would create an atmosphere favourable to the selection of persons who are guided by the interests of the State'. It was felt that the creation of such a local public opinion would ensure that all local matters would be looked at from the point of view of Catholic morality.[36] The 'evil literature' question,[37] the possibility of divorce legislation, and the Seanad elections, were also important factors in the society's organisational drive, together with the fear of contaminating the workers with questionable theories.[38] The campaign was helped by the Bishops' Lenten pastorals.[39] Similarly, they secured weekly columns in newspapers including: *The Irish News*; the *Cork Examiner*; the *Munster News*; *The Irish Catholic*; the *Ulster Herald*; the *Frontier Sentinel*; the *Tipperary Star*, and the *Westmeath Independent*.[40] Hugh Allen, a person with considerable press experience, was appointed in early 1925 as a full-time organising secretary.[41] According to the Society's report for that year, the only way 'to repel attack, was to meet organisation with counter-organisation'. Organisation would create branches, and branches would create public opinion, 'which would radiate'.[42] *Catholic Action* was decided upon as the title of the Society's new magazine. By early 1926, sixty branches with thousands of members were operating throughout the country.[43] Not only that, but sales of pamphlets had reached 'new records of achievement', selling one million that year. Compared with the figures for 1918, that was an increase of 337 per cent.[44] Similar results were achieved with its sales of Catholic newspapers and magazines.[45] Of course, these figures were helped by the fact that, in 1926, 92.6 per cent of the population of the Irish Free State was Catholic.

THE SYNOD OF MAYNOOTH AND THE DECREES ON CATHOLIC ACTION

By 1927 the country was beginning to settle down. The wireless was starting to make its appearance in some homes; a new political party, Fianna Fáil, had entered the Dáil; dancing, jazz and cinema attendance were becoming increasingly popular; and the Catholic Church decided to call a National Synod.[46]

The purpose for the 1927 Synod of Maynooth was 'to take spiritual stock after the havoc of the Great War which shook the whole world and was accompanied by grave troubles among ourselves'.[47] Of even greater significance, however, was its function to give effect to the provisions of the 1918 Code of Canon Law and to bring into conformity with it the legislation of the previous National Synods of 1850, 1875 and 1900.[48] The Code, which the Synod endeavoured to put into better effect in Ireland, was the disciplinary counterpart of the Pope's assertion of papal infallibility in 1870.The Code completed an internal tightening of the ranks, made for increased homogeneity and uniformity of action within the Irish Catholic Church, and ensured the strict dependence of the whole clerical army on two levels of command – the Pope and the Bishops. The 1927 Synod of Maynooth was to have a powerful effect on Irish society, similar to that of the 1850 Synod of Thurles on nineteenth-century society.

The Synod, with its call to Catholic Action and to the laity to join Catholic organisations, had its own guiding principles. In a strictly hierarchical Church, Catholic Action organisations would be controlled by the clergy and would operate in accordance with their agenda. The assertion of Catholicism in Ireland and its defence were part of that agenda and lay organisations were to be the levers to ensure its completion.

Some of the more important decrees of the Synod 'as they affect the laity', were numbers 233 to 248, relating to Catholic Action.The laity of Ireland were called upon to unite, 'in suitable societies to form an organised army which shall put forth all its powers to mould the public conscience in accordance with Catholic principles, to foster religion, to defend it in public and private and to restore the Christian mode of life' (Decree No.233).[49]

Particular societies were recommended: the Catholic Protection and Rescue Society of Ireland; the Society of St Vincent de Paul; the Catholic Truth Society of Ireland.The last of these was described as 'that excellent organisation for the defence and propagation of Catholic truth'. Fears of socialism were expressed and parish priests were exhorted to encourage organisations of workers and farmers that would be in conformity with Catholic principles.[50] Through these Catholic Action organisations, which would be 'amenable to ecclesiastical authority', the clergy would be able to 'expand and defend their rights and duties'. Other issues such as the problem of dances, 'evil literature' and women's fashions, were also examined in the decrees.[51]

The growth and development of specifically 'Catholic' organisations that had been developing since the CTSI had been established in 1899 was given a tremendous stimulus by the Synod of Maynooth. Organisations flourished and expanded, all intent to respond to the clarion call to Catholic Action and to be 'up and doing'.

THE PUBLICATION OF THE HANDBOOK OF CATHOLIC ACTION, 1928

According to its Annual Reports, the attitude of the CTSI in the years 1927–1928 was that their 'organisation work is the most important activity on hand'.[52] To enhance and further develop this aspect of its work, it was decided to publish a small book dealing with Catholic Action in Ireland, and 'with special reference to the CTSI whose function it is to develop Catholic Action'.[53] They felt that with the establishment of definite structures and strategies, 'the way is now perfectly clear for a big advance in Catholic organisation'.[54] The new publication was called *Up and Doing – A Handbook of Catholic Action* and was a lengthy eighty-page 'charter' for the Society's activities.[55] It clearly spelt out the purpose of the organisation's endeavours, 'to create in Ireland a thoroughly Catholic environment, a thoroughly Catholic atmosphere, a thoroughly Catholic public opinion'.

Organisations would 'affect the whole thought and outlook and conduct of Irish Catholics', with a view to 'strengthening' Irish Catholic life with a 'robust Catholic public opinion'.[56]

Organisations were to counteract the 'forces' and 'enemies' arrayed against the Church. Every person was seen as a 'soldier' in the 'war' between the Church and her enemies. There could be 'no neutrality'. The 'neutral' was in fact the enemy. The war against the Church was being intensified 'by almost the entire press, newspaper, periodical, and book: and by the cinema and theatre'. Catholics were exhorted to join lay organisations, because, 'CATHOLIC ACTION NEEDS THEM'.[57]

Pius XI's new encyclical on Catholic Action, *Non Abbiamo Bisogno* (1931), gave the movement a further spirit of urgency. In Ireland, a spate of manuals, books, articles, and pamphlets were published subsequent to the encyclical. Typical of the manuals was *A Manual of Catholic Action* (Dublin, 1933), which set out to refute the infamous forty 'current erroneous systems'.[58]

The introduction stated, 'The object of this publication is to furnish those engaged in Catholic Action with the knowledge needed for combating the "pernicious errors" current at the present time and the unscrupulous propaganda by which these errors are disseminated'.

The *Manual* consisted of 150 pages, 73 of which were devoted to 'errors', 36 to Catholic sociology, and nearly 40 pages to 'organised Catholic Action and how it could be strengthened'.

Other important publications in the early 1930s included: *Catholic Action, Principles and Practice*;[59] *The Serried Ranks of Catholic Action*;[60] *Catholic Action in Ireland*;[61] *The Catholic Social Movement*,[62] and *The Splendid Cause*.[63]

Lynn Doyle, the writer who was appointed to the Censorship Board in the mid-1930s, much to the annoyance of the CTSI, captures the atmosphere of the country in his work *The Spirit of Ireland* (1935). According to Doyle:

...the tourist will, if he looks attentively at newsagents', posters and shops, gain insight into the heart of Ireland in an essential particular. It is necessary that one should learn and take account how much religion enters into the life of an Irish Catholic. There are half a dozen Catholic weeklies – their circulation in the aggregate is enormous. All are militantly Catholic – some of them at times exhibiting a little more zeal than meekness – buttresses of the Church, and allies to the clergy. The Irish are justified of their boast that they are today the most Catholic people in the world. Their religion is part of their daily life.[64]

Catholic organisations reinforced this culture. The CTSI itself launched a new magazine in these years called *Catholic Action*. This was later changed to *Up and Doing*, and still later to the *Catholic Truth Quarterly*.

The proliferation of organisations and publications meant that campaigns and vigilance activities were also stepped up. John Swift, a senior trade unionist, and a member of the Secular Society,[65] recalled the 'proliferation of Catholic Action lay groups who attracted the zealots who harassed and intimidated those promoting objects at variance with theirs'.[66] 'Intellectual terrorism' was the term he used to describe the atmosphere of the time. The Secular Society met in premises in Lincoln Place, Dublin. According to Swift, in order to avoid disruption of its meetings by 'Catholic Action devotees', attendance was strictly monitored.

The CTSI did, however, manage to penetrate the organisation, and drew adverse publicity to it in the columns of *The Irish Press* and *The Irish Catholic*[67] who, in the opinion of Swift, 'resorted to the normal intimidation of the time'.[68] Not long afterwards they were forced to move premises. If 'intellectual terrorism' was the experience of Swift, the CTSI preferred the term used by the Free State's Director of Broadcasting, T.J. Kiernan, who referred to the need for 'intellectual protectionism' in an article on Catholic Action he wrote for the *Capuchin Annual* in 1934.[69]

DENOMINATIONAL ISSUES AND THE GROWTH OF ORGANISATIONS

The motivation for a number of Catholic organisations which flourished in these years was the determination that Irish life in the new Ireland should bear a Catholic complexion and that Catholic power should assert itself unambiguously in social and economic terms, as it had been unable to do so in the past. The result was the restructuring or founding of a number of specifically 'Catholic' organisations, with the emphasis on countering the 'Protestant' or Ascendancy influence in the emerging Irish nation.

A Jesuit priest, Fr Stephen Browne, was instrumental in establishing the Central Catholic Library in Dublin in 1922, with the specific aim of catering for the expected needs of 'Catholic' journalists and politicians.[70] Another Jesuit, Fr Richard Devane, who had been active in the Limerick vigilance campaign of 1911 and who had helped Frank Duff in his anti-proselytism and anti-prostitution activities, was the inspiration behind the founding of the Irish Guild of Catholic Nurses in the same year.[71] The popular writer Annie M.P. Smithson, a convert to Catholicism, was for many years the Secretary of the Guild.[72] Ruth Nicholls, one of the CTSI's committee of management, was the editor of the *Irish Nursing News*, and she saw this early initiative as being like 'early Christians creeping out of the Catacombs – afraid at every turn of going too far; practically unrecognised by the Catholic hospitals, haunted by the fear of creating difficulties in the undenominational training schools – for no Catholic Doctors' Guild stood beside us for ten years'.[73] She believed that these circumstances in a way 'unconsciously forced them' to Catholic Action, as they became conscious of the 'purely Protestant atmosphere' and viewpoint which was being applied to moral–medical problems.[74] This symbiotic development was frequently a manifestation of organisational initiative.

In 1922 also, the Dublin-based Columbian Knights (founded in 1909 by members of the Catholic Defence Society) amalgamated with the Belfast organisation, the Knights of St Columbanus. The new order advised Archbishop Byrne that 'the united body now represents the best elements and most energising influences in the Catholic laity of Dublin'.[75] They sent their *Constitution and Laws* to the Archbishop for approval the following year. Amongst their objectives were the following:

1. The promotion of Catholic interests and well-being; to promote and foster the cause of the Catholic faith and Catholic education, subject always to the approval of the Church.

2. To afford Catholic men a means of intercourse, whereby Catholic principles of social order and social reform may be studied and disseminated.

3. To foster the sentiments of Catholic unity and mutual co-operation in social matters.[76]

By 1924, the Order's membership was given as 3,000, with thirty primary councils (branches) in the country.[77] Nearly ten years later, in 1933, the Knights were able to further clarify their objectives to include, 'fostering a Catholic conscience and securing adequate recognition for Catholic doctrines and practices in all phases of life, social, public, commercial and professional'.[78] By then they had 108 branches and 5,387 members.[79] The organisation's main activities in the 1920s were concentrated on the 'work of organisation' and the building up of a branch structure throughout Ireland. Because of this they felt they were unable to engage in any 'work of Catholic activity on a large scale', but despite this, 'a really useful Catholic work has been attempted and done'. This work they saw as being 'Catholic Action' work.[80] This vagueness in terms of what the Society was actually doing, this discretion, is evident as far back as 1917, and is admitted in the *Ritual of the Knights of St Columbanus*, which points out that it was adopted from a similar one of the American Knights of Columbus.[81] These rituals and secrecy the Knights regarded as a necessary and reasonable precaution in the face of the power and influence of the established interests. These Ascendancy interests had their own organisations and secret rituals.

These new organisations held the common belief that social reconstruction on a definitely Catholic basis was both possible and necessary. The Annual Report of the CTSI for 1926-1927, issued in mid-1927, set the tone.[82] The report indicated that progress had been made since independence, in that 'the Catholic is substantially in control of Government, the Civil Service, the Judiciary, the Army and the Police', and the 'learned professions boast of many distinguished members', yet in two important respects the Catholic:

> ...still suffers as a result of the Penal Laws — in industrial and commercial life he is still suffering from the poverty under which he started a century ago: the Protestant still continues to maintain the ascendancy in social life; the cultivated pose of superiority in the Protestant oppresses us.[83]

The report concluded that the Society's future role lay in assisting 'the completion of Catholic Emancipation'. National organisation of the Catholic laity of Ireland was to be the only way forward for this necessary 'regeneration'. The CTSI stance was representative of much of the kind of feeling expressed by many in the 1920s, with the emphasis on the explicitly denominational nature of the social and economic order.

That feeling was underpinned by the employment and occupational patterns of the Protestant and Unionist population, which remained in the Irish Free State after the Civil War and partition, according to the Knights of St Columbanus.[84] The Protestants, despite their numerically inferior position, in fact maintained a high socio-economic profile, doubtlessly a legacy of their pre-independence days. In the agricultural sector, Protestants were disproportionately represented in all the large farm size categories, right down to fifty acres. In 1926, 22.5 per cent of the owners of farms over 200 acres were Protestants. In the non-agricultural sector, this disproportionate percentage was also reflected in the strikingly high proportion of Protestants in management and administration, in big business, including banking and brewing, in wholesale, retail and catering spheres, and above all, in the professions. In the higher socio-economic occupations, 33 per cent of the total consisted of Protestants, despite their low population numbers. Even among typists over one quarter of them were Protestants in 1926 – an almost threefold rate of over-representation.[85] The political shift towards a Catholic ethos in the Irish Free State did not seem to be changing these hard facts. But the situation was to be the dominant factor in influencing Catholic organisations to become more vociferous as the decade wore on.

The CTSI pointed the finger of the collective consciousness at the malevolent Protestant influence, and other Catholic organisations would grasp that nettle with different strategies.

FR EDWARD CAHILL AND THE 'UN-CATHOLIC' FRAMEWORK OF IRISH SOCIETY

The Jesuit priest Fr Edward Cahill, who had been a contributor to the *Irish Messenger* office's *Social Action* series of pamphlets since they were inaugurated in 1914, informed Archbishop Byrne in October 1926 that a new society, An Rioghacht – The League of the Kingship of Christ, 'has already been at a tentative stage for some months'.[86] The Provisional Committee of the new organisation consisted of M.J. Lennon BL, J. Durnin, Sir Joseph Glynn, George Gavan Duffy BL, Patrick Waldron, and three priests. This organisation was to be an important element in the intellectual drive behind the Catholic Action movement. Duffy had participated in the Anglo-Irish Treaty negotiations of 1921. Another prominent member was Mrs Berthon Waters, an economist. One member, Eoin O'Keefe, owner of Duffy's Publishers, was a personal friend of Éamon de Valera, as was Peadar O'Loghlen TD. Gabriel Fallon, the well-known critic, was also an active member. Michael Lennon was a district justice, and Waldron a prominent lawyer. Two senior civil servants, Maurice Moynihan and O.J. Redmond, were also activists.[87] Fr Cahill consciously drew to An Rioghacht a select body of men and women, and through them, and by means of his own personal contacts and writings during the 1920s and 1930s, won recognition and influence for the work and aims of the organisation. Cahill was very aware of the general intellectual weakness of Irish Catholicism and he sought to ensure that the top rank members, the Associates, all made a serious study of Catholic social principles. There were six branches in Dublin, two in Cork, two in Kilkenny, and one each in Waterford, Mullingar, Nenagh and Bray.[88] Membership ran to several hundred at any one time. Cahill was more concerned about the training of men and women rather than the numbers in his organisation. His organisation differed from others in that respect, as he actively encouraged them to move on once trained.[89] Writing in 1951, to celebrate the silver jubilee of the organisation, one of the founders, J. Waldron (brother of Patrick), declared, 'Not least among the achievements of An Rioghacht has been the training of members, who have carried into their various spheres in public life a sound knowledge of Catholic social principles, in the Judiciary, the professions, the civil Service, Trade Unions, in local bodies and in commerce.'[90]

It was Cahill's hope that An Rioghacht would aim at doing for Ireland something similar to what the Volksverein and kindred Catholic associations were doing in Germany and other continental countries. He hoped that this would lead to the adoption of a national programme based on these principles and covering the social, economic, and educational spheres. The League intended to achieve this through organisation, lectures, pamphlets, the establishment of an Irish Catholic press, summer schools, and an annual Catholic Congress.

Shortly after the founding of the new organisation, and coinciding with the impending Synod, Cahill issued a pamphlet defining An Rioghacht's object as, 'a society for social study and Catholic Action'.[91] The need for such a type of organisation arose from his conviction that the organisation of the laity was vital to counteract highly organised anti-Christian forces and movements. For Cahill, then, 'there was no phase of contemporary history more striking than the rise of the great Catholic lay organisations during the past fifty years. These organisations are already an immense force in many continental countries'.[92]

Cahill saw the situation in Ireland as showing a special need for such organisations because, although the people were predominantly Catholic, 'the framework of the society in which they live is still largely un-Catholic'. He saw the civic institutions and social organisation of the country as being out of harmony with the 1922 Constitution because for centuries the country had been dominated by non-Catholic and anti-Catholic foreign influences. This, according to Cahill, had led to Ireland losing touch with the traditional Catholic culture of Europe. Echoing his fellow Jesuit Fr Stephen Browne, he regarded the English literature upon which the minds of the people were largely formed, as predominantly Protestant.[93]

One of Cahill's plans was for an Irish Catholic weekly. He drew up a draft policy for what the weekly would represent and promote.[94] Irish nationality would be a major theme. He would publish articles on the following:

1. Economics – whereby national control of credit would be necessary for national wellbeing. Home markets were to be encouraged, as were natural resources such as agriculture, fisheries, mineral resources and forestry.

2. Social wellbeing. The functions of the State were to be defined by Catholic teaching. In urban areas the poor and the workers needed to be housed. Unemployment had to be tackled. In rural areas labourers should be given land.

3. Literature and the Press – a Catholic Press.

4. Art. 'Native genius' was to be encouraged with emphasis on simplicity and 'lastingness' in manufactured products. Control of the theatre and cinema would be vital and the national theatre would represent true concepts of the Irish national character.

Cahill believed that 'Catholic organisation' was the pre-requisite for the co-ordination and the development of united aims and conscious purpose. Organisation would facilitate 'Catholic defence' and would be useful for 'public demonstrations'.[95] He was a firm believer in supporting rural life and he emphasised that agriculture was the mainstay of the Irish economy. With the help of members of An Rioghacht, in 1928 he drew up a 'Scheme for Social Re-construction', which proposed the revitalisation of rural life through the establishment of 'Catholic Agricultural Colonies'.[96] The 'Colonies' would counteract the attractions of the city and would stem the tide of emigration. Above all, they would 'save the historic Irish nation from final extinction' and would 'build up again the fabric of Christian social organisation'.[97]

During the 1920s Cahill was Professor of Social Science in Milltown Park, and published many articles on similar themes in the *Irish Ecclesiastical Record* and the *Irish Monthly* between 1924 and 1930. The same matter formed the basis of a series of weekly lectures which he gave to the Central Branch of An Rioghacht. The cumulative effort of his writings and lectures on Catholic Action and social science eventually led to the 1932 publication of his magnum opus, *The Framework of the Christian State*.[98]

Another abiding concern that was attracting Cahill's attention was international freemasonry. In August 1926, in the course of his research on the topic, he received a letter from Colonel Claude Cane, Deputy Grand Master of the Freemasons of Ireland.[99] Cane informed Cahill that there were practically no Catholic Freemasons in Ireland but, he added, 'it is true that many, if not most, of the big businesses in the country were controlled by Protestants'. He was adamant, however, that freemasonry in Ireland was certainly not a 'secret society' and had between 60,000 and 70,000 members throughout the country. Cahill was not impressed by the assurance and during the years 1927-1928, he published five lengthy articles on the subject in the official clerical journal, the *Irish Ecclesiastical Record*.[100]

Cahill was not alone in having strong views on the subject. The Holy Ghost priest Fr Denis Fahey also wrote a series of articles on the subject under the title, 'Secret Societies and the Kingship of Christ' in the *Catholic Bulletin* in 1928.[101] The Dominican publication *The Irish Rosary* followed suit in 1929, with a number of articles on 'Freemasonry in Ireland'. *The Irish Rosary* described freemasonry as, 'almost a miracle of silent, relentless, determined, organisation; while the ordinary Catholic people of this nation remain unorganised and disorganised, fighting over silly questions of politics, while the common enemy laughs at their folly, and gathers in the spoils'.[102]

But the issue was not confined to Ireland. In England, America, France and Belgium, during the 1920s, there was an upsurge in publications examining the anti-Christian movement of 'Masonry and its Jewish allies'. It was not until 1931 that the CTSI decided to publish booklets on the subject, the first called *Freemasonry: Its Origin, Aim and Methods*, by a Fr Clune. The booklet had a particularly striking cover, with a silhouetted devilish face with horns on its head, painted on a gloomy red and black background. This cover was intended to evoke feelings of the horrific and the macabre. The Society followed this by publishing booklets written by Fr Cahill on the subject.[103] All writers on the issue quoted Pope Leo XIII's encyclical on freemasonry, *Humanum Genus* (1884).[104]

In 1929, Cahill's *Freemasonry and the Anti-Christian Movement* was published. This book became an immediate bestseller and within a few months a second edition was published.[105] Such propagandist work coming from the pen of one of the highly respected Jesuit Order was not questioned at the time. Rather the contents were accepted as fact, not open to criticism. Because of this, Cahill's inflammatory and provocative writings stirred the angry embers of post-independence failure and pundits jostled to lavish their praise, while punters drank his vitriolic language and partook in creating a splenetic, vindictive and fearful Catholicism.

The Leader, still under the editorship of D.P. Moran, remarked in early November that Cahill's book 'was a revelation' to them and begged the question, 'should freemasonry be suppressed? Mussolini put an end to it in Italy'.[106] True to its own unique style, *The Leader* echoed Cahill by declaring that, 'in the Catholic Saorstát we have been dragooned, bludgeoned, and legislated into a Protestant country'.

It recommended that the book should be widely read so that people could wake up to the reality of Masonic influence in the banks, railways, Dublin University, the RDS, and some of the medical institutions.

On the same day as the *Leader* review, and about six weeks after the appearance of the first edition of Cahill's work, a letter of protest from Col. Claude Cane, the official spokesman of the Freemasons of Ireland, appeared in the *Irish Independent* and the *Belfast Telegraph*. The letter drew forth rejoinders, which were published throughout the month of November 1929, and the controversy aroused keen public interest. Practically all the Irish Catholic weeklies and monthlies devoted considerable space to it, week after week. Neither *The Irish Times*, nor the *Cork Examiner*, nor any of the Dublin evening papers alluded to it.[107] In March 1930, some of the Bishops' Lenten pastorals warned once more of 'secret societies', including freemasonry.[108]

In retrospect, it can all appear to have been greatly overdrawn. Yet contemporaries of the 1920s and early 1930s frequently remarked on the reality of Freemason influence in business and commercial life, particularly since it was well known that many of the great business houses were owned by Protestants.

One organisation which in particular kept the Irish Catholic hierarchy well informed on the demerits of the Freemasons was the Ancient Order of Hibernians, and especially the Mountjoy Square Dublin branch, whose secretary was John D. Nugent. The AOH published a number of leaflets during the 1920s, which seemed to gather fresh momentum as the years passed by. The first, *The Hidden Hand in the Mexican Atrocities*, warned that Irish Catholics should take note as 'the Masonic organisation is getting its grip on the Free State'; its membership had increased by over 50 per cent between 1920 and 1925, 'and is still growing'.[109] Another leaflet, *Have You Ever Given a Thought?*, indicated that in 1925, despite the retirement of the British Army and British military officials – the two sources from which the Masonic organisation was largely recruited in the days of British rule – there were 540 lodges and 43,000 members in Ireland, an increase of 15,000 members during the years 1920 and 1925. (Col. Claude Cane gave a larger figure to Fr Cahill.) In Dublin alone, according to the AOH, eleven new lodges had been established in these years.[110] In a later leaflet, *Freemasonry's Duplicate Personality* (1928), the organisation posed the question as to whether the Irish Free State should 'be left to the mercy of this Masonic influence'. The AOH saw direct links between Bolshevism/communism, Jewry, and freemasonry, which they described as 'this unholy combination'.

However, the problem as John Nugent saw it was that no Catholic organisation could accept responsibility or be publicly identified with the fight against freemasonry, which he believed was working, 'through a process of peaceful penetration, seeking to consolidate its hold on every position that might give it an influential, if not dominating, position in the new Free State'.[111]

Catholic organisations, according to Nugent, could not 'expose' themselves. It was a difficult task to 'compete for an existence with a solid Masonic influence on the one hand and a disorganised Catholic laity on the other'. He did believe, however, in the vital part to be played by Catholic organisation of the laity in creating a 'healthy public opinion'. Young men should join the AOH, the Knights, or the CYMS, he argued. The more the laity joined these organisations the better, as they would benefit from widespread Catholic propaganda. The wide distribution of leaflets was part of the propaganda work of the AOH itself, in its efforts to create an 'informed' public opinion.

The need for Catholic organisation was a constant theme of the AOH. At their November 1927 conference held in Dundalk, the well-known Cork solicitor John J. Horgan, a member of a number of Catholic organisations and author of *Great Catholic Laymen* (CTSI, 1905), said that unless Catholics became 'more organised ... Catholic interests might be seriously affected'. He believed that the Hibernians should seek to strengthen and develop the alliance of their Society with lay Catholics because 'the business of the country was in the hands of the old Ascendancy Party' and he regarded this as being largely due to 'Catholic apathy and lack of organisation'.[112] His views were shared by a number of other speakers at the conference. A Waterford delegate, J. McDonnell, said that the time had come for the AOH to be reorganised along 'militant Catholic lines'. Any influences at work to the detriment of Catholic interests were solely because Catholics were not organised. Another delegate, this time from Louth, was glad to be able to say that in his county they never separated Hibernianism from politics and were always able to return a Hibernian identified with the national spirit of the country. J. Coburn, the standing TD for Louth, was one of the delegates present at the conference.

The National Secretary of the AOH, in his concluding speech to the conference, cited the successes of the German Catholic Centre Party, which 'brought Bismarck to his knees'. By unity and organisation in the Free State, Catholics could 'counter the forces' that were 'always the deadly enemies of Irish Nationalism and Irish Catholicism'.[113] Several delegates agreed strongly with this view and re-emphasised the need to continue to pursue this agenda through politics. Plans for greater organisational strategies were also agreed upon by delegates representing branches in Dublin, Longford, Cork, Donegal, Mayo, Kildare, Westmeath, Sligo, Kilkenny, Wexford, Tipperary, Meath, Kerry, Limerick, Waterford, Wicklow, Louth, and the border counties. Dublin was represented by a number of delegates from different branches.[114]

Both the Knights of St Columbanus and the AOH placed great emphasis on the crucial importance of an organised Catholic laity during the 1920s, but even more so after 1927. This process was to bear fruit during this and the following decades, and Catholics were enabled to acquire greater influence in professional, commercial, industrial and business life. This emphasis on Catholic organisation echoed the hopes and aspirations of the earlier organisations at the beginning of the century – the Catholic Association and the Catholic Defence Society. John Horgan, a veteran of the earlier campaign, can be seen as the link in this historical process, which attempted to develop a significant and dominant Catholic influence in social and economic life. The campaign continued with greater vigour after independence and under the added protection and aegis of the energising Catholic Action umbrella.

THE ROLE OF Fr AMBROSE CROFTS

At the end of the 1920 CTSI annual conference, a paper was read on 'The Potentialities of the CYMS'. P.J. Daniel of the CYMS asked his audience the following, 'Why should not the CYMS educate their fellow Catholics as to their economic power, and how to use that power for the purpose of obtaining justice for those to whom it is denied at present?'[115] He saw the Society's potential in 'aiming for the removal of the obstacles which obstruct the path of Catholics' in obtaining their social position in society.

By the mid-1920s, with the CTSI opening branches all over the country, the Kilkenny CYMS heard Bishop Downey of Ossory advising them at their AGM, of the importance of extending the influence of Catholic societies.[116] In 1925, a Dominican priest, Fr Ambrose Crofts, had written an article in the *Irish Monthly* on 'Catholic Organisation in Belgium', in which he argued that 'our great want is real Catholic social organisation'.[117] For Crofts, they 'could do nothing without organisation'. He suggested that Ireland should imitate Catholic organisations in Belgium, 'unity must be their strength, and their battle-cry that of the Catholics of Belgium, "For God and Country"'.[118] Crofts had just returned to Ireland after completing a year's study in practical sociology in Brussels. He suggested to the CYMS that a federation of all the scattered branches would be required in order to revitalise it.[119]

The task of reorganising the CYMS was a difficult one, and it was recognised in 1927 that it would take years to produce results. John Costello, who was a very active member, became full-time secretary. In 1931 he was to write, 'the state of the Society was truly appalling and in such a condition that we despaired of ever achieving success. The position is a curious one. Almost every county has a branch but not one branch seems to have anything in common with the others.'[120] Not only that, but according to Costello the branches appeared to have overlooked the fact that they were supposed to be part of a Catholic organisation. He believed the situation had to change, as 'the Irish Bishops' call to Catholic Action in 1927 was too strong'.[121]

To give the organisation stronger focus and direction, Crofts, Costello and the new national council undertook to draft a new constitution and rules for the Society. Two of the aims would be: 1. The grouping and co-ordinating of the forces of the Catholic young men of Ireland, and 2. Supporting, recommending, encouraging and engaging in Catholic Action through the co-operation of affiliated branches.[122]

A further development gave tremendous impetus to the Society's forward movement in making branches 'real centres of Catholic activity' (as a correspondent informed Archbishop Byrne), in early 1928, with the holding of Dublin's first Catholic Social Week.[123] The week, which occurred in April 1928, had been Crofts's idea, and received its inspiration from the very popular Catholic Social Weeks in France. According to the souvenir programme of the week, 'one of the most powerful institutions for Catholic Action and social propaganda on the continent has been undoubtedly the Social Week. The Social Week should open up a way and prepare the ground for practical Catholic Action'.[124]

One of the principal speakers was a Herr Serrarens from Holland, who had a reputation as a Catholic organiser and was closely identified with the Catholic Labour Movement in Holland.

Crofts, by linking Catholic organisation in Ireland with the successes of Catholic organisation in Holland, was ensuring that a rejuvenated laity could no longer remain indifferent to the successes of the Catholic movements on the continent. Indeed, the Catholic Social Week did help to infuse new vigour into the Society. At last the CYMS had a *raison d'être* – Catholic Action. According to the week's programme, the Society felt that 'the time is now ripe for Catholic Action on the part of the laity'.[125] The Society now saw itself as being in the vanguard of this new, 'organised campaign of Catholic Action to promote and strengthen the influence of the Catholic Church'.[126]

The programme also quoted liberally from the encyclicals of Pius X and particularly Pius XI's *Ubi Arcano* on Catholic Action. Similarly, the Maynooth Synod's call to Catholic Action was emphasised.[127] The drive towards unity in the organisation, the National Council argued, would make the CYMS 'a powerful Catholic force not only in Dublin but throughout Ireland'.[128] The *Irish Rosary*, in a comment on the Social Week, saw it as spelling 'a triumph for the recently formed Federation'.[129]

THE 'NEW WOMAN' AND THE RESPONSE TO THE SYNOD

The 'New Woman' emerged in 1918. With her short hemline, her boyish bob and clipped sardonic speech (faithfully recorded in Evelyn Waugh's fiction), she embodied a rejection of the deluding romanticism that had led to such slaughter in the Great War. She also reflected the 'anything goes' hedonism of the 1920s – 'Après la Guerre/There'll be a good time everywhere' – and the changed role of women in the workplace brought about by the wartime labour shortages in Britain.

In Ireland, however, the *Irish Independent*, reporting on the CTSI annual conference for October 1926, captured the Catholic Church's attitude to this challenge to their vision of society. One speaker declared:

> The women of Ireland heretofore renowned for their virtue and honour, go about furnished with the paint-pot, the lip-stick … and many of them have acquired the habit of intemperance, perhaps one of the sequels to their lately adopted vogue of smoking. A so-called dress performance or dance today showed some of our Irish girls in such scanty drapery as could only be exceeded in the slave markets of pagan countries.[130]

Throughout the 1920s and subsequent decades, the Bishops regularly warned mothers that they were failing in their responsibilities by allowing their daughters to go to dances, immodestly dressed, unchaperoned and unprotected.[131] The Bishops feared the possibility of emancipation inherent in post-war amusements, and the levelling effect such amusements had on women in particular and the population in general. Modern dress defied social hierarchy and did not signify one's place in the class structure in the was nineteenth-century fashion had done.[132]

The cinema equally offended Irish ecclesiastics because of the challenge to Catholic perceptions of morality and stability. According to the *Irish Monthly* for early 1925, films portrayed alluring lifestyles that left young women 'sick with discontent' at the grim contrast presented by the realities of their own drab lives.[133] Therefore young women going to the cinema would be both morally corrupted and culturally dissatisfied.

As expected, the Bishops fears were given particular prominence in the decrees of the 1927 Maynooth Synod. The need to challenge the post-war emancipation movement then sweeping Europe, saw the Bishops repeatedly criticising 'immodest fashion'. Not only that but they linked modesty, the dance hall, the cinema, the 'bad book', and the indecent newspaper, with the modern practice of contraception. For the Bishops, 'chastity was a most beautiful gift. No flower in the field exhales so sweet a fragrance. It is a pearl of great price. In women especially, purity is the crowning glory.'

Difficulties for chastity began in the dance hall. Dancing led to immodesty and vice versa, and on to the abuse of intoxicants. And in the newspapers, 'concealed by the beautiful imagery and elegant diction, falsehood and immorality drape themselves'.[134] Public hoardings also came in for criticism, for 'occasionally flaunting suggestive advertisements'. Modesty in female attire was therefore essential. The Bishops were not slow to play the cultural nationalism and economic orthodoxy cards, 'the adoption of these exotic modes of dress is a crime against our country, because the imported articles are not only out of joint with traditional usage, but mean moreover, an injury to our native industries, and a loss to our trade'. It was hoped that soon, 'Celtic refinement will expel from our shores all these debasing fashions in dress and forms of pastime which minister to the lowest instinct'.[135]

Such concern for the native distilling industry was never expressed throughout the temperance campaign in the early 1920s. In this situation the Church was conscious of what they saw as even greater threats – the cinema, fashion, dances, etc. These challenged women's aspirations in a way never experienced before, and in the process challenged the very basis of Catholic Church control and influence in society.

Even worse in the eyes of the Church, was that contraception was directly linked to the issue of women's fashions. In Decree 217 of the Synod, every effort had to be made to prevent 'this unutterable crime, hitherto unheard of in our midst' from ever taking root.[136] This link was also given particular prominence in the submission of the CTSI to the Commission on Evil Literature in 1926.[137] The Synod and the CTSI's concern reflected the wider Catholic European stance. The German Catholic theologian Uta Ranke-Heinemann argues that the anti-contraception battle became particularly intense in the post-war period. The Belgian Arthur Vermeersch (d. 1936), was the leading moral theologian of the day, and was particularly adroit in influencing Belgian, German and Austrian Bishops to issue pastorals denouncing contraception.[138] The motives of the French and German Bishops, Ranke-Heinemann felt, were derived from a nationalist and militarist spirit that needed to be encouraged after the war because of the high human losses. Contraception was seen as undermining the necessary growth in populations. The Irish Bishops followed suit in 1926 and 1927, and also played the patriotic card. When the French Bishops spoke of the criminal freedom of contraception, the Irish Bishops spoke of the 'unutterable crime'.

One result of the Synod's exhortation on women's modesty was the establishment of a new organisation in late 1927, 'The Modest Dress and Deportment Crusade' (MDDC), which within a few months had a membership of 1,000.[139] The MDDC saw its inspiration coming from as far back as 1917, when the issue was first addressed in an article by Mary Butler in the *Irish Monthly* entitled 'The Ethics of Dress'. Butler wrote about her attendance at the International Federation of Catholic Women's Leagues, where it was decided that 'modern fashions are indecent, often injurious to health, and almost extravagant'.[140] Similar sentiments were also expressed, according to Butler, at the recent German Catholic Congress, and furthermore, concern was expressed that many of the leading fashion houses in Paris and other continental cities 'are almost all in the hands of Jews and Freemasons'.[141] Butler described as 'monstrosities' and a 'scandal', the 'slit-skirts, glove-tight costumes, and very décolleté costumes worn out of doors'. She quoted Pope Leo XIII's *Instruction to Christian Women on Fashion* to indicate that the Church was 'vigilant' in the matter. Butler, however, added that 'in no domain does the Church find greater difficulty in securing compliance with her wishes than in this realm of fashion'.[142] She emphasised above all the 'extravagance' aspect, which she believed would lead to fewer marriages, wreck existing ones, and therefore undermine 'the future of the race'. But crucially, this 'extravagance' was seen as leading to the emancipation of women by conferring on them equal economic power with men. This was in stark contradiction to the Church's conception of male–female relations, which the 1930 encyclical on marriage, *Casti Connubii*, so clearly spelt out – the man was the 'head' and the woman the 'heart'. Women were subject to men in the marriage relationship and 'extravagance' by women in fashion, or accepting birth control, would undermine this relationship and therefore the stability of society.[143] One of the recommendations of the Catholic Women's International Congress at Vienna was the fostering of national and local costumes. The 1927 Synod did just that, as indicated in their post-Synodal pastoral address to the people of Ireland.[144]

In the same year, the attention of the CTSI was drawn to 'Six Special Lectures for Women' being given in Dublin, and the Society made arrangements 'to have these watched in the Catholic interest'.[145] Also in 1927, the *Irish Messenger* office published a pamphlet, *Modern Fashions in Ladies Dress*, which quoted extensively from Mary Butler's article of ten years previously and particularly emphasised that the 'originators of objectionable modes were trying deliberately to de-Christianise society'.[146]

The Modest Dress and Deportment Crusade spread rapidly through the country, having originated among students of the Mary Immaculate Training College, Limerick. The founders, sixty in number, drew up a code of rules as a standard of modesty and deportment for all who should join the crusade. The code was published in booklet form in early 1928, under the title *Wanted – A New Woman*. The 'Modern Woman' was rejected because she was seen as cultivating 'mannish manners' and 'indecent fashions', and was adopting customs of 'the lowest type of humanity, the savages of Central Africa'.[147] The MDDC followed the European and Irish Bishops' example and played the nationalist card, 'is the grand record of fifteen hundred years of Irish culture to be swept away at a blow by the women of Ireland? Is this a proper sequel to the fight for nationality which cost so many of the men of Ireland their lives within the past dozen years?'[148]

That the subject was an abiding issue for the Catholic hierarchy was again evidenced by the late-1927 address of Bishop Coholan to the Cork branch of the CYMS. He warned parents about the dangers connected with dress and dances, and appealed to Catholic mothers to strive to maintain in their daughters their tradition for purity and modesty.[149] He warned mothers that unless they took this matter in hand immediately and removed the 'evil', then, 'ecclesiastical action will be taken in the line of excluding them from the sacraments'.[150] The campaign was widening, and the *Irish Rosary* also took up the cause during 1928-1929.[151] In their correspondence pages in October 1929, under the heading of 'Feminine Fashions and Shoddy',[152] one writer deplored the importation of 'pagan surplus stock too nasty for English girls to wear'.[153]

Meanwhile, the numbers in the MDDC had risen to 12,000 by the end of 1929.[154] Principals of schools throughout the country were starting to establish branches of the 'Children's Guild of Modesty', and members of the Children of Mary Sodality were being canvassed to join. The Registrar of the MDDC, in a letter to the *Irish Rosary*, said that she would have expected the Catholic leaders of Irish feminism to 'take a bold and uncompromising stand' against 'pagan indecency in dress'. She criticised the 'country girls' who exclaimed that they would be 'awful frights' if they wore their dresses four inches below the knee, as the society enjoined them to do.[155]

Another organisation with similar aims was established – Our Lady's League. They published a one-page leaflet for distribution, entitled *Summer Modesty*, in which they stated that, 'the creation of a personal, high standard of modesty is a lofty sphere of Catholic Action worthy of the co-operation of any young woman'.[156]

Both organisations were still active up to and during the years of the Second World War, which in fact gave the campaign a new lease of life.[157] In 1942, the CYMS reported that they were actively supporting and co-operating in the MDDC campaign.[158]

THE NATURE OF THE CLERGY–LAITY RELATIONSHIP

Independent lay initiative was not welcome in the sphere of Catholic Action, as evidenced as far back as 1902, with the difficulties faced by the Catholic Association. In 1927, both the Catholic Boy Scouts of Ireland and the Catholic Girl Guides of Ireland were established. The latter organisation proved a testing ground for clerical power.[159]

The defeat of Margaret Loftus and Brigid Ward at the hands of the chaplains for control of the Guides was a clear indication of the determination of the clergy to maintain control of Catholic organisations despite very spirited opposition and independence. The CTSI were strongly reprimanded by Archbishop Byrne for advocating socio-economic themes for their conferences in the mid-1920s.[160] The Catholic Women's Federation were effectively snubbed by Bishop Michael Browne when they were giving evidence before the Commission on Vocational Organisation in the early 1940s.[161] However, the treatment meted out to Frank Duff, founder of the Legion of Mary, by Archbishop Byrne and his successor Dr McQuaid, highlights the fear the hierarchy and clergy had of a laity possessing independence, initiative and imagination.[162]

Elizabeth Kirwan, a member of the founding committee of the Legion of Mary in 1921, was the strength behind the organisation in the difficult early years.[163] And it was probably because the early members were attached to the St Vincent de Paul Society, had their own families, and lived through very hard times, that they retained a sense of their independence in the face of the difficulties that emanated their way from Archbishop's Palace, Drumcondra. In a letter to Archbishop Byrne written in November 1928, the founder Frank Duff declared:

> For a long time past, Your Grace has regarded me with considerable disfavour. I have exhausted every effort to get in touch with you in order to bridge the misunderstanding but without avail. Of late, some particularly injurious statements have been made about me, ascribable to Your Grace's attitude toward me. The policy adopted in my regard is not warranted.[164]

In this spirited letter Duff examined the criticisms and rumours that had been brought to his attention. One of these was that he had founded the Legion of Mary 'without authority' and therefore in breach of a fundamental Catholic Action principle. Duff indicated that the reason why 'formal sanction had not been sought', was that 'all concerned were afraid to approach you', having heard that the Archbishop was 'most averse to me and to anything with which I was connected'. The breaking up of Monto by the Legion in 1925 formed the basis for another charge of 'unwarranted action'. The opening of the Morning Star Hostel for women in 1927 was the occasion of several charges against Duff, including: 1. of falsely stating that the Archbishop approved of it, and 2. that Duff had endeavoured in some discreditable way to foist the scheme upon the St Vincent de Paul Society.[165]

When Duff opened another hostel for women, the Regina Coeli, in 1929, further charges were levelled at him. He had to advise the Archbishop, through Sir Joseph Glynn who acted as an intermediary, that, 'the girls had not corrupted households into which they were sent as servants. Men had not been cajoled into marriage with the girls. Girls have not been let out on the streets to ply their trade and allowed to use the Hostel as their centre.'[166]

Duff, although staunchly Catholic, did not fit into the hierarchy's vision of a stable member of society. For them, Catholic Action aimed at, amongst other things, securing the civil–ecclesiastical relationship. Duff, in their eyes, went beyond the strict mandate given to lay organisations. Because of this, the Legion of Mary never received full ecclesiastical approval in Dublin, although this was not the case elsewhere.

The Legion was a very orthodox organisation, with thousands of moderate and reasonable Catholics. In fact, the organisation attracted a broad spectrum from all strata of society, but in particular included huge numbers of civil and other public servants in its ranks. This was possibly because Frank Duff and Leon O'Broin (private Secretary to Ernest Blythe, Minister of Finance, and later Secretary of the Department of Posts and Telegraphs), founding members, had attracted their fellow civil servants. The Apostolic Work Society (1924), the St Joseph's Young Priests' Society (1895), and the St Vincent de Paul Society also attracted these people into their ranks in large numbers. An offshoot of the Legion was a group called the Patricians, which had W.T. Cosgrave (one of

Duff's greatest supporters in the 1920s), Patrick J. Little (Minister for Posts and Telegraphs) and General Seán MacEoin as members of one branch.[167] Eleanor, Countess of Wicklow, was also a very active Legionary.

Maria Legionis, the journal of the Legion, suffered severe ecclesiastical censorship in the 1930s over its publication of the story of the demise of the infamous Dublin red-light district, Monto, and the crucial role of the organisation in the developments.[168] The situation did not improve under Archbishop McQuaid, who gave Duff a 'blanket refusal' to continue publishing the story.[169] Duff declared to O'Broin on more than one occasion that he had more than a fear of Archbishop McQuaid's censorship. He was beginning to wonder whether McQuaid was singling the Legion out for castigation, but that did not appear to be the case. The St Vincent de Paul Society and other organisations were also receiving 'curt, hurting messages of disapprobation'.[170] According to O'Broin, 'the Archbishop was chameleon like – you never knew what face he was going to show'.[171]

Muintir na Tíre was also frowned upon because they operated as a Christian rather than a purely Catholic body. An Rioghacht were criticised for their strong stance at the Commission on Banking and Credit in the 1930s.[172] Such was the lack of confidence in the hierarchy with various lay organisations that Peter McKevitt, Professor of Catholic Sociology and Catholic Action in Maynooth College, was requested to draw up a report on the Catholic Action movement in 1939.[173] The result of his deliberations ensured that in the 1940s a far tighter rein was kept on the actions of various organisations. McQuaid would assign good reports to those laity who pleased him and would punish and freeze out those who disobeyed him. It would appear that he was particularly prone to flattery, which would have clouded his judgment and limited the advice given to him.[174] Above all, he did not accept lay initiative that challenged the very nature of the Catholic Action relationship – participation by the organised laity in the hierarchical apostolate.

As a result, two ecumenical organisations that Frank Duff founded, the Mercier Society and the Pillar of Fire Society, were both suppressed by McQuaid in the early 1940s. Among those who attended the Mercier Society (whose motto was 'Towards Mutual Understanding' and who engaged in dialogue with Protestants) were: Leon O'Broin; Joseph Walsh, Secretary of the Department of External Affairs; Desmond Fitzgerald, former Cumann na nGaedheal Minister; Lonan Murphy, President of the St Vincent de Paul Society; F.H. Boland, later President of the UN General Assembly; John Betjeman, the future poet laureate (at the time war-time Press Attaché of the British Embassy in Dublin); William Fay, the future Ambassador to France; the well-known artist Mainie Jellet, and George Otto Simms, Church of Ireland Minister, future Archbishop of Armagh, and expert on the *Book of Kells*.[175] The fact that the Society was attended by intellectuals and addressed by scholars and senior Catholic and Protestant churchmen gave it a seriousness that distinguished it from a mere convert movement. According to Fr Michael O'Carroll, a very close friend of

Frank Duff and one of the founders of the Mercier Society, McQuaid 'did not trust us', including the Spiritual Director, Fr Leen, a fellow Holy Ghost Father who McQuaid himself had appointed. The Archbishop felt that the organisation did not represent the Catholic position adequately, seeing the discussions rather as a 'series of gladiatorial contests to be won at all costs'. He told them that non-Catholics were not to expound 'their heretical opinions'.[176] At this point the Society was forced to close down.[177]

The Pillar of Fire Society had similar aims as the Mercier Society,[178] this time reaching out to Ireland's Jewish community at a time when anti-Semitism was encrusted in the mainstream of European civilisation, including Ireland.[179] On the Jewish side at the meetings were the entire Jewish Representative Council, with many of the country's most eminent Jews in attendance. However, the organisation's lifespan was even shorter than that of the Mercier Society. It was ordered to discontinue by McQuaid and told to close down.[180]

The whole situation was doubtlessly extremely frustrating for Frank Duff, and in an uncharacteristic but particularly revealing angry outburst in 1947, he declared that, 'Anybody who wants to work in Ireland will be cribbed, cabined and confined. Religion has become routine. A terrible conservatism exercises relentless sway, and tells the Irish people that they must walk by outmoded ways. Plainly we are looking at Jansenism, and not true Catholicism'.[181]

Frank Duff was in a most invidious position.[182] Seán Ó Faoláin, writing in *The Bell* in the mid-1940s described the Legion of Mary as 'Miraculous Meddlers' and as indulging in 'snooperism'.[183] Leon O'Broin argued that they were in fact 'pressurised into promoting local vigilance activities for the safe-guarding of morals' by the Archdiocese of Dublin.[184] Such may have been the case, but Ó Faoláin regarded Duff as the 'chief exponent of Catholic Action in Ireland' and one who could not disassociate himself from what had happened to the church's teachings 'in the hands of ignorant people'. Ó Faoláin described some of these people as 'a secret Gestapo wearing the mask of Catholicism'.

By this time of course, vigilance activities were nothing new; the CTSI, the CYMS, An Rioghacht, and the Knights of St Columbanus were all well accomplished in this area. The crucial foundations had been laid in the Byrne era but under McQuaid it seemed to take on an added urgency and momentum. As a result, he was able to use fear as an essential instrument for achieving uniformity and discipline amongst the clergy and laity in his Archdiocese. He seemed to thrive on receiving covert information from the strong and indispensable network of lay organisations. The sources of information ranged from all sectors of society, from what was being discussed in the Cabinet room in Merrion Street to the private behaviour of nuns, priests and laity.[185] Across his desk passed confidential reports from his spies and collaborators in Government Departments, the Dublin Corporation planning department, the medical, legal and teaching professions, the Army and the Garda Síochána.[186] Particularly vigilant were the members of the Knights of St Columbanus, with which he was associated. That organisation was regarded as elite in the ranks of Catholic Action. Some of the politicians who were members included Fianna Fáil Ministers Seán Lemass, Seán MacEntee, and Seán T. O'Kelly, and from the Opposition benches, Richard Mulcahy, Seán MacEoin, William Norton and Joseph Blowick.[187] Whereas Archbishop Byrne had been in ill health and rather aloof and reclusive during the 1930s, McQuaid had gained his experience working with lay organisations during this decade. Not only that, but he had a particular admiration for the espionage work of J. Edgar Hoover in the FBI, which had been directed against trade unionists with suspected communist leanings. In fact, when Hoover heard of McQuaid's interest in his work, he sent him a copy of his book *Masters of Deceit* and thanked him for his support.[188]

By the 1940s, Catholic Actionists had so entrenched themselves in every stratum of Irish society that they had become, in reality, the eyes and ears of every Bishop's Palace in the country, thus ensuring that the Catholic hierarchy's control and influence in Irish life and society was particularly significant.

REALITIES OF INDEPENDENCE: THE ECONOMIC DIMENSION

That Kevin O'Higgins should appeal, in his address to the crucial 1923 CTSI annual conference, to the Catholic social doctrines of his Church, highlights, in some respects, the crisis facing the new government. The crisis was not just political, but also social and economic, and in the face of potential anarchy and revolution the Catholic Church was a necessary ally. The Church, as was its practice, sided with the lawful government. The Church's support was even more vital as the years passed, since the dreams of Griffith and Pearse were not coming to fruition. In particular, the economic problems besetting the infant state called for austere and unpopular measures.

These measures were not what people had hoped independence would bring. Arthur Griffith had offered hope that a system of protective tariffs would be a means of building up new industries in an independent Ireland. In just 1920, a young Irish economist called George O'Brien had written an economic history of the Famine period, which constituted a strong argument in favour of protectionist government. But the country, without mineral resources and lacking any tradition of industrial skill or of that confidence which comes from successful enterprise in the past, had inherited an awful legacy of neglect and discouragement. Not only that, but the exclusion of Northern Ireland in 1920 had deprived the Free State of Ireland's principal industrial population. The new State was overwhelmingly agricultural, and agriculture entered a period of such intense depression after the European War that any experimental policy of protection would be a risky proposition.[189]

It was believed that agricultural prosperity, if unimpeded, would gradually stimulate wider economic development. George O'Brien, who was a member of the government-appointed Fiscal Inquiry Committee, writing in the *Irish Free State Handbook* nearly ten years after the committee's report was published, emphasised that the 'keynote of the Report was the necessity of caution in framing fiscal policy'.[190] In 1932 he was able to say that, 'until 1932 the recommendation of the FIC has been followed in the main by the Government'. Retrenched expenditure and financial orthodoxy were the key strategies of 1920s government thinking.[191]

THE REPERCUSSIONS OF ECONOMIC POLICY

A corollary of the economic policy of the 1920s was the necessity of keeping budgetary costs to a minimum, so that taxes should not handicap rising exports. This meant that welfare expenditure was not expanded. This policy was facilitated by emigration, which reduced unemployment from the high levels of the early 1920s. The relatively low priority given to welfare expenditure also meant that comparatively little was done to improve housing conditions in the larger towns that had inherited extensive slums from the nineteenth century. In Dublin, the housing situation had eased little in ten years. This was to be a crucial factor for the rise of certain Catholic Action organisations, such as the Legion of Mary (1921) and An Rioghacht (1926). Frank Duff in many respects represented the shared consensus of both Church and State. Neither possessed strategies or coherent philosophies that would have facilitated deeper involvement in social infrastructures.

While O'Higgins's paper at the CTSI conference in 1923 underlined the strains facing the new government, Alfred O'Rahilly's paper, given at the same conference, pinpointed the inadequacies of the Church's response. O'Higgins stressed the importance of Catholic social doctrine, whereas O'Rahilly's paper, 'The Catholic Layman in the Labour Movement', insinuated that the Church's social doctrine, in the presence of the existing labour/industrial impasse, had no influence and the blame for this lay at the Church's own door.[192] His paper was significant, particularly at a time, when the country was experiencing the effects of the July–October 1923 dockers' dispute. O'Rahilly himself was instrumental in ending the dispute in Cork with the proposal to establish the Cork Arbitration Board. At the conference, however, he bemoaned the lack of a 'Catholic' public opinion to consider the government's economic policies. He pointed to the Catholic Workers' College in Oxford, which was taking the lead in educating Catholic workers. There was no such initiative in Ireland.

The post-war years witnessed much labour unrest in Ireland, sustained initially by prosperity and the continuation of government intervention in the economy, politicised by the national revolution, and facilitated by the breakdown of policing during the War of Independence. It seemed, and this was echoed at many of the CTSI conferences, that labour was set to be a major player in the new Ireland. However, 1920 saw a crisis of overproduction and prices started to tumble. Employers started to clamour for the restoration of pre-war rates. By 1923, labour had succumbed to the wage-cutting offensive. Trade Unions were not just defeated, they were discredited.[193] The 'retreat from revolution' had begun.[194]

At the 1923 CTSI conference there was a determined mood amongst some of the participants to aim to calm this unrest. O'Rahilly, however, was not slow to criticise the Church's efforts in this regard. He quoted from an article in the English Jesuit periodical, *The Month*, entitled 'Ireland in Transition', in which Bishop Coholan of Cork was compared, to his disadvantage, to Bishop Ketteler, the founder of the German Catholic Social Movement, and to Cardinal Manning:

> The question naturally suggests itself – how is it that these labour troubles have arisen in a population mainly Catholic, when the moral principles which should govern relations between labour and capital are so clearly expounded in the teachings of the Church? Perhaps because there have been no prominent public men like Ketteler or Manning to proclaim magisterially these duties and these rights which make for just and peaceful dealings. Or perhaps, because neither clergy nor laity in spite of the trumpet calls of Leo XIII, have sufficiently realised in the past the profoundly ethical character of political economy, and have blindly accepted the godless system elsewhere as consistent with Christianity.[195]

O'Rahilly's remarks that Catholicism had no special influence or programme in the country did not go unchallenged. The 'pretender' (as O'Rahilly called him) to Ketteler's throne, Bishop Coholan, hit back in the *Cork Examiner*, arguing that O'Rahilly's claims were untrue in the light of 'the unreasonable claims or practices which cannot be defended on moral grounds'.[196] O'Rahilly was quick to respond to these charges and criticised Coholan again in the following day's *Cork Examiner*.[197]

The issue shows once more that the Catholic Church was not willing to accept criticism, even from the most prominent Catholic layman in the country. Most importantly, the Church was finding refuge in the blanket expression 'moral grounds' and this all-encompassing escape route was to be a feature of its attitude for many decades to come. The focus was to be on dogmatic ethics rather than on justice. In another respect, however, it was not necessarily deviating from state thinking, which at the time was crucially important, since the Church was trying to come to terms with its previous theological understanding of the role of the state, in the light of the state being ousted by the nation. Henceforth, its allegiance would be to the new State, and so offering alternative views on what constituted sound government economic policy would only jeopardise an already fragile political stability. Also, by excommunicating Republicans, the Catholic Church had effectively indicated where, what and who it stood for.

THE CATHOLIC CHURCH'S RESPONSE TO THE SOCIAL QUESTION, 1923-1926

Certainly *Rerum Novarum* was not at the top of the Catholic Church's list of priorities. Rather, the encyclical on Catholic Action, *Ubi Arcano* (1922), was, as it echoed the fears of the Irish episcopate and offered solutions. Although Archbishop Byrne had spoken in 1924 of the 'dead weight of unemployment', he was only able to suggest that it was 'the most difficult problem to solve'.[198] Meanwhile, in 1924, the government had cut old-age pensions from 10s to 9s a week. The levels of social expenditure in Britain could not be expected of a poor country seeking to finance public services out of current revenue. The St Vincent de Paul Society expressed concern at the 'acute situation of the poor and the largely increased numbers that will require relief' because of soaring unemployment.[199] By 1925, the Society's membership had increased to 8,000 with 288 branches.[200]

The response of the Legion of Mary was to direct their energies against prostitution in Dublin's inner city.[201] For Frank Duff the issue was first and foremost a moral problem. He was able to use his position as a senior civil servant to enroll the assistance of William T. Cosgrave, and General Murphy, the Commissioner of the Dublin Metropolitan Police, as well as the Jesuit Fr Richard Devane, in his campaign to close down the notorious and infamous Monto district of Dublin. According to General Murphy, 'the raid on the area was a success, and the consequences a marked success'.[202] Victory was not measured in terms of tackling the underlying causes and issues, but in sweeping away the problem. One of the consequences of their 'success' was the rapid growth and influence of the Legion of Mary. Moral solutions to economic problems were henceforth to be the way forward.

REACTION TO THE HOUSING ISSUE

The accommodation crisis in Dublin became the inspiration for some of the addresses at the 1924 CTSI annual conference, most likely because of Sir Joseph Glynn's involvement with the Society, as well as his position in the St Vincent de Paul Society.[203] Fr Fitzgibbon's paper, 'Housing in Dublin', was an appeal to the public conscience to apply the principles of Catholic sociology to the question.[204] Dr Myles Keogh TD, and some Dublin Corporation officials, also spoke. But as was to be expected, no radical solution was put forward. All agreed that it would be foolish to minimise the difficulties of the task and it would be insane to ignore its pressing urgency.

However, the Statistical and Social Inquiry Society of Ireland responded to the Society's initiative in publicly debating the issue, and in early 1925 they published a paper, 'The Housing Problems in Ireland and Great Britain and the Essentials to the Solution'.[205] They rightly argued that the problem was in fact more acute than the CTSI had imagined. However, while the Statistical and Social Inquiry Society were critical of the CTSI's non-committal stance on the problems of poverty, they were in a similar dilemma. The author of the paper, J. Maguire, recognised that a solution outside the principles of government was required, and in a concluding comment indicated and encapsulated the difficulties facing Catholic organisations, 'it makes for freedom and good government to limit rather than enlarge the sphere of the State's activities – it cannot afford to be generous'.[206]

However Archbishop Byrne was not happy with the public controversy generated by the CTSI.[207] The Society itself was not exactly noted for its emphasis on the social question and of 130 new publications issued in the years 1922-1929, only four were specifically related to the subject: *Religious Ideals in Industrial Relations* (1923) by Cardinal W. O'Connell;[208] *Catholic Organisation in Holland* (1924);[209] *Healthy Children and How to Keep Them So* (1925),[210] and *Medieval Trade Guilds* (1929).[211] It did, however, make a small grant through the Priests' Social Guild to the Council of the Unemployed Workers.[212] By 1925 however, the Society was considering expanding the platform at its conferences to include discussions on social matters, and with members of its committee of management such as Fr Coffey and Sir Joseph Glynn, this seemed a distinct possibility.

Fr Peter Coffey had already had some of his ideas published in pamphlet form by the Society in the previous decade: *The Church and the Working Classes*;[213] *Between Capitalism and Socialism: Some Landmarks for the Guidance of Catholics*,[214] and *The Social Question in Ireland*.[215] The second and third of these were published in 1919 and expressed the Church's fears about the growing demands of the labour movement. Coffey's thinking was influenced at different times by James Connolly, G.K. Chesterton, Hilaire Belloc (particularly the Distributist ideas of the latter two), and *Rerum Novarum*. His varying sympathies, however, landed him in trouble with the ecclesiastical censors, who refused the CTSI request in 1922 to publish in pamphlet form his *Catechism of the Labour Question*.[216] Despite this, Coffey was one of the principal speakers at the controversial 1924 conference.

It was decided to seek Archbishop Byrne's approval before widening the conference's subject area.[217] Plans were drawn up in 1925 for the 1926 conference, and Frank O'Reilly of the Society was authorised to meet the Archbishop in December 1925 to discuss the changes. The Archbishop told O'Reilly that, in the best interests of the Society, he was going to speak quite plainly, 'so as to show his full mind'. He pointed out that the CTSI seemed to place more stress on 'Society' rather than on 'Catholic Truth', and that sociology received more than its fair share of notice at its conferences. Because of this, Dr Byrne told

O'Reilly that, 'the proceedings there always gave rise to a certain nervousness among the Episcopacy, who never felt sure that at some time or another they would not hear some theories advanced that were not orthodox'.

He added that 'he personally had always experienced this sense of trepidation' and from what he had heard, he was convinced that the feeling was not his alone. O'Reilly indicated to Dr Byrne that he hoped that the Archbishop was aware that since the latter's previous expression of disapproval over the society taking part in discussions on the social question, they had in fact made great efforts to steer clear of the subject and to concentrate on non-controversial subjects at the conferences. But the Archbishop was not appeased, and in a very irate tone asked O'Reilly, 'Why all these questions? Why all these problems? Why all these theories and fads?'

What he wanted to hear at the conferences in future was solid doctrine and solid Catholic truth. He did not want the Society modelling its conferences on the Social Weeks held on the continent. He told O'Reilly to keep away from 'theories that lead nowhere'. O'Reilly was adamant in his stance and pointed out that the laity was not too keen on discussing what the Archbishop had in mind, i.e. religious and dogmatic subjects. The Archbishop had shown how reclusive he really was by expressing surprise that they were disinclined to discuss subjects of this kind. He would not budge on the issue and dismissed O'Reilly bluntly with, 'this was the view for the time being'.[218] Accordingly, the 1926 conference and subsequent conferences until the mid-1930s concentrated on 'Church' matters. The Society's committee of management tried to resurrect social issues in 1927 by appealing to Archbishop Harty of Cashel, who was President of the Society, but to no avail.[219] Instead the organisation's efforts were redirected into actively pursuing censorship legislation and organising branches throughout the country. It was to be left to the religious orders, the Jesuits in particular, as well as the Dominicans and the Holy Ghost Fathers, and the lay organisations under their direction, to develop and foster a public opinion on the social question.

The Archbishop's attitude was of course in keeping with that of the papal encyclicals on social issues. The Catholic Church was willing to countenance gradual, ameliorating, socio-economic change, but it was not prepared to encourage the poor or the workers to engage in confrontation.[220] Nor was encouragement to be given in developing a strong trade-union movement. In Ireland, the trade-union movement went into decline after the failure of the numerous strikes of 1922-1923.[221]

Of vital concern to the Catholic hierarchy also, was the crucial issue of allegiance to the State. At a practical level they were always anxious for close co-operation between Church and State. At a philosophical/theological level they had a conception of civil authority which required them to emphasise the duty of obedience and submission. Finally, at a psychological level, there was the fear of revolution. The strikes of 1922-1923 and the return of Jim Larkin preaching, in the words of Seán O'Casey, his 'divine mission of discontent', would doubt-lessly have alarmed Archbishop Byrne, who would have held the prevailing Catholic view that the obligation to work for an equitable social order was not one of justice but merely of charity. Hence we see the rise in the membership of the St Vincent de Paul Society at the same time as the Archbishop was tell-ing O'Reilly which course of action the CTSI should adopt. In the mid-1920s there was no concept of social justice as an issue (as opposed to the rhetoric) in the institutional Catholic Church, with the result that the focus of Catholic Action was a particularly narrow one.

PROSELYTISM

The Catholic Church's response to the difficulties of the mid-1920s was similar to its response in 1913. Once more recognising the existence of a slum problem, it was more concerned with how Church membership would be affected. In 1925, the Bishops of Ireland issued a major statement entitled, *The Evils of Proselytism*.[222] (It must be said, however, that the issue of proselytism was not just confined to the Catholic Church. The Church of Ireland was similarly concerned.) Three years previously, Archbishop Byrne had granted formal approval for the Rules and Constitution of the Catholic Protection and Rescue Society of Ireland.[223] In a letter to Mr Mahoney of the Society, the Archbishop had underlined the 'urgent need for concerted action on the part of Catholics to combat the activities of proselytising agencies'.[224] This 'concerted action' was in line with the Pope's hopes for Catholic Action, and Dr Byrne spelt out exactly what he expected from the Society, 'to counteract the demoralising campaign, efficient organisation is needed. Now that the Constitution has been revised the society is brought into closer touch with diocesan and ecclesiastical authority'.[225]

One year after the bishops' 1925 statement, the issue was still foremost on their agenda. A position paper entitled 'Proselytism, Its Operation in Ireland', was read at the annual Maynooth Union meeting by Fr Creedon, who had already been active with Frank Duff in anti-prostitution activities in Dublin's Monto area. Creedon examined the manifestations of the problem and sug-gested some solutions.[226] It was felt that a wider circulation of CTSI pamphlets would give people a 'religious backbone'.[227] The meeting appointed a provi-sional committee to examine the question further. Sir Joseph Glynn and Frank Duff were co-opted onto this committee and a report was submitted to the hierarchy's October meeting. One feature that particularly stood out in their report was the terrible plight of unmarried mothers in Ireland.[228] It cited the work of the CPRSI in this respect. For the first nine months of 1926 the latter society had to deal with 600 cases. The report pointed out that the 'present system of dealing with unmarried mothers is chaotic. There is no provision for the expectant mother except the Union.'[229]

The report did not offer a solution, but suggested there was a need for a 'carefully prepared plan of campaign' for dealing with the matter of countering proselytism. This concern for the religious/moral welfare of Catholic girls and women is also seen in the Annual Reports of the International Catholic Girls Protection Society, who operated a hostel in Dublin's Mountjoy Square for the thousands of women who emigrated every year to Britain and the USA.[230] Emigration was accepted as a fact of life in 1920s Ireland.

FUTURE DIRECTIONS

The Bishop of Kildare, Dr Fogarty, in his 1926 Lenten pastoral indicated the direction of Catholic Church thinking by rejecting any criticism of the government's handling of the economy.[231] He wrote:

> To their credit it must be said that their excellent young Ministers had displayed admirable courage and success in facing unpleasant problems inspired by the public good and regardless of popularity. They seemed, unfortunately, to be the only body in the community that had disinterested fortitude to do so. The least they might expect in return was sympathy, encouragement and loyal co-operation. Instead of that there was hardly a goose that cackled but insulted and belied them.[232]

Furthermore, he asked whether the people realised what their lives would be like 'if the government was to break down under the stress of such discouragement'. The only avenue open to the Church in this climate was their belief that social reform could only be accomplished by moral reform – to elevate the life of the people they would have to 'lift up their souls'. War and Civil War had left the people so exhausted that they had little energy with which to re-imagine the national condition. The 'retreat from revolution' was in full swing.

With all these Catholic organisations emerging and developing in the 1920s, we see the forging of a stronger Catholic Irish identity, building upon the foundations that had been laid in the previous century with the devotional revolution. At the same time, Catholicism helped to legitimate and to give cohesion and identity to the fledgling Free State. The crucial 1923 CTSI annual conference illustrates the informal consensus at work between the bishops, priests and politicians about the nature of Irish society and what Irish people needed. Within the Catholic nationalist mindset, there was a similar vision of Irish society. This shared consensus was not only greatly facilitated by the relationship between Church and Nation that had evolved over the previous few decades, but also by the wider Catholic Church's critical assessment of the importance of utilising the Catholic laity in organisations and under clerical control, for its own defence and protection, in the face of changing political and cultural circumstances in Europe in the post-War years.

In the new Irish Free State therefore, the most fruitful activity for Catholic organisations would be in the area of 'vigilance' on behalf of and at the behest of the Catholic Church. This is most evident in the 1920 CTSI 'Re-organisation Plan', which drew up a strategy for future development with the express intention of focusing on 'vigilance' and 'propaganda' as the most important spheres of activity. The establishment of the Irish Free State in 1921 also coincided with the urgent call to Catholic Action, that is the participation of the organised laity in the hierarchical apostolate, by the new pope, Pius XI (1921-1939). Catholic organisations that had been evolving in Ireland over the previous two decades were given a new mandate and new organisations sprang up to answer the call.

The annual conference of the CTSI in 1920 had as its theme, 'Lay Co-operation', as did practically every subsequent conference for the next fifteen years. The CTSI became the major sounding board for Catholic opinion in Ireland. The fact that they were able to call upon prominent government ministers, politicians, and members of the business, trade union and legal communities, to grace their platforms and committees, indicates the respect and attention they were able to command.

But the relationship between clergy and laity was at times an uneasy one, and always dependent upon the 'mandate' and goodwill of the hierarchy. Archbishop Byrne's ire was often directed at the leaders of the Catholic Girl Guides, the Legion of Mary, the CTSI and An Rioghacht. The CYMS was often regarded as 'the' Catholic Action organisation because of its repeated compliance to the hierarchy's wishes. Such were the difficulties between Frank Duff and Archbishop Byrne that when the latter threatened to close down the Sancta Maria hostel for women and force it to halt its rehabilitation work for prostitutes, Duff growled, 'Tell the Archbishop to put it in writing and I'll nail it to the door'.[233]

These difficulties were further exacerbated under Archbishop McQuaid. By then there were thousands of members working in the various organisations throughout the country, constantly feeding information to the Catholic Church on local and national developments and thus helping to secure the Church's hegemony in the Irish Free State.

Also of crucial importance for the spread of Catholic Action, were the economic difficulties facing the embryonic nation. These seemed to fuse with the evolving concept, principle and direction of Catholic Action so as to create a forceful vehicle straining for a Catholic cultural renaissance, which found expression in the 1929 Catholic Emancipation Centenary celebrations and the 1932 Eucharistic Congress. The way was being prepared to enshrine the Catholic moral code in law.

III

INFLUENCE, CONTROL AND CENSORSHIP

LEGISLATION FOR PUBLIC SAFETY AND TEMPERANCE AFTER THE CIVIL WAR

The restoration of law and order in the wake of the Civil War was the most important task for the Cumann na nGaedhael government in 1923.[1] Primary responsibility lay with Kevin O'Higgins, the Minister of Home Affairs (later called Justice), who was to make an impassioned plea for civil order at the annual CTSI conference in late October. In the same year, he introduced the Public Safety Act to counteract the violence and lawlessness that still flourished.[2]

Associated with these problems was the issue of excessive drinking. There was a general consensus in the country that Ireland was drinking beyond its means. The decision of the new government to tackle the drink question legislatively, through the Intoxicating Liquor Commissions and the Licensing Acts of 1924 and 1927, reflects the nearly unanimous feeling that there was a need for an improvement in the moral and religious tone of the new Irish Free State.[3] Eoin O'Duffy, the new Chief Commissioner of the Civic Guards (later the Garda Síochána), enthusiastically endorsed the increasingly vocal temperance organisations, such as the Pioneer Total Abstinence Association and the Father Mathew Union.[4] The government, under increasing pressure to act, both from the temperance organisations and the Licensed Vintners Association, took the issue seriously, and Kevin O'Higgins initiated reform such was his concern. In a Department of Justice memorandum it was stated that the licensing law reform and its attendant challenges was, 'practically the biggest and most urgent social problem that there is before the Government'.[5]

It would appear that an important factor for temperance legislation was the determination of the Minister to effect change. His determination coincided with episcopal obsessions with the long-running temperance campaign that peaked after the Civil War.

The CTSI had already played an important part in the temperance movement prior to the enactment of the Intoxicating Liquor Act, 1924, when through its numerous publications and conferences it helped to create that groundswell that was so necessary for any changes or improvement in legislation.[6] Some of its publications on the issue included: *The Evils of Drunkenness* (1918); *Proposals for Legislative Restriction* (1922) by Professor Coffey of Maynooth College; *The Liquor Traffic in Ireland* (1922); *If We Didn't Manufacture Alcoholic Drinks* (1922), and *The Alcoholic Road* (1924).[7] These publications coincided with a major campaign for legislative restriction of the liquor traffic, which was being undertaken by the Catholic Total Abstinence Federation of Ireland (CTAFI), the umbrella group for the increasing number of temperance organisations. Since 1914, yearly congresses had been held by this body.[8] Prior to 1914, the founding of the Pioneer Association in 1899 marked the beginning of the most successful temperance movement in Ireland since the 1840s.[9]

Since 1915, there had been calls for the overhaul of the drink laws. In that year, Fr Coffey suggested in a pamphlet, *Aids and Obstacles to Ireland's Progress: The Enemy Within Our Gates*, that, 'one of the first things the Irish people should demand of their own Parliament (i.e. Home Rule) in Dublin was a change in the maladministration of the Irish licensing laws'.[10]

English licensing laws had been overhauled in 1915. The post-war years witnessed the 'Prohibition' drive in the USA. The campaign in Ireland gained increased momentum in the years 1922-1924.

The CTSI booklet *The Alcoholic Road* was an address delivered at the CTAFI congress in September 1923 and refers to the programme advocated at the event.[11] It called on the government to implement the following proposals:

1. The reduction by one-half of the number of licensed houses.

2. The closing of licensed houses on Sundays, election days, and occasions of public excitement and danger.

3. The curtailment of the hours of opening on other days and the abolition of the '*bona fide*' farce.

4. The separation, at least structurally, of places for sale of groceries, hardware, etc. from places where intoxicants were sold.[12]

At the congress, Thomas Fullerton of the CTSI, delivered a paper on temperance legislation and called on the government to immediately curtail and restrict 'our excessive drink traffic'.[13] The eventual draft legislation was very similar to the recommendations made at the congress. The CTAFI had been canvassing individual Dáil deputies since early 1922. It was Fr Coffey's view that, 'the Gaelic League and Sinn Féin are indebted for their success to the temperance movement and temperance people have a right to expect that triumphant Sinn Féin will now pay back the debt by giving reasonable help to the temperance cause'.[14] His organisation sought persistently to have deputations received by members of the Cabinet. In December 1923, a deputation was met by Kevin O'Higgins, the Minister of Home Affairs, and Eoin O'Duffy of the Civic Guard. According to the CTAFI, the government had shown itself 'thoroughly alive to the situation and freely discussed and adopted practical preventative measures' suggested by the deputation.[15] This was not surprising, since O'Higgins had declared in the Dáil that 'we need a genuine licensing code, not a bewildering maze of statutes and decisions'.[16]

The Dáil appointed the Intoxicating Liquor Commission to examine the situation.[17] The CTAFI only expected a moderate measure of legislation since they were aware of the 'greater economic clout of the liquor interests and liquor trade who in fact contributed to the funds of Cumann na nGaedhael'. In June 1924, a large temperance demonstration was held in Dublin in which 10,000 members of the Pioneer Association marched. A resolution was passed, which demanded that the moderate measure of temperance reform introduced in the Dáil should be passed in its entirety and in fact improved.[18] It was some measure of the success of the temperance movement that the Liquor Commission had recommended reducing by half the number of licensed houses in the Free State.[19] Of particular significance was that the first draft of proposals for temperance legislation was very close to the association's proposals, although the later one was perhaps less so. The drive for legislation was, it would seem, not motivated merely because of the pressure exerted by the temperance bodies. In fact, the government tried to balance the conflicting demands of those bodies with the competing demands of the Licensed Vintners Association, and also with its own recognition of the vital necessity for reform. O'Higgins, on one occasion, informed the Dáil that he was not 'indulging prohibitionists masquerading as temperance reformers'.[20]

The *Irish Catholic Directory* for 1926 recorded that:

> ...not for many years was the feast of St Patrick celebrated in a manner more akin to the spirit of the Apostle than was the case this year. For one thing, it was a day of sobriety beyond all precedent, thanks to the new licensing legislation, which ordains the total closing of public houses on St Patrick's Day.[21]

The enactment of temperance legislation points to a number of enabling factors besides the advantages conferred by a planned and organised Catholic campaign. Most importantly, the campaign coincided with the government's preoccupation with the need for law and order and its various manifestations in the wake of years of civil disruption. The temperance lobby itself was often divided on fundamentals and could rarely agree on the targets of their campaign. Many of its witnesses at the Liquor Commission proceedings showed little practical knowledge of the problems with which they were dealing. In fact, temperance legislation might well have happened irrespective of the clamour of the CTAFI, but their presence bolstered the government's plans in the light of the very strong anti-change lobby in the campaign. Most significantly, the campaign highlighted the fact that the legislation was not the result of Catholic triumphalism or Catholic assertiveness.

The campaign differed from the other major campaign of the 1920s – that for the censorship of publications – on a number of fronts. In the first instance, the government agreed with the need to have liquor legislation updated and improved. The initiative came from the government itself. There was no such recognition in the case of the 'evil literature' campaign. That initiative came directly from the CTSI. On the issue of censorship the government had mixed feelings, but they were forced to bow to the censorship lobby. One of the reasons for this was that the CTSI spearheaded a sustained, focused, co-ordinated and extremely well-orchestrated campaign – the reverse to that of the temperance lobby. The CTSI did their research on the subject, nationally and internationally, and no other organisation presented such a detailed or knowledgeable marshalling of the facts. The censorship lobby, despite some disagreements in the ranks, acted as one in calling for new legislation. The CTAFI was characterised as disunited, amateurish and fanatical. Catholic Action was more of a feature in the censorship campaign than the temperance movement, with a big emphasis on the power of organisation.

THE CAMPAIGN FOR CENSORSHIP OF LITERATURE LEGISLATION

The temperance movement had shown the widespread recognition in the Irish Free State of the need to return to the old standards. Similarly, censorship stood for a rejection of materialist, pagan, Anglo-Saxon and un-Irish values, and appealed to a leadership that had been influenced by the writings of the Irish-Ireland revivalist D.P. Moran. Catholic Action was to become the vehicle for the further expression of this process. The climactic event of this movement in the 1920s was the centenary celebrations of Catholic Emancipation in 1929, planned and for the most part organised by the CTSI. Independent Ireland brought with it the promise of the fulfillment of real Catholic Emancipation.

The Society's propaganda and vigilance campaign prior to independence ensured that the CTSI would be centre stage in any new campaign, and they would in fact be the spearhead of a movement in favour of enshrining the Catholic view on literature censorship in Irish legislation. They were helped by the Irish Vigilance Association (committee members of both organisations overlapped); the Catholic Writers' Guild; the Irish Retail and Newsagents Association; the *Irish Ecclesiastical Record*; the *Catholic Bulletin* (founded in 1910 at the height of the anti-modernist vigilance campaign); *The Leader*, and *The Irish*

Catholic. They were also helped by individuals such as the Christian Brother Br Craven and the *Our Boys* magazine, and the Jesuit priests Fr Stephen Browne of the Central Catholic Library and the Limerick vigilance campaign veteran Fr Richard Devane.

Of particular significance was the revival, by the CTSI, of the 'Catholic Newspaper Campaign' or, as it was also called, 'The Good Literature Crusade', which had been such a strong feature of vigilance work. From 1924, the purpose of the campaign was to ensure that a Catholic newspaper or magazine went into every home in Ireland every week.[22] This involved an aggressive sales attack against imported newspapers in an attempt to shift people's reading habits. Members of CTSI branches concentrated on a house-to-house canvass in every town and village. They were advised to 'use persuasion to procure orders'. If a person discontinued taking a subscription they were to be visited by a member of the Society to find out the cause of the lapse and to ensure a 'conquest'. People of this type were to be 'nursed', visited, and revisited until they gave an order. The *Handbook of Catholic Action* had stressed that Catholic Action 'really begins to bear fruit only when those not well-disposed are induced to take a newspaper or magazine'.[23] The Society's aim above all was to create a demand for Catholic reading material, and this was certainly achieved on examination of the sales figures for 1925-1929. An examination of branch reports also shows the results. In Tralee, 17,000 pamphlets and booklets, and 20,000 Catholic newspapers, fortnightlies, monthlies, and quarterlies were sold each year.[24] In Roscrea, 95 per cent of Catholic householders in the town were taking a Catholic publication from their local CTSI branch. Prior to the inauguration of the Society's campaign, the number interested in Catholic publications was practically nil. This must be one of the most crucial factors in our understanding of the process of shaping the mood and character of Irish public opinion that took place in the mid-to-late 1920s and during the legislation for censorship campaign. The swing was also facilitated by local newsagents throughout Ireland who had been won over to the campaign partly through moral pressure and partly by the fact that they would not be losing sales in the process.[25]

In Castlebar, Co. Mayo, the local CTSI branch undertook a complete survey of the town and surrounding region, dividing the area into thirty-one districts and listing all the householders who were then canvassed. Householders were not given an option, as each one received a CTSI *List of Catholic Weeklies and Periodicals* catalogue, and each was requested to make their choice from the list. According to the Castlebar Branch Report, 'the whole distribution system was carefully thought out – down to satchels made from American oil-cloth for each district'.[26] Not only that, but the branch, in analysing the expected recipients of Catholic publications, wanted to ensure that the subscription list would be 'truly representative of our Catholic population'. They attained their objective, and the list included, 'our leading merchants and professional men, as well as practically every teacher in the parish, the Gardaí – officers and men, shop assistants, artisans and farmers'. They also secured a column in *The Connaught Telegraph*, and they were happy to report that 'a Catholic atmosphere is given to our local newspaper, as it should be, in a district 99 per cent Catholic'. In 1929, the branch was able to report that since its inception in 1927, the year of the Synod of Maynooth, it 'has been in a vigorous and flourishing condition'.[27] Around the same time, Castlebar welcomed the establishment of a new CYMS branch in the town.

The CTSI was not slow in reproaching newspapers and magazines for publishing questionable articles or advertisements. *The Irish Times* was frequently tackled by Frank O'Reilly of the Society (which had at the time a long-standing policy not to advertise with that newspaper). After he complained to the editor of the popular satirical magazine *Dublin Opinion* about an 'objectionable' advertisement, for 'art pictures', O'Reilly was given an undertaking that the offending advertisement would not be repeated.[28]

English newspapers also came under constant scrutiny. When the *Daily Express* was brought to the attention of the Ennis branch of the CTSI because it carried birth-control advertisements, instructions were issued to Catholic Actionists to stop its distribution in the area. However, on this occasion, the local newsagent took umbrage at the Society's stance. He held the view that 'life in a country village like this is dull enough without being told what to read in one's spare moments'. O'Reilly at once informed the parish priest Fr Hehir that, 'he might like to know what is taking place in the village', and he added, 'you may like to be aware that Mr Doherty resents any dictation as to what the people are or are not to read in their spare moments'.[29]

Brother Craven, editor of the hugely popular *Our Boys* magazine, advised Archbishop Byrne of the need to use 'combinations of the laity' to keep back 'the tide of poisonous literature'.[30] His activities had resulted in seventy Dublin newsagents agreeing not to stock 'literary scavengers sent to us to be read, as if we were unclean insects that feed on filth'.[31] Fr Richard Devane expressed a similar view when he stated that 'legislation cannot run in advance of public opinion'.[32] He also felt that the value and efficiency of any proposed legislation depended upon the volume of pressure brought to bear on the legislature. He saw that pressure coming from 'systematic organisation' of the laity. *The Irish Rosary* applauded Brother Craven's efforts as showing what could be done 'when zealous local Catholics know how to organise'.[33] Writing in that journal in 1925, Craven referred to the 'cartloads of filthy literature', which was 'truly a picture to make angels weep'.[34] *The Irish Catholic* noted the mounting vigilance 'again gathering force'.[35] One reflection of the movement's growing influence was the offer by the Irish Retail and Newsagents Association, in 1926, to co-operate with Brother Craven and the CTSI.[36]

Lenten pastorals similarly recognised the need for 'organised' activity to influence public opinion. In early 1925, the Irish bishops appealed to the public 'to lend an enthusiastic support to the new forward movement now being organised by the CTSI'.[37] Archbishop Harty of Cashel, in his pastoral, said that a 'flourishing branch of the Society in each parish would go far to cure this festering sore'.[38] In Cashel, a branch was subsequently established to: 1. take steps to stop the sale of harmful literature in the town; 2. to co-operate with the pastoral's instructions in relation to 'dancing', and 3. to sell good literature.[39] The Tralee branch collected and forwarded to Dublin samples of Protestant publications 'designed to deceive Catholics into believing they were Catholic publications'.[40] In Tralee, according to the local branch, 'retailers have been warned'. Likewise in Dingle and Emly, where the branches 'were discouraging the sale of evil literature'. The Kanturk, Co. Cork, branch 'induced all the local newsagents to discontinue black-listed newspapers and to stock instead other newspapers, principally Catholic'.[41] In Cork City, the bishop promised that there would be Missions in all the churches during Lent to encourage the establishment of new CTSI branches.[42] By June 1926, the Society was able to state that a considerable proportion of its eighty-three branches had 'got the spirit of Catholic Action, and there was considerable promise of much greater achievement in the coming years'.[43] The Society's annual report noted that it was thanks to its 'energetic campaigning' that the CTSI had become an important factor in Irish life. Because of this success they were confident that 'it will not be difficult at any time to voice Catholic public opinion on any Catholic cause that may arise'.[44]

EASON'S AND THE CTSI

For two years, 1925-1927, the CTSI had Hugh Allen, its full-time organising secretary, touring the country, giving lectures and forming new branches. A newsagent in Tuam informed Eason's, the country's largest newspaper distributor and wholesaler, that 'all two penny novels are stopped here – not to be got here anymore'.[45] Newsagents correspondence with Eason's during and after 1925 from places as far apart Tipperary, Kildare and Cobh, point to the CTSI as the driving force. When Charles Eason, in a letter to the *Irish Independent* in October 1926, suggested that the papers banned in Canada could be kept out of Ireland without additional legislation, he drew down on his head an angry reply from Frank O'Reilly of the Society in a subsequent edition of the newspaper:

> Is Mr Eason not in favour of strengthening the existing law in the matter of all the objectionable literature? As one of the largest distributors of Catholic prayer-books in Ireland, I should have expected him consistently to be one of the most emphatic in favour of banning printed matter advocating foul practices condemned by the Catholic Church.[46]

Widespread intimidation had also become the order of the day, as Hugh Allen's organising reports indicate. Newspaper burning and seizure made its appearance. A letter from the Drogheda branch of the Society to Eason's referred to the possibility of violent action by others.[47] A report in *The Irish Times* in May 1927 related how masked men had seized thousands of copies of eleven English Sunday newspapers the previous day.[48] On 8 May, twelve armed and masked men had seized the newspapers at Killiney Station, Co. Dublin. Stormy scenes also took place in Cork, where members of the Cork Angelic Warfare Association were similarly active in the campaign. Brother Craven's campaign in the *Our Boys* reached its peak in 1927. In the spring of that year, he had 100,000 leaflets printed castigating 'evil literature', and he took a whole page advertisement in the *Irish Independent* with the heading, 'Satan, Smut and Company', which was directed against 'pamphlets and newspapers, any of which would be quite sufficient to change an angel into a devil'.[49] The General Assembly of the Presbyterian Church in Ireland published a report in the *Irish Independent* in June 1927, commenting favourably on the increased activities of the CTSI.[50]

In an article in the *Irish Ecclesiastical Record* of February 1925 entitled, 'Indecent Literature, Some Legal Remedies', Fr Richard Devane sought inspiration for a renewal of vigilance activity in the Limerick anti-modernist campaign of 1911.[51] His article referred to the 'memorable and effective attack on the filthy cross-channel papers at Limerick, and its effect on several centres in Ireland', which he believed 'must be quite fresh in the memory of many'.[52] He called for a similar 'crusade' with the same 'vigour and earnestness', which would result in legislation. In April, Fr Devane, along with Fr John Flanagan of the Pro-Cathedral in Dublin, representing the Priests' Social Guild (1915), met Kevin O'Higgins to try to persuade him of the necessity of introducing legislation relating to 'indecent' literature. Some years later, Fr Devane published a booklet, *The Imported Press: A National Menace – Some Remedies*, in which he implied that these efforts were successful, as some of his recommendations were included in later legislation.[53] In reality, he was only one part of a country-wide campaign under the leadership of the CTSI.

A colleague of Fr Devane's, Fr Stephen Browne, had established the Central Catholic Library in 1922. Writing in the Jesuit quarterly *Studies* in June of the same year, Fr Browne argued the need for such a library, because of the 'barrenness of Catholic religious literature in Ireland'.[54] He was particularly worried that with the achievement of independence, the new Ireland would still derive its views on political, moral and social questions 'from anti-clerical sources, filtered, in fact, from the rabid anti-clerical and Masonic Press of the continent through highly respectable English and Irish dailies'.[55] He believed that it was time for Irish Catholicism to resume its links with continental Catholicism. He intended his library to be a 'well-spring', a centre of Catholic thought for Irish journalists, politicians and professional people who would be able to go to 'authentic sources' in the future to ascertain where politics and religion intersected.[56] His *Studies* article was supplemented by another in *The Month* periodical in 1923 – 'A New Storehouse of Catholic Thought',[57] and in the *Irish Ecclesiastical Record* in 1924, 'The Central Catholic Library – An Apologia'.[58] Fr Browne's significance lies also in his work and reputation as an international Catholic bibliographer, working on, delineating and defining the existence of a 'Catholic' literature in English. He was one of the founders of the Catholic Writers' Guild (1926); the Catholic Association for International Relations (1937/1938); the Catholic Writers' Association, and the Academy of Christian Art. His published works include *A Catalogue of Novels and Tales by Catholic Writers* (1929) and *An Index of Catholic Biographies* (1930). In 1930 he founded the UCD Library School. He was an influential contributor to the *Irish Library News*, and most importantly, he was instrumental in shaping the 'Catholic' policies and ethos of the Irish library service for nearly forty years (*d.*1962).

Writing in *The Irish Rosary* in 1924 on the power of Catholic novelists, he declared that, 'without hesitation I would maintain that an immense number of novels now being written contain much deadly poison'. The only antidote to this was a distinctive Catholic view which the public would find in the 'considerable body of Catholic novelists of value'. His demand for a distinctly Catholic literature and a concomitant Catholic vision for any aspect of life, whether politics, art, sociology, literature, etc., lent much weight to the arguments in favour of imposing legislative controls on imported newspapers and periodicals.

EVIL LITERATURE REPORT OF THE CTSI

On 1 May 1925, a subcommittee of the Catholic Truth Society of Ireland held its first meeting to investigate the problem of 'evil literature' with special reference to legislation. This subcommittee was composed of nine legal members and three priests. Members included Professor William Magennis TD and Professor Michael Tierney TD, both of the National University of Ireland. Also present were Mr James Geoghegan BL, Judge O'Brien, Revd P. Finlay SJ and the Dominican priest Fr McInerney, chairman of the Irish Vigilance Association.[60] The Society, having being impressed by some of Fr Devane's arguments in his *Irish Ecclesiastical Record* article on the subject,[61] decided to 'inquire fully into the position as regards the banning of dangerous literature of all kinds', and to 'push forward their point of view to the fullest extent'.[62] It was the opinion of the CTSI that if they set forth 'reasonable and effective demands' and backed them by means of public meetings at their next annual conference, there would be every reason to hope that the government would take action.

The mobilisation of public opinion was an essential part of the Society's strategy to see legislation enacted. Already, in late 1924, their organisation subcommittee had decided that they should be in a position to tell the Minister

of Justice that, 'unless he complied with their request the Society would com-
mence immediately to take such steps to influence the voters throughout the
country to force the government's hand in the direction the Society desires'.[63]
The organisational drive and the activities of the Society's 'evil literature' subcommittee show how determined they were to take such steps.

Political lobbying was much in evidence during the 1925 Seanad elections
campaign. The Society tried to ensure that successful candidates would represent the Catholic viewpoint on divorce. Bishop Downey of Ossory expressed
his concerns to Frank O'Reilly about the 'merits of individual candidates' and
reminded him of the role the Society had in helping to ensure the return of
'reliable Catholics to the Senate'.[64] O'Reilly advised Bishop Downey that
this view 'confirms my own personal view as to what the society should do'
and he confidently declared that 'we are leading up gently to the creation of
a virile Catholic public opinion'.[65] For O'Reilly, 'religion as expressed in the
Ten Commandments must govern politics'.[66] He also thought it desirable that
candidates should give evidence of their good faith and guarantee to support
the Catholic point of view. He wanted to 'make these men unafraid to state that
they are Catholics'.

Consequently, the Society used the CTSI column in all the provincial
newspapers to recommend or criticise candidates in local and national elections. One successful candidate, Senator J.J. O'Farrell, accused the Society
of 'Waging a Holy War'.[67] He described O'Reilly and the CTSI as 'lay
professional Crusaders' who set out to 'save the Faith by knifing in the back
a fellow-Catholic'. He added, 'the whole wretched business was un-Catholic,
un-Christian, and untruthful from beginning to end. A malignant and venom-
ous propaganda was launched against me and all the Catholic voters were called
upon to have nothing to do with me'.[68]

He was convinced that it should not be left to 'a few lay Pharisees in Veritas
House to hurl the thunderbolts of their excommunications'. Such a reaction
from a successful candidate gives an indication of the determination of the
CTSI to proceed with its vigilance activities, whether in the area of divorce or
censorship legislation.[69] However, Dr Douglas Hyde, another candidate, was
not so lucky when he too incurred the displeasure of the Society. He lost his
Senate seat.

DRAFT PROPOSALS TO REGULATE SALE OF 'EVIL LITERATURE'

At the October 1925 CTSI annual conference, the principal address was
given by the Cumann na nGaedhael activist and prominent solicitor James
Geoghegan. The theme was the 'Rule of Christ and the Press Today'. He made
a strong appeal to the public to stand behind the Society's draft proposals to
regulate the sale of immoral and dangerous literature.[70] One reaction to his

call came from the influential Irish Retail and Newsagents, Bookseller and Stationers'Association, who wrote to the Society strongly approving of his proposals. According to the Society's annual report, 'the effect of Mr Geoghegan's paper was soon seen in the raising of the question in the Dáil by Mr P.S. Doyle TD [a prominent Cumann na nGaedhael and CTSI activist]. A Departmental Committee of Enquiry was set up as a result by the Government'.[71]

In late October, Doyle reported to the CTSI that matters were developing.[72] In February 1926, in accordance, as the CTSI put it, 'with an undertaking given some time ago', the Society succeeded in obtaining the appointment of a committee of five, 'to consider and report whether it is necessary or advisable in the interests of public morality, to extend the existing powers of the State to prohibit or restrict the sale and circulation of printed matter'.[73]

That the Society did have such influence on the government was corroborated by Mr J.P. Clare, the Secretary of the government-appointed committee, and an official of the Department of Justice. In a note he wrote in April 1926 to a representative of the Department of Posts and Telegraphs requesting his attendance before the Committee, he advised, 'In response made to him [Minister of Justice] by various religious associations and vigilance societies appointed a departmental Committee...'.[74] The CTSI was the most important and influential of these vigilance societies and had as recently as mid-1925 secretly assumed control of the Irish Vigilance Association.

A special meeting of the Society's committee of management was held on 26 February 1926, to discuss whether the CTSI should give evidence before the Dáil Committee.[75] They decided that it would be prudent to give evidence because:

1. They regarded that setting up of the Commission of Enquiry by the government as being largely due to the 'official' action of the Society and its pressing the government to remedy existing scandals.

2. If the Society did not give evidence it would be taken to imply that they no longer believed any grave abuses existed, or that they had no evidence to offer, or that they were indifferent to the issues at stake.

3. They were convinced that the evidence of a national, organised body would tell more powerfully with the Commission than that of individual witnesses.

4. They saw themselves as the representatives of a consensus of Irish Catholic public opinion, both clerical and lay, as 'no other Catholic organisation can speak so enthusiastically for the whole body of Irish Catholics' as the CTSI. At the same time they saw themselves in this role as 'supporting' the views and evidence of the Irish Catholic episcopate.[76]

In early March 1926, James Geoghegan BL, Mr F.T. Sweeney BL, Fr Peter Finlay SJ and Frank O'Reilly, were appointed to give evidence on the Society's behalf.[77]

The Society's evidence, *The Problem of Undesirable Printed Matter: Suggested Remedies*, a book of nearly 100 pages, was prepared by Frank O'Reilly, and presented by the subcommittee on 10 May.[78] They contended that the law as it stood was inadequate, and certain remedies were suggested, including the enactment of a law on more or less similar lines to the Cecil Bill recently introduced to the British Parliament, and the establishment of a Board of Censors.[79]

Much of the Society's evidence to the Commission dealt with 'Neo-Malthusian Birth Control Propaganda', and books, pamphlets, newspapers and advertisements came under scrutiny in the process.[80] The issue for the Society was that 'these neo-Malthusian methods allow their users full sexual pleasure without fear of procreation. Therefore the specific motive is sexual satisfaction'.[81] The 'primary end' of marriage was the 'begetting and bringing up' of offspring.[82] Large families were recommended as, 'it is clear that in a large family, the child is brought up in a most stimulating atmosphere of poverty, chastity and obedience – the three foundations of all stable society'.[83]

Birth control, in the eyes of the CTSI, would undermine large families, and ultimately the development and growth of the nation, a situation which would eventually lead to 'race suicide'.[84] Its strong concern for maintaining family structures was the dominant principle behind their drive for censorship legislation. The denial of access to literature was to be the unfortunate but necessary sacrifice for this aim. With this end in view, the principal and first recommendation of the Society to the Committee on Evil Literature stated, 'Neo-Malthusian birth control to be made illegal. All printed matter advocating birth control or publishing birth-control propaganda or sale of birth-control appliances or drugs to be banned absolutely under severe penalties'.[85] The Society's other three recommendations derived from this.

Their 'Submission', in its essence and entirety, focused on sexual immorality, contraception, and indecency and obscenity in people's reading. It argued that there was a 'clear association between the advocacy of contraception and the publication of obscene literature'.[86]

The CTSI did not stop with their 'Submission'. In a letter to Archbishop Byrne shortly afterwards, O'Reilly explained why:

> Our general impression is that the Committee are well disposed to our recommendations, and also to the recommendation that the existing law as regards indecency and obscenity should be codified. But we have the impression that some influence has been at work on the committee, suggesting that the existing law is quite adequate, but that it is not being taken advantage of.[87]

O'Reilly was of the opinion that this was in fact the official view, as instanced by replies to questions in the Dáil. He therefore felt that it was vital 'to rouse public opinion' in favour of immediate legislation in accordance with the Society's recommendations.

With this in mind, O'Reilly organised the printing of a circular which was sent to every parish priest in the country where a CTSI branch had not been established.[88] This was accompanied by a copy of the Society's 'Submission', and it requested that steps should be taken to give their parishioners an opportunity of giving public expression to their desire for the reform and amplification of the existing law. Some 200 parish priests had already co-operated with O'Reilly in providing statistics on imported newspapers – information which had helped him with the 'Submission'.[89] O'Reilly advised in the circular that, 'it is essential that public opinion should indicate to the government the need for legislation without delay. The CTSI has now taken the matter in hand, and it will continue its efforts until the country is thoroughly safeguarded from the avalanche of filthy literature.'[90]

He quoted Kevin O'Higgins's statement in the Dáil that the cure was 'a matter more for public opinion than for an official or officials appointed by the State'. For O'Reilly this made it all the more necessary that the Society should encourage more vocal demands for legislation. With CTSI branches being established up and down the country, public meetings could easily by organised. He emphasised the urgency of immediate action as the Report of the Committee on Evil Literature was anticipated within a few months. Branches were encouraged to 'use influence to pledge candidates for the Oireachtas to support adequate State action in this matter'.[91] He also suggested the outline for a resolution to the government to be endorsed at the public meetings. His circular proved very successful, and in the space of a few weeks large public meetings were held throughout the country, with numerous resolutions demanding State action being passed and sent to the Minister of Justice.[92]

In Cavan, the platform included representatives of the Urban Council, the Irish Farmers' Union, the proprietor of the *Anglo-Celt*, a local TD and the Chairman of the County Council. Some were appointed to the Standing Committee to 'co-operate with Veritas House'. In Clonmel, the Lord Mayor was among those presiding. In Kanturk, the local Irish National Teachers' Organisation branch supported the Society's call. The INTO had previously submitted evidence to the Committee on Evil Literature. In Emly, the CTSI branch passed a resolution stating that, 'we put before the Government and our local TDs the need for speedy legislation ... and we promise to assist in every legitimate way to bring about the desired effect'. In Newbridge, the Society was promised the support of the Urban Council and the local branch of the Irish Transport Workers' Union. Tralee saw the Gaelic League endorsing the Society's resolution. The Wexford branch organised a huge meeting, which was attended by representatives of the GAA, the Corporation, the St Vincent de Paul Society, St Iberius Club, the Workingmen's Club, the Pierce Institute, Irish National Foresters, Selskar Temperance Hall, Gaelic League, Sinn Féin Club,

Hibernian Social Club, Legion of Ex-Servicemen, the Merchants' Institute, the Third Order (a confraternity), and the Men's Confraternity. All pledged their support for the CTSI initiative. This was the general practice throughout the country, with representatives from business, agriculture, unions and local government, pledging their support.[93]

This support was vital to the Society in the light of the neutral stance the government appeared to be taking. James Geoghegan, in a note to Frank O'Reilly, expressed his annoyance that the government had been 'very casual, if not disdainful in the treatment meted out to the efforts of the CTSI and others interested in the question of debasing literature'.[94] O'Reilly agreed with Geoghegan's sentiments, as he too found 'the attitude of the Government difficult to understand'. He believed that it was time 'to protest against the Government's inactivity'.[95] In the important June 1927 election, which saw Fianna Fáil taking their seats in the Dáil, all 376 candidates were asked to 'give an undertaking to use their influence, if elected, to secure full legislative effect to the Committee's findings'.[96] Of the 376, only 114 replied and 112 gave the required undertaking. Kevin O'Higgins wrote to the Society informing them that the Bill was 'in preparation to give legislative effect generally to the recommendations of the Committee on Evil Literature' and promising that should he have responsibility in the matter after the election, 'the Bill will certainly be introduced'.[97]

The major victory for the Society at this stage was that the findings of the Report of the Evil Literature Committee corresponded with the evidence submitted and recommended by the CTSI. Secondly, they had a written promise from the Minister that legislation would follow soon after the elections.[98]

CTSI CRITICISM OF THE EVIL LITERATURE BILL

In May 1928, Frank O'Reilly had a meeting with Mr P.S. Doyle TD. Doyle had always kept him informed on developments with regard to the 'evil literature' question. He advised O'Reilly that it was the government's view that the problem was too large to be dealt with at one stroke. The committee of management of the Society decided therefore to consider options with a view to having the Society's recommendations carried out.[99] In June they sent a resolution to the government regretting the delay in the introduction of the legislation and urging them to take immediate action.[100] In August, the Society decided to further examine the Bill with a view to discussing it at their September meeting.[101] At this meeting it was agreed that the main criticisms centred on the size of the Censorship Board and its independence (it should not be dependent on the Minister's final decision). Some of the wording was also an issue, for example, where it was stated that the Minister 'may' act on the recommendations of the Censorship Board, the Society wanted to substitute the word 'shall'.[102] At a subsequent meeting to discuss the Bill, the society agreed that it should also cover publications that specialised in sensational and crime stories, and should not be confined to publications that offended in the area of sexual morality. They also felt very strongly about various attempts to 'whittle down' the Bill to exclude books from its purview. It was decided that a delegation should meet the new Minister of Justice, Mr Fitzgerald-Kenny, to lay their views before him.[103]

These views were given public airing at the Society's annual conference in Dublin's Mansion House in October 1928. The theme adopted was 'A Catholic Nation', and the proceedings attracted considerable attention at a time when there was much debate in the secular and religious press over the Censorship Bill.[104] One of the days was devoted specifically to discussing 'A Catholic Nation and a Catholic Press', and the conclusions were published subsequently in booklet form for widespread distribution.

Most of the newspapers gave the proceedings prominent coverage, including *The Tuam Herald*,[105] the *Cork Examiner*[106] and the *Irish Independent*.[107] Most coverage, however, was given by *The Irish Times*, which had been critical during the debates on the Censorship Bill.[108] They reported verbatim Archbishop Harty's opening address to the conference in which he refuted criticisms of the Bill, such as that it interfered with the liberty of the individual. He declared that the Bill did not say to the citizen, 'you shall not read', but rather it said, 'you shall not read what is harmful to you'.[109] *The Irish Times* editorial noted the society's 'unusual influence' in the campaign, 'Ministers are exceedingly unhappy about the Bill. Most of them dislike it; they are afraid of the educated criticism it will provoke and of the abuses it will engender. Nevertheless they are unable to resist the peculiarly effective pressure which is being put upon them by various religious organisations'.[110]

These sentiments expressed by *The Irish Times* were echoed by Professor Thrift TD, a member of the Committee on Evil Literature and the Dublin correspondent of *The Sunday Times*.[111] For Professor Thrift, 'the Society commands weight and influence, and might also be described as the sounding board of Catholic policy. The curtain was lifted on the part the Catholic Church was playing in the country's affairs'.[112]

It was made clear at the conference, he believed, that in a Catholic state, Catholic morality should pervade and direct the civil power and it should be the vital force in every aspect of the country's life. He saw the conference as possessing an 'inner and deep significance'. The Catholic Church was striving to call to its aid the civil power in order to 'forbid by law what by moral authority it is becoming powerless to prevent'.[113] His greatest fear was that an organisation such as the CTSI would have an influence in the censorship of books process.[114]

However, Professor Thrift himself was soon under attack from the CTSI in the columns of the *Irish Independent* because of certain amendments he tabled in the Dáil relating to the Censorship Bill. The Society's ire was also directed at Deputies Tierney, Law and Alton, who had all sought various amendments to the Bill.[115] Professor Tierney was reluctant to place books (other than birth-control books) within the scope of the Act at all. The Society was alarmed about engaging in public controversy with Dr Tierney, since he had been on the original CTSI subcommittee established in mid-1925 to examine the problems of evil literature. At all costs the Society wished to avoid confrontation, which they were convinced would undermine the united Catholic Action front on the issue.[116] Consequently, a meeting was arranged with Tierney which resulted in the Society agreeing to aspects of his amendment; in return Tierney agreed to push for a ban on periodicals that devoted an unduly large proportion of space to the publication of sensational matter relating to crime.[117] This was incorporated into the final Bill, as was Tierney's amendment that the Censorship Board would examine the literary and artistic merit of books that were drawn to their attention. Despite this agreement, Tierney was adamant that he could not assent to all of the Society's demands, and the CTSI were forced to the conclusion that unanimity at this stage was impossible.

Accordingly, at a meeting of the Society on 23 November 1928, they considered a statement to be published in the newspapers on 26 November, giving their criticisms of the Bill. They also sent a copy of the statement to every TD in the country.[118] One of the main criticisms related to birth-control propaganda. They saw the prohibition of birth-control propaganda as 'a vital section' of the Bill. They rejected the amendments of Deputies Law and Tierney to delete this section. The deputies wanted to substitute for Section 7 a new section, under which books advocating birth control would be put on an equal footing with those 'wholly or in general indecent or obscene', i.e. such books would require to be specifically and individually examined and prohibited before it would become illegal to sell or distribute them. The Society saw these amendments as weakening the Bill. For the CTSI, 'Christian principles of grave moral importance are here involved.' They wanted no whittling down of the proposal of absolute prohibition of contraceptive propaganda and they 'confidently look to their representatives in the Dáil to defeat these amendments'.[119]

The Society also rejected Tierney and Law's amendments which would have allowed any person to import any prohibited book or periodical for their own personal use, and a provision that books over the net price of three shillings should not be prohibited. They also challenged Professor Thrift's interpretation of the word 'indecent'. For Thrift, the word should be construed as meaning that which, in its purpose, suggests or incites to sexual immorality. The Society's counter-argument was that, 'indecency can surely, in writing, as in other things, exist without being intended'. They also claimed that indecency was most often found in the writings of persons who had no sense of decency at all, and who therefore had no indecent purpose.[120]

The eventual measures in the Censorship of Publications Act, 1929, went a long way towards meeting the Society's objectives. The final readings in the Dáil and Seanad were rushed affairs, as if the government were glad that the unpleasant experience was over. Most significantly, and in recognition of the standing and influence of the Society, a CTSI representative was always either the Chairman or a member of every Censorship Board from 1930 onwards.

Another pointer to the success of the Society's campaign was the eventual outcome of the problem concerning 'recognised associations'. The original Bill provided for the lodging of complaints against books and periodicals, through 'recognised associations' such as the CTSI, although the Society had not been mentioned by name. In its published statement in late 1928, the CTSI had indicated that they were willing to accept this brief.[121] The Minister concurred with this view but the Dáil rejected it and gave the initiative to complain directly into the hands of the citizen instead. This did not deter the Society, who decided to circumvent the deletion of the 'recognised associations' from the Bill. For the next few years, they lodged numerous complaints about publications with the Ministry and with the Taoiseach's Office. Looking through the records of the latter for this period indicates that the overwhelming majority of complaints lodged came from Frank O'Reilly of the CTSI. O'Reilly also informed the Society's committee of management that he had President Cosgrave's 'special attention' drawn to certain complaints.[122] O'Reilly bypassed normal procedures as laid down in the Censorship of Publications Act, and went directly to the Taoiseach. He was not slow to complain to Cosgrave that the office of the Minister of Justice was failing in its duty under the provisions of the Act.[123] He threatened to publish correspondence with them 'with comments' unless Cosgrave made efforts to 'induce a change of attitude in the Department'.[124] O'Reilly did not see the Act as merely 'a pious raising of the hat to Catholic sentiments', which was the impression the Department of Justice seemed to be conveying to him. Cosgrave informed Fitzgerald-Kenney's Departmental Secretary, O'Friel, that the Ministry was 'bound to do the work which the recognised associations were originally designed to operate'.[125] He also told O'Friel that he had a strong suspicion that the Act would be condemned by such organisations as the CTSI in cases where books were not banned which they believed should be. He did not want the Act to be attacked within a few weeks of its passing, and he was also mindful of the 'possibility of amendment'.[126] Cosgrave indicated that he regarded O'Reilly's approach as 'obviously an endeavour to get what he wants by means of threats'.[127] O'Reilly was using Cosgrave as a 'Court of Appeal'. Cosgrave recognised that they were, 'unfortunately in the position of having to tell him that his tactics have succeeded in the present instance, and this I am afraid, will only invite further trouble'.[128]

The Society's approach indicated that they had realised that, because of the cost factor, it would be difficult for the average citizen to fulfill the necessary requirements under the provisions of the Act to have books and periodicals examined.[129] In May 1930, *The Catholic Mind* gave considerable coverage to the arrangements made by the CTSI for the 'systematic examination' of items for the purposes of the Act. About 500 people 'of steady judgment' had been enlisted to 'co-operate in the heavy work'.[130] According to the Society, the

Minister's regulations had put additional financial burden on the CTSI and they had come to the conclusion that, 'these vexatious regulations cannot be regarded otherwise than as well designed to kill the Act. We protest against them; we interpret them as an attempt to make a bad Act worse.'[131] Throughout the 1930s, the Society appealed to the public to send them marked copies of objectionable periodicals so that they would take the matter up with the Minister. However, public enthusiasm soon waned and the Society was unable to devote sufficient resources required to tackle the issue full-time.

In 1937, they appointed a committee to draw up proposals for amending the Censorship of Publications Act, 1929. The committee included: Mgr Lyons (later Bishop of Kilmore); Dr Michael Browne (Bishop of Galway); Mr C.J. Joyce (later a member of the Censorship Board), and Frank O'Reilly.[132] The committee drew up a report, which concluded that the Act as it stands, 'fails in its purpose; for it does not ban the highest percentage of the worst books within the shortest possible time after publication; and it does not provide for sufficiently close supervision of periodical publications'.[133]

This report, together with proposals for remedying the 'faults in the existing Act', was submitted to the President of the Executive Council, Éamon de Valera, on 1 October 1937. Unsurprisingly, however, the government was not prepared to accept these suggestions, considering that the new Constitution of Ireland (1937) reinforced the provisions of the Censorship of Publications Act, 1929. In late 1938, the Minister of Justice advised the Society that it was the government's view that the Act had achieved its object to a very large extent.[134] The CTSI, however, was not to be deflected and persisted in pressing for a revision despite receiving private assurances from Monsignor Boylan, Chairman of the Censorship Board (and a member of the Society's committee of management) that 'the Board had in fact achieved a great deal'.[135] At a heated CTSI committee of management meeting, Boylan said that he disagreed with some of the conclusions in the report.[136] Professor Howley, who was also Chairman of the Library Association of Ireland, was similarly adamant that librarians took the best possible steps to exclude objectionable books from their shelves. He was supported by some other members of the committee, who argued that it was the Society who 'had all the books supplied to Irish libraries examined before issue'.[137] The committee eventually decided that the matter should still be pursued and that certain TDs should be lobbied.[138]

The Society's complaints were not of major significance. They related to the need to provide the Censorship Office with adequate funds for the purchase of books and periodicals, and the need to increase the number of staff in the office and on the board itself. It was believed that these improvements would make the system more efficient and expeditious. Other protests related to making 'such changes in the Minister's Regulations regarding the submission of complaints against newspapers and periodicals as are necessary to prevent evasion of the Act'.[139]

In 1941, however, the CTSI decided to tone down its campaign because of changing circumstances. The following statement was issued by Veritas House:

> This Committee, recognising that the adequate amendment of the Censorship of Publications Act could not be demanded of the Government at this juncture with due regard to national interests, has not pursued the matter further with the Minister. The question has been put back for post-war consideration. In the meantime the restrictions imposed upon cross-channel publishers as a result of the War have made the problem less pressing.[140]

In fact, the war years proved to be a boon for the CTSI in another respect. Sales of their publications increased to record levels. In 1939-1940 they had sold 738,586 pamphlets. By 1945-1946, this had risen to 2,312,338 pamphlets – its best year ever.[141] The post-War years and the 1950s, however, witnessed a revival of the vigilance campaign, with organisations such as the Legion of Mary and the Knights of St Columbanus taking more active roles.

THE 'CATHOLIC' THEATRE AND CINEMA MOVEMENT

It was in this atmosphere of control and discipline that more active calls were made for a central and legally binding cinema censorship.[142] In the 1920s, the Irish Vigilance Association were particularly prominent in this area. In the 1930s, An Rioghacht took over the mantle. Professor Lyons has suggested that 'censorship in its pristine form was at least part of an attempt to translate into reality the Puritanism that goes with revolution'.[143]

T.J. Deering of the Dublin Vigilance Association and the CTSI, went even further than the standards laid down previously, and in 1922 he called for a banning of all films and stage performances which were used for 'propaganda purposes' alien to Catholic and Irish ideals.[144] In particular, he referred to films that covered such issues as birth control, the unmarried mother and divorce. *The Irish Rosary* added its voice, and in a hard-hitting article, 'The School of the Cinema', argued that 'the time is more than ripe for a rigid censorship of the screen in the interests of the child'.[145] The Irish Vigilance Association, representing all similar-minded pressure groups, had remained active, particularly since the heady days of 1911. They were quick to take advantage of the new mood and changed circumstances. After a number of deputations to Kevin O'Higgins, they elicited a promise to enact legislation. The prevailing atmosphere, combined with the pressure of vigilance groups, easily facilitated the passing of the Censorship of Films Act, 1923. The new film censor was not to grant a certificate if he was of the opinion that the film was 'indecent, obscene or blasphemous', or 'would be subversive to public morality'.[146] The first chairman of the Appeals Board was Professor Magennis TD, an activist with the CTSI.

The Irish Vigilance Association kept up the pressure for stronger legislation.[147] The Censorship of Films (Amendment) Act, 1925, extended the powers of the censor to include advertisements. This was welcomed by the IVA, who subsequently passed a resolution congratulating James Montgomery, the first censor, and his colleagues, 'for the splendid work they have already accomplished in the censoring of films'.[148]

A strong and successful campaign against what was or was not staged, particularly in Dublin, was also undertaken simultaneously by the IVA and the CTSI. While the CTSI were involved in the 'evil literature' campaign they had managed to persuade Dublin Corporation officials to allow them to become unofficial censors for the burgeoning cinema industry.[149] In 1933, they transferred their attention to the stage, but great care was taken that 'no publicity' would arise as regards the Society's involvement and influence in this work.[150] From 1934 to 1938 they aggressively tackled theatre management with a view to controlling what the public saw on stage. In 1934, they noted 'with satisfaction' the promise of the Directors of Dublin's Gaiety Theatre with reference to the future conduct of the theatre. However, by 1938 they were still concerned that much needed to be done despite their best efforts, and consequently they arranged to meet the City Manager, Mr Hernon.[151] They requested that a vigilance committee be set up. Six warrants of Temporary Inspectors were granted to nominees of the Society, under the provisions of the Public Health Acts.[152] Though the CTSI held the view that some kind of legal action was really needed and had examined the issue of controlling the patents granted to Dublin's theatres, a more general feeling prevailed that vigilance would achieve all that was needed.[153] Such was the confidence they had in their own influence that when the appointments of the Temporary Inspectors was publicly announced, they ignored the criticism that was forthcoming in the columns of The Irish Times. In a confidential report on the censorship of theatres, the Society made it abundantly clear that they regarded criticism as only coming from 'pseudo-intellectuals' and that no attention would be paid to their protests. They would instead proceed with their plan to deal directly with the theatres.[154]

The theatre and stage industry itself soon saw an organisation developing to help in their Catholic formation – the Catholic Stage Guild. Besides the CTSI's campaign, there were other calls in the 1930s for a specifically 'Catholic theatre',[155] the need for 'Christian drama',[156] and the ending of the 'Ascendancy clique which controls the Abbey Theatre'.[157] The first president of the Catholic Stage Guild was the legendary film and stage actor Jimmy O'Dea, who, according to his biographer, took this position very seriously.[158] Another famous name in the Catholic Stage Guild, Eamonn Andrews, did not take it with equal seriousness, saying, 'I always felt a Catholic Stage Guild in Dublin was like forming a league of decency in a convent'.[159] Andrews's cynicism worsened over the years, partly because of the interference in the Guild by Archbishop McQuaid.[160] Another founding member was the great actor and singer Noel Purcell.[161]

The writer Seán Ó Faoláin believed that the worst censors were to be found among the laity. Writing of his native county he recalled, 'Cork's too-good people have almost ruined their theatre. They recently formed themselves into a Society of St Jude and exercised an unofficial censorship over plays'.[162]

In one of his short stories, *The Old Master* (1937), Ó Faoláin captures the atmosphere of Catholic Actionists at work outside the Cork Opera House. O'Sullivan, the main character, gets a shock at the entrance, when he hears his name 'pronounced in full'. Turning, he sees two men looking at him. One holds a notebook and is writing his name down. The other says, 'we're taking down the name of every man who enters the theatre tonight ... we think it an indecent performance'. He also notices a little procession of young men marching around carrying placards. Then O'Sullivan reconsiders the situation, bearing in mind his 'nice job', which has to be renewed by the County Council every year – sometimes a delicate business. O'Sullivan, as he walks away, hears one of the men saying, 'Cross out that name. Mr O'Sullivan is with us.'[163]

THE 'CELLULOID MENACE'

In June 1934, a CTSI branch called on the government to introduce, without delay, legislation prohibiting the attendance of all children under eighteen years at cinema performances, except those especially sanctioned. This did not represent totally the Society's view however; they felt that if films were marked 'unsuitable for children', the number of people viewing them would increase.[164] Professor Magennis of the Censorship Board said in 1935 that he considered censorship of films 'absolutely necessary' so long as people would go to films if they were warned not to go.[165]

In 1930, the Censorship of Films Amendment Act extended film censorship to sound films. In 1931, a paper on the 'Reform of the Cinema in Ireland' was read by a member of An Rioghacht at a meeting in Dublin.[166] Film was seen as being an 'insidious attack' on society. Not many shared this view, however, and in town and country nearly everyone was addicted to the Hollywood film. In village halls and city cinemas, the 1930s was the decade of the enthusiastic discovery of celluloid dreams from California. But 1935 saw the stepping up of a Catholic Action campaign against this pleasure.

By this time there were 181 cinemas in the Irish Free State, and 75 per cent of all films shown were from the USA, with the remainder from Britain.[167] The CTSI Catholic Action periodical *Up and Doing* declared, however, that the approval of a film by the American lay organisation, the Legion of Decency, 'is no guarantee that the film censor in the Free State won't be called upon to use his scissors or to reject a film'.[168] In March 1935, *The Irish Times* reported that a national association to secure cinema control was advocated in a statement issued by the governing body of An Rioghacht.[169] According to the statement, the object of the proposed association was to ensure that 'the immense influence exerted by the cinema in Ireland today should cease to be the hindrance which it actually is to the work of restoring Catholic ideals and native culture'.

An Rioghacht also rejected the control exercised over the cinema 'by a small clique of international capitalists, mostly non-Christian'. They regarded the existing censorship system as only a 'palliative', which did not tackle the root of the question. An Rioghacht's statement received widespread media coverage and support. The *Cork Examiner* quoted the Lord Mayor's criticism of films, indicating that there was 'plenty of room for reform in that direction'.[170] The *Mayo News* also supported the call.[171] An Rioghacht's statement also received considerable coverage from British trade publications such as *The Daily Film Renter*, *Kinematograph Weekly* and *Today's Cinema*. The last of these publications had an article on the situation in Ireland entitled 'Various Uplifters, Reformers and Enemies of the Screen in General'. Organisations such as An Rioghacht were described as 'zealous, bellicose, but aggressive patriots'. According to *Today's Cinema*, vigilance committees were cropping up all over the country. Churches were organising pulpit and doorstep campaigns. New bodies were being organised to clean up the cinema.[172]

Dublin's Lord Mayor, Alfie Byrne, reacted quickly to the growing clamour for a cleaner cinema. In late March 1935, he called a Mansion House conference to examine the matter.[173] As a result of the conference he went to the USA on a fact-finding mission to learn about their censorship system. On his return, he was quoted in the *Irish Independent* as saying that since the Mansion House conference, there had been 'a marked improvement in the type of cinema and stage shows presented in Dublin'. He declared that the 'unsavoury type of picture was quickly vanishing from the screens, and so was the gangster films'. He had been assured by the producers during his American visit that, 'no more pictures of a kind likely to have harmful effect on the juvenile mind would be made'.[174] It would appear from the report that Alfie Byrne alone was responsible for cleaning up the Irish cinema! More to the point, however, was the fact that American Catholic Action under the name of the Legion of Decency (directed by Joseph Breen, an Irish Catholic), was pressurising Hollywood producers to adopt the famous Production Code, which became the industry's self-censorship system.

The powerful Legion of Decency's influence in Hollywood reached a peak in the 1930s. It had started as a reaction against racist depictions of the Irish in some of the early films, which generated a nationwide backlash from Irish Americans and the Catholic Church. Boycotting was one of the early tactics used and the film industry quickly caved in to pressure. The Legion of Decency was successful in blacklisting any film it considered offensive. The Catholic Church, through Catholic Action, played a major role in determining what Americans saw or didn't see on the screen during Hollywood's Golden Age.[175] But Catholic Actionists in Ireland were not happy even with this. The Opposition Fine Gael TD John Dillon criticised *The Irish Press* in the Dáil for what he called a 'sort of hypocritical, fraudulent, and sloppy agitation about indecent films'.[176] Dillon said that *The Irish Press* were talking through their hats for the purpose of posing as the pious good Catholic newspaper that ought to be in the hands of every decent man.

The controversy did not die down, despite Dillon's protestations and Alfie Byrne's assurances. June 1935 saw the Jesuit Fr Richard Devane becoming embroiled.[177] His broadcast on Radio Éireann on the subject was widely reported and discussed.[178] He argued that it was necessary to change cinema from a plaything into a 'valuable national instrument'. He urged the development of the film trade in Ireland on national lines, as unfortunately the country was in a 'position of cultural dependence on Britain'. Devane's views reflected Catholic Church concerns that were evident in the frequent warnings in pastorals. Cinema was regarded by the Church as being an anathema to their view of a self-sufficient Ireland holding on to traditional values. The cinema encouraged the 'new woman', put ideas into her head, and therefore upset the Church's view of authority and the social hierarchy. Cinema brought to Ireland a view of the American and British ways of life, which offered men and women hopes and dreams. It was believed to be one of the factors that facilitated the exodus to Dublin, and to Britain and the USA in the widespread emigration of the 1930s.

Bishop McNamee of Ardagh and Clonmacnoise put the Catholic Church's views on the cinema very clearly:

> The emigration of girls to Great Britain ... they are lured perhaps by the fascinations of the garish distractions of the city, and by the hectic life of the great world as displayed before their wondering eyes in the glamorous unrealities of the films. For it is not the least of the sins of the cinema to breed a discontent that is anything but divine in the prosaic placidity of rural life.[179]

As a result of An Rioghacht's campaign, the government set up an inter-departmental committee to investigate film in Ireland. Fr Devane, a propagandist for strict censorship, was asked to suggest its terms of reference. One of the outcomes of the investigation was the imposition of heavy import duties on 35mm film. Funding was also to be provided for Irish language films and for a National Film Institute. In June 1938, the Minister of Finance announced in the Dáil a grant of £200 for a fifteen-minute, Irish-language film, *The Seannachie*. Eventually, in 1943, the National Film Institute was established with funding and support coming from both State and Church.

It was not only An Rioghacht who were active in this campaign. The 1937 *Catholic Action Programme* of the Drumcondra Branch of the CYMS called for a 'strict censorship of all film displays'.[180] The branch wanted to see particular attention paid to gangster films, to the elimination of bedroom scenes, bathrooms, hospital and surgical operating rooms, and all films likely to create views and ideas 'not in conformity with Catholic teaching'.[181] Moves were made by the Society to control the Irish Cine Club, which had been founded in 1936. By 1942, the Cine Club, one of the most flourishing and technically advanced of the amateur production groups in Dublin, had transferred its headquarters to the CYMS North Frederick Street branch.[182] The Irish Film Society, founded in 1937, constantly advocated the need for films to depict Irish versions of Ireland and not the American or British ones. In 1938 the Catholic Film Society of Ireland was established.[183] Based in Youghal, Co. Cork, it planned to teach doctrinal subjects by 'actual representation on the screen, using films already approved by competent ecclesiastical authorities'.

The Catholic Film Society of Ireland soon ran into difficulties with the ecclesiastical authorities, when they planned to screen the film *Golgotha*. The official Vatican newspaper, *L'Osservatore Romano*, regarded the film as 'the most important production of the year … a remarkable effort'.[184] Archbishop Byrne of Dublin did not share this view, however. According to James Montgomery, the film censor, the Archbishop had 'requested him not to pass certain types of Catholic films for general exhibition in the Irish cinemas'.[185] Montgomery had therefore banned the film as 'blasphemy'. When Hallessey of the Catholic Film Society queried this he was informed that, 'the scene of the Last Supper is too sacred for screening'. Montgomery further added, 'the canon of the Mass, and views of the monstrance in Benediction and procession are never passed by me for general exhibition'.[186] A very annoyed Hallessey contacted Cardinal Maggliore, the Pope's Secretary of State in the Vatican, who informed him that 'competent Catholic offices have been unanimous in their approbation'.[187] This did not help the Society's case. The situation brought pressure on the Society and they soon wound up. The Vatican's strict views on censorship were covered in the 1936 encyclical on the subject, *Vigilanti Cura*. It acknowledged the beneficial results of the campaign for clean films conducted in the USA by the Legion of Decency.[188]

Film censorship in Ireland, therefore, should be seen in this context of an international movement for control, except for the one fact that the ecclesiastical authorities and Catholic Action were not satisfied with this kind of campaign – it did not go far enough for them. Besides the influential work of the Legion of Decency in the USA, the British Board of Film Censors, founded in 1913, has been described in a recent work as 'a killjoy organisation whose pomposity, repression and downright ignorance would test the satiric talents of Jonathan Swift'.[189]

The overriding mood generated by Catholic Action can be summed up in the title of an article by the influential columnist, Gabriel Fallon, in the *Capuchin Annual* for 1938 – 'The Celluloid Menace'.[190] An Rioghacht, having been inspired by the successes of the Legion of Decency, had succeeded in making film censorship and control an important issue in 1930s Ireland.[191] The campaign did succeed in creating that public opinion susceptible to vigilance activities. The activities of the Legion of Decency were widely reported in *The Irish Press* and *Irish Independent*. The *Irish Independent* however took the saner view, hoping that, 'enthusiasts in this country who consider themselves better censors than Mr Montgomery and the Appeal Board will not allow themselves to be betrayed into stupidities which would only discredit themselves and the cause they hope to serve'.[192] The advice seems to have been ignored, and vigilance by Catholic Actionists of stage and cinema remained a facet of Irish life until well into the 1960s.

IV

THE COLLAPSE OF CAPITALISM – HALLMARKING THE 1937 IRISH CONSTITUTION

TOWARDS DIRECTIVE PRINCIPLES OF SOCIAL POLICY: THE ENCYCLICAL QUADRAGESIMO ANNO, 1931

The social encyclical *Quadragesimo Anno* was issued on 15 May 1931 by Pope Pius XI.[1] It reaffirmed the teachings of Pope Leo XIII on social justice. The new encyclical echoed many of the important points in *Rerum Novarum*, but it gave them a heightened sense of urgency because of the ongoing global economic depression. It condemned the evils of unconstrained and unprincipled capitalism, emphasised the unacceptability of the socialist state with its collectivism, statism and anti-Catholicism, and called for a fundamental re-organisation of society, one based on respect both for the worker and the employer. Pius proposed as an example of this cohesive, organic society, the trade or guild system that flourished in the Middle Ages.[2]

The encyclical was written in a very turbulent time of economic depression, when millions were unemployed, employers faced ruin, and farmers were burning produce they could not sell. In the face of financial collapse brought about by the Depression, the leftist parties of Europe were increasing in numbers among the working classes, while the extreme right was gaining among the working and middle classes.[3] In parts of Europe it was a time of disillusionment, as democracy's promises seemed to have been reduced to ineffective parliamentary wrangling. It was also a time of religious persecution in the Soviet Union, an anti-clerical war against the Catholic Church in Mexico and the beginnings of anti-clerical violence in Spain.[4]

The reputation of the prevailing economic system, capitalism, therefore, had never been worse, and people all over the world were seeking a new social order. Communism made many converts in the 1930s. So did the totalitarian movements of the right, such as the Nazis in Germany and the Fascists in Italy. Caught between the anarchy of traditional capitalism on the one hand, and the totalitarianism of the left and right on the other, Catholics believed that the Pope had shown a way out. All over the world, a new self-confidence, and a new precision in the formulation of objectives, could be seen in Catholic Action and its organisations after 1931.

In Ireland, this confidence was also in evidence, starting with the foundation of the rural revival movement of 1931, Muintir na Tíre. Yet developments in Ireland were marked by the two crucial hallmarks of Catholic Action – the dual strategy of vigilance and propaganda. The revived CYMS were regarded by the Irish Catholic hierarchy as being 'the' Catholic Action society, who would provide the ground troops to repel the perceived communist threat. On the other hand, Muintir na Tíre, An Rioghacht, the CTSI, and later in the decade, the CYMS, were to be the great propagandists of the theories of *Quadragesimo Anno*.

THE FEAR OF COMMUNIST INFILTRATION

On 18 October 1931, an important joint pastoral was issued by the Catholic hierarchy, which was read in every church in Ireland.[5] It made claims to 'growing evidence of a campaign of revolution and communism, which if allowed to run its course unchecked, must end in the ruin of Ireland, body and soul'. The IRA and Saor Éire were called 'whether separate or in alliance', 'sinful and irreligious'; no Catholic might 'lawfully be a member of them'. The pastoral described Saor Éire as a 'frankly communistic organisation, trying to impose upon the Catholic soil of Ireland the same materialistic regime, with its fanatical hatred of God, as now dominates Russia and threatens to dominate Spain'. The hierarchy were particularly wary of the same catastrophe befalling Ireland. Saor Éire was further castigated as a body which aimed at 'class warfare, the abolition of private property and the destruction of family life'; in fact, the 'overthrow of Christian civilisation'.

Meanwhile the government, on 14 October, had rushed through the Dáil the Constitutional (Amendment No.17) Bill, which became law three days later. The timing of the bishops' pastoral was perfect from the government's viewpoint. On 20 October, a military tribunal replaced the normal jury system for certain crimes. The IRA, Saor Éire, Cumann na mBan, Friends of the Soviet Union and eight other organisations were banned. Arrests and the suppressions of republican journals followed. *An Phoblacht* and the *Irish Worker* were also suppressed. *The Irish Catholic Herald* reported on 31 October, 'public satisfaction with the *Safety Act Enactment*' and that the government 'has at last grasped the communist nettle'.[6] They noted that de Valera had stated that there was no communist menace, 'only a scare manufactured for political purposes'. They agreed that there was no communist menace of the Russian variety, but disagreed where the IRA type was concerned.[7] The *Catholic Bulletin* was not as circumspect. In various editorials they referred to 'Soviety snakes in Ireland'[8] and 'Boiling Bolshevism'.[9] The *Irish Monthly* warned of the coming apocalyptic struggle in an article, 'The Coming Conflict: Capitalism versus communism'.[10] These staunchly Catholic periodicals (including *The Irish Rosary* [11]) were supplemented by the Catholic press and the numerous CTSI and *Irish Messenger* office pamphlets. The poet Austin Clarke in his autobiography, *Twice Around the Black Church*, recalls Dublin at the time:

> I glanced at the titles of the pamphlets in the glass case on the wall near me. The booklets about the saints, their wonderful lives and miracles, were no longer there to delight the young. Instead I saw the battle-array of religious action: *Communism and the Home*, and other bellicose covers were in that row among sundry liturgical tracts and explanations.[12]

The *Irish Independent*, too, was caught up in the bishops' concerns and had front page headlines such as, 'Satan's Terrible Anti-God Campaign ... The Communist Gospel ... Vigorous Warning ... The Irish Bishops' Advice'.[13]

Despite de Valera's dismissal of the communist threat in the Dáil in 1934 (Cumann na nGaedheal had used the 'red scare', unsuccessfully, as an electioneering strategy in the 1932 elections), there were many, irrespective of political allegiance, who took it very seriously. De Valera was convinced that communist activity was limited to Dublin, Kilrush and Castlecomer, and even in these areas the danger was insignificant.[14] The Church, however, did not share his optimism. Hence, when it was announced that the Revolutionary Workers' Group would be formed into a fully fledged Communist Party, Cardinal MacRory issued a warning that Bolshevism seemed to be spreading 'like a plague', and that it was time 'that all of us should feel called upon to prepare ourselves for this trouble that seems to be coming'.[15] A reaction was spreading that gave a veritable *raison d'être* to the resurgent CYMS.[16]

Bishop Collier of Ossory called for 'vigilance committees' in every parish to watch and expose the 'red menace', and a Catholic Able-Bodied Men's Association was set up to challenge the communist-led Irish Unemployed Workers' Movement.[17] The Lenten pastorals of 1933 were almost incitements to tackle the threat.[18] The people of Ireland were urged 'to combine' and not to tolerate it in their midst. Professor Hogan's *Could Ireland Become Communist? The Facts of the Case*[19] was published at a time when the printing presses of Catholic publishers were churning out anti-communist literature. In February 1935, the front page of *The Irish Catholic Herald* had the warning, 'Communism Advancing from Russia. Catholics must be in the Vanguard'.[20]

The CTSI were certainly active in this vanguard. Already, in April 1932, Sir Joseph Glynn had raised the question of Catholic Action organisations co-operating more closely in the distribution of anti-communist literature.[21] In early 1934, the Society agreed to distribute free literature on the subject to unemployed men.[22] Approaches were made to the Central Catholic Library to establish a special section for anti-communist material.[23] In 1937, the Legion of Mary and the St Vincent de Paul Society [24] were co-opted to help in the distribution of free copies of the new anti-communist encyclical, *Divini Redemptoris*.[25] In 1938, the CTSI established an Anti-Communist Propaganda Committee at the behest of Bishop Cohalan of Waterford and Lismore.[26] The committee presented a report to the Society in June 1938 entitled, 'The Production and Distribution of Anti-Communist Propaganda', which examined the whole question of counteracting the communist movement in Ireland.[27] The conclusion the report arrived at was that the communist position in Ireland was not strong, but was steadily growing, through the insidious spread of pamphlets, etc. amongst all of our workers'.[28] They established that there were several 'cells' in Ireland and that the organ of the British Communist Party, the *Daily Worker*, circulated in Ireland and 'has been actually been on sale in the official shop of the Irish Transport Workers' Union'. It was particularly amongst the transport workers that the Society noted communist agents. The CTSI had tried to counter pamphleteering with pamphleteering and had distributed over one and a half million copies of its own publications, 'Facts about Communism' and 'Workers of Ireland Unite against Communism'. The Society also published nine other pamphlets on various aspects of the communist issue, covering Labour, Papal encyclicals, and aspects of Catholic social teaching. At the same time they realised that pamphlets alone could not persuade the worker who 'wants to know how his own lot is to be improved'.[29] They saw a particular need for a newspaper along the lines of the *Daily Worker* and proposed that *The Standard* be improved. The suggestion was taken up by, amongst others, Professor Alfred O'Rahilly, and *The Standard* soon became a staunch promoter and defender of Catholic social teaching. The CTSI also recommended that a 'co-ordinated effort' on the part of all the Catholic Action organisations was necessary in the campaign.

Efforts were already being made in that direction. The CYMS were at the forefront of the anti-communist drive. The number of its branches had increased from six in 1927 to twenty-five in 1932.[30] The weekly columns of the 'CYMS Notes' in *The Irish Catholic* focused more and more on getting the society off the ground, so as to be ready to combat 'the most dreadful evil of our time, Communism'.[31] The Society regarded itself as 'a bulwark of Catholic defence and a cradle of true nationalism'.[32] In 1932, they were given a specific mandate from the Catholic hierarchy to devote their energies to countering the spread of communism.[33] In 1933, the growing organisation (which reached 15,000 members by 1939, with over 100 branches)[34] had already taken decisive steps in the face of the 'red menace'.[35] It was the lecture by the well-known priest Fr Owen Dudley on the 'Menace of Communism', given in Dublin's Theatre Royal, that precipitated their first embroilment.[36] It aroused a considerable response in the letters pages of the *Irish Independent*.[37] Mrs Charlotte Despard, secretary of the Friends of the Soviet Union – Irish Section, came in for attack from a CYMS writer. He asked why the CYMS had not done in Dublin what the society had done in Cork, 'smash the red menace the moment it made its appearance in the city'.[38] The Angelic Warfare Society was also involved in that activity in Cork. A Mr Horan of the Dublin CYMS wrote to the *Irish Independent* denouncing Mrs Despard and promising that the Society was not going to sit still while she promoted the communist cause.[39] In March 1933, the weekly newspaper, *The Irish Catholic*, reported that the CYMS no longer intended to be 'humble, passive, ignorant papists' who shrank from publicly asserting their religious principles. The Society had no intention of apologising for 'taking the offensive' against certain anti-Catholic movements.[40]

The CYMS focused their attention on the Irish Workers' College in Dublin's Eccles Street. The Society regarded it as being nothing more than 'a soviet university' and they challenged the college to publish its education programme and show it to the people of Dublin.[41] The college was accused of being full of 'communist adventurers and traitors'. The prospectus of the college was obtained and the names of the individuals on the governing board included four representatives from the ITGWU, two from the National Union of Railwaymen, one from the Workers' Union of Ireland, and two from smaller unions. The Society contacted the trade unions to verify their association with the college.[42] Those named contacted the CYMS and denied any connection with the college.[43] The society had the correspondence published in *The Irish Catholic*.[44] They regarded the outcome as a vindication of their vigilance.

In the same period, March/April 1933, the CYMS were also actively organising anti-communist demonstrations in Dublin. On 27 March, following the fiery Redemptorist Mission in the Pro-Cathedral, a mob attacked various properties belonging to the Communist Party. Shouting 'God Bless the Pope', they stormed Connolly House, headquarters of the Revolutionary Workers' Group, and set fire to it.[45] From there they moved on to the Workers' College and sacked it. They then attacked Unity Hall, headquarters of Larkin's Workers' Union, and Kevin Barry Hall, a republican meeting place.[46] When the mob turned to looting O'Connell Street, the Gardaí intervened.

According to the official *Irish Catholic Directory*, some of those who took part were members of St Patrick's Anti-Communist League.[47] This particular organisation consisted of members of the CYMS and the Catholic Boy Scouts of Ireland, groups that had been forging closer links, according to reports in the *Limerick Leader*[48] and *The Irish Catholic*.[49]

Further CYMS demonstrations were organised for Dublin. In early April, a meeting took place in Cathal Brugha Street calling for an end to the circulation of communist literature. It was organised by a group of young men who described themselves as 'representing the Catholic laymen of Ireland'.[50] Copies of communist newspapers, the *Daily Worker* and the *Workers' Voice*, were publicly burned. The Society called upon newsagents to cease stocking these newspapers, and requested all branches to 'enter the fight against Communism, to prevent the circulation of Communist literature in their districts, and by every lawful means to stamp out Communism'.[51]

The following month saw another CYMS-organised demonstration in O'Connell Street. According to a report in *The Irish Press*, Tom French of the CYMS, in his address to the crowd, referred to a Communist poster that described the Anti-Communist League as 'gangsters, hooligans and Hitlerites'.[52] They were not hooligans, he said, they were simply defending the Catholic faith against people whose sole aim was to crush it. In a strongly worded speech, he pointed out that the marchers were the 'first body which had the courage to come out into the open and tell the people that Ireland was not having Communism'. He continued, 'you have donned the gloves and entered the ring, and I appeal to you not to leave it until our opponents are beaten right through the ropes'.[53]

In June 1933, the *Sunday Independent* reported on the continuing activities of the Society, 'Ban on Communism Urged by the CYMS', and 'Members Should be the Church's Storm Troops'.[54] The Society's annual convention attracted record attendances and a resolution was sent to the government requesting them to suppress the communists. Vigilance committees in the branches throughout the country were told to 'take action the moment Communism, no matter what form it takes, appears'. Newsagents who sold communist papers were to be boycotted until undertakings were given that their sale would be discontinued. 'Catholic Action' was henceforth to be the Society's *modus operandi*.[55] The campaign went ahead despite a report in *The Irish Press* that the official number of communists in Dublin was only seventy-five, whilst in the rest of the country there were only about fifteen.[56]

The *Fairview CYMS Journal*, in an article, 'The Muskrat Menace', drew parallels between the prevailing concern in Ireland at the time with the burrowing properties of the muskrat, and the menace of communism.[57] At a public meeting organised by the Monasterevan branch, Fr Ambrose Crofts said that the defence of property rights was essential in counteracting the arguments of communism.[58] His book *Property and Poverty* (1938) combined with an earlier work, *Catholic Social Action* (1936), became indispensable reference works for Catholic Actionists.[59] For Crofts it was vital to look back to the Middle Ages and to Thomas Aquinas for the axioms of reform. He hoped that the CYMS would take a definite stand for the Church 'in the great campaign of Catholic Action'.[60] In 1934, Crofts was responsible for founding an organisation in Waterford called the Aquinas Study Circle. Shortly afterwards, the new society published a pamphlet on communism called, 'Workers of Ireland, Which Way?' The pamphlet called upon Catholic Action organisations to play a large part in Ireland's social reconstruction.[61] It called for the regaining of a Catholic consciousness in social matters.

The CYMS also directed their attention to Galway, having heard of a proposed communist meeting being held there. They organised a major conference to coincide with the communist meeting. The *Irish Catholic Directory* noted that the attendance of young men at the CYMS conference was 'the largest ever seen in a public building in Galway'.[62] *The Connacht Tribune* welcomed the conference to Galway with a front page story headed, 'CYMS – Answer to Communists'.[63]

According to Milotte in his work *Communism in Modern Ireland*, the bishops' call for Catholic Action 'met with a wide response and served to increase the isolation of the Revolutionary Workers' Group'.[64] Milotte states that, 'priests throughout the country were told to go on the offensive, through Catholic Action'.[65] In Galway the CYMS had a very active branch operating with a strong vigilance committee drawn from workers in the Post Office, the railways and the buses.[66] According to the branch report to headquarters, as a result of vigilance exercised, 'certain literature addressed to a Communist agent in Galway had not reached him'.[67] The *Irish Independent* reported in June 1934 that the Communist Party had written to the Minister for Posts and Telegraphs, drawing his attention to the fact that consignments of literature had not been received by them, due to the intervention of the CYMS.[68] We can equally presume that Catholic Action organisations were also directing their 'vigilance', not only at communist literature, but to any kind which they suspected to be indecent or obscene.

In Co. Kilkenny, Bishop Collier put his full weight and influence into the drive to see the CYMS established throughout the county. He also invited An Rioghacht to establish branches. The Castlecomer coal-miners' long-running dispute was the reason for Dr Collier's intense activity. Catholic Action branches were seen as an effective remedy against communist infiltration. In a New Year's Day pastoral of 1933, Collier declared that, 'no Catholic can be a Communist, no Communist can be a Catholic'.[69] He believed that since they had in Kilkenny the only coal-mining area in the country employing hundreds of workers, such an area was 'always the hope of the Communist agitation'. The communist activity in Kilkenny had, he said, 'the marks of the beast. We had the secret infiltration from headquarters, the paid agitator, the preaching of labour unrest, the veiled incitement to looting and rioting.' Because of this he felt there was a definite need to 'expose' and 'oppose', these activities in his diocese, by every means possible.[70]

Collier seems to have been completely oblivious to the harsh realities of the coalminers' working conditions, and the possibility that they might have legitimate grievances. Even the CYMS in Kilkenny admitted to the employers' 'blindness to the welfare of the workers', and the board of directors' 'hardness of heart'.[71] Collier wanted more branches of the Society established immediately and he pressed them to hold their annual convention in Kilkenny in 1933. In 1935, the CTSI were also persuaded to hold their annual conference in Kilkenny City. Addressing the CYMS annual convention in November, Bishop Collier told his audience that the Society should 'not merely be a social club, but should also be a stronghold of Catholic Action'.[72] He regarded the CYMS as one of the best means of countering attacks on the Catholic Church.

By July 1936 the Society had established eleven branches in the county, with a membership of nearly 1,000.[73] Kilkenny City had the largest branch, with 200 members, and Castlecomer the second largest, with 120. The Castlecomer branch was the last to be established, such was the ill-feeling generated by the excommunication of the miners' leader, Nixie Boran. His daughter, Ann Boran, writing on those difficulties a number of years later, described her father as 'a committed Catholic who fought for workers' rights despite the opposition of Church and State'.[74] She claimed that Boran had been a 'Professed Communist' until the mid-1930s, and he remained a socialist and a dedicated member of the Labour Party until his death in 1971.[75] It was his activities in Castlecomer and his writings in the *Workers' Voice* and the *Daily Worker* which aroused such opposition. In a letter to the *Kilkenny Journal* in March 1931, Nixie Boran indicated his intention, 'the ultimate overthrow of the capitalist system', which the miners believed would 'be the only genuine cure for the evils and miseries which the workers of Ireland are subjected to'.[76] The columns of the *Kilkenny People* and the *Kilkenny Journal* for the early 1930s amply show that the clergy saw the entire question as one of a communist threat. The miners were seen as uneducated, without views or opinions.[77] The legacy of bitterness and division in the parish of Moneenroe, Castlecomer, has not been forgotten more than seventy years later, according to a former parish priest Fr Gerry Joyce, writing in a recent work, *The Laity: Help or Hindrance?*[78]

Vigilance activity against the perceived communist threat stimulated the development of a vigorous intelligence network in the CYMS. This was particularly evident in the correspondence between the branches and the Central Vigilance Department in Dublin. John Costelloe, the organising secretary, was able to state in a confidential letter to one of the branches that, 'you may rest assured that you will be placed in full possession of all the facts relating to communism affecting any part of Ireland'.[79] This was Catholic Action at its most determined and ardent. Bishop Collier had information fed to him by the local branches.

In 1936, the Society's attention was drawn back to Dublin, where there was concern that the communist movement was going to make an effort to re-establish the party.[80] With this in mind, some Dublin members decided to picket a communist meeting in Rathmines Town Hall, where guest speakers from the British Communist Party were expected. The *Irish Weekly Independent* reported on the event with the headlines, 'Scenes at Dublin Meeting', 'Communist Speeches Cause Uproar' and 'Chairs as Weapons'.[81] Apparently, 'amazing scenes' were witnessed at the meeting, with 'chairs, pokers and sticks' being freely used as weapons. There were shouts of, 'We represent Catholic Action' during the scuffles, as CYMS members tried to break up the meeting. Outside, more young men carried banners with wording such as 'Dublin Rejects Communism'. Leaflets were distributed outlining the Society's case.[82] The Society's activities also gained front-page headlines in the *Irish Worker's Voice*, where it was stated that, 'Workers Route Rowdies', and that efforts by 'an organised gang, said to be members of the CYMS' to create a disturbance failed, and the 'hooligans were ejected'.[83]

In the 'CYMS Notes' in the *Irish Weekly Independent*, the society explained why they had given 'special attention' to the Rathmines rally; their original efforts to prevent communists from obtaining the use of the Town Hall from the Vocational Educational committee had failed.[84]

The year 1937 heightened fears of communism, which the new encyclical on communism, *Divini Redemptori*, did nothing to allay. Catholic Actionists from An Rioghacht and the Knights of St Columbanus had helped, covertly, to establish the Irish Christian Front to help the anti-communist effort in Spain. The Irish Christian Front had been founded in August 1936 and some of its meetings in Dublin, Cork, Waterford and elsewhere attracted huge numbers. The concept and principle of Catholic Action was the central ideological strain within the Irish Christian Front, although some of the leaders' (notably Paddy Belton TD) political objectives damaged the organisation in the long run. Many of the ICF's supporters and organisers had hoped that the organisation would be a populist, non-political, unifying Catholic Action movement. For advocates of Catholic Action, the ICF had the potential to develop into the long-awaited unifying body. The CYMS leadership in particular, were among the ICF's strongest supporters. Alfred O'Rahilly and Frank O'Reilly of the CTSI were initially very supportive, because of the ICF's anti-communist campaign, but became suspicious that Paddy Belton was intent upon establishing a Catholic political party. This disparity of objectives meant that the ICF had a very short life and petered out in late 1937. Other organisations took over the organisation of the pro-Franco campaign, namely the AOH, the CYMS and the CTSI. However, the immense popularity of the Irish Christian Front demonstrated Irish interest in Spain and the strength of anti-communism. In fact, by this time, for many people Catholic Action meant anti-communism.

The CYMS stepped up their vigilance activities. The *Dublin Evening Mail* reported a laundry van being stopped and searched for 'goods on behalf of the Reds in Spain'.[85] The young men involved were, according to the CYMS branch reports, their members.[86] Horan, the director of the Society's Vigilance Department, had circulated a confidential questionnaire to nearly 100 branches throughout the country, requesting further details on their intelligence activities.[87] He also advised the branches in a confidential 'News Bulletin' on where 'cells' were to be formed by the communists, such as in trade unions, the public service and even Catholic organisations.[88] The 'News Bulletin' advised members 'to deal effectively with agitators'. Places where meetings were or might be held were to be approached and 'convinced' of the wisdom of 'bowing to Catholic opinion'. Swift and effective action was to be the norm to stamp out the activities 'at all cost'.[89] This approach proved very effective in Castlecomer, with the miners soon going over to the ITGWU and abandoning their new union.

Despite strong anti-communist rallies being held in Dublin and elsewhere in 1937, the government did not share the Catholic Church's alarm.[90] In keeping with its policy of denying that there was a communist threat, it refused to take part in the anti-communist crusade, although it issued a strong statement condemning the war in Spain.[91] The government's overall policy *vis-à-vis* the Spanish conflagration was one of strict neutrality. As with the popularity of the Irish Christian Front, it is difficult to correlate the profound fear of communism which was central to the Catholic Church's reaction to the Spanish Civil War, with the marginal position of communism in Ireland. Their response demonstrates the importance the clergy attached to European events. This was in part due to the extensive coverage on anti-clerical atrocities in the Catholic press and the presence of Irish religious in Spain. The Catholic Church in Ireland astutely identified some of the issues it associated with Spain as threats to its power.

The Catholic Action campaign died down during the Second World War, though it became particularly active and vociferous in the late 1940s and 1950s because of the difficulties experienced by the Catholic Church in Iron Curtain countries such as Poland, Hungary and Yugoslavia, which had come under communist rule.

PROMOTING CATHOLIC SOCIAL PRINCIPLES: ECONOMIC NATIONALISM

The anti-communism campaign of the 1930s was paralleled by a propaganda strategy on the part of Catholic organisations to promote the benefits of Catholic social teaching based on the 1931 encyclical *Quadragesimo Anno*.

During the final years of the Cosgrave administration, the economic position deteriorated as the world depression deepened. Exports of meat and dairy produce dropped sharply and there was a big fall in the price of cattle and sheep. Many factories closed, unemployment soared and emigration increased as farmer incomes dropped. The government attempted to alleviate the crisis by decreasing public expenditure and reducing the salaries of some of those in public employment. These measures further decreased the popularity of the government. An additional weakening factor was that the government was divided on the question of tariffs. There was a widespread desire for political change. In the election campaign of 1932, Fianna Fáil emphasised economic self-sufficiency, promised larger doles, and the repudiation of debts to Britain. The support of the Labour Party, together with that of three Independents, was sufficient to enable de Valera to form a government.

Economic self-sufficiency involved the encouragement of tillage in agriculture and the development of native manufactures in industry. Overall, it was intended to create employment and thus decrease emigration. In agriculture the task was formidable. Against a background of world depression and the Anglo-Irish economic war (over the withholding of land annuities), agricultural exports plummeted. In this situation, self-sufficiency was pursued by decreasing dependence on the cattle industry, while giving maximum encouragement to home-grown produce. The establishment of tariff-created industries gave new employment opportunities as did the state subventions for house-building schemes.

It is the view of commentators such as R.J. Raymond that it was the conflicting visions of Seán Lemass and Éamon de Valera – progressive social reform versus an austere rural utopia – that may have slowed down the necessary proper management of the Irish economy.[92] Professor Mary Daly argues in her *Industrial Development and Irish National Identity, 1922-1939*, that the 'long-term efficiency of protected firms was further circumscribed by the dominant attitude of uncompetitiveness'.[93]

Competitiveness was certainly not a quality that was encouraged by the Catholic Church, whether through its control of the education system, or in public pronouncements. *Quadragesimo Anno* was in fact highly critical of what it regarded as the excesses of capitalism. Most of the important Catholic speakers and lecturers of the decade, Cahill, Hayes, O'Rahilly, Hogan, Tierney, Coyne, lay and clerical alike, constantly rejected the urban way of life in favour of the rural, because of the Church's perception of the materialism and immorality of town and city. The largest and most influential Catholic Action organisation in rural areas, Muintir na Tíre, had self-sufficiency as its cornerstone policy.[94] Catholic Action ideology helped to encourage fears that even modest social changes threatened the fabric of Irish society. Muintir na Tíre and An Rioghacht did much to facilitate acceptance of the urge to national self-sufficiency, by their conviction that life on a small Irish farm represented a purity and decency of life that could set Ireland apart from the more commercial societies that surrounded her.[95]

Economic nationalism was one manifestation of the prevailing ethos of the decade. This ethos was reinforced by *Quadragesimo Anno*, which in essence sought to strike a balance between the extremes of capitalism and communism by its advocacy of the principle of subsidiarity.[96] This principle embraced and reinforced political and national self-sufficiency, with its emphasis on devolving power from the state to lesser bodies or local communities. National self-sufficiency involved an independence from the orthodoxies and restraints of the international community, and subsidiarity involved a further independence within the national community. National self-sufficiency, then, was a characteristic impulse of 1930s Ireland. Catholic Action and its organisations, intent on cultural and religious exclusiveness, and propagating the vocational ideal, were useful vehicles for this process.

The international Eucharistic Congress was held in 1932. The CTSI had played a very prominent role in the organisation of this great event.[97] The English Catholic convert and well-known writer G.K. Chesterton, writing on his experience at the Congress, remarked, 'the poorer were the streets, the richer the street decorations'.[98] For him, Dublin was akin to passing through a 'supernatural toyshop'. Both the *Irish Independent* and *The Irish Press* published special *Eucharistic Congress Souvenir Numbers*. These were substantial publications running to nearly 100 pages each.[99]

The Irish Press supplement was also a Fianna Fáil political manifesto, with statements advocating self-sufficiency. Efficient tillage farming 'coupled with national co-operation' with other industries and national culture, was regarded as 'the only salvation for the country', according to one commentator.[100] The article declared the urgent need for 'economic self-reliance' and a return to Irish ideals. Abnormal conditions called for more than ordinary remedial measures.[101] In the same issue, Alfred O'Rahilly called for a 'Christian social policy for Ireland' and he echoed Fianna Fáil dogma by calling for a 'self-contained community', but one based on the 'medieval guild system' as advocated by *Quadragesimo Anno*.[102] His views, he said, came from the encyclicals, and he was glad that probably for the first time in Irish history, 'we have a government able and willing to adopt such a policy'.

The Irish Press also assured its readers in early 1933 that, 'there is not a social or economic change Fianna Fáil has proposed or brought about which has not its fullest justification in the encyclicals of either Leo XIII or the present Pontiff'.[103] When Fianna Fáil called a snap general election in early 1933, *The Irish Press* was able to claim that the party was the only one that cared for the poor.[104] Fianna Fáil's appeal to the poor, the pocket and the pope had the desired effect. The government's initial success with its housing programme, improving old-age pensions, and its tillage campaign, helped it to win the election. *The Irish Press*, now selling 115,000 copies per day,[105] continued to emphasise Fianna Fáil's Catholicity, 'in Catholic countries man has not yet lost his importance in the scheme of things'.[106]

De Valera's policies soon provoked his political opponents to develop a new party. Public disorder had been increasing, with clashes between the IRA and the Army Comrades Association (ACA, founded 1932). The ACA aimed at protecting Cumann na nGaedhael supporters from IRA harassment. In March 1933, the ACA adopted the blue shirt as part of its uniform, and in July, General Eoin O'Duffy, the recently sacked Garda Commissioner, assumed leadership of the movement, now called the National Guard. It adopted a constitution with a vague corporatist commitment to form 'co-ordinated national organisations of employers and employed, which, with the aid of judicial tribunals, will effectively prevent strikes and lock-outs and harmoniously compose industrial differences'.[107] In September, the 'Blueshirts', the new Centre Party (old Farmers' Party) and Cumann na nGaedhael, joined together to form the United Ireland Party, soon known as Fine Gael.

FINE GAEL AND QUADRAGESIMO ANNO

Corporatist or vocational ideas on social organisation as recommended by Pius XI in *Quadragesimo Anno*, had a special appeal to those who felt that Ireland's Catholic nature must be expressed in her newly won independence. This could best be managed through a loyal, active obedience to Papal teachings on the social order. As 1932 progressed, fears grew among some Cumann na nGaedhael supporters, that communism was a real and immediate threat, and the IRA a communist or quasi-communist body. Despite having lost the 1932 election playing the communist card, some party stalwarts persisted in this view. The editorial in the Cumann na nGaedhael organ, *United Ireland* in October 1932, clearly expressed the view that the threat still existed.[108] The unrealistic and obsessive fears were fuelled by numerous ecclesiastical condemnations and warnings, as already indicated. Doubtlessly, the rhetoric of *Quadragesimo Anno* was also percolating down. The encyclical itself had been published amidst a background of economic and political instability, with widespread loss of confidence in democratic structures and old political ideologies. Even England did not escape, with the views of Oswald Mosely attracting some attention from Fascist hopefuls. Combine the international situation with economic and political problems in Ireland, and it is not surprising that *Quadragesimo Anno* should find echoes in the 1933 constitution of the National Guard, forerunner to Fine Gael.[109] The first point of the new constitution promised that the party would 'oppose Communism and uphold Christian principles in every sphere of public activity'.[110] Other *Quadragesimo Anno* ideas followed:

...to promote and maintain social order, to make organised and disciplined voluntary public service a permanent and accepted feature of public life; to promote the formation of co-ordinated national organisations of employers and employed; to awaken throughout the country a spirit of combination, discipline, zeal, and patriotic realism that will put the state in a position to serve the public efficiently in the economic and political spheres.[111]

These proposals marked the first tentative introduction of corporatist ideas by an Irish political movement. They were inspired by *Quadragesimo Anno* (sections 82, 86, 74, 79).[112] Organised public service, national organisations of employers and employed, and the spirit of combination were all subsidiarist principles.

According to *The Irish Times* in their commentary on the new constitution, the National Guard stood for 'unconditional opposition to Communism'.[113] In August 1933, O'Duffy unveiled his plan to remodel the Dáil.[114] Under his scheme, Parliament would consist of representatives of professional and vocational groups. Instead of election by constituencies, he would substitute election by these groups. In an organisation extending from the parish to the Central Council (also a Muintir na Tíre approach), each profession or vocation would select its representatives. No legislation affecting any trade or profession would be introduced without the sanction of any group directly concerned. O'Duffy attacked the party system as an 'English parliamentary system'. Party politics were banned within the organisation.

Among the founders of Fine Gael, which included the National Guard and its corporatist philosophy, was Peter Nugent, an active member of the AOH and a strong advocate of Catholic Action. Another founder was John Horgan of the ACA, who was, as we saw in an earlier chapter, a member of the Catholic Association, the Catholic Defence Society and the Knights of St Columbanus. Horgan was a firm believer in the essential need for disciplined organisation under Catholic aegis. In this respect, it was not surprising that the new party's plans should include strategies to establish industrial and agricultural corporations with full statutory powers.[115]

Both Fianna Fáil and Fine Gael drew on aspects of the subsidiarist/vocational ideal for different reasons, each realising it had something that could enhance their own political standing and opportunities. The new Fine Gael Party grasped corporatism as a plank for its own political survival. Within the new party, however, tensions soon developed between the conservative elements and the flamboyant O'Duffy. The latter was eventually forced out. In 1935, he founded the National Corporate Party which, after initial interest, soon faded into oblivion.[116]

THE CORPORATIST LEGACY

In December 1934, the Fine Gael organ, the *United Ireland*, claimed that the corporate state, 'as advocated by Fine Gael and as based on the principles of *Quadragesimo Anno*, could be carried into effect without what are regarded as the characteristic features of Fascism'.[117] The party was endeavouring to extricate itself from the excesses of O'Duffy and continental corporatism.

The columns of *United Ireland*, however, reflected the new party's wholehearted embrace of *Quadragesimo Anno* corporatism. The most important articles on the subject came from Professors Hogan and Tierney, such as one entitled, 'Fine Gael to Adopt Pope's Social Programme'.[118] Other articles were written under the heading of 'Corporatism'. Michael Tierney was Professor of Greek in UCD, and his many articles in *Studies* since 1922 reflected his abiding interest in the subject, an interest which coincided with the Catholic Church's reliance on the neoscholastics. He provided much of the intellectual basis for the rise of O'Duffy. His grasp and appreciation of ancient and scholastic philosophy, added to O'Duffy's organising skills, and combined with Hogan's reading of Reformation and Enlightenment history from the Catholic viewpoint, proved a strong and potent mixture.[119] The Catholic blueprint, *Quadragesimo Anno*, provided all three with the answer to contemporary difficulties in Ireland, whether economic or political.

Thanks particularly to Hogan and Tierney, the corporatist ideal did not die with the demise of the Blueshirts and O'Duffy, but instead lived on in the Catholic-Action-supported vocational movement. Tierney stressed as fundamental the passage in *Quadragesimo Anno*, 'The principal duty of the State and citizens is to abolish conflict between classes with divergent interests, and foster and promote harmony between the various ranks of society. The aim of social legislation therefore must be the re-establishment of vocational groups.'[120] Hogan shared this view. He felt strongly that the guild or corporate/vocationalist type of society was the normal type of society, because 'it is the only type of society that can succeed in reconciling the conflicting aims of collective and individual life'.[121] In 1935, he published his bestseller, *Could Ireland Become Communist?*, which helped fan the flames of the vigilance campaign and the activities of organisations such as the CYMS. Most significantly, Hogan and Tierney helped to sustain the drive for a corporate state for Ireland during the mid-to-late 1930s. Corporatism as a political philosophy disappeared quietly from the public agenda of Fine Gael, but it was kept very much alive through Catholic social teaching and Catholic Action organisations, and by Catholic lay and cleric intellectuals.

Political corporatism failed in the early 1930s, so great was Fianna Fáil's popular support. It had developed as a reaction, or as a further development of the Civil-War hatreds, rather than as part of the European movement. It would seem that Irish political corporatism borrowed from *Quadragesimo Anno* for strictly self-serving motives, rather than for the promotion of Catholic social teaching.

IDEOLOGICAL INTRICACIES

Irish Catholicism was placed in a dilemma as a result of European political developments, and in particular the events taking place in Italy. Enormous ideological transformations were the order of the day. The 1931 Catholic Action encyclical *Non Abbiamo Bisogno*, issued only a few weeks after *Quadragesimo Anno*, was a reaction to the fears about Fascist intentions.[122] It denounced harassment of Catholic organisations by Fascists in Italy, and vindicated Catholic Action. But as a compromise with the Fascists, *Non Abbiamo Bisogno* indicated that Catholic Action would henceforth have to be above and beyond politics.

Because of this stance, a contradiction emerged in the recommendations of *Quadragesimo Anno*, since that document recommended social reconstruction using a political model.[123] This inherent contradiction was to plague the Catholic Action campaign in Ireland during the 1930s and 1940s, particularly in the area of political initiatives. On the one hand *Quadragesimo Anno* pushed lay organisations into activity, but on the other, *Non Abbiamo Bisogno* pulled them back. Nell-Breunig, the principal architect behind the drafting of *Quadragesimo Anno*, reflecting a few years later on the encyclical's evolution, declared that it was 'a confused, ambiguous and vague reaction to the world economic and political upheaval'.[124] In one respect, the pope apparently admired the corporative/vocational model of society, but at the same time he feared the State's intrusion into the domain of the individual and the Church.

In Ireland there was a similarly confused reaction. Fine Gael supporters, such as Hogan and Tierney, promoted it under the guise of vocationalism. The Irish Catholic Church's reaction was very positive but always prepared to be reticent. In official Church circles there was particular confusion over the word 'corporatism'. Vocationalism was the preferred term. Attempts were even made to use the expression 'corporative' as an alternative. This word became the preferred option for many commentators and Churchmen. Other terms used from time to time were, 'Solidarism', 'Subsidiarity' and 'Functionalism'.[125]

The Jesuit Fr Edward Coyne saw the issue as being sociological rather than necessarily economic. He argued in 1934 that *Quadragesimo Anno* was about 'social order', 'social reconstruction' and 'social institutions'. For Coyne, the doctrine of the 'corporative organisation of society, of vocational corporations' did not stand alone, but was part of a much larger body of doctrines embedded in a Catholic social philosophy.[126]

'Solidarism' went even further than Coyne's limited sociological vision. It covered both economic and sociological principles and was developed by the German Jesuit priest Fr Heinrich Pesch, one of the most influential writers of his time. On the economic side, it accepted, with certain reforms, the main lines of the capitalist technique of production. But on the sociological side, it was opposed to both individualism and collectivism. *Quadragesimo Anno* adopted the principle of 'solidarism' as a golden mean. Another principle related to solidarism was that of subsidiarity. The social life of the community should not be exclusively concentrated in the State – it should be decentralised.

Coyne suggested that *Quadragesimo Anno* expressed approval of the corporative society, not the corporate state, the latter smacking of totalitarianism. He realised, however, the difficulties facing the acceptance of these ideas in Ireland. Society and social organisations were organic things; they must grow and they are not made by rule of thumb.

The *Catholic Bulletin* also tried to grapple with the difficulties of definitions. In a 1937 editorial, it indicated that it supported the Portuguese system of corporatism (similar to Italy's, but with a more flexible attitude on economic structures and a more harmonious relationship with the Catholic Church), but condemned the German system, where 'corporations were simply instruments of dictatorial government'.[127]

Even Fr Cornelius Lucey, the Catholic Church's expert on such issues, had problems over terminology. Writing in the *Irish Ecclesiastical Record* in early 1937, he postulated that the 'great aim of the Catholic social movement is, or at least should be the setting up of occupational Associations'.[128] He was unsure, however, of the 'chances' of such a movement setting up these associations. He was not happy with the word 'corporatism'. The only solution for Lucey was to prefix the adjective 'Christian' and use the noun 'corporativism'. He interpreted the new 'Christian corporativism' as both a movement and a social philosophy, 'with the vital principle of *Subsidiarity*'. In a prophetic statement, he said that this new name was essential because the Christian Corporative Movement suffered in democratic countries because it was confused with the Fascist movement, whereas in his view, 'there was a world of difference between the Fascist Corporate State and the Christian Corporative Society'.[129] Lucey suggested that in Ireland the only part the State had to play was to 'encourage' the movement, and to confer on each occupational association the necessary legal standing once it was sufficiently developed. This, in Lucey's view, was 'voluntary corporativism', as opposed to 'dictated corporatism'. The role of Catholic Action organisations was the 'popularisation of the ideals of the movement among employers and employees'. Lucey did, however, admit to the inherent contradiction of his proposal when he said, 'the occupational unions so constituted could still be instruments of disorder as much as order'.[130] The wheel had already been invented. Employees and employers already had their own associations and unions, which had developed through the exigencies and vagaries of Irish history.

Professor Denis O'Keefe, lecturer in Politics in UCD, found these vocational hopes of Catholic Actionists 'very remarkable'. Writing in *Studies* in June 1937, he argued that the 'corporative' organisation of society would not succeed in Ireland.[131] In fact, he could not understand how political theorists and practical statesmen could be convinced that the salvation of economic and social problems was to be found in the corporative organisation of society. Such a complex system would take a long time to emerge. The survival of individualist views, psychological as well as social, were factors which would make the introduction of the corporative system so difficult. A classless society was not the solution. History was not reversible. Corporative institutions in Italy presented an exclusively bureaucratic and political character, and if applied to Ireland would similarly risk serving political aims rather than contributing to the initiation of a better social order. O'Keefe regarded it as a 'maxim of prudence' to build upon institutions that already existed. He warned that, 'the whole subject bristles with difficulties, and to fail to recognise that would be naïve'.[132]

FROM TEXTBOOK TO CROSSROADS: A DEVELOPING CATHOLIC SOCIAL VISION

The public debate was partly a response to, and at the same time encouraged the emergence of, new publications which did much to promote the ideas of *Quadragesimo Anno*. The *Capuchin Annual* (1930); *Outlook* (1932); *Up and Doing* (1934); *Prosperity* (1935); *Hibernia* (1936); *Mother and Maid* (n.d.); *The Catholic Mind* (1930); *Maria Legionis* (1938); *CYMS Quarterly* (n.d.), and the revised *Standard* (1938) were all features of this growing movement. These publications were mainly associated with particular organisations, such as the CTSI, An Rioghacht, the League for Social Justice, the Guilds of Regnum Christi, and the Knights of St Columbanus.

The developing movement's ethos was reflected in the *Catholic Bulletin*'s call for a 'Catholic Economics' in an editorial in 1933.[133] The editor of *Outlook* saw as its principal purpose, 'assisting in the social and economic regeneration of Ireland', through 'propagating principles of social life which are in harmony at the same time with Christian teaching and Irish national tradition'.[134] *Studies* also took an active interest, with a number of articles debating aspects of *Quadragesimo Anno*. The CTSI produced a number of pamphlets on the subject, among them: *Medieval Trade Guilds*; *The World Economic Crisis and the Catholic*; *Bolshevism*; *Capitalism and Its Alternatives*, and *The Social Question and Some Answers to It*.[135] It must be noted, however, that of the 2,000 or so Catholic Truth publications issued between 1899 and 1949, only 130 related to social issues (the rest were mainly devotional, biography, history, liturgy and hagiography), and of these, scarcely a third related to social/economic questions and reform. This indicates the sense of proportion that the Catholic Church gave to these issues. Not so with the Jesuits, who throughout the decade published pamphlets in the *Social Action Series* through the *Irish Messenger* office. The purpose ostensibly was to encourage lay initiative via Catholic Action in the socio-economic sphere.[136] In this regard, the 1930s echoed the 1920s in terms of the different emphases within the Catholic Church. In the main, the official Catholic Church encouraged membership of charitable associations such as the St Vincent de Paul Society. One of its leading figures, Professor C.K. Murphy of UCC, was to write on the subject in his book *The Spirit of Catholic Action*. For Murphy, the spirit of Catholic Action was the spirit of charity.[137] And, crucially, Catholic Action had to be above politics. This was to become the ultimate contradiction in the Catholic Action movement in the 1930s. It was to be left to certain Catholic Action organisations like An Rioghacht, the League for Social Justice and the Knights of St Columbanus to push for structural change in the economic organisation of society. Radical action never accompanied the rhetoric of the Catholic Church.

But Catholic Action, despite the difficulties and contradictions, did propel the socio-economic problems to the forefront of public debate in the 1930s. As well as the aforementioned publications, works by nationally known Jesuits also appeared, such as Fr Cahill's *Framework of a Christian State: An Introduction to Social Science*[138] and Fr George Clune's *Christian Social Reorganisation*,[139] a work nearly matching Fr Cahill's in bulk. Holy Ghost priest Fr Denis Fahey published his *Kingship of Christ According to the Principles of St Thomas Aquinas*,[140] with a preface by Fr John Charles McQuaid, headmaster of Blackrock College. Like Cahill, Fr Fahey was a prolific writer and both were neo-scholastics and strong advocates and supporters of militant Catholic Action as a defence and bulwark against post-Reformation, post-Enlightenment, and Protestant liberal economic individualism. Other major works offering a remedy for the 'evils' of Capitalism and communism included Fr Crofts's, *Property and Poverty, A Treatise on Private Ownership According to the Principles of St Thomas Aquinas*.[141] That neo-scholasticism underpinned the Catholic Action movement was also shown by two other publications exhorting the supreme advantages of the 'guild' system, a system emphatically recommended by *Quadragesimo Anno*. These were Webb's *The Guilds of Dublin*[142] and Clune's *The Medieval Guild System*,[143] both of which became two of the standard works on the subject. The CTSI also issued a pamphlet, *Medieval Trade Guilds*, advocating the advantages of the system. The English Catholic Social Guild's pamphlet *The Guild Social Order* was widely available in Ireland through the CTSI.[144] The most prominent individual behind the drawing up of the encyclical, Fr Oswald Von Nell-Breunig, had his work *The Re-organisation of the Social Economy* published in 1936. This argued that, 'at a previous time there existed a better organised condition of society'.[145] Such was the emphasis on the Middle Ages and on medieval guilds in 1930s Ireland, that it was not hard to come to the conclusion that the Catholic Church was insisting that history could roll itself back to pre-Reformation times. The Church wanted to return to a medieval paradigm in which they had power and authority. Their ideology of history, which was as self-righteous as it was simplistic, claimed that the Reformation and the Enlightenment had led to the chaos of the twentieth century.

Anti-modernists had a conservative prejudice for the 'good old days' and they therefore propagated a counter-Enlightenment aiming for a Catholic restoration. Catholic Action was an indispensable lever for this strategy.

James Hogan, UCC Professor of History, sympathised with this view of history, as did Professor Alfred O'Rahilly and so many leaders of Catholic Action. It was an interpretation widely disseminated in the 1930s' Catholic world by, amongst others, the famous Catholic writer Hilaire Belloc (1870-1953), who wrote his major work, *The Great Heresies*, in 1938.[146] They all agreed with the assertion of *Quadragesimo Anno* that, 'following upon the overthrow and near extinction of a rich social life, which was once highly developed through associations of various kinds, there remains virtually only individuals and the State. The social order which met in a certain measure the requirements of right reason, had long since perished'.[147]

The loss of the workers' guilds had 'disastrous effects'. Now, faced with the impending collapse of the capitalist system, combined with the threat of communism, the only option for the Catholic Church was a revival of the old medieval guild system. This system would guarantee a role for the Catholic Church in society. Pope Pius XI was impressed by the system, which seemed similar to those already working in Italy, Austria and Portugal.

From the Irish point of view it was a useful interpretation of history, since it corrected the nearly universal Whig interpretation of British history, which attributed Britain's greatness to her Anglo-Saxon and Protestant background. Crofts, Cahill, Tierney and Coyne were of similar mind. But possibly it was an interpretation as dogmatic as that which it tried to replace?

Professor Tierney's son Niall recalled how his father was a great friend of Canon Hayes, founder of Muintir na Tíre, who, he recollects, had met and much admired Mussolini's achievements. Dan Norrison, a leading trade unionist, who had worked with both the Larkins, also recalls Canon Hayes being impressed by the work of Mussolini, particularly the reclaiming of the Pontine Marshes around Rome.[148] This appreciation of Mussolini's work and political system by influential Catholics (though Mussolini's fidelity to Catholicism is very doubtful) helped the movement aiming for a reconstruction of Irish society along the lines of Catholic social principles. During the 1936 CYMS Catholic Social Week, Professor Tierney reiterated the Catholic interpretation of history. For him, 'the colossal error of Protestantism shook civilisation' and led to the urgent necessity of Catholic Action.[149]

Edward Cahill, in his *The Framework of a Christian State*, was of the same view, 'the social system in which the Irish people live is not of their own making, it is as a result of centuries of oppression and is fashioned after an English Protestant model'.[150] For Cahill, too, Catholic Action was the only way forward for a Catholic restoration.

For Professor Tierney the first requisite for an 'ordered' society was the devolution by the state to other organs, both local and national, of the 'terrific powers it had gathered into its hands'. According to Tierney, 'if what is left of Christendom is to be saved, we must put behind us the whole complex of errors in which the secular and the materialist nation-state has grown to its terrible beauty'.[151] Canon Hayes had responded to this call. At Catholic Action gatherings he argued that the countryside was the 'power-house of Catholic social re-construction'.[152] Cities were viewed by the Catholic Church as the cause of the growth of nineteenth-century secularism and the waning of its influence. Therefore the neo-scholastic/subsidiarist outlook in ecclesiastical circles in Ireland promoted Hayes's vision for a rural country. He regarded Catholic Action as the 'prerequisite' for bringing Catholic sociology and Catholic economics from the textbook to the crossroads.

Muintir na Tíre's organisational structures were inspired directly by Italian Catholic Action organisation. Civardi's *Manual of Catholic Action*, translated from the Italian, was an important handbook for Catholic Actionists in Ireland.[153] Muintir na Tíre aimed at helping the farming community become as self-reliant and independent as possible, along the lines of the earlier co-operative movement and similar to the Boerenbond, so successful in Belgium.[154] By organising the rural communities into Parish Guilds and Parish Councils, it was hoped to regenerate rural life in Ireland.[155] Professor Sheedy of UCD, writing in the *Handbook of Muintir na Tíre* on 'Self Sufficiency in Foods', put succinctly what the organisation was striving for, 'a permanent policy of self-sufficiency in foods would facilitate the balance of trade' and would 'stabilise employment conditions and promote rural prosperity'.[156] In 1940, *The Irish Times* commented that, 'we believe that this organisation has hit upon the truth. It is a view that the land is the making of Ireland: that Ireland's prosperity depends upon the farmer.'[157] It hoped that organisations like Muintir na Tíre would 'preach to farmers the decency of self-reliance'.[158]

Another organisation founded in 1933 also advocated the importance of co-operation. The Guilds of Regnum Christi was established in Dublin by a Legion of Mary activist, Dr Hugh Daly.[159] It became affiliated to the English lay organisation the Catholic Social Guild. Fr John McQuaid of Blackrock

College, encouraged the organisation in the city.[160] According to its handbook, the *Manual of the Guilds of Regnum Christi*, one of the aims of the new body was to develop and encourage co-operation with a view to 'bringing about harmony between the various professions and industries in the State'.[161] It emphasised the need to 'organise' Catholics along 'guild' lines.

The CTSI developed an organisation to further promote the vocational idea. In an article in *Catholic Mind* in February 1934, 'Clearing the Ground for Catholic Action', Frank O'Reilly and Hugh Allen proposed an organisation along the lines of the Catholic Defence League or a League of Social Justice.[162] They argued for the need of a more co-ordinated and centralised movement in Ireland. It was not, however, until November 1935 that O'Reilly was able to call a meeting of those interested in his plans.[163] The meeting, held in Dublin's Catholic Commercial Club, included a cross-section of lay and clerical advocates of Catholic social reform: Professor Busteed (UCC and private economic adviser to Éamon de Valera); Sir Joseph Glynn (CTSI and the Society of St Vincent de Paul); Frank Duff; Alfred O'Rahilly; Dr Peter Coffey (UCD); Fr Ambrose Crofts (CYMS), and Fr McQuaid. The meeting produced a memorandum and a decision to attempt to organise a League for Social Justice and Charity.[164] The new organisation would give its full support to the State implementation of Catholic social principles, irrespective of political party. In early 1936, O'Reilly wrote to Archbishop Byrne advising him that the new organisation would 'foster, form and maintain public opinion to the point of insistence on the application of Catholic social principles in every domain of life'.[165] They would 'assist' all duly elected governments in implementing those principles. It was O'Reilly's contention that governments should be 'directive rather than executive', and he strongly emphasised that vocational groups, 'would be entitled to initiate legislation for their own domain'.[166] However, O'Reilly's organisation and plans had to be postponed because of the CTSI's involvement in the distribution of the new encyclical on communism in 1937.

At the same time, the founding of the Irish Christian Front in August 1936 raised hopes among leaders such as O'Reilly that it would act as a strong and populist Catholic Action organisation and would include on its agenda the plans of the League for Social Justice and Charity. O'Reilly's correspondence with the Archbishop does, however, show the strength of feeling and purpose held by many Catholic Actionists in the 1930s, and their determination to insist on the widespread acceptance of Catholic social principles.

THE KILKENNY CONGRESS: SUMMER SCHOOLS, RURAL WEEK-ENDS, CATHOLIC SOCIAL WEEKS, CONFERENCES

Frank O'Reilly was the organiser of the huge CTSI Annual Congress for Kilkenny in late June 1935.[167] Kilkenny was chosen as a symbolic and real show of strength of Catholic Action forces in the wake of the difficulties Bishop Collier had with the coal miners of Castlecomer. Average daily attendances in the city for the various meetings and ceremonies was 35,000.

The theme of the Congress was the social question from a Catholic perspective. The editorial of the *Catholic Bulletin* described the gathering as 'a really triumphant success and a most excellent specimen of Catholic Action'.[168] Undoubtedly, the approach of the society in organising huge Catholic events, with maximum national publicity, must have had an enormous impact on public opinion in Ireland. In the space of a few years they had organised the 1929 Catholic Emancipation Centenary Celebrations, the 1932 Eucharistic Congress and now this nationally important social question National Congress. It was given wide publicity, with photographs in all the dailies, weeklies and provincials, showing the large crowds, the ceremonies, processions, the prominent personalities in attendance, and the lecturers and speakers.[169] The *Irish Independent*, in one of many articles covering the Congress, adopted a triumphal note when it referred to St Canice's Cathedral as having once 'stabled Cromwell's horses'.[170] *The Irish Times* and *The Irish Press* also gave substantial coverage.[171] The *Kilkenny People* and *Kilkenny Journal* reported all the speeches verbatim. Every provincial newspaper from *The Clonmel Nationalist* to *The Dundalk Democrat* covered the event.[172] If nothing else, the media coverage of the 1935 event gives a picture of Ireland's complete loyalty, obedience, reverence and acquiescence to the Catholic Church. A thoroughly compliant and conservative press was a useful arm for lay organisations promoting Catholic Action. It is also of interest that the Congress did not put forward any radical solution to the social question. It was as if Catholic ritual alone was enough to banish Ireland's socio-economic difficulties. The Congress instead reiterated the central Catholic dogma of the 'rights of property', with a codicil that it had 'duties' as well. These 'duties', however, were not spelt out. This stance showed that the Catholic Church was not necessarily prepared to challenge institutional structures, although *Quadragesimo Anno*, which they were advocating, called for a reconstruction of society. The Catholic Church's response seemed to have been ill-defined in essentials, so as to leave it room for manoeuvre. It would be three years yet before the challenge was to come. The difficulties would be compounded because Catholic organisations took for granted, in their interpretation of the social encyclicals, that the Catholic social principles did envisage changes in society.

One of the principal ways Muintir na Tíre spread its message was through its Rural Weeks and Rural Week-Ends, which were based on the French *Semaines Sociale*. The first such week was held in 1934 and was attended by Dr Ryan, Minister for Agriculture. The number of parishes sending representatives to the Weeks reached 50 in 1939, 100 in 1942 and 200 by 1949. As with the CYMS Catholic Social Weeks and the CTSI congresses and conferences, they can be considered one of the most important channels through which the new focus of Catholic social teaching became known in Ireland. Fr Cahill, addressing the Rural Week at Ardmore, Co. Waterford, in August

1937, said that he saw the object of the organisation as 'educating the people of the land to a better realisation of the excellence and dignity of the agricultural calling'.[173] The organisation also acted as a unifying force and a balm at a time when many farmers were reeling from the effects of the 'Economic War' with Britain. It was particularly fortuitous for the Fianna Fáil government that Catholic social teaching was conservative rather than radical.

Along the lines of the Rural Weeks were the Summer Schools and Weekends organised by Fr Cahill's An Rioghacht. These began in 1935 and continued until 1939.[174] Old Clongownians had responded imaginatively to Dublin's slum crisis in the early 1930s, by forming the Family Housing Association in 1933 to provide housing for Dublin's working classes.[175] They had purchased premises in Blackhall Place with this end in view. Since many of the Old Clongownians were members of An Rioghacht, they decided to go further and hold Summer Schools along the lines of those held by the Catholic Social Guild (and the Fabians) at Oxford. The Summer Schools organised by An Rioghacht examined all aspects of the social question – the corporate state, work, wages, profit, property, vocationalism, the Banking Commission (1934-1938), *Quadragesimo Anno* and the encyclicals. Prominent business people, trade unionists, labour leaders, and well-known university lecturers attended. Over 200 attended the 1937 School.[176] It was a very heated event, with trade union leader Senator Farren declaring that if (as someone had said) Labour was flirting with non-Christian principles, then Capitalism was married to them! Professor Smiddy suggested in his paper that they should examine the vocational guild as a possible solution to industrial conflict. Professor O'Rahilly gave an account of a flour-milling guild that he had planned, which, although accepted in principle by both the workers and the owners, had never been put into practice.

By the mid-1930s, the CYMS was turning its attention to members attending 'study circles'. Study of Catholic social principles was emphasised through the pages of the Society's publication, the *CYMS Quarterly Review*, as being crucial to the success of Catholic Action. The Cork branch had built up a library of Catholic social teachings running to 19,000 volumes.[177] This gives some idea of the commitment of the movement in the city. Branches in Tuam, Tipperary, Dublin and elsewhere revived the Catholic Social Weeks first started by the Society in 1928. In 1939, a CYMS report noted that there was 'a re-awakening of the people, not alone in Dublin, but throughout Ireland generally, to face up to the problems of the day, and to apply their minds to a solution by the study of Catholic social principles'.[178] This was clear considering the reported 'overcrowded attendances' at CYMS meetings.[179] Dublin, by 1939, had twenty active branches with over 2,000 members.[180]

Such was the importance attached to the study of Catholic social teaching that the Knights of St Columbanus had, since 1930, been endowing Maynooth College with a Chair of Catholic Action and Sociology.[181] Throughout the 1930s, they concentrated on countering the discrimination against Catholics in agricultural, economic, industrial and professional life.[182] In October 1936, Fr Peter

McKevitt was appointed Professor of Catholic Action and Sociology. He had spent some time in Italy studying Catholic organisations.[183] In 1938, *Hibernia* became the official publication of the Knights when the *Columbian* magazine was discontinued. One notices from then onwards in its editorials and articles, a particular commitment to espousing the importance of Catholic social ideas.[184]

For Fr Cornelius Lucey of Maynooth College, it was thanks to the social congresses and study circles, and their being given prominence in the press and the radio, that public opinion had been 'won over to the cause' of subsidiarity and vocationalism.[185] That robust public opinion does help to explain the attitudes of the leaders who were drafting the new 1937 Constitution of Ireland. It is in the context of the growing Catholic Action movement, with all its diversity, that we can understand the making and the shaping of the Constitution of Ireland and in particular its 'Directive Principles of Social Policy'.

CATHOLIC SOCIAL PRINCIPLES AND THE DRAFT CONSTITUTION OF 1937: ON THE EVE OF THE CONSTITUTION

On October 4 1933, Seán T. O'Kelly, Vice-President of the Executive Council, and member of the Knights of St Columbanus, while attending a meeting of the League of Nations in Geneva, delivered a speech to the Cercle Catholique.[186] In the course of his address, he indicated that he was pleased to hear Chancellor Dolfuss at the League saying that Austria was engaged in providing herself with an economic and political constitution answering to her needs, and inspired essentially by the principles set forth by the Pope for the solution of social problems. O'Kelly said that there was one other government that was inspired in its very administrative action by Catholic principles and Catholic doctrine – the Government of the Irish Free State. That government, according to O'Kelly, was endeavouring to do for its people what Chancellor Dolfuss declared his government was trying to do for Austria. Its programme of economic and political reform was founded on the same Catholic principles. The social encyclical of Pius XI, *Quadragesimo Anno*, had had a profound effect throughout the world, but, he added, 'in no country was this inspiring pronouncement read and studied with greater eagerness and interest than in Ireland'. According to O'Kelly, 'what the Irish Government was attempting was Catholic Action in practice'.[187]

In the same year, de Valera had been conferred by the Pope with the Grand Cross of the Order of Pius IX. His reputation as a Catholic statesman, greatly enhanced by his presence at the 1932 International Eucharistic Congress in Dublin, went much higher in September 1934 after his address to the League of Nations, in which he praised the Christian philosophy of life. While the 1930s witnessed the emergence of a Catholic Church characterised in more strident form by clericalism, juridicalism and triumphalism, the influence of Catholicism on public life was particularly reinforced by such stances.

However, on the eve of the publication of de Valera's Draft Constitution, the strands, personalities, organisations and publications all showed that there was diversity of currents within Irish Catholicism. These would have made its writing more difficult than might first be realised. Competing Catholic groups and individuals are evident in the drafting, with well-known Catholic Action leaders such as Cahill, Fahey, McQuaid and O'Rahilly being the most vociferous.

Work first started on the drafting on a new constitution in 1934. In the summer of 1936, Fr Edward Cahill contacted de Valera, offering the benefit of his advice with the work in hand.[188] Cahill had already written on the subject of a Catholic constitution in his book *The Framework of a Christian State* (1932).[189] Fr McQuaid of Blackrock College was also interested in the drafting of the new constitution, having been involved in various organisations of Catholic Action. The debate over the influence of Cahill and McQuaid on the deliberations and drafting of the constitution must be seen as a secondary issue, albeit an important one.[190] Whether de Valera preferred McQuaid's advice to that of Cahill's did not necessarily matter. Both clergymen were advising de Valera on the exact same principles. Both were ardent scholastics and medievalists. Both were grounded in the same Catholic social teaching of the neo-Thomists Leo XIII and Pius XI. Both were well acquainted with the Code of Social Principles drawn up by the Catholic Action organisation, the Malines Union. In fact, McQuaid only referred de Valera to sources which Cahill had already pinpointed in *The Framework of a Christian State*. On receipt of that volume, de Valera wrote to Cahill thanking him for the book, 'It is worth reading and re-reading, and I believe it will be consulted for advice and guidance in the years ahead'.[191] It is not too presumptuous to imagine that he had not forgotten the theme of Cahill's work when, on 30 April and 2 May 1935, he instructed John Hearne, the legal adviser to the Department of External Affairs, to draw up the heads of a new constitution.

Cahill had also been actively involved in organising the Clongowes Wood Summer School, which in 1936 had discussed the subject of 'The Constitutional Problem from the Catholic Viewpoint'.[192] More than 200 of Ireland's leading Catholic laymen were in attendance that July. Among those present were Sean Moynihan, Secretary to the Executive Council and brother to Maurice Moynihan, de Valera's private secretary. Maurice Moynihan, with John Hearne, was part of the chosen group picked by de Valera to frame the constitution. Others in attendance included the Director of Broadcasting Dr T.J. Kiernan, Professor Busteed, and James Meenan, another prominent economist. Leading Catholic churchmen included Frs Cornelius Lucey and Michael Browne. The Jesuits were represented by Frs Cahill, Canavan and Coyne.

Prominent Catholic Actionists included Dr James McPolin of the Knights of St Columbanus and the Guild of Catholic Doctors, Frank O'Reilly of the CTSI, and Sean O'Cuiv TD and Patrick Waldron, both of An Rioghacht. Many of the country's most prominent legal experts were also in attendance. The significance of the 1936 Summer School was that it brought the country's most important Catholics together to discuss a new constitution. De Valera's biographer states that the President of the Executive Council also read carefully the writings of both Lucey and Browne whilst the draft was being prepared.[193]

In September 1936, Cahill wrote to de Valera enclosing a long submission for a new constitution. His advice stressed the need to make a definite break with the liberal and non-Christian type of state.[194] De Valera found Cahill's submission to be 'useful as indicating the principles which should inspire all governmental activity so as to make it conform with Catholic teaching'. He pointed out, however, the difficulty of trying to embody the ideas into a new constitution:

> I can see that some of the principles might be set forth in a preamble, but I fear that there is not much that can be incorporated into the body of the Constitution. If you could find time to put into the form of draft articles, with perhaps a draft preamble, what you think should be formally written into the Constitution, it will be very helpful. I could then arrange, when I have seen your draft, to have a chat with you about it.[195]

A Jesuit subcommittee on the constitution was organised, which included Frs Cahill, Bartley, MacErlean, Canavan and Coyne. The group met five times between 24 September and 18 October 1936.[196]

It was decided that the preamble should be modelled on the Polish constitution. It was also decided to draft articles on the following subjects:

1. The rights of the family, particularly with regard to the education of children.

2. The teaching of religion in all schools, which were to be denominational.

3. The State being unable to dissolve marriage.

4. The definition of relations between the Catholic Church and the State by a Concordat.

5. Freedom of religious worship.

6. Ecclesiastical property.

7. Private property.

8. Freedom of speech and the press and the limitations of this freedom.

9. Any other matters that might be suggested by a study of Concordats and existing constitutions.

Irish Catholics were constantly called to 'Stand and Deliver' and to be 'Up and Doing' for 'The Splendid Cause' of militant Catholicism and Catholic Action, as illustrated by this booklet cover.

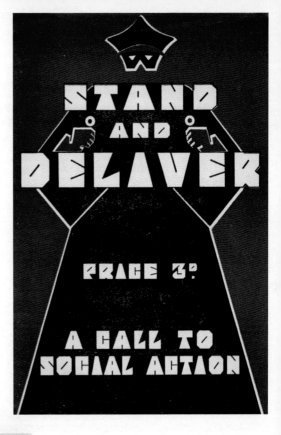

The Catholic Truth Society of Ireland (CTSI) came into being to provide popular, imaginative booklets for the ordinary people, to help give them a better grasp of their religion and of their Irish traditions. The booklets sold in their hundreds of thousands every year in Ireland and, in the age before television, had an enormous influence on Irish attitudes and behaviour, an influence that continued until the 1980s.

This booklet gives a grim account of the world economic crisis and the stark choices facing Irish Catholics.

This cover illustrates how the Irish Catholic Church perceived the nature, function and scope of militant Catholicism and Catholic Action; a view shared by Catholic lay activists.

That Ireland was in grave and mortal danger from a Communist offensive was a major theme of Bishops' pastorals and pronouncements in the twentieth century.

Fr Crofts was the Director of the Catholic Action organisation the CYMS. Here, he offers Irish Catholics the bleak choice between the Catholic Church and communism/totalitarianism.

Stand fast and firm with the teachings of the Catholic Church is the strong message of this booklet.

The Great Depression of 1929 and the harsh economic climate of the 1930s led to a loss of confidence in capitalism. The Catholic Church sought a middle way between the excesses of capitalism and totalitarianism.

An Agnostic in An Irish Village

This CTSI booklet cover is both a warning to Irish Catholics to be vigilant and also a challenge to them to evangelise.

There can be only one future for you if you have any atheistic tendencies, as illustrated by this CTSI booklet cover.

Fr Edward Cahill was one of the leaders of militant Catholicism in Ireland and did much to warn of the dangers of freemasonry.

This CTSI booklet cover evoking Satan and freemasonry struck fear and trembling into the hearts and minds of Irish Catholics. The evils and perils facing people, as shown in the CTSI booklets, ensured that the publications were quickly snapped up and avidly read, and they coloured the attitudes and behaviour of generations of Irish people. These booklets were able to reach into the furthest rural homes, which is why they sold in their millions.

Symbols of freemasonry as illustrated in this cover did much to warn of its inherent and grave dangers.

An expert on marriage, relationships and many other topics, Fr Daniel Lord's chatty and frank style had enormous appeal in Ireland, from the 1940s onwards.

Over 100,000 young hopefuls rushed to buy this title to see where they were going wrong.

The evils and perils of 'Celluloid Menace' (and the need for 'vigilance') was one of the major themes of Catholic Church pronouncements in the twentieth century. The campaign for censorship of printed matter led to the Censorship of Publications Act of 1929, which had a profound effect on subsequent Irish politics and society, including the divisive 1983 Pro-Life (Constitution of Ireland) Amendment campaign.

Unfortunately for the solidarity of the Catholic Action movement, this sub-committee was to give a hint that there were cracks appearing in the united stance. Cahill's fellow committee members were somewhat wary of the *enfant terrible* in their midst. As a result, a form of indirect censorship was agreed upon so that his singular approach would not dominate the proceedings. The merits and limits of the movement, not to mention attitudes within the Jesuits, were thrown sharply into focus by their constitution submission in late October. They had, in fact, no real intention of involving themselves in the business of constitution-making, but because of Cahill's initiative they had little choice.[197]

The agreed submission was modest enough by the standards of the day. It revealed none of Cahill's views about the liberal state and suggested no substitu-tion of new structures for the established forms of parliamentary democracy.[198] It did include a number of features to make the constitution conform to Catholic values. According to the proposed preamble, the people of Ireland, 'as a united and independent Christian nation' would 'sanction' the constitution 'in the name of the most Holy Trinity and our Lord Jesus Christ, the Universal kind'. The 'unique and preponderant position' of the Catholic Church was to be recognised, and a concordat with the Holy See was envisaged to regulate relations. According to the author of a history of the Irish Jesuits, Louis McRedmond, 'relations with other Churches were to be determined by agreement between the State and their official representatives'. There would be no divorce and the rules of the Catholic Church would be dominant if one or both parties were Catholic. The family was to be recognised as the 'fundamental unit' of society, possessing 'natu-ral, inalienable and imprescriptible rights, prior and superior to all positive law'. (The eventual wording of Article 41 in the new constitution was to be practically the same.) The constitution also laid down that, 'all citizens and associations of citizens were to have the right to found, own and administer schools'.

McRedmond argues that the Jesuit submission seemed to have 'envisaged a State which would take steps to respect and protect all organised religions rather than impose the beliefs of one Church on everybody – except in the sensitive areas of divorce and "mixed marriages"'. He suggests, in fact, that the submission displayed, 'very much the same principles as the constitution actu-ally enacted, and the contents of which it seems to have had more than a little influence'.[199] He was of the opinion that it 'may however be judged to have laid down more equitable principles on the subject of property than was done in de Valera's Constitution'. It wanted the State to be empowered to ensure that, 'the use which owners make of their property, especially goods of a productive nature, is in accord with the common good and with social justice'.

The 'common good' was to be the crucial principle behind any alteration of property rights, and a much more equitable distribution of land was needed in this respect. This latter hope was of course an abiding passion of Fr Cahill. De Valera, however, in his 'Directive Principles on Social Policy' in the Draft Constitution, opted for vaguer provisions.

On 13 November, Cahill followed the Jesuit submission with additional suggestions.[200] The suggested article on religion had noted that, 'The Catholic faith,
which is the faith of the vast majority of the nation, and which is inseparably
bound up with the nation's history, traditions and culture, occupies a unique
and preponderant position'. He changed the Jesuit subcommittee's word 'preponderant' with his own word, 'special'. It was Cahill's wording which de Valera
eventually put into the constitution (Art.44.1.2*). It would appear, then, that
both the main Jesuit submission and the additions from Cahill influenced de
Valera's deliberations, if not directly, then certainly indirectly.

At the same time, it would seem that Cahill and the more extreme exponents
of Catholic Action would have gone much further than the Jesuit submission if
allowed. Cahill had taken further steps in that direction but de Valera assured him
in May 1937 'that he was keeping his suggestions in mind'.[201] De Valera added
that it had not been possible to talk with Cahill generally on the constitution.[202]
While this would indeed appear to be a rebuff and might point to McQuaid's
greater influence on the drafting, I would not agree with Faughnan's assessment
that, 'the fact that de Valera did not meet [Cahill] is simply one more indication
that the work of the Jesuits was not an influential source in the drafting of the
Constitution'.[203] In fact, when one actually compares the Cahill and the Jesuit
submissions with the Draft, there are remarkable similarities. But it could not
be any other way since the Catholic principles underlying and underpinning
the constitution were not variable. That the final draft reflected Catholic principles is far more significant than de Valera's preference for personalities.

De Valera may have sidestepped some of Cahill's more extreme suggestions
(such as those on the economy and agricultural colonies), as he did McQuaid's
(his *Article on Religion*, for instance), but he did not do the same with regard to the
main Jesuit submission. It would seem more likely that the submission became
the framework to which McQuaid added flesh. And even if McQuaid had totally
ignored it, he would still have had to refer to the same sources as the Jesuits and
Cahill; the papal encyclicals (particularly *Rerum Novarum*, *Quadragesimo Anno*, and
Casti Connubii), the *Code of Social Principles* and neo-scholastic philosophy. One of
the number of books sent by McQuaid to assist de Valera was the *Manuel Social* by
Fr A. Vermeersch, a Belgian Jesuit and author who Cahill references heavily four
years previously in *The Framework of a Christian State*. The suggestion by J.H. Whyte
that it was McQuaid who brought the *Code of Social Principles* to de Valera's attention[204] ignored the fact that Cahill had used it extensively in his major work. Keogh
argues that the influence of the Holy Ghost Fathers (referring to McQuaid) can be
found particularly in Articles 41-45 (Family, Education, Private Property, Religion,
Directive Principles on Social Policy).[205] This is not necessarily the case, since the
Jesuit submission also referred strongly to them. These fundamental Catholic principles were similarly analysed in Cahill's work. McQuaid's particular influence
was more likely to be found on Article 42 – Education (he was headmaster of
Blackrock College and also chairman of the Catholic Headmasters' Association).

McQuaid was particularly influenced by Fr Denis Fahey, who, along with himself and Fr Kirwan SJ frequently addressed meetings of the Guilds of Regnum Christi and other Catholic Action organisations.[206] Both Fr Fahey and Fr Kirwan were well known to de Valera as former students of Blackrock College and, according to the historian of the College, 'he was made aware of their thinking in the matter of bringing State legislation into line with the social and political teaching expounded in the encyclicals'.[207] De Valera had known Fahey well, not merely for his rugby prowess when they played together on the Castle team, but because of his reputation as the brilliant student who had secured first place and first-class honours in 'Civil and Constitutional History, Political Economy and General Jurisprudence' at the Royal University.[208] It was as a specialist in this sphere that de Valera consulted him. Fahey was also regarded as a specialist in the area of papal teaching on social and political questions. But as with Cahill and McQuaid, de Valera did not feel compelled to accept without question Fahey's conception of the relations between political and theological positions. He consulted several authorities. De Valera modified the guidelines offered to suit his conception of what the Irish situation required.

Sean Faughnan's assertion that, 'the failure of the Jesuits to influence the drafting of the constitution contrasts sharply with the powerful influence exerted by the Holy Ghost priest Fr John Charles McQuaid',[209] does not stand up to closer scrutiny. McQuaid, already indebted to Fahey's ideas, could not have possibly added substantially to the ideas of the Jesuits and Fr Cahill. According to Vincent Grogan, parliamentary draughtsman at the time (and later Supreme Knight of the Knights of St Columbanus), the abiding principles behind the wording of the constitution, in particular the precepts of natural law, saw it as accepting the Thomistic philosophy of the natural law.[210] This particular Catholic view of the natural law, which became the anchor of the constitution, underpinned both the Jesuit and the Holy Ghost Fathers' thinking.

The issue only serves to contrast the uniformity of Catholic social thinking with the lack of unanimity as regard its actual implementation. The Jesuits differed among themselves; so did the Holy Ghost Fathers. Both had different emphases on the importance of the social question. McQuaid stressed the importance of Catholic education; for the Jesuits, infrastructural and social change was possible. De Valera's preference at times for McQuaid could also be explained by some of Cahill's economic policies. An Rioghacht were, at this time, in the process of challenging de Valera's economic policies through their representatives at the 1934-1938 Banking Commission. In a note to de Valera in early May 1937, Cahill argued that, 'effective social reconstruction along Catholic lines is impossible without monetary reform'. He considered it 'very imprudent' to allow anything in the constitution to close the door against it.[211] In the light of this, de Valera might have been cautious about accepting detailed advice from Cahill. But while de Valera was inclined to accept advice, from whatever quarter, on principles, he was not prepared to take directives.

Some of Cahill's views were shared not only by Fahey and prominent Jesuits such as Devane and Gannon, but also by Cardinal MacRory, who greatly admired *The Framework of a Christian State*. On the delicate issue of the Catholic Church being the 'one and true Church', Cahill, McQuaid, Fahey and MacRory shared the same views when de Valera was drawing up Article 44 on religion. De Valera, however, chose to ignore them all, as he was conscious of Protestant feeling in the Six Counties. He was also mindful of Fianna Fáil aspirations for a united Ireland. By bypassing the various strands of Catholic Action with regard to Article 44, he pre-empted a Church–State crisis, for it was only on this particular issue could he have united them against him.[212] Instead, he appealed directly to the Vatican for an acceptance of his particular wording. Rome reluctantly agreed not to interfere in his decision. This neutral stance enabled de Valera to ward off a triumphal recognition which the leaders of Catholic Action and Irish Catholicism in general sought. De Valera's dilemma was in persuading his Cabinet colleagues, on the one hand, that the provisions were not sectarian and offensive to Northern Irish sentiment, whilst on the other, that he was doing enough to acknowledge the 'special position' of the Catholic Church.[213]

In the end it was Cahill's phrase of 'special position' which appeared in the Constitution of Ireland, a constitution which gave less evidence of de Valera's republicanism than it did of the Catholic Church. It visualised a state that, while democratic in practice, would be theocratic in precept.[214] Overall, it would appear that it was de Valera's strong pragmatism that had the dominating influence. It was fortunate in one sense that he represented a current of Catholicism which, although conservative, was not as radical or as extreme as many of the ideas prevalent in Irish society in the 1930s, and from which he sought advice. Confessional lobbies at this time were particularly vocal, since nationalism and Catholicism were still seen as two sides of the same coin – Irishness. Part of de Valera's achievement in this heated atmosphere was that he was able to use Catholic Action to good advantage by taking on board Catholic principles from its main propagandists, while at the same time providing the necessary restraint for a movement which was disunited but ambitious. This is evident in the response of Cahill's organisation, An Rioghacht, to the Constitution of Ireland; they issued to the press a wholehearted and positive statement.[215]

The strength of differences in Catholic Action can best be seen in some of the reactions to certain draft articles in the constitution. We have already seen that the reaction to Article 44 united the strands of Catholic Action against de Valera. Had these substantive differences over the wording of the article become public, the chances of having the constitution passed by the people would have been remote. The fear of public controversy over the religious clause, led by an influential sector of the Catholic hierarchy and supported by Catholic Action, necessitated de Valera taking a risk and opting for the 'special position' wording.[216] De Valera also left the wording 'Church of Ireland' in the final draft (Art.44.1.3*) of the constitution. This drew considerable criticism from MacRory, Cahill, and other influential Catholic leaders. Cahill called the use of this phrase as nothing less than 'authoritative approval of a piece of lying propaganda'.[217]

However, it was not just the article on religion that attracted criticism. De Valera's views on the place of women in Irish society remained that of his adviser on the subject, Fr McQuaid, who suggested to him that the feminist critics of the clauses 'were very confused – both *Casti Connubi* [encyclical on marriage, 1930] and *Quadragesimo Anno* answer them'.[218] In fact, the Jesuit Fr Edward Coyne had far more liberal views on the subject than McQuaid. Coyne's reservations focused on the omission of the 'vast interests involved in women's life and work in the home – as wives, mothers, educators, buyers, etc.'. This omission he regarded as, 'reducing to insincerity' much that had been written elsewhere in the constitution and much that was said about women's place in the community.[219] But de Valera had also refused to accept the analysis of Bennett/MacArdle/Kettle, all activists for women's civil rights. The social clauses relating to women in the constitution blended prevailing Catholic concepts with popular attitudes rooted in the social structure. Article 41 therefore emphasised her place 'within the home'. De Valera's image of women was widely cherished in Ireland, not least by women themselves. But one commentator, Ita Mallon, writing in the Knights of St Columbanus's *Hibernia* in mid-1937, could not help exclaiming, 'the most Christian deterrent against mother and child labour was a decent wage for husbands'.[220] Needless to say, male wages were not raised to relieve mothers of poor families from the necessity of eking out their husbands' miserable pittances. The great illusion fostered by the constitution was that Irish society placed special value on motherhood. Ita Mallon saw through this illusion and argued that the State must be urged to bring about better economic conditions for men and women. Family allowances would have to be provided, which would give fathers of families a wage sufficient to enable the mother remain at home. Each increase in the family should bring an appropriate increase in income. Education should be directed to prepare young people 'technically and morally' for family life. Even the Knights themselves had high hopes that this would be the case. In an editorial lauding the Draft Constitution they declared that, 'it is not often that principles are thus courageously translated into practice'.[221] However, only individuals such as Ita Mallon and Edward Coyne recognised the naivety of such a hope. The Knights, in the main, did not see the constitution as an instrument or hope for social justice, unlike certain Catholic Actionists such as Coyne and members of An Rioghacht. Instead, when the plebiscite was over, they called for the 'blending of our united energies to welding a new and sharp instrument for the freeing of the people from the old slavery of an outworn political and economic system'.[222]

In May 1937, An Rioghacht issued a statement to the press on 'The Social Status of Women', in which they declared that the Catholic Church 'has always been the great champion of the rights, the dignity, and the true interests of women'.[223] The statement was issued in response to the controversy that the article on the family had generated. The Ard Comhairle of An Rioghacht also issue a public statement welcoming the new constitution, 'Since one of the aims of An Rioghacht is to strive for the effective recognition of Catholic Social Principles in Irish public life ... they were satisfied at the noteworthy manner in which basic Catholic principles are recognised'.[224]

However, these public utterances belied the fact that the organisation was quite unhappy with a number of the Articles. Writing to de Valera in late May 1937, they drew his attention to 'some points of detail' that they regarded as important.[225] Their first difficulty lay with Article 6.1 which covered the State and the powers of government. The clause, 'the people whose right it is to designate the rulers of the state', was in the eyes of the organisation 'a theological opinion' which, though tenable, was hardly in accord with the general democratic trend of the constitution. According to Mr Justice Gavan Duffy and other legal opinion in An Rioghacht, theologians differed on the sources of civil authority – some held that it came from God, direct to the rulers of the State – the people's function being only to 'designate the rulers'. The other opinion was that authority came from God 'direct to the people themselves', who then transferred it to the rulers.

The Article on the Family, in particular the section on Marriage (Art.41.3.1.), caused the organisation to raise some further questions.[226] The subsection in the article stated that, 'the State pledges itself to guard with special care the institution of marriage, on which the family is founded, and to protect it against attack'. Subsection 3.2. also declared that, 'no law shall be enacted providing for the dissolution of marriage'. An Rioghacht advised de Valera that since the article dealt with a very complicated question, it should be so worded 'as not to preclude legislation which experience may show to be necessary'. To bolster their argument they made two points. Firstly, the Catholic Church could, and sometimes did, grant divorce in two cases (non-consummation of marriage, and in accordance with the Pauline Privilege). It therefore could be held that under the new constitution the state could not recognise the dissolution even by a special law. In another set of cases a marriage, apparently valid, and registered as such by both Church and state, might be dissolved by a 'decree of nullity' declaring that no valid marriage had taken place in the beginning. Here again it could be held that the State could not recognise such a decree. Secondly, in the area of 'mixed marriages', the constitution did not address the Catholic view. Marriages between a Catholic and a non-Catholic in a registry office or in a Protestant church, 'while known to all Catholics to be invalid and merely legalised concubinage', was accepted by the State as a valid marriage.[227]

It was An Rioghacht's contention in all these circumstances, that, since the Catholic Church was accorded a special position of pre-eminence in the constitution, the State should have regard for the marriage laws of the Church.[228] But de Valera chose not to be moved by the suggestions. Catholic Action was divided on the issue and unlike the Article on Religion, could not provide a united front. The issue which de Valera had been warned about was to overshadow later generations of politicians and influence later Catholic lay organisations.

Some of An Rioghacht's heaviest criticism was directed against the preamble of Article 45,[229] which declared:

> The principles of social policy set forth in this Article are intended for the general guidance of the Oireachtas. The application of those principles in the making of laws shall be the care of the Oireachtas exclusively, and shall not be cognisable by any court under any of the provisions of this Constitution.

The last clause of this preamble, 'and shall not be ...' they saw as toning down the strength of the sections which followed, and therefore 'deprived them of due sanction'. They regarded the phrase as seeming to preclude all means of obtaining a decision that a law in violation of them was unconstitutional. Fr Cahill had similar reservations. The final letter in the Cahill papers from Fr Cahill to de Valera contains his reflections on the Draft Constitution.[230] He raised the question of how a constitution framed along Catholic lines would be interpreted by judges trained in a different tradition. Cahill pointed out that phrases such as 'social justice' and 'personal rights' conveyed different meanings to Catholic social thinkers, as distinct from the judiciary and the legal professionals brought up in the individualistic and liberal tradition of English jurisprudence.

Cahill stressed that there was 'a real danger that the intentions aimed at in the draft constitution may be frustrated except it is made clear in the constitution in what sense such terms are understood'. He argued that Article 45, which was intended to guide the State in social policy, would need to be cognisable by the courts if a range of social problems were to be tackled. Had this happened the implications for juridical interpretation of the constitution would have been immense.

An Rioghacht regarded the whole of Article 45 as being 'carefully contrived to appeal to instinct without damaging interests'.[231] For them, it completely undermined the endeavours of Catholic organisations and their striving for social justice. It would appear that de Valera, having enunciated radical sentiments about the primacy of the public good over private gain, then explicitly declares a restraint on the application of the same principles. He had used theological advice as a short cut for political expediency. An Rioghacht also rejected the notion that, 'the principles of social policy set forth in this Article are intended for the general guidance of the Oireachtas'.[232]

Despite these reservations, however, Fr Cahill was not slow to praise aspects of the 'Directive Principles of Social Policy'. In an article on the Constitution of Ireland in the journal *Revisita Javeriana*, he pointed out that the 'Directive Principles' were in direct opposition to economic liberalism, and implied a revolt against the teaching of 'the so-called Manchester School ... whose influence has had ruinous effects in Ireland during the last century'.[233] Cahill conceded that, in several details, the constitution fell short of providing for the full realisation of a Christian State. But nowhere does his article exclude the possibility of such an ideal being reached. Cahill understood de Valera's dilemma, and was sympathetic to it. McQuaid, on the other hand, did not conceal his disappointment; he expressed it, and subsequently apologised to de Valera.[234]

The Cahill/McQuaid contributions to the Draft Constitution indicate divisions in Irish Catholicism in the mid-1930s. There was a lack of uniformity of vision and purpose with regard to the implementation of the social encyclicals, or in fact the feasibility of such an undertaking. For de Valera, the social encyclicals provided the outline principles, but Fianna Fáil provided the actual answers. For many Catholic Actionists, the encyclicals provided the real and literal fundamentals for change. Most significantly for the Catholic Action movement was that the application, as opposed to the acknowledgement, of Catholic Action ideals was certainly not an integral part of de Valera's vision of Ireland's future.

V

THE ECONOMY AT THE CROSSROADS

Fianna Fáil's economic policy of national self-sufficiency was at best a partial success. Dependence on imports – now more often in the form of raw materials for new Irish factories – remained high, and the agricultural sector continued to provide 90 per cent of all exports. The new industries were too costly and inefficient to compete in export markets. The campaign for industrial self-sufficiency was accompanied to some extent by the phenomenon of increased state intervention in the economy in general. In 1933, the Industrial Credit Company and the Irish Sugar Company were formed. The Turf Development Board (later Bord na Móna) was established in 1934. The Irish airline Aer Lingus was founded in 1936. The Irish Life Assurance Company and the Irish Tourist Board were both established in 1939.

Besides these state-sponsored bodies, stimulus was given to the house-building industry by the Housing Act of 1932, which provided for generous state subventions for house-building schemes operated by local authorities. However, Fianna Fáil did not preside over an economic miracle in the 1930s, with emigration increasing in the latter part of the decade.

The Banking Commission, appointed by Seán MacEntee, Minister for Finance, in November 1934, was critical of the increase in the national debt, and by implication, the government's self-sufficiency policy and housing programme. The Reports of the Commission of Inquiry into Banking, Currency and Credit (1938) laid particular emphasis on the dangers associated with the accumulation of deadweight debts, much of it contracted by the local-authority housing schemes.

Four reports were published simultaneously in 1938: a majority report and three minority reports. The majority report generally reflected Department of Finance concerns about the need for budgetary restraint, whilst the remaining reports, in the main, reflected the attitudes held by some Catholic organisations and individuals (such as The League for Social Justice, An Rioghacht, Professor Busteed and Professor A. O'Rahilly) on Catholic social teaching. The four reports indicated that cracks were appearing in the apparent outward consensus on Catholic social teaching. Most significantly, Catholic Actionists appeared to be divided on fundamentals, as evidenced by three minority reports. The Banking Commission showed that different strands were at work in Militant Catholicism, and also in Irish Catholicism in general, facts that were also evident in the drafting of the Constitution of Ireland.

THE CATHOLIC ACTION AGENDA

The new Fianna Fáil government had decided that the Banking Commission was necessary, although there were many dissenting voices, notably that of Seán Lemass, Minister for Industry and Commerce.[1] The terms of reference were as follows:

> To examine and report on the system in Saorstat Éireann of currency, banking, credit, public borrowing and lending, and the pledging of state credit on behalf of agriculture, industry and social services, and to consider and report what changes, if any, are necessary or desirable to promote the social and economic welfare of the community and the interests of agriculture and industry.[2]

The Chairman of the Banking Commission was Joseph Brennan, late secretary of the Department of Finance. There were twenty other members. The personnel reflected the government's purpose (or Department of Finance's influence) in establishing it. The majority of the members, as would be expected, proposed a conservative and orthodox brand of economic and fiscal policies. A substantial minority were known to favour a greater or lesser departure from such policies, so as to deal more effectively with the country's grave social problems of unemployment and emigration. Among this latter group were: Sean Campbell, treasurer of the Irish Trade Union Congress; William O'Brien, Secretary of the ITGWU; Peadar J. O'Loughlin TD; Bishop MacNeely of Raphoe; Professor Busteed, Professor of Economics at UCC, and Professor Alfred O'Rahilly.

In May 1937, in the course of correspondence regarding the Draft Constitution, Fr Edward Cahill advised de Valera that he was 'convinced' that effective social reconstruction along Catholic lines 'is impossible without monetary reform'.[3] By this he meant the introduction of a system of distributive justice in the area of taxation, the ending of the link with sterling and the rejection of the teachings of the 'Manchester' school of economics. The agenda of Catholic organisations was widening still further.

At the beginning of 1936, a small group consisting of Fr Cahill, Mrs Waters (an economist) and Bulmer Hobson (who had been a key figure in the IRB) formed a new organisation, The League for Social Justice.[4] The name had been suggested by the CTSI's Frank O'Reilly at a meeting in Dublin's Catholic

Commercial Club in 1935.[5] In the early 1930s, Hobson had edited a small monthly paper called *Prosperity*, which aimed at arousing public interest in social issues. With the founding of the new organisation, he changed the name of the periodical to *Social Justice*. The group held meetings to discuss Catholic social principles, and a series of pamphlets under the general heading *Towards a New Ireland* was published.[6] Membership came from a cross section of existing Catholic organisations. There was one Fianna Fáil TD on the committee – Sean Brady. The new organisation disregarded the economic theories of the day, wishing to see the social and economic teachings of the encyclicals given practical effect in the State.[7]

On the Banking Commission a watching brief was held for Fr Cahill by the Fianna Fáil TD Peadar J. O'Loghlen. In March 1935, Mrs Waters, helped by Brian McCaffrey and J.A. O'Rourke, two members of An Rioghacht, presented evidence to the Commission.[8] Her evidence can be summarised by focusing on five points:

1. The system of allowing private syndicates, such as banking companies, to control credit, was regarded as being altogether incommensurate with the risk involved. This policy was seen as being economically unsound, socially injurious, and morally wrong.

2. Mrs Waters also saw it as particularly undesirable that the currency, credit or monetary policy of the Irish Free State should be controlled, directly or indirectly, by any institution or body outside the country.

3. The function of issuing credit, on the security of the community, which affected the welfare of the people, should belong to the State and should be exercised solely in the interests of the common good.

4. Mrs Waters also regarded it as very desirable that the State Bank or Commission which had the responsibility of controlling the issue of fiduciary money and credit should not be a Government Department.[9]

5. The social and economic system of the Irish Free State should operate in accordance with Catholic ideals.[10]

Fr Cahill advised Mrs Waters and the rest of the delegation on various strategies to be adopted. He pointed out that one 'obvious point of attack' was the meaning 'we attach to the term credit'. His view was that the safest answer to adhere to was 'the meaning the Pope attaches to it'.[11] Fr Cahill's representatives also kept in close contact with particular members of the Commission who shared their commitment to Catholic social principles – O'Rahilly, Busteed and a number of trade unionists including Campbell and O'Brien.[12]

When the preliminary report of the Commission appeared in late 1936, *Social Justice* attacked the rumours that the Commission had advised the government to retain the existing system.[13] Mrs Waters contacted Fr John McQuaid of Blackrock College (then active with the Guilds of Regnum Christi), and suggested to him that the solution to the problem of the distribution of wealth (a divisive issue during the Commission's deliberations) lay in the fundamental redirection of the monetary system of the Irish Free State. Another member of Cahill's two organisations, Eoin O'Keefe, a lifelong friend and supporter of de Valera, told the Taoiseach of his misgivings that the Commission would merely endorse the existing practice of the Department of Finance. In an adroit response, de Valera suggested that those members of the Commission who favoured economic policies more in harmony with national development needs, should combine to produce a report to that effect.[14] Consequently, O'Keefe, O'Loghlen and Mrs Waters all tried to persuade Alfred O'Rahilly to join them in producing such a report. Characteristically, he insisted on producing his own. Eventually three minority reports were produced, together with the majority one. The third minority report, signed by Peadar J. O'Loghlen, had been drawn up by Mrs Waters, Cahill and Hobson.

The majority report, running to 571 pages, reaffirmed the correctness of Cosgrave's (as opposed to De Valera's) economic and social policy. It criticised the increase in the national debt, demanded a policy of debt redemption that would have required the abandonment of the government's housing programme, and found that the commercial banking system adequately served the needs of the country.[15]

Of particular significance from the Catholic Action perspective was the imprimatur given to the majority report by the Catholic Church, through its representative Bishop MacNeely. MacNeely, in Appendix 15, declared that he 'was not convinced that the Irish monetary and banking system can be fairly blamed for such social injustices or economic evils as may exist in the Free State'. He continued:

> We do not believe that this system prevents the carrying into effect of a morally desirable social policy. That a better instrument might in pure theory be conceived is possible: but we do not feel justified in thinking that any practicable changes we could suggest would produce such a notable moral and social improvement as would compensate for other inevitable disadvantages – even in the moral and social spheres – which would result. We do not claim that the present system produces perfect social justice or is ideal from a moral point of view: such perfection is impossible in human affairs.[16]

The Catholic Church therefore, through its representative, appeared quite happy with the status quo, and MacNeely referred quite confidently to de Valera's St Patrick's Day broadcast in 1937, where government policy was reiterated 'to strive earnestly to make social justice and social charity imbue all the institutions of our public life'. Bishop MacNeely felt it was legitimate, therefore, to assume that social legislation in the Free State would be based on Christian principles.[17]

Staunch Catholic Actionists were not as optimistic, as understanding or as accepting as the Catholic Church's representative. In fact, the socio-economic theory of An Rioghacht and the League for Social Justice, as enunciated in the third minority report, proved very critical of the Department of Finance, and in consequence of certain developments under the Cumann na nGaedheal Government. They blamed the poor quality of the Fianna Fáil housing pro-gramme on the scarcity of money, imposed by the existing methods of issuing money. They saw local authorities compelled to build down to a price, instead of being able to build up to a standard.[18] They saw the need for better housing for the poor as a matter of extreme urgency and said that it was 'very doubt-ful if we are any nearer to-day to the abolition of the slums than we were when the Irish government took over control'. Not only that, but they saw the root cause of the slum problem as the absence of adequate rural employ-ment. Irish agriculture suffered because of the link with the British currency, 'we have been persuaded by the Banking Commission of 1926 to relinquish all but the appearance of control over such important and vital national interests as our price level'.[19] Net deadweight and net debt charges had accumulated rapidly in the period of 1924 to 1937, thereby placing a further burden on the community. An Rioghacht's overall conclusion emphasised that Irish finan-cial policy was, without regard to the social consequences, 'grinding to pieces' the lives of the people.[20] The 'economic waste' represented by unemployment and emigration, they interpreted as being enormous – a 'drain which the Irish economy cannot stand for an indefinite period'.[21] Social stability and internal order could not be maintained permanently unless they adopted measures to provide employment. The third minority report also argued that rural employ-ment could be significantly boosted by the initiation of forestry and drainage schemes. It recommended that an Economic Development Commission be established to promote employment, and that monetary policy be shaped to further the Commission's work. An appendix to this report discussed economic aspects of the social encyclicals.

Alfred O'Rahilly's opportunity to tackle the majority report came at the 1938 Muintir na Tíre Rural Week in Ardmore, Co. Waterford, where he was one of the principal speakers.[22] The Majority Report of the Banking Commission, according to O'Rahilly, had no measure to suggest what would help to check the decline in population. On the contrary, it considered that farms should be enlarged, forgetting what was to happen to the displaced population. Such a policy was contrary to the trend of agricultural development in Europe, where, apart from in England and Russia, a mixed farm of thirty or forty acres was typ-ical. The situation in which the Irish farmer found himself was unenviable. The level of agricultural production was at a very low ebb. This was mainly caused by a price system that was unfair to the agricultural producer. Farmers could produce abundant food for the people, but the people had not the money to buy it. At the heart of the problem was a lack of purchasing power. O'Rahilly was particularly worried that in the depressed economic climate which existed in Ireland, financial advisers advocated even more belt tightening and a further restriction of credit. This he regarded as being at total variance with Catholic social philosophy. Only by the interpretation of that philosophy, he declared, would the country's agriculture revive. He called for a 'crusade' to pursue that end.[23] He was to have his opportunity the following year, when de Valera appointed him to the Commission on Vocational Organisation.

O'Rahilly's rejection of certain provisions of the majority report was supported by another member of the Knights of St Columbanus, Vincent Grogan (later Supreme Knight).[24] In an article in the Catholic quarterly *Bonaventura* in late 1938, Grogan quoted Article 45 of the new Constitution of Ireland, which, with regard to land purchase, laid down the broad lines of State policy, 'The State shall in particular direct its policy towards securing … that there shall be established on the land in economic security as many families as in the circumstances may be practicable'.[25]

In Grogan's view, the majority report recommended the cessation of compulsory acquisition of land by the Land Commission. Its principle objection was that it added seriously to the deadweight debt, and that the division of farms into smaller allotments made for 'lessened efficiency' in production. Grogan pointed out that this argument was refuted by O'Rahilly's first minority report. He also thoroughly disagreed with the suggestion that 'efficiency' should be the first consideration, and he felt that this would soon be rejected by all who realised its implications. In his view, what efficiency really meant was cheaper food for fewer people. Echoing Fianna Fáil's economic policy, he said that the reason behind land division was to make it possible for an increasing population 'to subsist on the land in frugal contentment [*sic*]'. But the Commission had contributed little or nothing at all towards a solution of the problem. The economics of a stationary State would not solve the problems of a hundred years of neglect and maladministration. Unemployment, emigration and depopulation had not been tackled. Combating these issues should be the first and constant aim of economic and monetary policy. Grogan also expressed his rejection of the majority report's separation of ethics and economics.[26]

The Knights of St Columbanus journal, *Hibernia*, in its editorial of September 1938, was similarly critical of the majority report.[27] *Hibernia* congratulated O'Rahilly and O'Loghlen for basing their recommendations on fundamental Catholic principles.[28] The editor questioned whether Ireland had wasted hundreds of years in revolt against foreign domination only to 'accept it freely in the end'. For once they felt obliged to agree with *The Irish Times*, an 'organ of the ex-Unionist rentier class', who, while warning the government to act on the majority recommendations, exposed the whole weakness of the case against the new Irish policies in one startling sentence, 'In many respects the report is so conservative that it almost might have been prepared in Manchester fifty years ago'.[29]

That Catholic Actionists felt aggrieved at the findings of the majority report was nicely balanced by the Department of Finance's attitude towards Peadar J. O'Loghlen and Alfred O'Rahilly. According to Professor Joseph Lee, 'great umbrage was taken in Merrion Street at those members of the Commission so churlish' as to pen minority reports.[30] The Department intended the Commission to reassert the validity of eternal economic truths, following threats of deviance in the early Fianna Fáil years. The majority report reflected their expectations. But they were particularly incensed at the insensitivity of O'Rahilly. He was on reasonable terms with de Valera, and so his arguments had to be taken more seriously than the Department of Finance would have wished. In his report O'Rahilly called for a more interventionist financial policy generally. The Department went to great lengths to write a 136-page memorandum refuting O'Rahilly's arguments and referring to the 'irrational instability of judgment and purpose which characterises every paragraph of Minority Report No. I'.[31] The Department were not short on vitriol and spleen in their condemnations, referring to O'Rahilly's 'windy polemics', 'blatant contradictions', 'cloudy generalisations', and concluding that his report was 'a compact of fallacies' and a 'rubbish heap'.[32]

Criticism was not limited to O'Rahilly. The Department of Finance insinuated that O'Loghlen's minority report was penned with unworthy motives.[33] They sought to discredit their liking for the 'economic panaceas which formed the stock-in-trade of the Labour Party here', and smeared their report as 'Labour policy'. De Valera must have infuriated the Department when he then declared that, 'as far as our social aims are concerned, we are at one with the Labour Party'.[34] He also referred to the 'social objectives' of the third minority report as deserving particular praise.[35] According to Ronan Fanning in his work on the history of the Department of Finance, the reaction from the Department sprang from An Rioghacht's 'exceptionally hostile underlying principles' and stances.[36] The organisation's strong criticism of the Department angered them even more when An Rioghacht had 2,000 copies of their report printed and distributed. Fanning refers to Finance's 'preoccupation with emphasising the unholy parentage of their opponent's ideas'.[37] They did not find it easy to persuade the government of the merit of the policies enunciated by the Banking Commission.[38] In the event, the response was muted and the situation was something of a draw – no monetary reform but more deadweight debt. However, according to Mary Daly in her study *Industrial Development and Irish National Identity*, Fianna Fáil's attempts in the 1930s to develop a self-sufficient national economic policy ultimately floundered in the face of the resolve of the Banking Commission.[39] Any attempts within the party to explore alternative economic ideas or systems met with Finance's determination to undermine them.[40]

The Department of Finance never recognised the social encyclicals of the Catholic Church as economic doctrine but merely as recommendations for social reconstruction along vocational lines. Appendix 15 of the majority report clearly spells this out, 'The economist must be left with a certain discretion in deciding how the principles laid down by the encyclicals should be applied to a particular country at a particular time'.[41]

The Catholic Church seemed to agree with this, as already indicated. Its equivocal attitude showed it implicitly colluding with the Department in its acceptance of unemployment and emigration (or perhaps recognising that Catholic social teaching was no solution). But this view was not shared by An Rioghacht, who saw themselves as 'the first society for the promotion of social justice' and who 'actually debated the social problems' that existed.[42] Some ten years later, these principles were to be part of the political manifesto of Clann na Poblachta. Seán MacBride was still taking advice from members of An Rioghacht and the League for Social Justice.[43]

Fr Edward Coyne, writing in *Studies* in late 1938 on the Report of the Banking Commission, was severely critical of the report for 'failing to address the question of how the social welfare of the country was to be achieved'.[44] He also found fault with both An Rioghacht's and Alfred O'Rahilly's minority reports as 'purporting to obtain social values and welfare at an economic cost to no one'.[45] The significance of Coyne's criticism highlighted the fact that Catholic Action had not achieved a consensus on fundamentals, and might not manage to do so. The divisions also reflected the basic contradiction between *Quadragesimo Anno* and *Non Abbiamo Bisogno*, and within *Quadragesimo Anno* itself.

Coyne pulled no punches in his article. He regarded the economic teaching of the majority report as being 'ultra-conservative' and claimed that the Commission 'had made a serious error of judgment in omitting to take full cognisance of post-war thought and theories on its subject matter'. He asked if any of the Commission had come to a considered judgment of the work of John Maynard Keynes, and questioned how his *General Theory of Employment, Interest and Money* could be ignored. He saw the report as becoming nothing more than a 'museum piece' because of this dereliction.[46] He also saw the report as concentrating disproportionately on the 'economic' welfare of the community. This was the difference between the majority and the minority reports. When it came to the first and third minority reports, he was 'in complete disagreement' with much of their economic content. As far as he could see, the signatories of these two reports seemed to be 'trying to obtain the social values and welfare at the economic cost to no one'.[47]

Coyne didn't stop there. In a follow-up article in the *Irish Monthly* in early 1939, 'The Papal Encyclicals and the Banking Commission', he denounced the 'extraordinary bold claim' of the signatory of the third report, which he felt 'can hardly pass unchallenged'.[48] He objected first and foremost to An Rioghacht's 'blatant' criticism of the majority report, particularly since, amongst the signatories were Bishop MacNeely and Professor George O'Brien, 'a Catholic bishop and a conservative professional economist of strictly orthodox economic views', both of whom 'carried weight'. Coyne was somewhat wary of certain types of 'earnest, zealous Catholics eagerly trying to secure the acceptance of some specific remedy' of their own. Coyne saw these Catholics, by recommending the remedy as they saw it in the encyclicals, as being 'a serious danger to the whole cause of Catholic social reform'. He agreed with O'Rahilly's views that the Church could not be held responsible for the detailed schemes selected'.[49] Coyne interpreted Catholic Action's function as training Catholics to be leaders of social science, to imbue them with principles, to prepare them to use and defend their rights, and to encourage them to give practical application of their formation in their syndical and political activities.[50] Catholic Actionists were to be encouraged to go forth, 'provided we do not engage the responsibility of the Church for our proposals'. Those leaders, in Coyne's mind, who had 'quasi-official' training, conducted under the aegis of Catholic Action, 'should never, as Catholic Actionists, claim that they have the authority of the Church for their purely technical, financial, or economic solutions'.[51] He agreed that there should be unity among Catholics on 'principles', but not necessarily on specific, concrete measures and policies. An Rioghacht, in his view, had fallen into the trap of trying to use the authority of the social encyclicals to 'force people who disagree with the proposal on economic or technical grounds to give it their assent'. The organisation's failing, as Coyne perceived it, was that they did not demonstrate the soundness of their economic or social arguments. The soundness of their proposals was guaranteed by the encyclicals. For Coyne this was both 'indefensible' and 'very dangerous', since he regarded their proposals as having no objective link with the encyclicals. They did not flow from their principles and did not lead to their ideals.[52] So incensed was he at An Rioghacht's 'unjustified claim' that he called on Catholics to reject nearly all the recommendations in the third minority report.

Peadar J. O'Loghlen TD, An Rioghacht's representative and signatory of the third minority report, immediately challenged Coyne's criticism in a stinging response in the *Irish Monthly* of March 1939. He cited 'several contradictions' in Coyne's argument.[53] Contrary to Coyne's thinking, O'Loghlen said that the encyclicals were in fact 'very explicit' and 'specific and concrete' on the vital issue of social justice.[54]

That An Rioghacht had absolutely no intention of backing down was made obvious in the *Catholic Herald*, where they repeated the claims made in the third minority report that, 'the first step towards a cure for our troubles is the establishment of an independent economic and monetary system organised in accordance with the teachings of the Papal Encyclicals'. They cited Portugal as an example of a country that had tackled problems similar to Ireland's successfully. The link with sterling would have to be broken since the root cause of Ireland's problems was 'an alien economic regime' forced on the country by the Act of Union.[55]

An Rioghacht's views on the economy were stoutly defended by Fr Denis Fahey writing in *Hibernia* in 1938. Under the heading 'Off Sterling', an article critical of the majority report, Fahey recommended that, 'Ireland Should Assert Her Fiscal Autonomy and Undertake the Management of Her Own National Currency'.[56] He strongly objected to subordinating the Irish monetary system to that pursued by London.

THE SILENCING OF FR EDWARD CAHILL

The difficulties facing a united Catholic Action front were further compounded by the silencing of Fr Cahill in late 1938 by his Jesuit superiors. Cahill's problems had originated in 1933. Hitherto he had achieved widespread popular acclaim, both at home and abroad, for his major work, *The Framework of a Christian State* (1932).[57] However, in October 1933, one of his colleagues complained about the content of his lectures to a superior:

> ...no later than today complaints were made to me regarding Fr Cahill's lectures. What he said – or was purported to have said – is liable to give great offense to many of the clergy and laity of the country. I think he should only be allowed to speak from MSS which has first been censored.[58]

Cahill had referred once again to the Judaeo-Masonic influence in Irish banking circles, which he believed undermined the economic life of the country. In 1934, Cahill's pamphlet *Capitalism and its Alternatives* was rejected by the Jesuit ecclesiastical censors, but he managed to persuade the CTSI to publish it in 1936. Cahill's reaction was that the censor's criticism was 'manifestly exaggerated and ill-balanced'.[59] The censor had refused permission on the grounds that it was unsound in doctrine and 'dangerous in tendency and orientation'. The publication was particularly critical of the 'abuses' of the capitalist system, the 'oppression' of the workers, and the 'enslavement of the people under the control of a certain despotic and half hidden power which is identified with the international controllers of credit and finance'.[60] He also stated that, 'the control exercised by the great banking syndicates is the most comprehensive and far-reaching evil of capitalisms'.[61] Such was the Jesuits' suspicion of Cahill's works that *The Framework of a Christian State* was never reviewed or mentioned in the prestigious *Studies*, despite being favourably reviewed in other Irish, English, American and European Catholic journals. *Studies* seemingly had little time for Cahill's ideas and only published one article of his in 1915 (on secondary education in rural Ireland). Fr Coyne, on the other hand, merited twenty-three articles, mainly on socio-economic issues.

Cahill's difficulties worsened in 1935 when he invited Éamon de Valera to a meeting of An Rioghacht. The Jesuit Provincial was alarmed by this, taking the view that the incident 'might affect the interests of the Province at large' particularly since the visit had been covered by the *Irish Press*.[62] In April of the same year, Cahill requested permission to give evidence before the Banking Commission, on the grounds that he had been advised by Professor Busteed that it was important that the authentic Catholic view on the general principles governing it should be placed before the Commission.[63] Permission was refused, but Cahill ensured that the lay representatives of An Rioghacht and the League for Social Justice would give his views anyway.

Cahill's views on the findings of the Banking Commission were widely reported in *The Irish Press* and *Irish Independent*, and, once more, they particularly alarmed his superiors. In August 1938, Muintir na Tíre held a Rural Week-End at Douglas College, Ardmore, on the subject of vocationalism.[64] Cahill was one of the principal speakers. He castigated the majority report as an exposition of the old liberal economics in vogue before the publication of the social encyclicals. According to Cahill, the majority report was asking the country to throw aside its Christian principles and to settle down to the English system. His views were echoed by Dr Cornelius Lucey of Maynooth College, who said that at last they were beginning to realise that the Christian social teaching to which they were committed insisted that they must have vocational organisation if class strife, economic depression, and excessive State interference were to be avoided. Cahill, in the closing address to the Rural Week-End, was adamant that Ireland's currency was merely a 'reprint' of the English one that dominated their whole economic system.[65] Referring to the third minority report, he said that it had clearly been founded on the Papal encyclicals, but it had hardly been referred to in the newspapers. He hinted:

> There has been a kind of concerted effort to brush this aside. There has been a kind of propaganda going on to blind the Catholic public to the real facts and to glorify the acceptance of a measure which, I feel, will ultimately mean the ruin of Irish agriculture and the rural population.[66]

Cahill's apocalyptic speech, which was widely reported, did nothing to allay the concerns of his superiors.

There were a number of heated reactions within the Jesuit community. *Studies* refused to publish an article by Cahill on the findings of the Banking Commission. Its editor, Fr Connolly, advised him that he preferred to follow the findings of the Commission rather than those not expert in the 'highly technical matter of money'.[67] Another prominent Jesuit, Fr Bartley, pointed out that Cahill's remarks on the Irish currency were 'entirely unfounded'. The Irish pound was 'anchored' to sterling just as the French franc was since the abandonment of the gold standard. Such arrangements entailed no economic subservience. Bartley also said that it was 'ridiculous' to suggest that the relationship was going to destroy the rural population. And the fact that one of the signatories of the majority report was a Catholic bishop demanded a more temperate discussion.[68]

The Jesuit Provincial, Fr Kiernan, sent cuttings from the daily newspapers to another senior Jesuit, Fr Canavan, requesting his views as to whether: 1. Cahill's observations were correct and judicious; 2. They were opportune (were they 'not rather political in character?'); 3. It was prudent for a Jesuit to criticise in public the Report of the Banking Commission, which had been signed and 'presumably approved' by the Bishop of Raphoe.[69] Canavan replied the very next day, pointing out that it was not the first time that he had given his opinion of Cahill's competence in economic and financial questions, 'He simply does not understand them'.[70] In fact, Canavan firmly believed that Cahill's judgment was unbalanced, chiefly because he was 'incapable of keeping all the elements of a complex problem in his mind and of giving each of them its weight in the solution. In brief, he has not the natural ability nor the training to give authority to his statements'.[71] He regarded Cahill's statements in Ardmore as 'injudicious', and he saw it as a mistake to 'evoke destructive passions especially in such matters as finance which are governed so much by self-interest'. It was Canavan's view that Cahill was always looking for the 'hidden hand, the Masonic influence and all the rest of the devil's armoury in those who did not adopt his theories whole and entire'. He regarded this as a 'childish' attitude.[72] It had been Canavan's long held opinion that, 'Cahill was not a suitable person to make pronouncements in public about politics or finance in Ireland'.[73]

The strongly worded statements of Canavan and Bartley cast a shadow over the whole Catholic Action movement as it existed in the late 1930s. If one of the leaders of such a movement, which was ostensibly working towards the reconstruction of aspects of Irish society according to a Catholic blueprint, did not have the confidence of the much respected Jesuit community, it certainly put a question mark over Cahill's influence and achievements. These divisions effectively destroyed any hope of their being a united Catholic Action movement. Not only that, but there was obviously a fundamental difference over principles, over the interpretation of the encyclicals, over the right to comment publicly on socio-economic matters. What was particularly damning in the criticism of Cahill was that his main critics were Coyne, Bartley and Canavan, men who had, like Cahill, been appointed by the Jesuit Provincial to 'advise [de Valera] on certain matters connected with the Constitution' of 1937.[74] With the publication of the Report of the Banking Commission, this consensus broke up, personality clashes erupted, and confusion and differences arose over the application and interpretation of crucial Papal documents.

Coyne's criticism of Cahill was given public airing in the September 1938 issue of *Studies*. But Coyne himself admitted that this article was only 'mildly critical' since the Jesuit censor had 'tackled' it.[75] Coyne saw no need for reluctance or reticence in his private correspondence with the Jesuit Provincial. He regarded Cahill's Ardmore speech as 'dangerous and foolish'. Ireland's economic troubles were not as easily remedied as Cahill seemed to imply. He also felt 'appalled and disgusted' by some of Cahill's other comments, particularly the accusations levelled against Joseph Brennan, George O'Brien, Sean Moynihan, J.J. McElligott and others, that they were prepared to 'throw aside Christian principles'. In addition, Coyne rejected the input into the third minority report of Bulmer Hobson, 'a Quaker or Protestant' whose 'technique was well known'. According to Coyne, Hobson 'gets a number of prominent or semi-prominent people to join forces and he then uses them as a means to propagate his fads'. He repeated his view that An Rioghacht's scheme, which in O'Loghlen's definite opinion was clearly founded on the Papal encyclicals, was 'quite untrue, most unwise, injurious to the encyclicals and would bring them into disrepute with educated Catholics, or would lead to the uneducated to believe that the third minority report really was a concrete remedy backed by the Pope'.[76]

In late October 1938, Cahill was advised by his Jesuit superiors to submit to the Jesuit censors anything he proposed to say in public on the Banking Commission.[77] He was advised that his remarks were 'likely to be offensive to some good Catholics'.[78] Cahill had ignored hints dropped to him after his Ardmore speech, and he continued to lecture on the same at An Rioghacht meetings. His superiors then decided that they had no other option but to silence him.

The plethora of recriminations and accusations pointed to serious fractures in the movement. These divisions became even more damaging when criticisms levelled against An Rioghacht and O'Rahilly became public, and the controversy ensued in the pages of Catholic periodicals and the daily press. The difficulties did no damage to the strengthening Catholic ethos, but they played into the hands of the Department of Finance, faced with an opposition divided on fundamentals. Significantly, the strong movement which had developed under the aegis of Catholic Action, and which was successfully creating a determined Catholic public opinion, was not able to challenge effectively selective economic orthodoxies, because of differences of opinion on principles. Not only that, but experts like Professors George O'Brien, Busteed and O'Rahilly, could not agree on the technical matters. In fact, O'Brien and O'Rahilly frequently came to blows over such issues.

O'RAHILLY AND O'BRIEN AND THE 'MONEY' QUESTION

The 1942 Central Bank Bill, which was the outcome of one of the majority report's recommendations, saw the debate over a vocational order for Ireland take a new turn and further indicated the sharp divisions in Irish Catholicism with regard to Catholic social principles.

George O'Brien, Professor of Political Economy in UCD (1930-1961) and Professor of National Economics in the same university (1926-1961), had dominated the proceedings of the Banking Commission. He had played a large part in the examination of witnesses and the drafting of parts of the final report.

Professor O'Brien and other influential members of the Banking Commission had expected that O'Rahilly would attempt to have discussion of the social aspects of economics as outlined in the various encyclicals included in the report. But as earlier discussed, they had managed to elude his demands, and he had to settle for an appendix in the final deliberations. The effect on O'Rahilly was predictable. According to O'Brien, 'I think it was this appendix that finally aroused Alfred O'Rahilly to dash off his minority report, his large volume *Money* and his incessant articles in *The Standard* attacking the Commission in general and me in particular'.[79]

A different account of the genesis of *Money* (1941) is evident when we recall Fr Coyne's stinging criticism of O'Rahilly's first minority report. O'Rahilly had quickly responded, totally rejecting the criticisms in a series of articles in *The Irish Press* in 1938.[80] In late 1939, he delivered a series of lectures on the subject of money under the auspices of the UCC extension course. *Money* was published jointly by the Cork University Press and Blackwell's of Oxford. It was quite a massive tome, running to 652 pages. It received a great deal of public attention, mainly because O'Rahilly availed of every opportunity to demonstrate weaknesses in current accepted economic wisdom. The first edition sold out within six months and a second and enlarged edition appeared the following year.[81]

The main points covered in *Money* related to:

1. The inadvisability of amassing sterling assets during the war years.

2. The multiplier effect of banking, the fact that the operation of the banking system *ipso facto* creates money.

3. The importance of ensuring that Irish money was invested in Ireland and not overseas.

4. The need to have a currency related to, but independent of sterling.

5. The establishment of a Central Bank with the power to regulate all banking activity in the interests of Irish polity.[82]

There was nothing particularly unorthodox in O'Rahilly's economic thinking except that it was very difficult to invest in anything during the Second World War, and a breach with sterling would have meant no imports, since the country had no non-sterling assets. Unfortunately for O'Rahilly, his views did not coincide with 1940s Irish economic thought. Writing in *The Standard* in March 1941, Fr Peter Coffey, Professor of Logic and Metaphysics in Maynooth College, welcomed the book's exposition of the 'many fetishes such as sterling assets, sterling parity, liquidity and foreign investments by which we have been mesmerised, and the whole host of shibboleths that have hypnotised us into adopting the timid do-nothing policy'.[83] In a substantial review in the *Irish Independent* one month later, Fr Edward Coyne, who by this time was actively engaged in the work of the Commission on Vocational Organisation, contended that none of O'Rahilly's proposals were revolutionary or unorthodox and that most of them were accepted practice in other countries.[84] With an eye on sceptical economists, financiers and officials in the Department of Finance, Coyne did however urge caution, and emphasised the importance of trying to forecast the economic and social results that would follow the proposals, and in deciding whether these results would be more socially desirable than the status quo. In effect, Coyne echoed earlier criticisms which he had directed at O'Rahilly and the other signatories of the Banking Commission's minority reports. This time, Coyne was rather more reticent in his criticism, since he had to work with O'Rahilly on the Commission on Vocational Organisation. Overall, he regarded it as a 'vigorous book, possibly too vigorous at times, impatient of humbug, impatient of jargon, possibly too impatient of the necessary technical terms and traditional methods and modes of economic analysis'.[85] Relations remained strained between the two men for a number of months after the review, until Bishop Michael Browne of Galway eventually managed to heal the rift.

The reaction of professional economists was not so restrained. Professor George O'Brien was so upset by the book that, according to his biographer, James Meenan, he tried to pretend that it did not exist. Such an attitude took its toll, and eventually it became known that to commend O'Rahilly in any way caused O'Brien to be seriously disturbed. The writer Louis MacRedmond recalls his amused reaction and that of his fellow undergraduates, when, at their first lecture on economics, O'Brien, after recommending a reading list, fairly bristled and warned them against reading O'Rahilly's book.[86]

Economists had to take cognisance of the book. James Meenan, a junior colleague of Professor O'Brien's, reviewed *Money* in the *National Student* in May 1941.[87] He was quite dismissive of the book. James Beddy, secretary of the Industrial Credit Company, writing in *Studies* on 'Monetary Policy in Eire', concluded that while no one could disapprove of O'Rahilly's ultimate aim – the provision of full employment through maximum utilisation of national resources – he could not expect the same measure of agreement as to his suggested remedies to this end.[88] O'Rahilly, in a series of articles in *The Standard* in November 1941, challenged practically every detail of Dr Beddy's critique.[89] These were followed by scathing attacks on the monetarist views of Sir John Keane, governor of the Bank of Ireland.[90] In *The Standard* he also continued his articles (begun in 1938) on Finance's economic policies. In 1942, the Department's Secretary, James McElligott, wrote to Thomas J. Coyne, head of censorship during the Emergency, complaining that *The Standard* had been 'conducting a violent campaign' against his Department.[91]

Economists were united in their opposition to O'Rahilly and referred to him and his circle as 'nationalist economic amateurs' and 'credit cranks'.[92] This reaction was not surprising considering that in *Money* O'Rahilly referred to the 'economist-cult' as an 'alleged science'.[93] He regarded O'Brien and his colleagues as 'showing incipient signs of doubting their own dogmas'.[94] He regarded the majority report as 'reactionary, negative and out-of-date'.[95] He was also equally critical of the 'kind of advice' McElligott was giving to the government.[96] These people had long 'dazed' the public and it was time that the leaders and their financial advisers 'awoke from their dogmatic slumber', he declared.[97] He regarded O'Brien as being 'hallucinated by the humbug of finance'. George O'Brien was later to write in his memoirs:

> [O'Rahilly] has forgotten all about his attacks on me and would be surprised to be told that I had anything to forgive. I have forgiven, but I have not forgotten. One does not forget being bitten by a mad dog. But the mad dog frequently forgets that he has bitten his victim.[98]

In the longer term, there was something more significant than the personality clashes. The debate in a way represented a watershed, a shifting from previously held positions. The clash was between different theories and philosophies for the organisation of society. Writing in *Studies* in 1943, O'Rahilly defended scholastic principles, 'It would make an enormous difference if the dominant and accepted outlook of society were attributed to St Thomas'.[99] O'Brien, on the other hand, argued that, 'the modern liberal economist insists that the State has great powers for good as well as for evil'.[100] Despite O'Rahilly's assumption that no one except himself was aware of *Quadragesimo Anno*, O'Brien insisted on the ethical content of economics. In one of his earlier and most influential works, *An Essay on the Economic Effects of the Reformation* (1923), he argued that, 'the science of economics is a branch of the science of ethics'.[101] He also wrote favourably on the medieval economic system, which *Quadragesimo Anno* frequently referred to. In an earlier work, *An Essay on Medieval Economic Teaching* (1920), he praised the fact that in the Middle Ages, 'man did not exist for the sake of production but production for the sake of man'.[102] Not only that, but he also suggested that the teaching of the medieval Church on distribution and its insistence that it must be regulated on a basis of strict justice, showed that, 'the teaching of the medieval appears in most marked contrast to the present day'.[103]

In October 1942, he gave the presidential address to the Statistical and Social Inquiry Society of Ireland. In his paper on 'Economic Relativity' he again defended the economic system of the Middle Ages, because it rested on a general agreement on political, legal and moral standards.[104] The Christian ethical system imposed upon European culture had 'at least the semblance of moral agreement' right up to the nineteenth century. He felt that since the Middle Ages, Europe had been living upon 'inherited religious capital'.[105] Doubtlessly, he would have been echoing O'Rahilly and *Quadragesimo Anno* when he declared that, 'the world to-day recognises no such international morality'. The traditional Christian standards had been replaced by the idealisation of the State as in Fascism or Marxism. In countries where liberalism survived, instead of politics deriving its values from an ethical system, current ethical judgments seemed to be based on political decisions. For O'Brien, the crucial solution to this twentieth-century disharmony was a political rather than an economic one. If the advantages of liberalism were to be restored, the social and political framework would have to be refashioned so as to 'ensure that there will be a concurrence rather than a conflict of interest in the economic sphere'.[106]

Whereas O'Rahilly and Catholic Action wanted a return to the economic order of the Middle Ages, O'Brien sought a 'middle way' between unregulated individualism and totalitarianism. This would depend upon securing a sufficient social and political integration to enable the forces of competition to work harmoniously. Underpinning this integration would be the absolute necessity for some code commanding universal assent to provide norms of individual and international behaviour. O'Brien was aware that fundamentally, economics had to be the servant of politics rather than its master in any new order of things. Catholic Action, however, subscribed to the view that economics and politics should both be at the service of religion, as was perceived to be the case in medieval times.

The primary difference between O'Rahilly and O'Brien, and their views on Irish social and economic development in the early 1940s, can be summed up in O'Brien's own words:

> ...the one statement that can be safely made without due temerity is that revolutions move forward and not backward. The institutions of tomorrow will not revert to those of yesterday. Every attempt to remedy the evils of the present by restoring the conditions of the past is doomed to failure. The problems of today cannot be solved by the theories of yesterday.[107]

Effectively, he was rejecting the social theories of Catholic Action. He understood the Catholic interpretation of Reformation history. It was because of that interpretation the Catholic Church had adopted a 'defensive' attitude towards innovations of thought. That interpretation was, in fact, directly responsible for whatever there was of 'narrowness or reactionism in modern Catholicism', he declared.[108]

O'Brien argued that economists themselves had to engage in a high degree of flexibility and adaptability in their theories; economic laws would need to be revised if they were to keep pace with reality.[109] He lectured his students on Keyne's *General Theory of Employment, Interest and Money* (1936) within months of its publication.[110] But above all, for O'Brien, capitalism was not in decline, but merely in transition. He did not believe that the solution was to be found in adopting vocational corporatist models for society's organisation.

The question remained; what was to be the wider effect of the O'Rahilly–O'Brien clash? We have seen how O'Rahilly had completely alienated the economic and financial establishment, a situation that did not augur well for the outcome of the deliberations of the Commission on Vocational Organisation. The Department of Finance had quickly grasped the fact that the Catholic Church had no economic expertise, but rather a vague social aspiration, an abstract obsession, a Catholic blueprint based on a romantic theoretical medieval paradigm. Some Catholic Actionists, on the other hand, were determined to tackle some of the socio-economic issues of the day, with the help of Catholic social principles.

Fr Edward Coyne, economist, principal facilitator of the Commission on Vocational Organisation and the architect of its final report, had no real difficulties, despite some reservations, with O'Rahilly's economic theories. The various clashes within Catholic Action, and between O'Rahilly and O'Brien, did not necessarily mean that rejection of the Report of the Commission on Vocational Organisation was inevitable. However, they certainly indicated that there were winds of change in Irish attitudes and Irish society. There was to be no consensus on the future direction of the country in terms of socio-economic strategies.

Fr Cahill, an inspiration behind the widespread growth and popular success of the late 1920s and 1930s Catholic Action movement, died in July 1941, just over two years after the establishment of the Commission on Vocational Organisation. Taoiseach Éamon de Valera and members of the Oireachtas attended his funeral in Dublin's Glasnevin Cemetery.[111] An Rioghacht, however, was to survive as an influential force in Irish life for nearly twenty more years.

THE FLIGHT FROM STATISM AND THE QUEST FOR POLITICAL POWER

CHANGED RULES, CHANGED CIRCUMSTANCES: NEW DIRECTIONS FOR CATHOLIC ACTION

The activities of the various strands of Catholic Action working in the late 1930s persuaded the Catholic hierarchy that closer supervision was needed if the organisations were to act in strict accordance with the 'mandate' given to them by the bishops under the provisions of the encyclicals on Catholic Action. Many of the hierarchy were not happy with the independence shown by the Legion of Mary and An Rioghacht. Similarly, the activities of the Irish Christian Front had greatly alarmed the hierarchy, despite their initial enthusiasm for the organisation. The ICF had no formally constituted membership comparable with the CYMS. It had no agreed criteria for membership, no agreed constitution or objectives, no elected leadership and often little contact between the branches and the steering committee. Not only that, but there was a conflict of interest between many of the leaders of Catholic Action, such as Alfred O'Rahilly, Frank O'Reilly, and the leadership of the ICF itself (which seemed to have certain political motivations). Catholic Action advocates who backed the organisation because of its anti-communist rhetoric had a very different agenda from the clique of minor politicians who comprised the Dublin leadership. For them, the ICF had fortuitously appeared at an important point in the development of the Catholic Action movement. That the leadership may have had hopes to form a Catholic political party was completely unacceptable to the leaders of Catholic Action and the hierarchy.

Likewise, the activities of An Rioghacht and the League for Social Justice put a question mark over the whole area of lay initiative. It is not surprising, therefore, that in 1939 Fr Peter McKevitt, Professor of Catholic Action in Maynooth College, presented the Catholic hierarchy with a report entitled, 'Proposals of the Initiations of a Scheme of Catholic Action in Ireland'.[1]

REPORTS ON CATHOLIC ACTION IN IRELAND

The McKevitt Report reflected the hierarchy's ongoing wariness of lay initiative, and especially the views of Archbishop Byrne of Dublin. In fact, the whole report seems to reek with a tone of suspicion vis-à-vis lay organisations. The Catholic Action movement, according to the report, should be more involved in the process of 'formation' and 'inculcation of self-denial'. Organisations should be ensuring 'effective obedience to pastoral directions'. McKevitt recommended the establishment of a central directive committee. Women's organisations were to have representation on this central controlling body. Each member of this committee would have to 'enjoy the confidence' of the hierarchy. McKevitt also felt it necessary to have a priest in attendance to guard against the dangers of precipitate action. Besides, he believed that the 'inexperience' of laymen required such an adviser who would exercise a 'healthy' influence on the general direction of operations. Similarly, the constitutions of existing organisations would have to be changed to ensure that they were 'pliable to meet the exigencies of Episcopal control'.

The McKevitt Report examined a number of organisations. Despite the expansion of the CYMS during the 1930s, McKevitt was still not happy that the results were in proportion to what the bishops had hoped for. In the light of their involvement in the Banking Commission, An Rioghacht came in for much criticism. If the organisation was to be recognised under the new scheme of things, it would be necessary to ensure that its members, 'and especially its lecturers', should receive a definite training in social science.

The Knights of St Columbanus, on the other hand, would be most welcome, despite the 'secrecy' problem. They had a large membership (approximately 5,000) and to assign it a definite place in the Catholic Action reorganisation scheme would bring it under episcopal control, and would 'secure the support of the professional and business classes which the organisation embraces'. Muintir na Tíre could be entrusted with the organisation of Catholic Action in rural districts, where it could build up family life.

McKevitt emphasised that organisations must be grouped around the parish church, as this would be vital to secure full episcopal control. Hitherto they were often attached to a religious order, such as the Jesuits, the Dominicans, or the Holy Ghost Fathers, rather than a parish. Organisations such as the Legion of Mary and the Knights of St Columbanus were attached to neither structure but were dependent upon dynamic personalities such as Frank Duff, or were surrounded by a web of secrecy. Only with greater control could Catholic Action become an 'effective instrument' of the Catholic Church. Only then, owing to the 'authoritarian character' of the priest's office, would his decision be adopted. McKevitt was adamant that 'appropriate action was absolutely necessary', as it was 'vital that the Catholic Action movement should not weaken the control over the laity' exercised by the Church.[2] Initiatives such as those of

An Rioghacht, and particularly the organisation's failure to influence the deliberations of the Banking Commission, had alarmed the Church, and were seen
as major threats to its own influence and control.

That such influence and control was possibly shifting was indicated by the
militant and independent attitudes expressed by other individuals and organisations. The Drumcondra Branch of the CYMS bemoaned the tameness of its
activities. What they wanted was 'real activity, real Catholic Action', according to its secretary, J. Sheridan.[3] He wanted further powers to be given to the
CYMS so that a national Catholic Action body could be formed 'to harness the
energies of the Catholic forces'.[4] He wanted the Society to be more active on
the socio-economic front and to tackle politicians on various issues.[5]

Dr James McPolin, a well-known speaker at Catholic Action meetings, also
felt that Muintir na Tíre needed a change in direction and focus; 'a serious
study of socio-economic problems needed to be undertaken' by the organisation, he declared.[6] He deemed the Irish education system as being 'totally
unsuitable for the needs and interests of the rural population'. For McPolin,
the economic difficulties stemmed from a 'deformed' education system, which
was not geared towards the agricultural community.

Dr J. Waters, husband of Mrs Berthon Waters of An Rioghacht, and Master
of the Irish Guild of Catholic Doctors, gave a number of addresses in Cork and
Dublin in 1938 on the need to redirect Catholic influence away from vigilance
activities and towards economic affairs, so that pressure could be brought to bear
on the State 'to make the security of families its primary concern'.[7] In Waters's
view, Catholic Action energies were misdirected and wasted. Fr Roland Burke
Savage, long-time editor of *Studies*, was in agreement with these views. He was
of the impression that the 1937 encyclical on communism made more impact
in Ireland in the 1930s than did the teaching on social questions.[8] Attention
centred on the need for vigilance, on anti-communism activities and protests,
rather than on tackling the country's problems. Writing in the *Irish Ecclesiastical
Record* in 1939, he argued that as a consequence of this state of affairs, the lack of
trained leaders was 'the great problem of Catholic Action'.[9]

However, a confidential report, 'The Present Position of Catholic Action in
Ireland', drawn up by the Irish Jesuit community in 1936, had criticised the 'lack
of leadership' on the part of the hierarchy and clergy generally.[10] As with the
McKevitt Report, it pointed out the need for a centralising organisation, which
would direct the actions of the other organisations without hampering their ability. This would give the 'whole Catholic Action movement the cohesion it now
lacks'. Of particular significance also was the Jesuit report's insight into the hierarchy's fears and the fact that the bishops 'shared the confusion prevalent' about
the precise meaning of the term 'Catholic Action'. For this and other reasons they
were 'suspicious' of the movement and were therefore 'reluctant' to encourage it.
In fact, the Jesuits agreed that the bishops 'did not know what it implied' or what
urgent need there was for it. Consequently, they were especially 'slow' to approve

of any organisation which was 'not completely and in all details subject to the control of the diocesan clergy'. The Jesuit report also suggested that the bishops were 'jealous of their authority and they seem to think that they have the right to confide the direction of all forms of Catholic Action to the Diocesan clergy'.

Religious orders such as the Dominicans and the Jesuits, who were very active with lay organisations, were by implication not trusted with the task. The report quoted Alfred O'Rahilly and his view that 'the Bishop of Cork is most jealous of his rights over Catholic Action'. Consequently the bishops and the clergy had 'failed' to lead in the matter of Catholic Action, a factor which undermined the movement and which led to 'a growing feeling amongst Irish workmen that they or their interests are being altogether neglected by the clergy'.[11] The report also referred to the many clergy who were 'wanting in a sense of obligations to their flocks', who showed a 'lamentable lack of interest' in lay organisations, who were 'rather worldy and indifferent' and who displayed a 'lack of zeal for social work'.[12] This indictment further illustrates the seriousness of the divisions that hampered the movement. The Emergency years would show the reaction of the hierarchy to the McKevitt Report in particular, and the direction the movement would consequently take.

THE EMERGENCY YEARS: CRUCIBLE FOR CHANGE

The war years were a prelude to greater governmental planning, intervention, and strategic decision-making. In 1939, the government had felt compelled to invest itself with powers to cope with the new situation – The Emergency Powers Act. The establishment of the Department of Supplies fulfilled the role of a central planning department in Ireland's economic life.

During the winter of 1940/41, the Second World War, then in its second year, was seriously affecting neutral Ireland. Worst hit by the scarcities, caused by rising costs and shortages of essentials, were the poor in the towns and cities. Fuel became scarce. The army was drawn in to stockpile huge pyramids of turf in Dublin's Phoenix Park, since coal was practically unobtainable. Factories were closing because of the shortages of raw materials. There was widespread unemployment. An advertisement for boot polish in one of the newspapers ran, 'Please use sparingly, supplies are short'.[13] A song at the time had a line, 'God bless de Valera and Seán MacEntee, they gave us brown bread and a half ounce of tea'. Even soap was rationed. Food ration books were issued to every household. Huge numbers emigrated to the munitions factories of Britain. The pawnshops of the towns and cities did a thriving business (Dublin alone had forty).[14]

Some efforts were made in the early years of the Emergency to offset the hardships of those in dire need. A play called *Marrowbone Lane*, depicting the plight of destitute families in Dublin's inner city, so shocked audiences that the Samaritan Relief Fund was launched. Judge Wylie's Guilds ran 'Goodwill Restaurants' to help feed the poor.[15] In 1942, the Irish Housewives Association was founded in response to the dreadful conditions.[16] According to Professor Mary Daly in her work *The Spirit of Earnest Inquiry*, the Statistical and Social Inquiry Society of Ireland 'devoted considerable attention to the medical and social problems of Dublin's working class'.[17] One of the society's papers for 1941 showed that life expectancy was almost ten years higher for a baby boy born in Connaught than for one born in Dublin. A later paper of the Society, according to Professor Daly, showed a 'strong positive association between tuberculosis and poverty, over-crowded housing and poor living conditions'.[18] The role of that Society in Irish life was of particular importance since it facilitated, Professor Daly declared, civil servants discussing public policy issues with a certain freedom of expression in a supportive environment. As we shall see, it was a forum which played an important part in the evolution of public policy making.

The towns and cities were worst hit during the war years. The Annual Reports of the St Vincent de Paul Society give a clear picture of the day-to-day poverty experienced by so many.[19] One notes from the reports that the war years themselves did not create all the conditions for a crisis, but rather brought to a head a festering problem.[20] Problems associated with high rents were a feature of the reports. Highly priced, substandard accommodation was the lot of thousands of town and city dwellers in Cork, Dublin, Waterford, Limerick and elsewhere. Unemployment exacerbated the difficulty. Requests for money to help pay for infants' funeral expenses, or to help people to emigrate, were also strong features. Constant references were made to poor people being transferred to Crooksling TB Sanatorium on the outskirts of Dublin. There was also much co-operation between the Society and the Sick and Indigent Roomkeepers' Society because of the sheer extent of the problems.[21] Both organisations considered the question of fuel for the poor to be of paramount importance, and they welcomed the fuel and food voucher scheme introduced by the government. They actively participated in their distribution.[22]

During the war years, the rate of deaths due to TB (which had been falling) rose substantially, reaching a peak in the period 1942-1945, with an estimated 147 deaths per 100,000 of the population being attributed to some form of the disease.[23] In regional terms, Dublin and its environs suffered the highest mortality rate, and the number of deaths from TB was consistently above the national average. The Sick and Indigent Roomkeepers' Society noted in a report in 1943 that the epidemic was a growing problem.[24] The previous year, a National Anti-Tuberculosis League was founded to combat the growing menace. Public awareness was increasing rapidly. In 1941, the Royal Irish Academy of Medicine had published a report that proposed organising a network of TB dispensaries and sanatoria.[25] The report had blamed bad housing, lack of fresh air and shortages of fresh food as the major causes of the rising mortality. Although they recognised that improving living conditions was the long-term solution, improved medical services were also a matter of urgency.

In 1942, Dublin's Lord Mayor, Alfie Byrne, called a conference to discuss the problem of TB, and shortly afterwards representations were made to the government with a view to tackling the problem of footwear and clothing for the poor. The *Evening Herald* introduced its 'Herald Boot Fund' to help tackle this issue.[26] The Belvedere Newsboys' Club, consisting of members of the College's Past-Pupils' Union (PPU), stepped up their activities in helping Dublin's newsboys. But it was not until 1944 that a government 'Footwear Regulations Scheme' was launched, which provided free footwear to all children of persons in receipt of public assistance. The Emergency appeared to be accelerating the advent of social and other forms of legislation.

Of particular significance in the context of the campaign for a vocational, subsidiarist Ireland, was that when the government started to examine the case for the introduction of a Children's Allowances Scheme in Ireland, it took notice of the 1942 Beveridge Report, 'Social Insurances and Allied Services', which was the subject of much discussion in Britain. Indeed, in introducing the Bill in the Dáil in 1943, Seán Lemass, Minister for Industry and Commerce, quoted part of the report.[27] Developments in Britain were setting the example for how best to promote the health of poorer people.

Plans for community feeding had been drawn up as part of the emergency measures but greater state involvement proved to be a source of some unease.[28] *The Standard* grasped the nettle when they pointed out that while numbers attending Dublin Corporation's food kitchens were increasing, they posed a worry that mealtime, 'the very foundation of family life and intercourse', was being impaired.[29] In 1944, Archbishop McQuaid expressed his preference for 'private charity' over 'public relief schemes'.[30]

Greater state intervention was gradualist. State assistance was often introduced as a last resort or as a response to public demands, rather than as a result of radical thinking, Catholic or otherwise. From the government's point of view, the optimum deployment of supplies and resources remained the primary objective, as demonstrated by the establishment of the Department of Supplies early in the Emergency and the number of Emergency Powers Orders. But the poor living and health conditions of thousands of families was a contributing factor in persuading the government to take strong action on the question of public health. It was recognised in government circles that major reforms of the health services had become necessary. Seán MacEntee, Minister for Local Government and Public Health, became convinced of the need for a separate Ministry of Health. The result of this shift in thinking was the Public Health Bill of 1945.[31]

All this was happening at a time when the Catholic Action campaign wished to see the curtailment, rather than the extension of State activities and when the Commission on Vocational Organisation, which was appointed in 1939, was reaching conclusions on its deliberations for the establishment of subsidiarist structures in Ireland.

CATHOLIC ACTION AND THE SOCIAL ISSUE: NEW STRATEGIES

The early years of the Emergency saw the Catholic Action movement developing in a number of ways. On one hand, the establishment of the Catholic Social
Services Conference (CSSC) in 1941 saw Dublin's new Catholic Archbishop, Dr
John Charles McQuaid, firmly grasping the issue of independent lay initiative
and redirecting it, in accordance with Professor Peter McKevitt's recommendations, in a new, unified, yet non-confrontational manner. An indication of this
new approach was quickly apparent in his suppression of the Mercier Society
and the Pillar of Fire Society, which were two new ecumenical organisations
established by Frank Duff, much to the latter's great disillusionment.[32] Also in
1941, the Christus Rex Society was established among the clergy 'dedicated
to the cause of Christian Social Reform',[33] indicating the transfer of ultimate
control of the 'cause' to strictly clerical influence.

On the other hand, the CYMS and Muintir na Tíre came to the forefront of
Catholic Action activities because of their organisation of Catholic Social Weeks
throughout the country, at which widespread publicity was generated for the
cause of vocational organisation and against the need for greater state intervention. Muintir na Tíre were also involved in parish schemes during the Emergency,
and the CYMS helped local authorities organise allotments for the needy.

Christian Social Reorganisation by the Jesuit Fr George Clune was published in
1940.[34] It was a major work running to over 500 pages, and was an effective follow-up to Fr Edward Cahill's *Framework of a Christian State*. While emphasising the
'positive obligation' of Catholics to engage in the work of social reconstruction,
the new publication also reflected the concerns of the hierarchy that Catholic
Action organisations should henceforth carry out their mission 'according to a
plan determined by the hierarchy'.[35] The essential elements of Catholic Action
were therefore reasserted as 'assisting the hierarchy in its mission', and in this, being
'subordinate' to that hierarchy. As to the specifically social question, the business
of Catholic Action was to 'train' men to deal with the question, to teach them the
principles to guide them in their work and to lay down rules from the encyclicals
in accordance with which the movement should be organised. Clune strongly
emphasised that 'beyond that it does not go'. The vocal and autonomous Catholic
Action of An Rioghacht and the Irish Christian Front was not to be repeated.

In the light of this, the founders of Christus Rex saw one of the tasks of the
new society as educating the clergy in the area of Catholic social teaching.[36]
The clergy in turn would then promote the study of this teaching among the
laity. In this way, they hoped that Irish public opinion would be enlightened
and informed under the 'guidance and control of the Catholic hierarchy'. The
CYMS became more prominent in the 1940s because they had been granted
a Catholic Action 'mandate' in 1934 and were regarded by the hierarchy as an
ideal Catholic Action model because of their strict conformity to clerical control and approval. By the early 1940s they had a membership of 15,000 in more

than 120 branches. Dublin had 20 branches with over 2,000 members. With the publication of the Report of the Commission on Vocational Organisation in 1944, they became galvanised into action and were the leading activists in the campaign for a National Vocational Assembly.

It was with the establishment of the CSSC in 1941 that the dual strategy of the Catholic hierarchy with regard to Catholic Action was most evident.[37] The CSSC was the first stage in their plan for a vocationalist Ireland. At the same time, the new organisation acted as a focus for the energies of the lay organisations that had been developing during the previous twenty years. By embracing poverty and by emphasising the rule of charity, they were effectively discarding any radical or confrontational interpretation of the social problem. Most important of all was the fact that Dr McQuaid, by encouraging Catholic Action organisations to help the poor and needy, thereby reduced the need for State intervention. In his eyes, the task of the State was to facilitate organisations such as the CSSC and their work in the community, and not to supersede them if they were working with reasonable effectiveness.[38]

The CSSC co-ordinated hitherto disparate activities by a number of groups into a relatively efficient organisation, providing food and clothing for those in need. With this approach, Catholic Action, unlike their challenge to the Banking Commission in the late 1930s, would be politically innocuous and could enjoy cross-party patronage. Hence Muintir na Tíre, an organisation that did not seriously advocate the reorganisation of Irish society along vocational lines, could enjoy the patronage of bishops and politicians, who frequently graced their platforms together. Furthermore, its reasonable aims for the rejuvenation of rural life, while on the one hand appealing to vocational instincts, were also an integral part of Fianna Fáil policy of self-sufficiency.[39] Muintir na Tíre did not alarm the hierarchy, rather they promoted their aspiration to see rural life re-emerge as a viable alternative to the materialistic culture that they perceived to be prevalent in Irish cities. They were ideally placed also to fit in with Archbishop McQuaid's plans for the CSSC.

The immediate initiative for the CSSC sprang from a letter of appeal to help Dublin's poor, which appeared in *The Irish Times* on 11 March 1941. It was signed by the founder of Judge Wylie's Restaurants, which were a Protestant initiative.[40] In response, Dr Stafford Johnson, Supreme Knight of the Knights of St Columbanus, became the principal mover behind the establishment of a Catholic organisation having the same aims. He organised the preliminary meeting in Ely House on 12 March, at which representatives of over thirty Catholic societies attended.[41] Frank O'Reilly of the CTSI, who attended the first meeting, noted that a certain urgency surrounded the proceedings. An immediate statement for the press was prepared, to let the public know the new movement had been established, so that 'they would not be stampeded into supporting Judge Wylie's scheme'. According to O'Reilly, the meeting had in fact been arranged since 8 March, and the various representatives had been contacted on that date, since 'Ely House knew of Judge Wylie's move on that date'.[42]

O'Reilly and John T. Lennon of the Society of St Vincent de Paul, however, regarded the planned work of the new organisation as completely 'outside the scope of Catholic organisations'. They were both surprised at the political dimension of the draft plan which was presented to the meeting.[43] O'Reilly queried one of the plans of the CSSC which related to the encouragement of migration of labour from the cities to the countryside.[44] It was envisaged that single, unemployed men from rural districts, of not more than five years residence in Dublin, would be returned to rural areas to work on schemes for the production of food and fuel. O'Reilly regarded this as being directly contrary to the Constitution of Ireland. Lennon thought that 'very little good' would come from some of the ideas put forward. On 20 March, Lennon, Stafford Johnson and Frank Duff met Éamon de Valera in Ely House (headquarters of the Knights of St Columbanus) to discuss the project. But although he seemed 'courteous and interested', de Valera was not prepared to offer specific co-operation, and the only request he made was for information regarding the condition of the poor in Dublin.[45]

Despite the dissenting voices in the new organisation, a majority vote accepted the plans. Shortly afterwards, O'Reilly was advised by Eugene Kavanagh, the Supreme Secretary of the Knights, that the Archbishop had given his 'hearty approval' to their efforts. Immediate steps were then taken to implement the suggestions discussed at Ely House.[46]

The work of the CSSC was to be co-ordinated under several departments: food; clothing; maternity welfare; housing; youth; fuel, and employment. Executive committees drawn from thirty-nine Catholic societies were to oversee these seven departments. Four further committees were responsible for organisation, finance, storage and distribution, and publicity and propaganda.[47] The organising committee focused on linking Catholic organisations with parish councils, industrial, professional and commercial bodies, and rural local authorities. The finance committees remit included providing and creating employment, accessing cash and credit contributions, and acquiring land, housing, equipment, etc., from local authorities. They were also to be responsible for the issuing of long-term development loans, and for initiating farm-machinery leasing activities. They were to ensure that unclaimed deposits in banks totalling £4 million were to be put into production. In the area of food, Muintir na Tíre was to operate practically as an alternative Department of Agriculture, such was the range of its designated responsibilities. They were authorised to organise interest-free loans to farmers, the intensive development of vegetables, the production of crops, the management of equipment, and storage facilities.[48]

All these plans would, of course, take a long time to actually implement, but in the short term the CSSC transformed the nature of social work in Dublin and elsewhere. A single large organisation provided a focus for charity, and many thousands of pounds were taken up annually in Church collections. Grants were also forthcoming from central and local government funds; in the years 1941 to 1943 these covered nearly 20 per cent of its overall outlay. The bulk of its resources, income and labour, however, came from voluntary sources.[49] The success of the new organisation gave Archbishop McQuaid a model of what the most fruitful balance of State and voluntary enterprise would be. It was to be a significant step in the campaign for a more subsidiarist society.

The years 1941-43 were two of intensive development of social services, according to the *Catholic Social Services Conference Handbook*.[50] New services were established, including maternity welfare centres, food and clothing depots, and youth councils. *The Social Worker's Handbook* was published in 1942 for use by 'Catholic' social workers in Dublin. The 118-page handbook was a very comprehensive and detailed reference work, which epitomised Catholic Action efforts in the area of voluntary charitable work.[51] It was compiled by the Society of St Vincent de Paul, An Rioghacht and the Legion of Mary. It helped to bring social work to a new, more organised and professional plateau. To this day, the role and example of voluntary initiative, which reached a high point in the early to mid-1940s, plays a crucial part in Ireland's social-service structures. Shortly after the handbook was published, and 'in response to suggestions from a number of Muintir na Tíre Parish Councils' and other societies and individuals, a *Guide to the Social Services* was published by the government. This publication ran to only thirty-five pages.[52]

The CTSI, although initially reluctant to involve itself in the new movement, did in fact participate by producing a number of useful booklets such as *Food Supplies, Foods and Dietetics, Dirt and Health, Consumption* and *Infectious Diseases*.[53] During the war years, the Society were selling more than two million copies of its booklets and pamphlets each year in Ireland.[54] Extending its publishing endeavours to non-religious material enhanced the profile of both the CTSI and the CSSC.

While the CSSC was rapidly developing its activities and influence, the second part of the Catholic Action strategy for a vocationalist Ireland came to the fore, with the publication in late 1943 (though not available until 1944) of the Report of the Commission on Vocational Organisation. The experience gained by lay organisations working together in the CSSC was to prove invaluable in the campaign to have vocational structures adopted in Ireland.

THE SENATE AND VOCATIONAL ORGANISATION COMMISSIONS

At the beginning of their second term in office, de Valera and his colleagues were exasperated at what they regarded as the obstructionist tactics of the Senate, which was controlled by the Opposition, especially with regard to Constitutional Bills. Tension grew between the government and the Senate. On 21 March 1934, the Senate rejected the Wearing of Uniform (Restrictions) Bill, which had been prepared by the government to meet the challenge posed by the Blueshirts. The following day, de Valera introduced a Bill in the Dáil to abolish the Senate. With the passing of the Constitution (Amendment No. 24) Act, it ceased to exist on 29 May 1936.

Less than two weeks after the winding up of the Senate, the government appointed a Commission to, 'consider and make recommendations as to what should be the functions and powers of a second chamber of the legislature in the event of its being decided to make provision in the Constitution for such a second chamber'.[55]

The Commission reported to the government on 1 October 1936. Attached to the report was a substantial additional report containing observations, most of which were at variance with the majority report.[56]

This minority report was drafted and completed by Alfred O'Rahilly, and was signed by him and by Professor D.A. Binchy, Sir John Keane, E. Lynch, Frank McDermott, Sean Moynihan, Michael Tierney and R. Wilson. This report proposed the selection of a second chamber, 'on a professional and functional basis', so as to minimise party conflicts and bring people with experience into public life. Most members would be elected by the Dáil from four panels: farming and fisheries; labour; industry and commerce, and education and the professions. O'Rahilly's obsession with vocational organisation surfaced in the suggestion that the ideal model would be direct election to the House by the 'functional and vocational councils' mentioned in Article 45 of the 1922 constitution.[57] For O'Rahilly, the main purpose of the Second Chamber would be to safeguard democracy and human rights.[58] For this reason it would have the power to demand a referendum on any Bill. The House would also have the right to veto Dáil resolutions and to dismiss judges and the comptroller and auditor-general. O'Rahilly's view was that, because of the number of Catholic Action organisations advocating vocationalism, there would be no shortage of Catholic Actionists ready to take their rightful seats in the Second Chamber. This was exactly what Catholic Action was aiming for – a Catholic parliament controlled by themselves.

It was O'Rahilly's report that formed the basis of the structure of the new Senate. The fact that de Valera's close adviser Sean Moynihan was also one of the signatories of the minority report was doubtlessly an important factor. That the acceptance of O'Rahilly's report by de Valera was a stroke of political opportunism was subsequently shown to be the case, when O'Rahilly reacted belligerently to the 1937 Draft Constitution version. According to Senator Connolly, a friend and former adviser to de Valera, who was a member of the Senate Commission, the chief charge against the Draft Constitution was that under the system of voting, it was not impossible for an aspirant for senatorial honours to secure his return by the judicious expenditure of a certain amount of cash![59] In fact it was Connolly's view that de Valera's form of Senate never had the approval of the country:

> It has been made the haven or refuge for party candidates who have suffered defeat in the elections for the Dáil. In no sense has it ever had any claim to being a democratically elected representative body, and until it is such, it is futile and provocative of derision to have a Senate at all.[60]

De Valera had adroitly used O'Rahilly's minority report, not for the furtherance of Catholic social principles, but for his own political advantage. That being the case, it is also equally true that de Valera, faced with intransigent Catholic militancy (as well as a difficult Opposition), had to devise a strategy which would give him leverage to protect the rule of democracy. His Senate provisions were therefore the ultimate *coup de grace*. At the same time, de Valera had shown his abiding interest in Catholic social principles. The application, as opposed to the acknowledgement of Catholic Action ideals, was certainly not an integral part of de Valera's vision of Ireland's future.

O'Rahilly quickly responded to de Valera's ingenuity, when he wrote a 'critical analysis' of the provisions for the Senate in a long article in the *Irish Independent* in mid-1937.[61] Most significantly, he objected to the assertion that de Valera was following the report that O'Rahilly had signed, and he declared, 'Personally I would prefer no Senate at all rather than this contraption.' When it came to the provisions in the constitution for vocational councils, he was even more vehement. Article 15.3 stated, 'The Oireachtas may provide for the establishment or recognition of functional or vocational councils representing branches of social and economic life of the people.' O'Rahilly had no hesitation however in denouncing this as 'pious claptrap'. As far as he was concerned, Fianna Fáil had not the remotest intention of taking *Quadragesimo Anno* quite so literally. He criticised the government's provisions as 'blatant hypocrisy'.[62] Article 19 of the Draft Constitution stated that, 'provision may be made for the direct election by any functional or vocational group or association or council'. For O'Rahilly, this translated into, 'it may be made, but is it likely?' He knew that the government was not likely to abandon the power of election and patronage which 'the delightfully elastic method of senate election' put in their hands. O'Rahilly saw too late that de Valera's Senate, in contrast to his version, 'has no real power'.[63]

De Valera's clauses were indeed nebulous. He only paid lip service to vocationalist ideals. The Seanad limped along, very much under the government's control, and while it could be argued that its structure was a victory for the outspoken vocationalist lobby, it was much more a monument to the politics of patronage. De Valera placated the Catholic Action lobby by setting up the Commission on Vocational Organisation in 1939. This was one way to deal with a difficult and persistent lobby, which contained individuals such as O'Rahilly, who was described by *The Irish Times* as 'a cross between Thomas Aquinas and Jimmy O'Dea [the well-known Dublin actor]',[64] and as having 'the best mind of the twelfth century'.[65] Seán MacEntee, Minister of Finance in the 1930s, revealed the mindset of the government towards the irritating movement when he declared that 'there was nothing like a group of self-appointed experts getting on with the job of proposing solutions'.[66]

Despite recommending Portugal as an example (in paragraphs 49-58), and concluding that Ireland should have a National Vocational Assembly (paragraphs 700-711), the Report of the Commission on Vocational Organisation, which was finally published in August 1944, cautioned that it was still too early to judge the corporative system in Portugal by results.[67] It was Professor Joe Lee's contention that the commission's commitment to corporatism was 'more visceral than intellectual'.[68]

The Commission devised the most comprehensive blueprint for the reordering of society along Catholic lines and principles. Its massive 300,000-word report analysed the faults of Irish government and recommended sweeping changes as a consequence. Particular concern was expressed about the dangers of bureaucracy.[69] It was careful not to condemn state intervention when it was necessary for the good of the people, but it reserved its censure for state control merely for administrative convenience or for its own sake. Vocational organisation, on the other hand, would be the 'very antithesis of bureaucracy'.[70] As an alternative to a highly centralised and bureaucratic society, the Commission recommended the formation of a National Vocational Assembly, representing all the major interest groups, to advise the government on policy.[71] They envisaged such groups to be from the professions, agriculture, industry, commerce, transport, and the financial sectors. These interests would remedy the issue that economic planning was 'sectional, local, piecemeal, and unbalanced', by providing the 'necessary unity of economic structure'.[72] The Commission was highly critical of existing planning, which it saw as having been 'devised and executed bureaucratically by ministers and their official advisers'.[73] Many of those engaged in the agriculture, industry and commercial areas had been consulted only 'tentatively and rarely or not at all' in matters where their expert knowledge might have been valuable and their interests were vitally involved. The National Vocational Assembly, as envisioned by the Commission, would be far more 'democratic' and would give them a real voice.

The three main functions of this new Assembly would therefore be co-ordination, planning and consultation.[74] It would also be the 'final court of appeal' in cases of disputes concerning vocational matters. The Assembly 'should be the supreme centre of vocational effort' for industrial peace and regulation of production. Another main function would be in the area of social and economic planning.[75] In matters such as unemployment and emigration, for example, the Assembly would consider the problems, examine the remedies, calculate the cost and 'propound for adoption' the policy or procedure. Following on from this, as a safeguard against bureaucracy, and as a means of securing 'collaboration', the Assembly 'should be the recognised consultative body' on general vocational or economic questions, to which 'the Government should apply for information, suggestions or advise on the best means of attaining national policy'.[76] The Assembly would also expect that such advice and reports given to the government would be published in *Iris Oifigiuil*, and within three months an official statement should be issued, indicating whether they had been accepted and if not, the reasons for rejection. Similarly, the Assembly would expect, in order to fulfil its consultative functions, that it would be given powers by law to have the right to obtain information and statistics from government departments, and to inspect and report on all statutory orders and regulations, quotas, licences, tariffs and exemptions. Crucially, the Commission expected that the governing body of the new Assembly would be given an opportunity to advise on the preliminary drafts of all Bills dealing with economic or social subjects before introduction into the Oireachtas, and on commercial treaties or agreements under negotiation.[77]

The final part of the report refuted the main criticisms directed at the whole idea of vocational organisation that the Commission had encountered during their work since 1939. Two of these charged that vocationalism merely produced a new form of bureaucracy and that it would in fact result in a duplication of services, thus worsening the position of the consumer.[78] But the Commission argued that the conditions, methods of working, and outlook of vocational bodies would be 'the very antithesis of bureaucracy'. The names of members would be known to all, their policy would be determined by the bodies which employed them, and their tenure in office would depend entirely on the satisfaction they gave these bodies. In numbers and cost, the staffs of the vocational bodies would be 'insignificant' compared to a single department in the civil service. The new vocational system would be designed as a response to what the Commission itself had called for: the elimination of the bureaucratic mentality, methods and conditions, with a view to avoiding that rigidity, and lack of initiative which tended to arise 'when salaries and conditions are not dependent on results achieved'.[79] The Commission also placed great emphasis on 'voluntary service' as an important factor in eliminating 'bureaucratic evils'.

The Commission also swept aside criticisms from the Department of Finance, who had argued that vocational organisation would actually expand the civil service, as the State would have to maintain departmental machinery to supervise vocational groups.[80] The Commission's solution was quite straightforward, but equally startling – 'redundancy'! If and when a vocational body took over the responsibility for a public service, the Commission expected that an inquiry should be made as to 'whether certain sections of the civil service thereupon become redundant and, if it be so found, that immediate steps be taken to secure reduction of staffs'.[81] It was their strongly held view that there were many instances whereby existing State agencies or operations could be transferred to vocational bodies.

Although the report was presented to the government in November 1943, it was not until August 1944 that it was finally published. Given the Commission's deprecation of politicians and civil servants, it was hardly surprising that it received a frosty reception in government circles. In the light of such a dogmatic and prescriptive report, it was equally unsurprising that there was such an energetic silence. Suggestions referring to the 'corruption' of some politicians, and the need to dispense with the services of many civil servants, can only be seen as a naive and preposterous attempt to subvert the democratic process. Politicians were elected and civil servants were directly answerable to the Minister, but this would not be the case with vocational organisation and the members of an Assembly. At the same time, such had been the vitriol of Catholic Action elements that to engage in public debate would have been futile. That spleen had reached its highpoint in October 1943, just before the report was handed over to the government. O'Rahilly, writing in *The Standard*, had been highly critical of the Irish economic and financial establishment. The publication of a special 'economic and financial survey' of Ireland in the July issue of *The Banker*, had given him his final opportunity to attack the powers that be.[82] Ministers Seán T. O'Kelly and Seán Lemass, economists John P. Colbert and James Meenan, and Joseph Brennan of the Central Bank had contributed to the survey. In *The Standard*, O'Rahilly gave little quarter in his comments on their contributions. None of them, as far as he could see, had 'any glimpse into the real problems or how to deal with them'.[83]

Of course the government's real and immediate concern related to two elections in 1943 and 1944, in which they enjoyed renewed triumphs. On no account would they be prepared to abdicate office to a National Vocational Assembly as a non-party power centre in Irish life.[84]

Of significance also for understanding the government's silence was the April 1944 publication of James Meenan's book *The Italian Corporative System*, an exhaustive examination of the whole process of corporatism in Italy from 1922 to 1943.[85] It was more than a coincidence that Professor O'Brien's colleague should have been working on this subject during the Commission's deliberations, and at the height of *The Standard*'s campaign. The work could also help to explain the reluctance of the government to comment till Meenan published his findings. The book certainly pointed out the dangers to Ireland of going down the corporatist road, at a time when the Commission was recommending the Portuguese system.[86] The Jesuit periodical *Studies* pointed out that the book could be read, 'with even greater profit by those ill-informed evangelists who find in the blessed word corporativism – largely because it is polysyllabic and unfamiliar – something which dispenses them from the hard work and clear thinking involved in the drafting a real programme of social reform'.[87]

This *Studies* critique once again highlights the different and contradictory strands of the Catholic Action movement, since another very prominent Jesuit and economist, Fr Edward Coyne, was one of the principle authors of the Vocational Report.

In his book, James Meenan called the whole 'corporative' system 'a thing of shreds and patches'. For him it simply meant the extension of totalitarian technique to the economic processes. Whether it was destined to benefit the employer or worker, or both or neither, was a question of secondary importance. Absolute control by the State was the alpha and omega of corporativism. The principle of independent vocational organisation was never admitted. In an oblique reference to O'Rahilly and *The Standard*, he warned that the admirers of the Fascist brand of corporativism in the Irish Catholic press should take note of what Mussolini was doing and saying in Italy.[88] Irish politicians would hardly have failed to take heed of his warning. Similarly, General Eoin O'Duffy was not a forgotten memory. Meenan stressed the vast difference between theory and practice that characterised so many corporatist institutions. In other words, between the hope and the reality of vocational organisation for Ireland, there was a kaleidoscope of contradictions.

The *Studies* review was particularly blunt in this respect. It argued that while a 'true vocationalism' designed to limit rather than exaggerate the power of the State over the individual, had obviously much to commend it, it certainly was not the 'universal solvent of our present discontents which some of its more ardent advocates claim it to be'.[89] Another Jesuit publication, the *Irish Monthly*, also warned that 'the best laid plans of mice and social reformers often suffer radical modification when an attempt is made to translate them into practice'.[90] This journal, echoing Meenan, hoped that few states would be tempted to imitate the Italian experiment.[91] Amongst those who read Meenan's work was the Minister for Local Government and Health, Seán MacEntee, whose radical local government changes in the 1941 County Management Act (which in effect jettisoned any hope of recognition for subsidiarist or vocational structures) had so incensed the vocationalist lobby. The Minister's annotated copy of Meenan's book gives some insight into MacEntee's views on the subject. For him, corporatism and fascism were one and the same. He saw the basic concept of corporatism as 'the individual participating in the State as a producer not as a citizen'.[92]

The October issue of *Dublin Opinion* captured the attitude of the government. It used the very popular 1944 black comedy *Arsenic and Old Lace* as its inspiration to encapsulate the unspoken feelings of de Valera and his Ministers. The Frank Capra film portrayed Cary Grant as the nephew of a couple of mad aunts with a penchant for mercy-killing old gents: the front cover of *Dublin Opinion* depicted de Valera and Seán T. O'Kelly as the aunts and the Vocational Commission members as the old gents.

According to Professor Fanning, during the years 1942 to 1945 one can trace the beginnings of a debate on issues which were to demand the energies of the Department of Finance in the post-war period.[93] This, in turn, he saw as being related to the 'gradual impact of the economic ideas of John Maynard Keynes upon the Department of Finance'.[94] By late 1943, the winds of change had already overtaken the authors of the Report of the Commission on Vocational Organisation. The initial governmental silence reflected a gradual deep-seated awareness among some members of the government that the country's future was already being shaped by international political and economic events. Individuals such as Meenan and O'Brien had already given hints of developments. O'Brien and O'Rahilly were quite familiar with the writings of Keynes, although both took different interpretations.[95] The 1940s was marked internationally, not least because of the experience of the war itself, by an appreciation of the value of planning, and increasing sophistication of employment and social policies, foreshadowed by Keynes and the British governmental adviser William Beveridge. According to Seán Lemass's recent biographer, John Horgan, it was 'not remarkable that Lemass was part of this international growth of consciousness'.[96] But unfortunately for Lemass, not all his colleagues shared his enthusiasm for the new ideas. De Valera's St Patrick's Day speech in 1943 was certainly not marked by any indication that he was abandoning self-sufficiency.

Despite this, there was certainly evidence that change was afoot. Professor George O'Brien was part of this new movement. He penned two very important articles in *Studies* in 1944, which reflected the new mood. The first, 'Capitalism in Transition', declared that the 'great age of capitalism has passed' (although this idea was certainly not new, and had been a widespread response to the Depression) and the new society would be more egalitarian that the old. There would be less poverty with the help of the Beveridge scheme. Social security would provide against the risks and hazards of life.[97] This new society would be devised through a 'tradition of public service'. Moreover, the British 'bureaucracy' had already shown the way by being equal to the colossal tasks presented by the war. But either way, with regard to the new order of things, as far as O'Brien was concerned, 'that it is on its way is certain. Its outline is unmistakable, its advent inevitable.'[98] Writing later in the same year, he further developed his ideas in an article, 'A Challenge to Planners'.[99] He argued that the fundamental principle of liberalism was capable of an infinite variety of applications involving different degrees of State intervention. He believed that modern conditions in industry called for an increasing amount of public supervision and control. At the same time, the 'socialised' sector of life was growing and would continue to grow. Consequently, 'planning' was an essential feature of contemporary economic conditions. For O'Brien, planning was compatible with freedom; governments need only create conditions in which competition would be as effective as possible, or supplement them when the need arose. These tasks provided a 'wide and unquestionable field for State activity'.[100] He certainly did not share the fears of the Catholic Church that the drift towards totalitarianism was inevitable. Likewise, he did not share the fears of the Vocational Commission that planning could not be left to the Civil Service.

Writing on the impact of the war on the Irish economy, O'Brien argued that whether it be a matter of rejoicing or regret, State intervention would extend still further in the future.[101] He was also president of the Statistical and Social Inquiry Society of Ireland at this time. In early 1945, a debate on the problem of full employment took place at the Society.[102] Two departmental officials, Patrick Lynch (Department of the Taoiseach) and T.K. Whitaker (Department of Finance), took a leading part in the debate, and their contributions revealed the impact of the new Keynesian policies in Ireland.[103] Both officials recognised that controlled and planned State intervention would be required for the proper direction of the Irish economy. An attitude or a policy of self-suf-ficiency was no longer enough. The dynamic force of the government was needed to lift the economy.[104] Small-farm values, shared by both the Catholic Church and Fianna Fáil, were being questioned. According to an editorial in the *New Statesman*, Keynes made it his life's work to 'save capitalism by altering its nature'.[105] George O'Brien shared this view. He believed an 'individualist society could be purged of its abuses'. Crucially, for him, 'the main structure of capitalism must therefore be retained and its foundations strengthened'.[106]

The new Keynesian interventionism, which was helping to shape the think-ing and aspirations of Seán Lemass, was not however shared by the Catholic Action movement. In early 1943, Professor Peter McKevitt pointed out that 'the Beveridge Plan was particularly intended for British conditions; it was not for export'.[107] Speaking on 'The Beveridge Plan Reviewed' at a series of meetings organised by the CYMS during the Catholic Social Week in Dublin, he agreed that the country needed plans, but it would have to do its own thinking. It was for Irish employers and employees to collaborate to give the country a plan of its own. The choice lay between the doctrine of the papal encyclicals and the omnicompetent State. He also pointed to the progress which had already been made in tackling poverty and unemployment through the work of the CSSC.[108]

It was not just the discussions of the merits of the Beveridge Report of 1942 which had alarmed vocationalists. Seán MacEntee's local government centrali-sation policies had alarmed the Vocational Commission. The appointment of County Managers in 1942, and the accompanying new codes governing the activities of local authorities, substantially increased the already formidable powers of central authorities in relation to local authorities.[109]

MacEntee's efforts were the culmination of a process which had been ongo-ing in the area of local government since independence, and even before. Unfortunately, the process coincided with vocationalists fears of 'Statism'. Not only that, but MacEntee's reforms reinforced the principle of ministerial responsibility. Any diffusion of authority to vocational groups or local govern-ment bodies would in fact derogate from this principle. His reforms solidified the process of ensuring that local government would function merely as an agent of central government. Local initiative would henceforth be effectively stultified. Most importantly, MacEntee's efforts frustrated the principle of subsidiarity, since local administration was seen to be subordinate to national government. Local democracy was effectively weakened and subsidiarity was forced to retreat, as henceforth the organisation of local government would be a pyramidal one, with the apex of the structure securely fixed in Dublin.

Professor Mary Daly argues in her work *The Buffer State – The Historical Roots of the Department of the Environment*, that the change in the county management system which MacEntee helped to usher in, 'was very much in character with the general tone of public administration during the Emergency, which was primarily concerned with efficiency, often at the expense of consultation and democracy'.[110]

MacEntee agreed with McKevitt's rejection of the Beveridge Report, but he did not close his eyes to it. The subsequent British White Paper, *A National Health Service* (1944), made an impression on him, and he was well aware of the political gain from improved health services in Ireland.[111] Shortly afterwards, steps were taken to establish a separate government ministry devoted to health, public assistance and national insurance.[112]

The vocationalist lobby was not slow to respond to MacEntee's decision that the health services should be improved as a matter of urgency. Bishop John Dignan of Clonfert, the government-appointed Chairman of the National Health Insurance Society, produced a report on the subject. Dignan's report was a reaction to Beveridge, and Catholic social teaching was given particular prominence. He put forward a different strategy for overhauling the health services. *Social Security: Outlines of a Scheme of National Health Insurance* (1945) postulated that the services were not built on the strong foundations of the Church's social principles but on the 'shifting sands of economics', and should not undermine a father's obligation to support his family.[113] He envisaged removing the health services from the control of local government altogether and transferring responsibility to a governing body under the National Health Insurance Scheme. His plan was an explicit alternative to a state-organised medical service. Referring to the issue of subsidiarity, he argued that the Church would have to be represented on the central and regional committees which would supervise the service.[114]

The government's response to Dignan's plan was hostile. Seán MacEntee refused to argue the issues raised in the plan but instead condemned Dr Dignan for publishing it without submitting it to him first and also for exceeding his terms of reference as chairman of the Insurance Society.[115] When, in August 1945, his term as chairman was up, Dr Dignan was replaced by a civil servant, D.J. Donovan.

But being politically astute, MacEntee was at pains to distance himself from the Beveridge Report. His views on the Beveridge social security, which he expounded in a lecture in March 1945, were widely reported. He pointed out that a totalitarian state was needed for the successful operation of the Beveridge Report and he declared that, 'if Beveridgeism could eradicate poverty, sickness and unemployment, then so could we'. The Irish system would be 'constituted by a community of free men and women, whom the State will exist to serve, and not they to serve the State'. He wanted 'no stamp-licking Irish serfs'.[116] Although MacEntee embraced the Church's concerns over totalitarianism, he did not share their confidence in the corporatist/vocational solution. His reading of Meenan guaranteed that he was cured of any such infection.

It was a difficult time for vocationalists, since Dignan had not been the first advocate to be publicly reprimanded. A few weeks earlier, in February, Seán Lemass gave his view of the Report of the Commission on Vocational Organisation. He called it a 'slovenly document', which contained an 'extraordinary number of misstatements of facts' and 'self-contradictory recommendations'.[117]

The controversy aroused considerable interest in the country. *The Irish Times* welcomed the Dignan Plan in an editorial, and gave much space to summarising the Report of the Commission on Vocational Organisation.[118] As expected, the organs of Catholic Action showed a particular interest in the documents. *The Standard* gave extensive coverage to both. The annual conference of An Rioghacht welcomed the Dignan Plan.[119] Both the Muintir na Tíre Rural Week and the CYMS Catholic Social Week devoted sessions to considering the proposals of the Report of the Commission on Vocational Organisation.[120] Professor McKevitt's new book, *The Plan of Society*, which the CTSI published in October 1944, called for the 'immediate adoption of corporatism in Éire'.[121] He noted that the danger of bureaucratic 'encroachment' on personal liberty, which the extension of officialdom constituted to democratic control, would be prevented with the establishment of 'corporations', which would be 'consulted' by the government when relevant legislation was being contemplated.[122] His book was an apologia for Catholic sociology, and borrowed heavily from the writings of Fr Edward Cahill, Alfred O'Rahilly and Portugal's Salazar.

Whereas James Meenan's *Italian Corporative Organisation* had served as a salutary warning that with this system, employers and employees 'have been united in inferiority to the State',[123] McKevitt's study served as a naive statement of Catholic Action ambitions, when it declared that 'vocationalism is really the fulfilment of trade union ideals'.[124] That the latter statement was certainly not the case we shall examine shortly. However, McKevitt's writings and speeches in late 1944 were to be a springboard for a further stage in the campaign for a National Vocational Assembly.

The strongest response to the two reports came from the Dublin Archdiocese where, in May 1945, representatives from a number of Catholic organisations formed the Catholic Societies Vocational Organisation Conference (CSVOC) to press for the implementation of the Report of the Commission on Vocational Organisation.[125] The CYMS persuaded the various lay organisations to unite in support of the recommendations.[126] In late 1944, they decided that the report should become a 'charter for action' throughout the country.[127] A meeting was held on 12 February 1945 at the Society's headquarters in North Frederick Street, Dublin, which was attended by representatives of most of the country's Catholic societies. Professor McKevitt presided, and John Ryan, editor of *The Irish Catholic* newspaper, was appointed honorary secretary. Shortly afterwards a statement was issued to the press outlining the meeting's plans for the new organisation:

1. That the ultimate object of the CSVOC was to secure the establishment of a social structure in the country based on the principles of vocational organisation, with particular regard to the recommendations of the Vocational Commission.

2. That the immediate object was to 'enthuse' the members of existing Catholic organisations in favour of vocational organisation, and also to influence in that direction by 'propaganda' as many members of the wider community as possible.[128]

With the latter aim in mind, the new organisation quickly produced two booklets. The first, *A Synopsis of the Recommendations of the Commission on Vocational Organisation*, ran to sixty-seven pages with the first edition of 5,000 copies rapidly selling out. The inside cover of the *Synopsis* boldly stated:

> Hundreds of thousands have heard of the Vocational Report, tens of thousands have read it. Thousands have bought it. Hundreds perhaps have studied the Report thoroughly. Here at last is a book for the hundreds of thousands who have not the time to digest the full Report but who will surely wish to know what exactly are the recommendations.[129]

A second publication soon followed, *The Diagrammatic Representation*, which presented the commission's recommendations in graphic form.[130]

Through its constituent societies, the CSVOC had the support of thousands of Catholics throughout the country, and in Dublin, in particular, it was for some years an effective pressure group. That the opposition in the Dáil showed themselves sympathetic to vocationalism, though in different degrees, does show, however, that the campaign achieved some measure of success. The rejecting and shelving of the report did not deter Catholic Actionists, who pressed on for at least another ten years with publications, lectures, marches and articles on the subject.

The Standard, of course, gave the CSVOC its wholehearted support. A front page in June 1945 heralded the organisation with the headline, 'Catholic Action Plan for Vocationalism'.[131] *The Standard* regarded Lemass's 'slovenly document' description as 'an attempt to discredit the Report by abuse and false accusations', and to prevent people from even bothering to read it.[132] They also supported Bishop Michael Browne's strong defence of the report during the annual St Thomas Aquinas lecture in UCG. Browne had rejected Lemass's accusations that there was an atmosphere of unreality about the Report, and that the workers and employers would not accept the new functions to be given to them. In an angry outburst, Bishop Browne told the packed hall that he would like 'to teach public men to control their tongues and not to utter false accusations or gratuitous insults'.[133] The heady and sharp reaction of Browne stimulated considerable interest throughout the country, with the *Irish Independent* and other news media covering the issue.[134]

The reaction had the hallmarks of a campaign heating up. It showed the widening rift emerging in Ireland between different philosophies of government – the vocationalist/corporatist model, with the emphasis on decentralisation and subsidiarity, versus the interventionist, market-driven, model of Seán Lemass, and the centralist, managerial, conservative and financially orthodox, model of MacEntee. The latter two models overlapped at times and they were united in their opposition to the vocationalist model. Similarly, the vocationalists did not differentiate between the latter two models, preferring to categorise them both as 'statists'.

'PEACE IN INDUSTRY': REACTION OF THE LABOUR MOVEMENT TO THE CAMPAIGN

The CSVOC initiated a 'Peace in Industry' campaign that aimed at encouraging better employer–employee relationships. Certain companies responded favourably to the campaign, but the organisation was soon forced to admit that 'there appeared to be little interest among industrialists in the work of the CSVOC'.[135] It would seem that Lemass's diagnosis of the Report of the Commission on Vocational Organisation was correct; trade unions and employers would not accept the new structures. They had no intention of reneging on the organisations that had evolved through conflict and circumstance. Also, the Federated Union of Employers had been established as recently as 1942.

The strongest signal to this effect, however, had already been given anyway by those trade union members who had been on the Commission and who refused to sign the Report. Jim Larkin did not sign, and Luke Duffy, past president of the Irish Trade Union Congress and Secretary of the Labour Party, disassociated himself from it also. Other trade unionists such as Senator Campbell and Louie Bennett of the Irish Women Workers' Union and President of the Irish Trade Union Congress (1948), included reservations disassociating themselves from any suspicion of fascist tendencies that might be read into the recommendations. The former Labour Party leader and senator Thomas Johnson, who had been a key player in the Labour–Fianna Fáil alliance during the 1930s, wrote in November 1944 that, 'the line of policy for the future that is advocated is in many respects reactionary and its criticism very often ill-founded'.[136] He was also keenly aware that the Labour Party itself was under the close scrutiny of 'militant Catholicism as exemplified in Catholic Action'.[137]

Partly because of this scrutiny over alleged communist infiltration of the party, from 1944 to 1950 the Irish Labour Party divided into two rival groups, Labour and National Labour. Tensions between Jim Larkin and William O'Brien, which led to a major split in the trade-union movement, also exacerbated the Labour movement's difficulties during the war years.[138] But what is of particular significance is that Catholic Action failed not only to win support for its cause from prominent trade unionists, but that it alienated them even further from vocationalism. *The Standard*, in highlighting the communist leanings of Labour, as well as reflecting the Catholic Church's long-held distrust of the trade-union movement, did much to sabotage any hope that Labour or trade unionists might see some benefit in new social structures. John Swift, an avowed communist, who was elected president of the Irish Trade Union Congress in 1946, had little time for the Report of the Commission on Vocational Organisation. He found the Commission's disavowal that it was not recommending a corporatist state, implausible. He offered his own interpretation:

> To the members of the Vocational Commission … in the early years of the 1939–45 War, with the victories of the fascist powers, it must have seemed that fascism was invincible. Then, in 1943, came what is accepted as the decisive turn of the War, the Battle of Stalingrad. The subsequent collapse of the fascist forces was not without its message for those who championed the corporatist state, including its advocates on the Vocational Commission.[139]

Dan Norrison, a leading trade union activist who had worked with both Larkins, junior and senior, put in a nutshell the trade-union movement's reason for their unwillingness to accept vocationalism outright – they regarded it as a strategy to prevent strikes.[140] Being co-operative with employers in vocational councils would, they felt, take away their power to negotiate. Vocationalism attacked fundamental trade-union rights and strengths. It would end their strongest weapon – the right to strike – which trade unionists believed would be to the advantage of employers. This attitude was particularly vindicated in 1945 when women workers in the public laundries of Dublin, members of the Irish Women Workers' Union, voted for strike action to secure a fortnight's holiday.[141] On 21 July, 1,500 workers withdrew their labour. The strike lasted fourteen weeks. On 30 October, an agreement between the IWWU and the Federated Union of Employers conceded two weeks' holidays with pay. It was a victory, not just for the laundry workers, but for all trade unionists, who soon followed the women workers' example and secured two weeks' holidays.[142]

It comes as no surprise, then, that the CSVOC campaign made little or no impact on industry in Ireland. Approximately thirty industries made some small attempt to give effect to the application of Christian social principles in the running of their enterprises,[143] but these were merely a superficial recognition of Catholic devotional practices rather than concrete efforts. Factories were dedicated to various patron saints; statues were erected at entrances to places of work or near shop floors. The workers in the Irish Glass Bottle company built an oratory.[144] In Wexford, the sea-aring families combined to build a ten-foot-high statue to Our Lady. In Dublin, thanks to dockers' contributions, a huge 100-foot statue of Our Lady was built at the entrance to Dublin Bay.[145] In the boot factory in Kilkenny, the workers erected an oak crucifix, a replica of the Cross of Cong.[146] There were similar projects at the Dublin foundry of Tongs & Taggart, Roscrea Neat Products, Pye Radio, Sunbeam Wolsey Ltd in Cork, and CIE depots throughout the country (see entrances to Broadstone and Ringsend Garages in Dublin).[147] These efforts did not help the vocational campaign but rather helped to preserve Catholic pieties, devotions, practices and traditions. The CSVOC, however, while failing to achieve its objective of a National Vocational Assembly, persisted through its constituent organisations. These did not become moribund; rather they survived, their energies being deflected to other arenas. But the CSVOC did achieve one of the Catholic Action aims, that of reinforcing the Catholic ethos by placing Catholic social principles at the forefront of public debate in Ireland.

The Standard was convinced that 'popular pressure' was sufficient to ensure that the Vocational Commission's recommendations would not go by default.[148] In 1946, Dr Kinane, Coadjutor Bishop of Cashel, told the Catholic Social Week organised by Muintir na Tíre, that the diffusion of Catholic principles of sociology 'have now become a matter of extreme urgency' because of the collapse of the social order in many countries devastated by the war.[149] The annual conference of the CYMS heard a warning from its president, Mr J. Taylor, that they had to be ready to 'go on the defensive' at a moment's notice.[150] This was unfortunately the received wisdom of the Irish Catholic hierarchy for decades – they consistently adopted an internationalist view and applied it to the Irish situation. They persisted in fearing that what was happening elsewhere was bound to happen to Ireland, or else they adopted solutions found elsewhere as being altogether appropriate for the country. What the papal encyclicals recommended in the context of Germany, Italy or Russia, for example, was taken as to be applied diligently to this country. Dr Kinane told his audience that the whole social fabric was being 'assailed' by anti-Christian forces. That may well have been the case elsewhere, but not in Ireland. Kinane also shared Bishop Browne and Bishop Dignan's assumptions that the moral law was there for all to see, and that it could be applied in only one way. It was a worryingly simplistic application of Catholic moral precepts to the Irish social situation. It was assumed that since the Catholic hierarchy were the guardians of the moral law in society, they could claim to determine which social policy was acceptable.

As a consequence, Catholic Action adopted a defensive outlook. The Knights of St Columbanus's organ *Hibernia* reflected this. An article in late 1945, 'Catholic Action from Day to Day', was highly critical of those 'intent upon sabotaging' the Report of the Commission on Vocational Organisation.[151] The Knights directed their criticism at the 'insidious attempts' of those senior civil servants who they saw as creating a 'fixed line of propaganda' against vocationalists. The Knights were confident in this assertion, having gleaned this information from some of their own members who were senior civil servants in various government departments. They had found that people who had initially favourable views on vocationalism later became hostile and critical. It soon became obvious to the Knights that contact with 'certain officials' in government departments had invariably the same result: a belief that the Report was 'repetitive, redundant, impracticable and uninformed'. But they also directed their ire at many of the public representatives who were regarded as being more interested in their allowances than in the welfare of the people.[152] Maurice Glynn, a prominent member, wondered how these 'sons of the Revolution' had been robbed of their 'mental resiliency', and now seemed averse to 'evolutionary' progress, not to mention 'revolutionary'. With an understanding of the Irish psyche in the 1940s and the conflicts of the different political strategies, he asked, 'Is it that pathetic devotion to the status quo has become an obsession, or are they so determined to hold on to their privileges so that reform of any shape is to be resented?' It was Glynn's contention that if the 'ingenuity' used in discrediting vocationalists and the energy used in 'sabotaging' them was devoted to correcting the serious defects in the country's social life, much could be done to improve the country.[153] The Knights were impressed by what Salazar had done to bring stability to Portugal. *Hibernia* described him as the 'Catholic Actionist Prime Minister of Portugal'.[154]

A number of publications were produced in these years to further the aims of vocationalists, including George Clune's *The Medieval Gild* [sic] *System* (1943).[155] Professor Charles Murphy, President of the St Vincent de Paul Society and Dean of the Law Faculty in UCC, had his work *The Spirit of Catholic Action* published in the same year.[156] Murphy emphasised the importance of charitable endeavours to alleviate poverty. In 1946, under the aegis of Alfred O'Rahilly, UCC began a series of courses for trade unionists based on Catholic social teaching. In 1948, the Jesuits, and Frs Coyne and Kent in particular, established the Catholic Workers' College (later the National College of Industrial Relations) with a similar objective. In 1950, the Archdiocese of Dublin followed suit, with the opening of the Dublin Institute of Catholic Sociology. The fact that some trade unionists had established their own People's College in 1948 was a factor prompting this step. The People's College faced enormous opposition from Archbishop McQuaid, O'Rahilly, *The Standard* and the Jesuits, amongst others.[157] As was its norm, *The Standard* undertook its crusade against the People's College with missionary zeal in excess of anything undertaken by any other opponent. UCD withdrew its support and some trade unions boycotted it. The atmosphere in the mid-to-late 1940s was not conducive to undenominational activities or any kind of activities not in accordance with the strictly regimented Catholic ethos.

While the CSVOC and its constituent organisations were having little success in their campaign, Mrs Berthon Waters of An Rioghacht was advising Seán MacBride on the drafting of economic and social policies for the new political party, Clann na Poblachta.[158] He was the leader of this party, which had been founded in the summer of 1946. Of particular significance was the fact that these policies derived their inspiration and content to a great extent from the Dignan Plan and the third minority report of the Banking Commission.[159] The rejection of the Dignan Plan by the government had played into the hands of their critics, and Clann na Poblachta gladly grasped the ready-made social policy which had the imprimatur of the Catholic Church. They included it in their manifesto and called for its immediate implementation. Seán MacBride strongly endorsed the Dignan Plan in the party's electioneering literature and in particular in their propaganda film *Our Country*.[160] MacBride also used large chunks of the third minority report in his economic policies. Mrs Waters had, with Fr Edward Cahill and Bulmer Hobson, helped draft this report. Consequently, she enjoyed particular influence with MacBride. She wrote numerous economic reports for him, both before and after he became Minister in the inter-party government which supplanted Fianna Fáil in 1948.[161] Evidence of An Rioghacht's influence in the area of economic policies was prominent in his electioneering, with the emphasis on the repatriation of sterling assets, an intensive programme of capital development, afforestation, land reclamation, public-authority housing, and ending the link with sterling. The Clann's policies on TB eradication won them widespread support.

The party's existence generated enormous excitement at a time when the political landscape seemed dull and impervious to change. They won ten seats in the 1948 election, which gained them two ministerial posts in the new government. MacBride and Dr Noel Browne became idealistic, innovatory and talented Ministers. It was partly thanks to the new party that Fianna Fáil were ousted from power after sixteen years.

Nearly all the parties in the new government had expressed some degree of sympathy for vocationalist ideas. A questionnaire sent to all parties by the CSVOC, asking for their views on vocational organisation, had elicited favourable replies from Fine Gael, Labour and Clann na Poblachta.[162] It remained to be seen how they would react in government, and how they would tackle pressing social issues.

VII

REACTION AND CHANGE:
THE STATE, THE FAMILY
AND THE CONSTITUTION

Many of the organisations that were involved in Catholic Action since the 1930s still exist today and, although their numbers are lesser, they remain influential, such as the CTSI (now part of the Catholic Communications Institute/Veritas), the CYMS, the Knights of St Columbanus, Muintir na Tíre and the Legion of Mary.

The theme of this book, that of 'Militant Catholicism', may be illustrated in looking briefly at the organisational structure of the Legion of Mary. It was one of the most influential of these organisations throughout the twentieth century, and was founded by a former civil servant, Frank Duff. The organisation of the Legion was modelled on the Roman Army, starting with the *Praesidium* as its smallest unit, and going up from there. The *Praesidium*, usually a group of four to twenty members, meets weekly in its parish. The *Curia* is the next level up, and one *Curia* supervises several *Praesidia*. The next level is the *Comitium*, which is in charge of several *Curiae*, usually over an area like a big city or a part of a province. The following level is the *Regia*, in charge of larger territories like a province or state. The *Senatus* is the next highest level, and it generally has control over the *Regiae* in a very large area, usually a country or very large territory. The *Concilium* is the highest level. It has its seat in Dublin, Ireland, and has control over the entire Legion.

In 1965, Pope Paul VI invited Frank Duff to attend the Second Vatican Council as a Lay Observer, an honour by which the Pope recognised and affirmed his enormous work for the lay apostolate. These activities were numerous, including work in the area of prostitution, provision of housing and sheltered accommodation, censorship and evangelisation.

TYPES OF MEMBERSHIP

Active members regularly attend the weekly sessions of their *Praesidium* and recite daily the prayer of the Legion, the *Catena Legionis*, which consists essentially of the *Magnificat* and some shorter prayers. Their main role lies in 'active' apostolate for the Legion and the Church. Active members under the age of eighteen are not allowed to give the 'Legion promise' until they reach that age. Members aged eighteen and under are considered Juniors, and are able to hold any office except President in their *Praesidium*. Above the level of the *Praesidium*, no Junior may serve as an officer.

Auxiliary members support the Legion through their prayer. They pray the whole booklet of Legion prayers, the *Tessera*, every day. The *Tessera* consists of the *Invocation*, prayers to the Holy Spirit, the Rosary, the *Catena* and the concluding prayers of the *Tessera*.

Praetorians hold a higher grade of active membership. In addition to their duties as active members, *praetorians* pray the Rosary, the Divine Office and go to Holy Mass daily.

Adjutors are a lever higher again. They additionally pray the *Divine Office* and go to Holy Mass daily.

Praetorians and *Adjutors* do not have higher status or higher rank inside the Legion system. The meaning of these grades is only a desire for a more devotional life, not for higher status. Entering the grade is done by registering with a list of *Praetorians/Adjutors* and by subsequently observing their duties. All this highlights that the Legion of Mary took its role as a Catholic Action organisation particularly seriously.[1]

ONWARD MARCH

A number of other developments illustrate the militant and integralist spirit that was becoming more pervasive in the 1940s and '50s. Fr Denis Fahey was disillusioned with the fact that the 1937 constitution was not Catholic enough. As a result, he established the Marie Duce organisation in late 1945 to campaign not only for vocationalism but also, more importantly, that the State should formally recognise the Catholic Church as the one true Church. The State had already acknowledged, under Article 44 of the constitution, 'the special position of the Holy Catholic Apostolic and Roman Church as the guardian of the Faith professed by the great majority of the citizens', but this, in the eyes of Maria Duce, was not nearly good enough. In late 1949, it proceeded to organise a petition, *Memorandum to Hierarchy, Public Bodies, TDs and Senators*, for the amendment and strengthening of this article. The organisation seemed to reflect some of the tendencies of the decade. It published a journal called *Fiat* with a circulation running into the thousands. Including associate members, it had 5,000 to 6,000 members.

Initially inspired by Catholic social teaching, which it interpreted in a fundamentalist fashion, it was rabidly anti-communist and spearheaded a campaign to amend Article 44 of the constitution to recognise the unique truth of the

Catholic Church's teaching. Fr Denis Fahey died in 1954 and the movement survived until the 1960s as An Fhírinne (the Truth).

In 1946, a member of An Rioghacht, George Gavan Duffy, was promoted to the Presidency of the High Court. He had a major input into Article 40 of the Constitution of Ireland [on Fundamental Rights]. As with Fr Edward Cahill, the founder of An Rioghacht, Duffy often equated Irish Nationalism with Irish Catholicism (an attitude widely held and expressed in Ireland during those decades), and tended to interpret it in the light of Catholic teaching, as in the famous Tilson Case of 1951 (on the Father's right to control a child's education in a 'mixed' marriage). Reflecting current fears of 'statism' among vocationalists, he was a staunch defender of individual rights against the State. In the mid-to-late 1940s, as a result of his rulings, he gave Irish law a more distinctly Catholic cast.[2]

While Maria Duce was working to exalt the juridical status of the Catholic Church, other lay organisations were working on a more mundane level to improve the material status of Catholics. In this respect, the nearly forty organisations that constituted the Catholic Social Services Conference deserve credit.

THE KNIGHTS AS THE 'COMMANDOS' OF MILITANT CATHOLICISM

Meanwhile, the Knights of St Columbanus were increasing the influence of Catholics on hospital boards, although one particular case, the Meath Hospital in Dublin, backfired, because of the over-zealousness of one particular branch of the Knights.

In the 1950s, its campaign against evil literature was stepped up with vigour when a flood of paperbacks and horror comics imported in bulk from the US flooded the country.[3] Furthermore, it was vigilant in the area of cinema and theatre censorship. Artists, intellectuals and left-wing activists who insisted on asking 'Why?', were seen as a disruptive and most unwelcome presence in these decades.

It was not only the official censorship, but also what UCC historian John A. Murphy has called the layers of unofficial, self-righteous, 'busybody censorship'. Then there were all the complex forms of self-censorship, overt and subtle, conscious and unconscious, direct and indirect. While there was no direct censorship of theatre, as there was with literature and cinema, the prevailing atmosphere of censoriousness took its toll there nonetheless. And as we have seen, other media, as well as print, have also been subject to censorship, both official and unofficial. In 1957, the producer of a play at Dublin's Pike Theatre was arrested under the obscenity laws. The court case surrounding the Pike's production of Tennessee Williams's *The Rose Tattoo*, the public outcry against the Abbey's production of Seán O'Casey's *The Bishop's Bonfire*, and the withdrawal of O'Casey's *The Drums of Father Ned* from the Dublin Theatre Festival were cases in point. Even so, there were those willing to swim against the tide and to set forth and defend a more humanistic, a more secular and more cosmopolitan perspective on what Ireland was, and what Ireland ought to be. But there was an uphill battle, as forces much more influential ensured that Ireland would 'keep the faith'.[4]

By the middle of the twentieth century, the Knights had become a particularly influential Catholic lay organisation, drawing its membership from the middle class more so than many of the other organisations. Bishop Neil Farren of Derry saw the Knights as, 'the cream of Catholic Ireland, the great purpose served by the Order is to make Catholic laymen realise their importance in the Church of Christ'. Dr Staunton, Bishop of Ferns, for whom the Knights were 'a dynamic group, full of initiative', said in 1951 that he was glad to note that:

> ... not too long ago there was much clerical action outside the sanctuary and too little lay. This situation is now reversed and the great interest of the Holy See is Catholic Action of all kinds. In this sphere – while I hesitate to make comparisons – I will say that the Knights are second to none. They are the *Commandos*.

Dr Staunton openly approved the methods pursued by the Order, 'methods which did not proclaim themselves to all and sundry, but which nevertheless conveyed a spirit of quiet, steady, enthusiasm'. He would wish others to be like the Knights, 'a hard core of men, sound and unflinching where Christian principles are concerned'.[5] For all his reliance on the Knights, Bishop Staunton failed to involve them in the Fethard-on-Sea Boycott of 1957, which developed following the break-up of a mixed marriage. The bishop's request was debated by the Supreme Council and was duly rejected. This was apparently one of those situations where the Knights believed there were sufficient protagonists in the field to justify their policy of non-involvement.

However, there can be no doubt that the Knights were involved in a huge number of activities. They pinpointed existing areas of communism in Ireland, all emanating from the Book Shop in Pearse Street, Dublin, which in turn was part of a complex comprising the Connolly Clubs in London, the National Committee in Belfast and the Central Committee in London. The Book Shop was 'the centre from which the tentacles of communism spread out in a number of directions'. The Knights were under no misapprehension about the infiltration of communistic ideas at all levels of society.

Their other projects included: the delivery of £5,000 and upwards to Archbishop McQuaid, requesting him to 'remit it to the Holy Father for the defence of the faith in Europe'; criticism of the Irish Football Association for acting host to a Yugoslav team, 'thereby condoning a communistic country which was persecuting the Catholic Church'; provision of funding for the St Vincent de Paul's Sunshine Home in Balbriggan, the Catholic Boy Scouts of Ireland and the St John Bosco's Holiday Homes for Boys, and raising the question of undeveloped areas through Order members in the Senate.

Policies of the Order extended to youth welfare, emigration, employment and a drive towards 'putting Christ back into Christmas' by encouraging the purchase of Catholic art cards produced by the Disabled Artists' Association. They stepped up their campaign against evil literature. They counteracted the activities of the Jehovah Witnesses, who they described as 'subversive, anti-Catholic, anti-Protestant, anti-Jewish and anti-Establishment'. They founded the Marian Invalid Fund in the mid-1950s, which was spearheaded by Peter Bailey of Dublin, with the view to transporting invalids to Lourdes. They also provided: excursions for the blind boys of St Joseph's, Drumcondra; Christmas dinners for Dublin's homeless; funding for the mentally disabled; funding for housing; assistance with the establishment of Listen-Look Groups with the advent of television to Ireland; practical and monetary assistance in the setting up of the Catholic Communications Centre (the CTSI advanced £55,000 towards the centre and the Knights gave a guarantee to the hierarchy of £35,000 from the Order), and the Dublin and Tullamore Councils of the Order took up the cause of Daingean and of Industrial Schools throughout the country. Their persistence in stressing the inadequacies under which these institutions laboured won a 'satisfactory' measure for Daingean from the Minister for Finance in 1969. The Minster agreed to double the capitation fee of £4 per week (the rate in Northern Ireland was £16) and to provide free health services to the reformatory. In the same way, council members in Inishowen 'adopted' Nazareth House in Fahan and they too succeeded in obtaining a better deal for Fahan, which, previous to that date, received 'no State aid, either under our social services schemes or from the local County Councils'. The escalating casualties of modern society became now the special concern of individual councils throughout the country.[6]

By the 1960s, Supreme Knight Dr D.J. O'Mahony was able to say that:

> Our Order is the source from which are derived many committees dealing with Catholic activities throughout the country and our members are to be found, officially and unofficially, in such diverse organisations as the Catholic Social Welfare Bureau, the Catholic Social Service Conference, the St Vincent de Paul Society, the Legion of Mary, the St John Bosco Society, the National Film Institute, the Catholic Societies' Vocational Organisation Committee, the Catholic Young Men's Society, Muintir na Tíre, Safety First, the Catholic Protection and Rescue Society, the Irish Society for the Prevention of Cruelty to Children...[7]

In the area of adoption, the Catholic Protection and Rescue Society of Ireland were able to claim in 1950 that the issue of proselytism had not gone away and that there were still some proselytising agencies 'quite active in the country. We actually removed six children from Protestant institutions and assisted a mother in recovering the custody of her three children from a Bird's Nest.'[8] (The Bird's Nest was the name of one of the best known of these Protestant orphanages, and is sometimes used as a generic term for them all.)

ST JOSEPH'S YOUNG PRIESTS' SOCIETY

Meanwhile, the St Joseph's Young Priests' Society, the organisation that fostered and funded vocations to the priesthood, had branches in every corner of Ireland. In particular its strength lay in having so many branches in the public services, among civil servants, teachers, Gardaí, etc. The estimated strength at the height of its influence ran to 300,000 members. Olivia Mary Taafe established it in Dublin in 1895, with the aim of promoting, fostering and sustaining vocations to the priesthood. In 1994, the membership was close to 100,000, with 439 branches in Ireland.

A major development in the history and influence of the society was the establishment of a civil-service branch in 1930. By the end of its first year 2,500 had been enrolled, and by 1935 it had 5,000 members. This figure rose to 10,000 in 1940 and to 17,000 in 1957, and the financial contribution to the society from the civil-service branch reflected a large membership. Within four months of the establishment of the civil-service branch an electricity service branch was set up, mainly from employees of the Electricity Supply Board (ESB), which had been established in 1927. Its membership had increased to 4,500 by 1958. By 1959, more than 4,000 primary teachers were enrolled in their own branch. Other branches were set up among railway workers, bus workers and other transport workers in CIE, and eventually they all amalgamated into the transport branch, with a membership of 10,000 in 1958, making it the second largest branch. The insurance branch had 2,000 members by 1962. Bank officials, local-authority employees, bacon-trade employees, licensed-trade employees, laundries, engineers, brewers and distillers, aviation employees, meat trade, motor trade, commercial, and legal, were all 'vocational' branches set up and developed in these years to give the society a huge membership throughout the country and a corresponding influence on the Catholic Action activities (emphasised by its new constitution in the late 1940s) and attitudes of the members themselves.[9]

MOTHER AND CHILD SCHEME CONTROVERSY OF 1951

In 1950/1, Dr Noel Browne, Minister for Health in the first inter-party government, drew up proposals for free medical care for mothers and for children under sixteen. This has been seen by some as the State's first steps towards taking responsibility for family life, including mandatory State entry to the home by health workers. Although Browne had apparently believed that he had secured the acquiescence of the Catholic bishops, they denounced the scheme as contrary to the Catholic principle of subsidiary function (that the State should not intervene in cases where a lower organisation, in this case the family, could provide what was needed).

John Costello, as Taoiseach and Seán MacBride, as Browne's party leader, joined in forcing Browne's resignation. Their action, accompanied by extravagant declarations of their obedience to Church teaching, enshrined the episode as a demonstration of the political power of the Church. But it also suggested that the powerful Irish Medical Association, whose members were reluctant to lose fee-paying patients to a State service, manipulated the bishops themselves. In 1953, Browne's Fianna Fáil successor, James Ryan, successfully introduced a broadly similar scheme, but excluded the 15 per cent of families in the highest income bracket.

Noel Browne had become Minister for Health in 1948, but he did not immediately introduce the scheme; instead he concentrated on other aspects of healthcare reform. Even before the introduction of the scheme, there was some disquiet among the Catholic Church and medical profession. Whilst in opposition, Fianna Fáil had pushed for the introduction of the scheme.

In 1950, Browne proposed introducing a scheme that would provide free maternity care for all mothers and free healthcare for all children up to the age of sixteen, regardless of income. It met with ferocious opposition from conservative elements in the Catholic hierarchy and the medical profession. The Catholic Church leadership was divided between those like Archbishop of Dublin John Charles McQuaid, who believed that it was the exclusive right of all parents to provide healthcare for their children, and younger moderates like William Philbin, who saw some merit in state assistance for families. Some bishops, like MacQuaid, also feared that it could pave the way for abortion and birth control. 'The State will become the Mother and Father to us all', warned the Bishop of Cork when objecting to the scheme. Though some Catholic Church leaders may have been privately sympathetic to Browne and wished to reach an accommodation, what was viewed as Browne's tactless handling of the Catholic Church forced the moderates into silence, allowing the anti-Mother and Child Scheme members of the hierarchy, under McQuaid, to set the agenda.[10]

Many doctors disapproved of the scheme, some on principle, others because they feared a loss of income and becoming a kind of civil servant, referring to the plan as 'socialised medicine'. Browne refused to back down on the issue but received little support, even from his Cabinet colleagues, most of whom he had alienated on other matters, notably his failure to attend many cabinet meetings and the lack of support he had shown them in other crises. Browne was isolated in cabinet as a 'loner' who did not consult with his more experienced cabinet colleagues.[11]

He also faced the hostility of his own party leader, Seán MacBride, with whom Browne had also fallen out, as he had with most members of the Clann na Poblachta Parliamentary Party, who resented his appointment to cabinet over the heads of more senior colleagues, and who were also offended by his treatment of them.[12]

In April 1951, MacBride demanded Browne's resignation as a Clann na Poblachta Minister. Browne duly submitted his resignation to the Taoiseach John A. Costello for submission to President O'Kelly.[13] The resignation took effect from 11 April 1951.

Some believe that doctors drew the bishops into the row, while John Charles McQuaid, the powerful Archbishop of Dublin, was himself a doctor's son with strong views about the status of the profession. When their views were invited, the bishops avoided stating whether the plan was at odds with Catholic morality but denounced it as at variance with the Church's social teaching.

At the root of their opposition was the perception that Browne's scheme would open the way to liberal family planning and contraception. The actual demise of the weakened coalition in the general election of May 1951 was not decided by the Mother and Child Scheme, however, but by the desertion of rural Independents over its failure to raise the price of milk.[14]

When Browne resigned from government on 11 April 1951 the scheme was dropped. He immediately published his correspondence with Costello and the bishops, something that had hitherto not been done. Ironically, derivatives of the Mother and Child Scheme would be introduced in Acts of 1954, 1957 and 1970.

JAMES MCPOLIN, DOCTOR AND CATHOLIC ACTIONIST

In his memoirs, James Deeny, Chief Medical Officer in 1944, described how the new State was confronted with a crumbling and neglected poor-law system, which had been badly run down. The country had the worst tuberculosis problem in Western Europe and a chronic typhoid problem. It also had a very high infant mortality rate, with large numbers of babies dying from enteritis, and a high maternal mortality rate. There was particular concern about these mortality rates – the most fundamental quality indicators of any public health system. New and radical proposals were needed to address this major problem and it was within this appalling context that Dr Noel Browne introduced the Mother and Child Scheme through the 1947 Health Act, which provided for state-funded healthcare. This was opposed by Fine Gael, who felt that general practitioners' private practices would be significantly affected. More ominously, the Catholic bishops feared that a State medical service would ultimately include sex education and information about contraception and abortion, and that the State might take control of Catholic hospitals.

Dr James McPolin, who was the Chief Medical Officer for County Limerick at the time, was particularly vocal in relation to this Act. He had previously had an altercation with the Department of Health, which considered suspending him because health services in Limerick were a 'black spot', and McPolin emerged as an ardent opponent of State medicine despite the fact that he was State salaried himself. In a series of articles he argued that State medicine contravened moral law, that it was the father's duty to provide medical care for his dependants and that it was the role of the family doctor and the church, and not the State, to educate mothers and children about health.

He had already voiced disapproval of any State interference in health provision for families in an article entitled, 'Public Health Bill', in *Christus Rex*, in 1947. The *Christus Rex* journal, in its early years, voiced these fears of 'Statism'. Contributors seemed more anxious to pass moral judgments than to spend time amassing the facts. More pages were devoted to denunciations of excessive state intervention than to any other subject.

According to Patrick Conway writing in *Christus Rex* on the subject, 'Self-help through Muintir na Tíre is preferable to state assistance and the regulations made through vocational organisations are better than Civil Servant's red tape.' Similarly McPolin, was critical of the 1947 Public Health Bill, claiming that it contravened natural law and the Irish Constitution. He had already written on the importance of the family and similar themes in the *Limerick Leader* on 28 December 1946, in an article called, 'The State is a Glutton for Power'. In this hard-hitting article McPolin warned of the necessity for vigilance against any threat to the family from the State. McPolin successfully lobbied public opinion and Church leaders to recognise the dangers ahead. The Catholic hierarchy obviously hadn't the time to examine every piece of legislation which passed through the Dáil that might contravene Catholic social teaching. It was the Catholic Action movement and McPolin in particular, who drew their attention to the possible dangers in the 1947 legislation. Also under McPolin's influence, the Limerick Branch of the Irish Medical Association had become the 'outspoken antagonists against the proposed changes'.[15]

The response of the Supreme Knight of the Knights of St Columbanus, Mr Stephen Mackenzie, to the crisis, may be seen in the following comment:

> Referring to the recent controversy over the proposed Mother and Child Scheme, the Supreme Knight said it was lamentable to see the large number of Catholics who disagreed with the teaching of the hierarchy and the number of highly educated people who did not appear to know the rudiments of the Catholic religion. 'The organ of the Protestant minority', he said, 'missed few occasions to discredit the doctrines and leaders of the Catholic Church, and this year it had openly attacked the religious leaders of the people. One aspect of the attack by *The Irish Times* was the confidence with which those who represented the Cromwellian traditions of Ireland were attempting to continue that tradition of endeavouring to drive the Catholic Church out of the life of the country.[16]

The reaction of Catholic Actionists after the crisis, then, was not to question the direction of their movement, but to reiterate current Catholic teaching with greater emphasis. There was never so many denunciations of State power as in the year or two after the Mother and Child Scheme crisis. Canon Hayes told a Muintir na Tíre gathering that the logical conclusion to increasing State power was to be found in the Kremlin.[17]

According to J.H.Whyte, in his *Church and State in Modern Ireland*,'the characteristic weaknesses of the Catholic Action movement were accentuated after the crisis. The dangers of State power were so much stressed that opposite dangers, such as that the State might not intervene enough to protect weaker citizens, were almost forgotten.'The major social problem of mass emigration was practically overlooked by the movement, which was still at an adolescent phase. First principles were still being applied too enthusiastically to particular situations without rigorous examination of the logic. The bishops' arguments too, in their pronouncements on social ethics, lacked cogency.[18]

Finola Kennedy, in her recent book, *Cottage to Crèche: Family Change in Ireland*, cautions that when examining the Mother and Child controversy, the role of the medical profession should not be minimised. This was as much a class conflict as anything else. The Catholic Actionist James McPolin, for example, not only excoriated the notion of the State interfering in the medical affairs of private families, but also objected to the scheme 'on the grounds that it obliterated a whole section of private practice for doctors'. Central to Kennedy's thesis is that economic influences were more important in the long term than the social and moral teaching of the Catholic Church – a significant challenge to more traditional interpretations of the power and influence of religion.[19]

As indicated, it was members of Catholic Action groups who alerted the Irish Catholic hierarchy to the impending threat from State involvement in family life.

THE RED PERIL AND THE IRELAND–YUGOSLAVIA
FOOTBALL GAME OF 1955

The reaction to perceived State encroachment was also illustrated in the response to the Ireland–Yugoslavia soccer match held in 1955. Catholic Actionists always saw communism as a huge threat, and any encroachment by the State in family and social issues was seen as being just a short step to full-blown communism in Ireland. The communist state of Yugoslavia was completely anathema to the prevailing Catholic orthodoxy in Ireland and represented and encapsulated the fears about communist infiltration and State control. That anyone should have any dealings with representatives of that country implied giving recognition to its politics.

According to writer Conor McCabe in 'Catholics, Communists and Hat-Tricks', a recent article about the controversial game, in 1955 the Irish political, cultural, and religious establishment found itself challenged by an unusual and reluctant opponent: The Football Association of Ireland (FAI). The clash arose over a friendly soccer game between the Republic of Ireland and Yugoslavia, which was played at Dalymount Park on 19 October of that year. The Catholic

Archbishop of Dublin, Dr John Charles McQuaid, one of the dominant figures in Irish twentieth-century life, called for the cancellation of the game. Various government ministers and senior civil servants echoed this, as did Catholic lay organisations. The Irish national broadcasting service Radio Telefís Éireann (RTÉ) declined to cover the game after its main sports commentator, Phil Greene, pulled out of the broadcast. The protests arose out of the continued persecution of the Catholic Church in communist Yugoslavia, and were similar in tone to other protests held in Ireland over the previous seven years.[20]

CATHOLIC ACTION OPPOSITION INCREASES

One of the first signs of opposition to the game came in August at a meeting of the Waterford District Football League. A Waterford clerk, Mr Leo P. Dunne, told the meeting, which was attended by the chairman of the FAI, Mr Prole, and its secretary, Mr Wickham, that the visit of the Yugoslav team was against all Christian principles, in view of the persecution behind the Iron Curtain. The meeting decided to take no action, as it was a matter for the FAI, but Mr Tim Galvin, who was the assistant branch secretary of the Waterford ITGWU, supported Mr Dunne in his protest. On Thursday 13 October, *The Irish Catholic*, in an article headed 'Tito's footballers in Dublin', reported that the Catholic Federation of Secondary Schools' Union had protested 'against the coming to Dublin of a team representing Yugoslavia'.

The response from the Irish laity was robust, as expected. In a letter to the FAI, Mr M.L. Burke, supreme secretary of the Knights of St Columbanus, wrote that 'it is most regrettable that your association, in which so many tens of thousands of Irish Catholics are found, has failed to realise how distasteful to Irish Catholics is this link with a communist-dominated country'. However, it was not long before a decidedly open hostility to communism emerged, when the Knights agreed that Ely House should be the centre for a combined protest from Catholic organisations condemning the executive of the Irish Football Association for acting host to the Yugoslav team, 'thereby condoning a Communist country which was persecuting the Catholic Church'.

The secretary-general of the Guilds of Regnum Christi, Mr M. O'Connell, told the press that his organisation supported the protests because the 'communist government of Yugoslavia would make capital out of it in its struggle with the Catholic Church'. The League of the Kingship of Christ released a statement on Sunday night, which emphasised 'the existence of a special bond of union between ourselves and our brothers who suffer behind the Iron Curtain, because they and we are members of one another in the mystical body of Christ', and that charity demands that asylum should be granted to any player who so wished it. The president of An Rioghacht, Mr Brian J. McCaffery, said that asylum should be offered to any player who wishes to remain in Ireland, while at the same time criticising the Department of Justice for the 'amazing and absurd guarantee which has been forced on the Football Association of Ireland'. This was in reference to the stipulation by the Department of Justice that the FAI should cover the living costs of any player who wished to seek asylum. The Catholic Association for International Relations wrote an open letter to the Yugoslav players, which stated that that while 'our football association is a free, voluntary organisation of sportsmen, having no connection with the government ... yours is under the control of a state department', and that the bulk of the Irish people 'are unhappy about your visit'.

The Chief Scout of the Catholic Boy Scouts of Ireland, Mr J.B. Whelehan, wanted the match stopped, and said that 'neither good relationship nor brevity of time can excuse want of principle or lack of courage'. He wrote:

> Must Irish Catholics stand calmly by while the tools of Tito disport themselves and are fêted in the capital of Catholic Ireland? Has the FAI forgotten the exploits of the gentle Tito, the tyrant-jailer of a prince of the Church ... and relentless persecutor of bishops, priests and laity, some of whom were petrol-soaked and set aflame with complete immunity by Tito's heroes?

Pre-match speculation on the possible attendance ranged from 5,000 to 35,000, 'the fixture having aroused such varying degrees of indignation and sympathy'.[21] In the end, the official figure for attendance was 22,000, although *The Irish Times* and *The Irish Press* put the figure at 21,400, with the *Press* adding that the gate for the game was £4,000. The average Dalymount gate for a game against a team of Yugoslavia's calibre was £40,000. Although there had been talk of a walkout by at least some of the Irish players, this proved to be unfounded, and the team played as named on 12 October. Gardaí and detectives were on duty at the ground, both inside and outside, but there were no incidents. John Cooney, in his biography on MacQuaid, wrote that the supporters 'had to pass a picket of Legion of Mary members carrying anti-communist placards'. Author Tim Pat Coogan, who wrote that the 21,400 showed up 'despite having to pass a large picket formed by Catholic Actionists', makes a similar claim. The only visible protest on the day, apart from the drop in attendance, came from one man who carried a papal flag as he walked outside the entrance to Dalymount Park. He was named by *The Irish Press* as Mr Gabriel Diskin, a Dublin-based journalist.[22] Diskin worked for *The Irish Press* at the time. However, the fact that only half of the normal attendance turned up, did indeed point to a victory for Catholic Action and the Church.[23]

HUMANAE VITAE AND CHAINS OR CHANGE

Towards the late 1950s and early 1960s, the ideological commitment of Catholic Action was less pronounced. However, the movement remained as active as ever, although certain organisations disappeared. The Legion of Mary sent Frank Duff as a lay representative to the proceedings of the Second Vatican Council. An Rioghacht petered out at about this time, but Muintir na Tíre, the Catholic Truth Society of Ireland and the Knights of St Columbanus remained vigorous, as did many of the lesser organisations. Muintir na Tíre sponsored the Limerick Rural Survey to investigate the actual needs of the Irish rural people. The Knights continued to be vigilant in the area of theatre and film censorship and indecent publications. Vocational organisation was no longer pressed and the CSVOC became dormant about 1960. The Catholic Workers' College was renamed the College of Industrial Relations.

The launch of Ireland's own television network, Telefís Éireann; the continuing attraction of the cinema; Pope John XIII and the Second Vatican Council; the arrival of John F. Kennedy to Ireland and the Beatles to Dublin; the dance hall and showband blitz; the changing of the old political guard with the advent of Séan Lemass and the influence on economic matters of T.K. Whitaker; the application to join the Common Market; Ireland's role in UN peacekeeping activities; the 1968 encyclical *Human Vitae* (On Human Life); the 'swinging sixties'; the international political convulsions and students' riots, and the rise of the Irish Women's Liberation Movement all generated a huge psychological shift, which jettisoned and challenged many of the settled beliefs, traditions and attitudes previous generations took for granted.

THE CONTRACEPTION CHALLENGE

As the psychological climate changed rapidly in Ireland during the 1960s, it was natural that laws inherited from past periods should come under increasing scrutiny. One Catholic document had, and still has, enormous repercussions for Militant Catholicism in Ireland – *Humanae Vitae* (On Human Life), issued by the Vatican in 1968.

Before this new encyclical was published, in Ireland the papal encyclical *Casti Connubii* (On Christian Marriage), issued on 31 December 1931, was regarded as the ultimate Catholic guide to the sanctity of marriage and the immorality of birth control. In a state with an overwhelming Roman Catholic majority there was little room for dissent, and in the prevailing social climate people were generally satisfied with the legal restrictions on divorce, contraception and abortion.

In the socially conservative climate of Ireland in the 1920s and 1930s, the family issues of divorce, contraception and abortion were settled with little controversy and were not to become major issues again until the late 1960s and early 1970s. Abortion was outlawed in Ireland under the Offences Against the Persons Act (1861). The advocacy and sale of birth-control devices were outlawed in the Irish Free State under the 1929 Censorship of Publications Act (which the main

Catholic Action group, the CTSI, were primarily responsible for initiating and monitoring) and the remaining loopholes regarding the importation of contraceptives were closed under the Criminal Law Amendment Act (1935).

Divorce by civil process was available in England from 1857, but extension of this process to Ireland was strongly opposed by both Catholic and Protestant clergy. In the early years of the Irish Free State, the introduction of private divorce bills in Dáil Éireann caused alarm and led to the official banning of divorce in 1925. To solidify this position the 1937 Constitution of Ireland had included an unequivocal ban on divorce.

Whereas the Irish State's legal position on civil divorce and abortion remained relatively uncontroversial until the early 1980s, the issue of family planning reared its head considerably earlier, primarily because of concerns regarding maternal health. Some doctors and Protestant clergymen on the Commission on Emigration in 1956 dissented from the commission's disapproval of 'family limitation', on the grounds that large families on low incomes weakened the health of women and children. From the 1960s, doctors were permitted to prescribe the contraceptive pill for menstrual regulation. In 1963, the pharmaceutical companies were able to introduce the Pill as a 'cycle regulator', but it was not advertised as a contraceptive. Nonetheless, it was at a grassroots level that change gradually began, involving key members of the medical profession and lay activists.

The fundamental reason for the power and impact of the availability of the Pill (a phrase loosely used to mean all artificial contraception) is that it handed over complete fertility control to women. It empowered (or seemed to empower) women.[24] A journalist called Mary Kenny was one of the founding members of the Irish Women's Liberation Movement in the late 1960s and in its time the Pill was seen as a 'wonder-drug' that changed the whole agenda of sexuality.

There was a general sense of optimism among Catholic liberals that the spirit of the Second Vatican Council would translate into some kind of a tacit acceptance of Catholics' right to limit their families by artificial means. The papal encyclical *Humane Vitae* was therefore considered a major setback, as it reiterated the Catholic Church's opposition to contraception. There was a bitter sense of being let down when the encyclical came out against all artificial contraception. The Archbishop of Dublin, John Charles McQuaid, used the encyclical to institute a ban on contraceptive advice being issued in the Dublin hospitals under his control.

In September 1968, the Knights of St Columbanus registered 'full and filial obedience to the encyclical *Humanae Vitae*' and recommended to its members to study the encyclical, to give the widest possible publicity to the teaching embodied in the document, and that in undertaking the study, be subject to the guidance of its own national hierarchy.[25] Dr Cornelius Lucey, Bishop of Cork, in his address at the Knight's Annual Meeting of June 1971 said, 'Knights, by definition, are people who dedicate themselves to a life of outstanding loyalty to some person or cause … the hard way, the uncompromising way, the traditional Irish way…'.[26]

Contraception was indeed one of the main issues of the day in 1960s Ireland. Not surprising, since, according to Mary Kenny in *Goodbye to Catholic Ireland*, 'there can hardly be anything that concerns a woman's life more directly than how many children she will have'.[27] The majority of Catholics were still guided by the traditional ban on 'artificial' birth control. Because the sale or prescription of contraceptives was also against the law in Ireland, people had to cross the border into Northern Ireland to get them. The new modernising spirit following the Second Vatican Council (1959-1963) suggested that the Council would relax the old rule.

When Pope Paul's encyclical *Humanae Vitae* was issued in 1968, it reaffirmed the traditional teaching of the Catholic Church. However, it sent shock waves across the world – and Ireland to a lesser extent. Fr James Good, a moral theologian at UCC, called the decision a 'major tragedy' and predicted that the 'majority of Catholic theologians and ... lay people' would reject it. The Irish bishops, however, publicly supported the Pope. A new organisation, the Irish Family League, campaigned vociferously against contraception. The Knights of St Columbanus likewise lobbied for a ban on the sale of contraceptives.[28]

However, the encyclical did mark a watershed: for the first time, a significant majority in Ireland chose to disregard a central teaching. Moreover, many clergy were encouraging them. In 1973, the Irish bishops issued a statement noting that when the Church's declared a behaviour wrong, it did not mean that the State needed to make it illegal. This remarkable concession was followed by two decades of increasing secularisation in Ireland, but precipitated decades of clashes between the Catholic Militants and some of the new generation of Irish people. As a sign of the changing face of Ireland, in 1972, nearly 85 per cent of voters approved a referendum to remove the reference to the Church's 'special status' from the Irish Constitution.[29]

Humanae Vitae of 1968 was the successor to *Casti Connubii* of 1931. It had a similar influence on Catholic Actionists as the previous encyclical. It re-invigorated them to defend the letter and law of the encyclical. Likewise it gave them the *raison d'être* to campaign to protect and defend challenges to the constitutional protection for marriage and family life. But *Humanae Vitae* was a catalyst in Ireland for a concerted reaction, which persists well into the twenty-first century.

UNDOING THE CHAINS: THE IRISH WOMEN'S LIBERATION MOVEMENT

From 1922, feminists opposed women's exemption from jury service, attacks on women's working rights in 1935 and their consignment to a domestic role in de Valera's constitution of 1937. Representatives of the 28,000-member Joint Committee of Women's Societies and Social Workers, the Catholic Federation of Women's Secondary School Unions, and the National Council of Women in Ireland stoutly affirmed their feminism to the Commission on Vocational Organisation in 1940, demanding that 'homemakers' be given an authoritative voice in the proposed vocational assembly. The Irish Housewives Association (1942) defined women's issues as everything from consumer issues to children's welfare and women's political representation. It was regularly attacked by the Christus Rex Society through the pages of its journal *Christus Rex* for its support of school meals and co-operative housekeeping ventures. It supported Dr Noel Browne's Mother and Child Bill of 1950/1.

In Ireland, the lack of ready availability of the Pill acted as a catalyst to challenge the law of the Ireland prohibiting other methods of contraception that, by the late 1960s, was being eroded by custom and practice.[30] Therefore, the ban on the Pill by law and by encyclical and the accompanying furore, combined with the developing feminist movement, was the mixture that led to decades of confrontation between Militant Catholicism (adhering to *Humanae Vitae* and its successors) and the new social forces (driven by ideological feminism) in Ireland. The focus on contraception and the ideas that the Pill unleashed, made for a heady mixture that spurred a very successful women's movement.

In the 1960s and 1970s, the high-profile, Dublin-based Irish Women's Liberation Movement attracted the most publicity. It sent shock waves through Irish society. The founders included a number of journalists like Mary Kenny and Mary Maher, who were to disseminate its message to the media. Other prominent activists in the new social revolution movement included Nuala Fennell, later an Irish Government Minister and founder of AIM (Action, Information, Motivation), which was to be an inspiration for much political change over the next twenty years, and future President of Ireland, Senator Mary Robinson. A manifesto, 'Chains or Change', was agreed and delivered to the people of Ireland on *The Late Late Show* of 6 March 1971. It contained five demands: equal pay, equality before the law, equal education, contraception, and justice for deserted wives, unmarried mothers and widows. An irreversible start had been made in making the status of women a political issue.

The issues of feminism and sexuality would become central and often troubling in Irish Catholic culture over the next twenty-five years. Traditionally, women in Ireland had upheld the Church. After the 1970s, a new anti-clericalism was apparent among women, some of it aroused by the birth-control question. Catholicism and feminism parted company on the issue of reproduction. The Catholic Church would not, and indeed, in consideration of its theology, *could* not agree that it was 'the woman's right to choose'. The Pill issue, and subsequently, the abortion issue, was an unavoidable course of collision. Consequently, on the major biological revolution of the time, the Catholic Church and Militant Catholicism would be feminism's foes.[31]

Women's issues became news on radio and television. *The Irish Press*, *The Irish Times* and the *Irish Independent*, in response to the chord that the movement struck, all started feminist 'women's pages'.[32]

However, the ongoing pressure put on the government by the Irish Housewives Association and the Irish Countrywomen's Association, among others, to appoint a commission to review the status of women, probably also had considerable impact. The Commission on the Status of Women in 1970 led to the Council for the Status of Women as a monitoring body in 1973. The feminists of the 1970s and 1980s, while they did build upon the earlier feminist concentration on women's household work, prioritised the redefinition of women's legal and social relationship to the family, economic resources, education, employment and public life. Key reforms followed, while groups like Irishwomen United, Irish Feminist Information, Cherish, Rape Crisis Centres and many others testified to the renewed popular interest in women's rights. It was in this new context – a veritable social revolution, a shift from patriarchal ideology – that the battle lines were drawn for the next twenty years and for more amendments to the Constitution of Ireland.[33]

The tide of change, then, was not stemmed. Women began to give sex education talks in some Protestant schools, and the Fertility Guidance Company set up a family-planning clinic in Dublin in 1969. The group of medical volunteers behind this company issued free advice and free contraceptives, circumventing the law by not selling the contraceptives. Small groups like Irish Women United, Contraception Action Programme, the Dublin Well Woman Centre, and the Women's Right to Choose Group developed to challenge the settled law, sometimes quietly and sometimes with high-profile events such as the 'Pill train', which carried contraceptives illegally from Belfast to Dublin. On 22 May 1971, the Irish Women's Liberation Movement travelled to Belfast on what became known as the 'contraceptive train' in order to bring back contraceptives across the border to the Irish Republic, thereby raising public awareness. Meanwhile, a young Catholic lawyer, Senator Mary Robinson drafted a bill to legalise contraceptives and placed her Criminal Law Amendment Bill before the Senate in March 1971. Both of Robinson's attempts to have her Bill ratified failed. In 1973, the Supreme Court's decision to reverse the High Court decision on the McGee case was considered a watershed in the contraception debate. Mrs McGee claimed that she had attempted to import contraceptives via the post for personal use and her package had been intercepted by customs. She had taken a case against the Attorney General, claiming that the Criminal Law Amendment Act (1935) was inconsistent with the section of the 1937 constitution that vowed to respect the rights of citizens. The Supreme Court's ruling that Mrs McGee's rights had been interfered with effectively annulled the previous legislation, and opened the way for Irish citizens to import contraceptives for their own use.

In 1979, the sale and distribution of contraception information was no longer 'obscene and indecent' and in the same year the Health (Family Planning) Act legalised the sale and distribution of contraceptives to people for *bona fide* family-planning purposes. Soon afterwards all restrictions on the sale of contraceptives were removed.

On 13 December 1978, Charles Haughey, the Minister for Health in the Fianna Fáil government, had introduced a Health (Family Planning) Bill, which allowed contraceptives on prescription to be available to married couples, and legalised the importation of contraceptives for sale in chemist shops. This law became operative in 1980, though it remained illegal until 1985 to sell contraceptives to anyone without a medical prescription.[34]

These huge developments precipitated some Catholic activists and organisations to respond and become revitalised in the 1970s. Those advocating the easing of Ireland's ban on contraception had thrown the gauntlet down initially. Catholic groups were dismayed by what they saw as the comparatively liberal Health and Family Planning Act (1979), which permitted the distribution of contraceptive devices by prescription. This development in particular suggested that the Constitution of Ireland was not completely secure from challenge, and pinpointed the urgent need to copper fasten it against abortion, the logical extension to the liberalisation of the contraception laws. This time Militant Catholicism would not be wrong-footed and would instead take the initiative.

FROM CONTRACEPTION TO ABORTION: THE CAMPAIGN TO AMEND THE IRISH CONSTITUTION

Militant Catholicism did not stand by idly in the face of these dramatic developments. Recognising the inevitable challenge to the Irish Constitution that would come from those who had been involved in the campaign to ease Ireland's contraception laws, Catholic activists had decided that their best strategy was to campaign for a constitutional amendment, which would copper fasten the legal ban on abortions in Ireland. In 1983, a new pro-life group made up of members from a variety of Catholic organisations, as well as doctors, nurses and lawyers, campaigned successfully for a referendum that added to the Irish Constitution a clause asserting the equal right to life of the mother and unborn child.

Abortion, outlawed in Ireland under the 1861 Offences Against the Person Act, became a significant political issue in the early 1980s. In 1982, Ireland had three different governments, so political volatility helped push the issue to centre stage. As power swung back and forth between Fine Gael and Fianna Fáil during 1982 and 1983, both parties were eager to appeal to the large pro-life constituency, and therefore, they backed the effort by Catholic lay activists in particular to amend the Irish Constitution. It was the Fianna Fáil wording that eventually went to the people in a referendum to amend the Irish Constitution. Pro-life groups quickly moved to use the new right-to-life amendment to prevent activity likely to lead to abortions.

The Pro-Life Amendment Campaign, or PLAC (which was simultaneously the name of an organisation as well as the name of a campaign) of the early 1980s, lobbied successfully for an amendment to the Irish Constitution to protect the right to life of the unborn, which led to the insertion of Article 40.3.3 into the Irish Constitution protecting that right (as well as the equal right to life of the mother). The Eighth Amendment of the Constitution of Ireland effectively introduced a constitutional ban on abortion, which was approved by referendum in Ireland on 7 September 1983 and signed into law on 7 October of the same year. It is often called the Irish Pro-Life Amendment. The very pro-active campaign also had an influence on the 1992 Maastricht Protocol that guarantees Ireland's Constitutional protection for the unborn.[35]

In 1985, the Society for the Protection of the Unborn Child (SPUC) took legal action against two Dublin clinics that counselled women and sometimes referred them to the UK for abortions. In 1986, these clinics were ordered to cease counselling. In 1992, the Supreme Court overturned a High Court decision to prevent a fourteen-year-old girl pregnant as a result of rape from leaving the country to get an abortion. A constitutional amendment recognising the right to travel and the right to information was carried by a referendum later that year.

The 1983 abortion referendum brought out into the open the bitter cultural conflict between Catholic, rural Ireland and secularised, urban Ireland (rightly did Tom Hesketh call it 'the Second Partitioning of Ireland'). It was far more rigorously pursued by lay Catholics than by the clergy. Hesketh shows that the impetus and the energy for the referendum came from populist lay Catholics – their opponents would describe them as 'fundamentalist right-wing Catholics' – to whom the politicians were quick to respond, and whom they were, indeed, anxious to manipulate. The referendum carried, but the pro-life advocates were to be mortified by the unexpected and notorious X Case of February 1992, when a fourteen-year-old girl was involved in an abortion controversy that shocked the world. There was universal sympathy for the girl who had been raped. Eventually, an entitlement to seek an abortion was conceded on the grounds of her alleged suicidal tendencies or a threat to her right to life. Pro-life activists believed that a *de facto* right to abortion had now been established and much of what they had campaigned for in the referendum had been overturned. But 1983 had established a kind of marker, that however human beings might fail to live up to the ideal, Irish society was essentially hostile to abortion. Within a few years, survey after survey would show that the influence of Catholic Ireland had decreased throughout all parts of society, and most particularly through the poorer parts. It is the 'underclass' that has most strongly lost its faith.[36]

According to Tom Hesketh in his book documenting the pro-life movement that blossomed in the 1980s (*The Second Partitioning of Ireland*), a 'former' member of the Knights[37] was 'a leading activist in the anti-contraception campaign during the 1970s … and perhaps the main instigator of the PLAC'. The activist spelled out the pre-emptive strategy of the entire pro-life lobby when he asserted, 'Attack is the best form of defence. The alternative would have been to wait and watch the abortion lobby erode our laws by court cases and private members' Bills, and by extensive abortion referral and by pro-abortion propaganda in the media.'[38] This kind of rhetoric is very reminiscent of the Catholic Action approach in the halcyon days of the movement. It lends credence to the assertion that the legacy of Catholic Action was that some members of the Knights of St Columbanus, the CYMS, and other activists acted as a bridge-head, a lever and a catalyst between the heady days of Catholic Action in the mid-twentieth century and the new generation of Catholic activists campaign-ing in the closing decades of the twentieth century and the first decade of the twenty-first century.

Authors Tovey and Share quote Emily O'Reilly's *Masterminds of the Right*, which recounts 'the remarkable influence of a committed individual', a member of the Knights of St Columbanus, in the public morality campaigns of the 1970s and 1980s (contraception, divorce, abortion, education, etc.).[39] According to Tovey and Share, her book is a 'highly conspiratorial account of social change, where appearances are deceptive and hidden interests work covertly behind organisational fronts'. In her book she quoted a member of the Knights from 1988 that, she alleges, said:

...an organisation or a group is never more powerful than when it influences events without itself being regarded as the initiator ... members of the Knights of Columbanus occupy positions of influence in many walks of life and at the high-est level. They are asked to be confidentially politically active.[40]

Moreover, the member is quoted as saying:

We also need to keep our eyes on hospital boards; ethics committees; school boards; parents' groups ... trying to keep the right government in power, or at least the one which is the lesser evil ... such a network (of activists) if well moti-vated and highly confidential could do wonders quietly without coming out openly as Knights.

According to Emily O'Reilly, a member of the Knights was involved or was instrumental in setting up a succession of Catholic organisations, from the Irish Family League to the Pro-Life Amendment Campaign (PLAC), from the Society for the Protection of Unborn Children, to Family Solidarity of the early-to-mid 1980s and the second pro-life campaign of the early 1990s. She traces the 'concealed hand of the Knights' within most of the Catholic organisations set up during the period, and in particular PLAC.[41] Whether this 'conspiracy' was the case remains to be seen.

In 1989, the Supreme Court ruled in favour of an injunction preventing the publication of phone numbers and addresses of British abortion clinics in student-welfare clinics in Ireland. The official figure for Irish women travel-ling to Britain for abortion services was 4,000 in 1990, rising to an estimated 6,000 in 1999. The so-called X Case brought the issue of Irish women seeking abortions abroad to a head and generated considerable national debate. The Supreme Court overturned the ruling in the X Case by a four-to-one margin and accepted that abortion was legal in limited cases where there was a real danger that the pregnant woman was suicidal. As a direct result of the X Case a referendum was held on 25 November 1992, in which the Irish people voted on the right to abortion information and the right to travel. The voting public affirmed the right to information and travel, but rejected the wording for a new amendment allowing abortion in cases of maternal ill health.

In 1997, another action, the C Case, brought the issue of abortion to the fore once again. The C Case involved a thirteen-year-old girl pregnant as a result of rape. The High Court ruled that, by virtue of the Supreme Court judgment in the 1992 X Case, a girl who was suicidal was entitled to an abortion within the Irish state. In September 1999 the Irish government published a Green Paper on abortion. An all-party Oireachtas Committee on the constitution was invited to collect written submissions regarding abortion.

However, long-established organisations such as the Knights of St Columbanus, the CYMS, the Irish Guild of Catholic Doctors and Muintir na Tíre continued their work and made submissions to the government-established inter-departmental working group on abortion in 2000. Other submissions also came from the newer organisations, such as the Pro-Life Campaign (although a veteran organisation in the pro-life movement since the early 1980s), Youth Defence, Human Life Ireland, and others that were established in response to perceived threats to Ireland's traditional Catholic ethos and in particular to threats to its marriage and family articles in the constitution. Approximately forty Catholic lay organisations made submissions in 2000, illustrating the vibrancy of Catholic activity.[42] The pro-life movement successfully lobbied to have another constitutional referendum to strengthen the constitutional protection for the unborn. Because of divisions within the ranks of the movement, with Catholic activists divided on principles and the precise wording of the text of the amendment (some being pragmatic, some being fundamentalist), on 6 March 2002, the proposed amendment was very narrowly defeated. The situation remains unresolved.

THE DIVORCE CAMPAIGN

The contraceptive and abortion battles evolved into a movement in the mid-1980s for a referendum on the constitutional ban of divorces in Article 42.3.2. The Fine Gael government announced a constitutional referendum for 1986. The pro-life movement quickly reorganised into an anti-divorce campaign with an almost completely Catholic lay leadership, and with William Binchy and Mary McAleese as its legal advisers. The lacklustre support of the government parties, combined with the well-organised conservative groups, played an important role in dooming the amendment to outlaw the ban on divorce. However, in a second referendum on divorce in 1995, a slim majority overturned the ban.

NEW CHALLENGES

As previously indicated, following the success in having the Irish Constitution amended (Article 40.3.3.), the PLAC campaign spawned a number of like-minded organisations, including Family Solidarity. Co-founded in 1984 by a Knight of St Columbanus activist and supporters of the campaign that led to the Eighth Amendment of the Constitution of Ireland, Family Solidarity campaigned in particular against the introduction of divorce. Other organisations established included Youth Defence, established in 1992 in response to the threat of abortion being legalised in Ireland, the Mother and Child Campaign, and Cóir. The Iona Institute, 'dedicated to the strengthening of civil society through making the case for marriage and religious practice', was founded by David Quinn, former editor of *The Irish Catholic* and *Irish Independent* columnist. The Family and Media Association, and the John Paul II Society have similar aims. All these organisations, and a number of others, are dedicated to defending marriage and the family as per the Irish Constitution and the papal encyclicals, and continue to be active in these areas and remain influential with the Irish voters (note the Lisbon Treaty debate).

Irish voters had rejected the Lisbon Treaty in 2008, partly due to concerns that it could weaken the protection that Irish law gives to unborn human life. Following that rejection, the Irish government sought and obtained legal guarantees from the other EU members that the treaty would not be used to undermine Ireland's abortion law.

During the campaign, several respected pro-life advocates, most notably former Fianna Fáil Senator Des Hanafin of the Pro-Life Campaign, assured voters that they were confident that, given the guarantees, the treaty did not threaten Ireland's abortion law. Clearly, many pro-life voters were persuaded by these assurances as there was a large swing in favour of the treaty in the second referendum of 2 October 2009. Other pro-life voters, however, remained sceptical of the government's promises, questioning the legal status of the guarantees and fearful that, over time, the European Court would use the treaty's Charter of Fundamental Rights to interfere with Irish law on abortion and family issues. The divisions on some fundamental principles and issues within the pro-life movement and within Irish society remain, and the battles continue.[43]

CONCLUSION

The roots of Catholic Action, laid in the crucial first decades of the twentieth century, were an outgrowth both of changing national circumstances in Ireland and developments in European Catholicism.

The European Catholic Social Movement played an important role, as an example of what could be achieved by organised Catholic lay organisations.[1] Similarly, Pope Pius X's call to Catholic Action in 1903 and 1905, when the term was first coined, did much to stimulate interest in Catholic organisations.[2] The modernist crisis of 1907-1910 shook the Catholic Church to its foundations when 'heresy' became a major issue.[3] The modernist debacle was to have a major impact on the shaping of aspects of twentieth-century Irish history, since the reaction of the Catholic Church in Ireland subsequently influenced and underpinned the whole censorship campaign. It gave rise to the growth of the Irish Vigilance Association (1911) and focused the attention of the Catholic Truth Society of Ireland (1899) not only on Catholic propaganda work, but significantly on vigilance activities.

In Ireland at the turn of the century, as powerful forces jostled for cultural and political supremacy, the Celtic revival in its many and varied manifestations and its reaction against cultural absorption and confusion, also greatly stimulated and facilitated Catholic Action and its diverse programme. D.P. Moran and Edward Martyn were two outstanding figures who concentrated the ambitions and grievances of a growing Catholic bourgeoisie and who helped channel their tensions through the Catholic Association (1902) and the Catholic Defence Society (1905).[4] In the place of the old paternalistic Protestant elite, a new Catholic ruling-class-in-waiting, made up of an alliance between the politicians of the Irish Parliamentary Party and the Catholic Church, was beginning to emerge. The journalist D.P. Moran, by inspired use of nicknames such as 'sour-faces' for Protestants, 'west-Brits' for the Anglo-Irish, and 'shoneens' for those native Catholic Irish who aped British fashions, exacerbated the Anglophobic element.[5] By such ridicule and constantly swiping at the Irish politicians at Westminster, Moran helped to foster an atmosphere conducive to the assertion of Catholic grievances. In the early 1900s, the equation began to develop in Ireland that to be an authentic nationalist one had to be an Irish speaker – and a Catholic.

Clerical concerns over independent lay initiative siphoned off any radical tendencies which were not mandated by the local bishop, and a different Church–State–Nation relationship ensured that an Irish Catholic Social movement along the lines of the European model would not arise.[6] Instead, the focus would be narrower and would coincide with the Catholic Church's fears, concerns and interests. 'Vigilance' was to be the watchword for the new Catholic lay organisations that sprang up during the modernist crisis, during the 1913 Dublin lockout and after the Sinn Féin election victory of 1918. The Catholic Church was forging a strategy that would take into account the new relationship it envisaged between itself and the nation in an independent Ireland.[7] Catholic lay organisations would play a crucial role in asserting the Catholic Church's influence.[8] Nationalism and Catholicism were not strange bedfellows, as both sought a certain kind of purification. Anti-modern traditionalism was part of that ideology to some extent.

It came as no surprise that both Church and State should share the same platform at the 1923 CTSI annual conference to discuss aspects of the future direction of independent Ireland.[9] W.T. Cosgrave and his colleagues had the task of state-building, and their collective style of government during the 1920s was to eschew flamboyance for a sober patriotism and a self-effacing zeal designed to return the country to normality. An impecunious government, burdened by the debt of destruction and faced with expectations that had been elevated unrealistically by the political rhetoric of 1919-1921, was unable to achieve rapid and radical social reform. Unemployment and emigration continued. In this difficult situation it was not surprising that the Free State remained predominantly Catholic and nationalist in ethos. Throughout the decade, the leaders of Church and State were prominent together at public and state occasions, including the platforms of the CTSI.

Although Pope Pius X was the first pope to use the term 'Catholic Action', stressing its importance in several encyclicals, it was Pope Pius XI (often called 'the Pope of Catholic Action') who gave it its classical definition as, 'the active participation of the organised laity in the apostolate of the Church's hierarchy'.[10] The concept was implicit in his first encyclical, *Ubi Arcano Dei* (1922). Pius XI gave Catholic Action a charter, a spirit and an apocalyptic urgency. He tended to restrict the term to action or work of the laity which was organised, apostolic and done under the special mandate of the bishop. A spate of manuals and handbooks developed these points and one in particular became a veritable bible for Catholic Actionists in Ireland – Civardi's *Manual of Catholic Action* (1933). Further stimulus was given to the movement with the call of the 1927 Synod of Maynooth for lay Catholics to join organisations for the defence and upholding of Catholic opinion.[11] A number of new organisations sprang up in Ireland during this decade including the Legion of Mary, the Central Catholic Library, the Guild of Catholic Nurses, An Rioghacht, the Knights of St Columbanus, and the Modest Dress and Deportment Crusade. Other established organisations, including the CTSI, the Catholic Protection and Rescue Society of Ireland, the CYMS, and the Ancient Order of Hibernians undertook increased organisational activities.[12] The 1930s and 1940s also witnessed the establishment of new organisations, such as the League for Social Justice, the Guilds of Regnum Christi, Muintir na Tíre, the Irish Christian Front, Christus Rex and Maria Duce. These organisations focused on different activities: the CTSI campaigned for censorship legislation; An Rioghacht were an elitist movement devoted to advancing Catholic social principles amongst those in influential positions in Irish public life; the revived CYMS found a *raison d'être* in vigilance and anti-communist activities and in organising Catholic Social Weeks. The CTSI were also particularly involved in the 1929 Catholic Emancipation Centenary celebrations and the 1932 Eucharistic Congress.

With all these organisations emerging and developing, the Catholic Irish identity was further strengthened. At the same time, Catholic Action helped to give cohesion and identity to the fledgling Irish Free State. The important 1923 CTSI annual conference illustrated the informal consensus at work between the bishops, priests and politicians about the nature of Irish society and what was necessary for its stability.[13]

The most fruitful activity for Catholic organisations would be in the area of 'vigilance' on behalf of and at the behest of the Catholic Church. This was already evident at the 1921 and 1922 CTSI annual conferences, when the bishops were protected by CYMS and AOH members in the face of angry republican demonstrators. Vigilance and propaganda activities were critical ideological principles of Catholic Action to which the corporatist and vocational were added in the 1930s.

The relationship between clergy and laity was not always an easy one. The success of Catholic Action was dependent upon the mandate and goodwill of the Catholic hierarchy. Archbishop Byrne of Dublin frequently expressed his distrust and annoyance at the activities of the Legion of Mary, the Catholic Girl Guides and the CTSI.[14] The situation did not change under his successor, Archbishop John Charles McQuaid, who quickly put an end to the activities of two ecumenical organisations founded by Frank Duff – the Pillar of Fire Society and the Mercier Society.[15] By the 1940s, however, there were thousands of Catholic Actionists at work throughout the country; every parish had at least half a dozen organisations acting as moral guardians and constantly feeding information to priests and bishops on local and national developments. They had become the eyes and ears of the Catholic Church (Séan Ó Faoláin referred to them as 'Miraculous Meddlers'; Peadar O'Donnell regarded them as the 'yahoo laity').

The CTSI's propaganda and vigilance activities prior to independence ensured that the Society would be in the vanguard of any new campaign. Consequently they spearheaded a movement, from 1925 to 1929, in favour of legislation for literature censorship.[16] Catholic Action became the vehicle for the expression in post-independent Ireland of that need for expurgation and redemption in the light of Civil-War excesses. It was also a placebo for failed expectations. The Committee of Enquiry on Evil Literature was established due to pressure brought to bear on the new government by the Irish Vigilance Association and the CTSI.[17] The findings of the committee reflected their concerns. The Censorship of Publications Act, 1929, reflected the submission of the CTSI, 'The Problem of Undesirable Printed Matter: Suggested Remedies'. The Society was subsequently represented on every Censorship Board for the next thirty years.[18]

The strong censorial spirit which found expression in the hearings of the Committee of Enquiry on Evil Literature was not absolutely echoed in Cumann na nGaedhael circles. However, they acquiesced in the demands of the vigilance organisations. When the legislation was enacted, the CTSI wanted it to be tightened up. A memo drafted by the Justice Minister's office in reply to a suggestion by the CTSI, triumphantly declared how successful the 1929 Censorship of Publications Act had been, 'As regards periodicals, in particular English Sunday newspapers, the Act has been, in the Minister's opinion, an unqualified success.'[19]

Catholic Actionists also turned their attention to the growing 'celluloid menace', with the CTSI and An Rioghacht in the forefront of the Catholic Theatre and Cinema Movement.[20] Efforts were made to ensure censorship in Ireland was even more rigid than that requested by the Legion of Decency in the USA.

National timidity and conservatism was also reflected on the Abbey Theatre stage. The latent forces, the energies and the pressures of Irish consciousness at this time seemed to manifest themselves on that stage. If the Abbey Theatre had to exist at all, it should be patriotic, pure and Catholic and it should not upset people with silly, foreign ideas. The campaign also highlighted the fact that censorship of literature and cinema was not just an Irish issue but was widespread in Britain, Canada, the USA, Australia and elsewhere.

In the 1930s, corporatism/vocationalism came to the fore as a motivating principle. These ideas stemmed from Pope Pius XI's 1931 social encyclical *Quadragesimo Anno*, which sought a middle way between what it saw as the excesses of unbridled capitalism and the threat to human freedom posed by communism and socialism. The new encyclical sought the elimination of class struggle. The aim was to ensure that the traditional division of society into upper and lower classes would be overcome by dividing society instead into various vocational groupings or 'corporations' (the agricultural sector, the business sector, etc.). Within each of the different corporations or vocational groupings there would be people of different social classes. This was the system adopted by the fascists in Italy, Portugal and Austria.

A number of factors helped make these Catholic social principles a dynamic part of the Catholic Action campaign in the 1930s and 1940s. Just as world economic depression influenced the writing of *Quadragesimo Anno*, so too it influenced the reception of the encyclical in Ireland. The ideal of vocational organisation in society was embraced enthusiastically by many Catholic social activists. Fianna Fáil's doctrine of economic nationalism had parallels in the subsidiary principle of *Quadragesimo Anno*. An attachment to corporatism and the social theories of the encyclical helped the establishment of Fine Gael as a political party.[21]

Coinciding with this new mood was the gradual development of a Catholic social vision. New organisations such as Muintir na Tíre, the Guilds of Regnum Christi and the League for Social Justice, new periodicals such as *Prosperity*, *Hibernia*, *Outlook* and *Social Justice*, new books including Fr Edward Cahill's *The Framework of a Christian State*, and Summer Schools, Rural Week-Ends, Study Circles and Catholic Social Weeks did much to harness public discourse and sympathy for this vision.

It was hoped in Jesuit quarters that efforts would be made to give centralised direction to the various strands of Catholic Action.[22] The enormous popularity of the Irish Christian Front, which had Catholic Action ideals as a propelling force, gave some activists hope that the movement would pull together into one united body. This was not to be the case, however, as divisions on fundamental Catholic Action principles and personality clashes came to the fore. The confidential Jesuit Report on Catholic Action, completed in 1936, pointed out that despite the fact that Catholic organisations were 'largely responsible for the passing into law of many important measures of social reform', there was still much ignorance and confusion over the term.[23] The Report on Catholic Action argued for greater cohesion of the Catholic Action movement, 'which it now lacks'. It saw no need for Catholic trade unions or a Catholic political party in Ireland. The report also suggested that the bishops 'on the whole seem to share the confusion prevalent about the meaning of the term Catholic Action'. Consequently, for this and other reasons, they were 'suspicious' of the movement and were reluctant to become involved.

The CYMS and the Irish Christian Front were at the forefront of the anti-communist drive in Ireland in the mid-to-late 1930s.[24] Mass meetings, demonstrations, attacks on communists and violent rhetoric were the order of the day. Fear of communism was central to the Irish response to the Spanish Civil War. As with the popularity of the Irish Christian Front, it is difficult to correlate the profound fear of communism, which was a central motivating factor in Catholic Action vigilance activity, with the marginal position of communism in Ireland. The pessimism that seemed to pervade bishops' pastorals was in stark contrast to the confident Catholicism in England, with converts flocking to become members. Hopes for a united Catholic Action movement in Ireland collapsed partly due to suspicions about the Irish Christian Front's political ambitions.[25]

In another area, An Rioghacht were making submissions to Éamon de Valera apropos his new 1937 Constitution of Ireland.[26] The organisation's founder, Fr Edward Cahill, whose book *The Framework of a Christian State* had been given to de Valera in 1932, had an important influence, both directly and indirectly, on the deliberations, as did Fr John Charles McQuaid, Headmaster of Blackrock College. Both individuals would have been indebted to the pivotal work on Catholic social principles, *The Code of Social Principles*, published in Malines in 1929 by a Catholic organisation, the International Union of Social Studies. A number of Articles in the new constitution were obviously marked by Catholic thought, including: Article 41 on the Family; Article 42 on Education; Article 43 on Private Property; Article 44 on Religion, and Article 45 on Directive Principles of Social Policy.

De Valera's provisions were criticised by some Catholic Actionists for not being Catholic enough.[27] By bypassing the various confessional lobbies on the issue of Catholicism being the 'one, true Church', he pre-empted a Church–State crisis, for it was only on this issue that they would have united against him. The wording eventually used in the constitution had been devised by Cahill, and referred to the 'special position' of the Catholic Church.[28] Even then, Professor Alfred O'Rahilly saw through the apparent sleight of hand of de Valera.[29]

For vocationalists there was some recognition of their principles in the provisions for the second chamber in the Oireachtas. Forty-three of the sixty senators were to represent the five vocational categories. But as with the clever compromise on Article 44, certain Catholic Actionists were quick to spot the flaws in the new arrangement (for example, members of the Senate could be political appointees having no interest whatsoever in the vocationalist cause), and so they denounced it.[30] In practice, the Senate never recovered its former glory. De Valera had combined Catholic principles with his own pragmatism to confuse the vocationalist lobby. For him, the social encyclicals provided the outline principles, but Fianna Fáil provided the actual answers. For individuals such as O'Rahilly and Cahill, the encyclicals provided the real and literal fundamentals for change. The application, as opposed to the acknowledgement of Catholic Action ideals, was certainly not an integral part of de Valera's vision for Ireland. Part of his achievement, then, was to use Catholic Action to good advantage by taking on board some of their principles, while at the same time he provided the necessary restraint to a movement which was disunited but ambitious.

This disunity was again in evidence in the Reports of the Commission of Inquiry into Banking, Currency and Credit, 1938. An Rioghacht and Alfred O'Rahilly penned the first and third minority reports. One of the signatories of the majority report was Bishop MacNeely, representing the Catholic Church. He was 'not convinced' that the Irish monetary and banking system could be fairly blamed for 'such social injustices or economic evils as may exist in the Free State'.[31] An Rioghacht members were not as optimistic or as understanding as the Catholic Church's representative. Their social theory was highly critical of the Department of Finance and the economic policies of Fianna Fáil, and they argued that it was 'very doubtful if we are any nearer today to the abolition of the slums than we were when the Irish government took over control'.[32] They concluded that Irish financial polity was 'grinding to pieces' the lives of the people.[33] Alfred O'Rahilly rejected the majority report's call for 'efficiency', as for him this meant 'cheaper food for fewer people'.[34]

The Knights of St Columbanus applauded both minority reports. However, the Jesuit economist Fr Edward Coyne took issue with all three reports.[35] He criticised the majority report for 'failing to address the question of how the social welfare of the country was to be achieved'. He also found fault with the minority reports as, 'purporting to obtain social values and welfare at an economic cost to no one'. The significance of Coyne's demolition of the reports only served to highlight the fact that Catholic Action was not the homogenous force it appeared to be. Rather it was a disparate and divided group. Catholic Action had not achieved consensus on fundamentals, and, in fact, might not. The divisions also reflected the basic contradictions within the encyclical *Quadragesimo Anno*, leading to different interpretations and strategies. One of the consequences of the divisions was that Fr Cahill, a well-known leader of Catholic Action, was silenced by his superiors.[36]

Alfred O'Rahilly's clashes with the economist George O'Brien over these issues, and particularly over the 1942 Central Bank Bill (which was one of the recommendations of the majority report), represented a watershed in Irish economic thinking. Whereas O'Rahilly and the Catholic Action forces wanted a return to the economic order of the Middle Ages (as recommended by *Quadragesimo Anno*), O'Brien sought the 'middle way' between unregulated individualism and totalitarianism. In fact, O'Brien crucially recognised the contrasting philosophies when he declared that, 'revolutions move forward and not backward – the problems of today cannot be solved by the theories of yesterday'.[37]

Irish Catholicism was not a socially or politically homogenous group. There were winds of change blowing, and there was to be no consensus as to the future direction of Irish economic affairs. The questionable value of Catholic social teaching was becoming apparent. Catholic Action did not allow itself to recognise the realities of the Irish situation – the adherence to liberal democratic standards and the dominance of the national question. There was also the ultimate contradiction in the movement – it was driven by two opposing principles. On the one hand, *Quadragesimo Anno* advocated the reconstruction of society according to a Catholic blueprint, with the help of Catholic lay organisations. But on the other hand, one of the stipulations of Catholic Action, as laid down in the encyclicals on the subject, and in particular in an encyclical of 1931, *Non Abbiamo Bisogno*, was that Catholic Action had to be 'above and beyond politics'. This might go some way in explaining the ambivalent alliance that existed between the clergy and lay organisations in the 1930s. The movement, therefore, seemed to be characterised by a push and a pull, as it was moving in opposite directions.

At their annual meeting in Maynooth in 1939, the Irish Catholic hierarchy considered the whole area of Catholic Action organisation, its validity in
Ireland and its future direction *vis-à-vis* Catholic social teaching.[38] The meeting
examined the findings of the Report on Catholic Action drawn up by Fr Peter
McKevitt, Professor of Catholic Action in St Patrick's College, Maynooth.
His report saw no room for those who wished to inaugurate a radical form
of Catholic Action. It recommended that Catholic Action would have to be
more centrally controlled by the hierarchy and the clergy, who would delegate responsibilities to a central board. The 'inexperience of laymen' was to be
avoided at all costs. An Rioghacht was treated with suspicion for placing the
Catholic Church in an embarrassing position consequent to its submission to
the Commission of Inquiry into Banking, Currency and Credit. There was to be
no room for radical political opposition arising from Catholic ranks. The bishops intended to ensure that those Catholic Actionists who demanded a more
integralist social order or who challenged the status quo, would not succeed
in compromising the Catholic Church's position regarding the State. Rather,
the bishops preferred forms of Catholic Action which were politically innocuous, and which enjoyed cross-party political patronage, such as that enjoyed by
Muintir na Tíre, the CTSI and the St Vincent de Paul Society, while at the same
time extending the Catholic Church's influence and interests. The opportunity
to implement this strategy would come with the establishment of the Catholic
Social Services Conference of 1941. This consisted of an amalgamation of the
efforts of nearly forty Catholic Action organisations. Directed charity was to
be the new order of things under Archbishop John Charles McQuaid. At the
same time, the CSSC was an example of the subsidiarist principle in action, as
recommended by *Quadragesimo Anno*.

All hopes for a vocationalist Ireland now rested with the Commission on
Vocational Organisation, which met for the first time in March 1939, to 'determine whether in the circumstances of the moment, it was practicable to develop
here a general form of organisation of that character'.[39] De Valera argued at the
opening session that the Commission's function would not be political, but
rather of a social and economic nature.[40] The Report of the Commission on
Vocational Organisation was not published until August 1944. It was very ambitious in its proposals, recommending the establishment of a National Vocational
Assembly, with the three-fold function of co-ordinating, planning and advising
on Irish socio-economic policy.[41] There was no doubt that politicians would
have to justify their decisions much more to an independent vocational assembly than to a partisan Dáil and dependent civil service. The government had no
intention of giving the vocationalists such power.

The reaction to the Report of the Commission on Vocational Organisation
clearly proved that the concept of vocationalism was not regarded as a feasible
option. And instead of a decrease in the State's interference in the economy
(as was recommended), de Valera's years in office saw a substantial increase, as

the government tried to deal with world economic depression, the economic sanctions with Britain and the consequences of a world war.[42] The wartime emergency stimulated a greater awareness of the importance of rational economic and social planning. The disruption of world trade necessitated fundamental changes in the role of government, involving a more managed deployment of resources, increased bureaucracy and a new consciousness, so that the Irish economy could be directed into desired channels to sustain economic growth.[43]

The message of *Quadragesimo Anno* and the vocationalist system it espoused strengthened the nation's Catholic consciousness. But its idealism and impracticalities meant that it would have no substantial influence on Irish political or economic life. The reality was that Ireland was not interested in the medieval guild system on which vocationalism was based. Not only that, but the employers had their own organisation, as did trade unions. The leading trade unionists who participated in the work of the Commission on Vocational Organisation either refused to sign the final report or signed with serious reservations. Trade unions were not prepared to surrender their ultimate sanction – the right to strike.

Leading vocationalists also had their doubts. Professor Michael Tierney questioned whether the sweeping social reorganisation necessary was practical, and he challenged the hagiography of the guild system.[44] Fr Edward Coyne SJ, on the other hand, challenged Professor Tierney's conception of vocationalism, and argued that what was required was a corporative society and not a corporative State.[45] Of particular significance was the recognition by some vocationalists of the near futility of their campaign. Archdeacon Kelleher of Waterford commented on the eve of a series of broadcasts on Radio Éireann in 1938, 'While the organisation must come from below upward and cannot be imposed by the State, still without sympathetic support and even initiative from the State, I see no basis for hope that it can ever be realised in this country'.[46]

The Catholic Action movement was not to be deflected, despite the government's shelving of the Report of the Commission on Vocational Organisation. An umbrella organisation, the Catholic Societies Vocational Organisation Conference (CSVOC), was established in 1945 to campaign for the increased recognition of vocational principles in Ireland.[47] Attention was diverted to challenging what the CSVOC regarded as an intrusion by the State into people's lives, particularly in the area of the government's planned reform of the country's health services. The compulsory medical inspection of schoolchildren, as envisaged in the government's plans, was strongly criticised because it was seen to interfere with the fundamental rights of the family, and it was also regarded as an increase in that State control which the vocationalists rejected. The establishment of the Department of Health in January 1947 was a landmark on the road to greater centralisation of the health services. The leading Catholic Actionist Dr James McPolin, an activist with the CTSI, the Knights of St Columbanus and the Christus Rex Society, was foremost in warning the Catholic hierarchy of the dangers posed by the recommended changes in the health services.[48] The foundations were being laid for a significant Church–State confrontation.

The Catholic Action movement was a two-pronged campaign concentrating on vigilance and propaganda activities on behalf and at the behest of the Catholic Church. The CTSI had as its objective the creation in Ireland of 'a thoroughly Catholic public opinion' and this society, as well as others in the movement, succeeded in this respect. When we examine the nature of the debate on social and moral issues in Ireland in these decades, Catholic Action had a decided influence. There were also the legislative achievements, which were referred to by the Jesuit Report on Catholic Action in 1936.

Similarly, when we examine the volume of Catholic pamphlets published and distributed by organisations such as the CTSI, we can see that the movement had an impact. By the 1940s the CTSI were selling approximately two million pamphlets per year.[49] That lay organisations were the 'eyes and ears' of the bishop's palace was also of particular significance.

Some organisations in the movement were determined to tackle social problems, but they lost their way because of their concentration on anti-communist activities and the divisive nature of the campaign. The establishment of the Catholic Social Services Conference elevated Irish social services to a new level, however. The establishment of the Department of Social Welfare in 1947 was certainly at least partly in response to Catholic Action raising public awareness of the social injustices endemic in Irish society. Similarly, the establishment of the Labour Court, under the provisions of the 1946 Industrial Relations Act, could be interpreted as a response to the vocationalists' call for a more harmonious working relationship between employers and employees. The voluntary nature of lay organisations also gave much credit to the whole idea of self-help and the collective role of the community in addressing issues. Catholic Action, through the multiplicity of organisations, acted as a binding force in Irish society. It helped to sustain the Catholic ethos in Ireland, while at the same time strengthening the Catholic Church's control over that society.

One reason for the influence of Catholic Action was that there was no alternative body of teaching that was seriously competing for the attention of Irish people. Catholic Actionists grasped the initiative in the early years of the Irish Free State, having seen some success in the first two decades of the twentieth century.

During the period of this study, Catholic social principles were offered as the solution to many of the social problems besetting the country. The fact that the government appointed the Commission on Emigration and Population Problems in 1948 does seem to indicate that, for many people, Catholic social principles were not seen as practical in dealing with the realities of the day. People looking for change in politics and society did not necessarily seek to work through Catholic Action organisations or vocational structures, but rather through existing political structures or new political parties, such as Clann na Talmhan (1938/1939) and Clann na Poblachta (1946).

Catholic Action in the late 1940s and 1950s concentrated more on vigilance activities. Fr Denis Fahey's organisation, Maria Duce (1945), was particularly active in this area, as were the Knights of St Columbanus. The Catholic Cinema and Theatre Patron's Association, the Legion of Mary, the St Vincent de Paul Society, PPUs, St Joseph's Young Priests' Society, and the CYMS all continued to be prominent. The post-war communist threat and the fate of Catholic prelates behind the Iron Curtain also focused the attention of Catholic Actionists.

The ambiguity surrounding the concept of Catholic Action came to the fore at the 1957 international gathering of representatives of Catholic lay organisations in Rome. By then, the term 'lay apostolate' was becoming the more acceptable expression, as it could be used to refer to all Catholic lay activity, whether organised or unorganised, whether episcopally mandated or not, without quibbling over terms. A report issued in 1966, Survey of the Organised Lay Apostolate in Ireland, showed that despite falling membership, there were almost thirty Catholic lay organisations active in Ireland.[50] There seems to have been some carry-over in leadership, personnel and ideas from the formative era of Catholic Action to the pro-life and divorce campaigns of the 1980s and 1990s. The cyclone of uniformity of the previous decades had created, with militant Catholicism, a reservoir of latent Catholic lay-activist energy and purpose. This concerned and organised laity, fearing that Ireland might take the same path as the UK and the USA and introduce legislation to allow abortion, decided to pre-empt any such cultural shift and threat. Some of the existing lay organisations such as the Knights of St Columbanus and the CYMS helped to face and energise this new challenge.[51]

EPILOGUE

Militant Catholicism, and in particular its expression, 'Catholic Action', as we have seen, was a rallying cry, or even a battle cry, for Catholic activity in the 1930s, 1940s and 1950s. Moreover, it was instrumental in giving expression and shape to and motivating individuals, organisations, campaigns and developments in the second half of the twentieth century, even after its heyday. The names of some of the Catholic Action organisations clearly spell out their militancy and intent: Angelic Warfare Society; The Catholic Defence League; Catholic Defence Society; Catholic Literature Crusade; Catholic Protection and Rescue Society of Ireland; Dublin Vigilance Society; the Knights of St Columbanus; the Legion of Mary; Maria Duce, and the Irish Christian Front.

Many of these organisations, such as the CTSI (now part of the Catholic Communications Institute/Veritas), the CYMS, the Knights of St Columbanus, Muintir na Tíre, and the Legion of Mary are still in existence in the first decade of the twenty-first century, albeit with reduced memberships, new formats and changed aims and objectives. Nevertheless, they are still influential.

Moreover, the movement was instrumental in giving expression to and in motivating individuals, organisations, campaigns and developments in the last quarter of the twentieth century, even after its zenith. Some of these later organisations also had military language in their titles, such as the Pro-Life Campaign and Youth Defence. One fundamental difference however, is that these organisations, unlike Catholic Action organisations, were not subject to a mandate from the Catholic hierarchy; they operated independently, were fewer in number and membership and their activities were limited to a single issue, such as the pro-life cause. Furthermore, this cause was not heralded as a necessarily Catholic (although taking ultimate inspiration from Papal encyclicals) or even religious one, but one that transcends religion.

Following the success in having the Irish Constitution amended (Article 40.3.3.), the PLAC campaign spawned a number of similarly minded organisations, including Family Solidarity. Family Solidarity was co-founded in 1984 by a Knight of St Columbanus activist and supporters of the campaign that led to the Eighth Amendment of the Constitution of Ireland. It campaigned in particular against the introduction of divorce. Other organisations established included Youth Defence, founded in 1992 in response to the threat of abortion being legalised in Ireland, and the Iona Institute, 'dedicated to the strengthening of civil society through making the case for marriage and religious practice', established in 2007. The Family and Media Association, The Mother and Child Campaign, Cóir, and the John Paul II Society were also established in these years with similar aims. All these organisations, and a number of others, are dedicated to defending marriage and the family as written in the Irish Constitution and the papal encyclicals, and they remain active in these areas and influential with the Irish voters (note the Lisbon Treaty debate).

Throughout the 1990s and beyond, the Catholic Church was rocked by a series of priestly scandals, and many observers believed that the 'Confessional State' finally died in November 1995, when Ireland conducted its second referendum on divorce. This is debatable; the scandals did more to damage the moral authority and reputation of the Church than the issue of divorce. The scandals effectively torpedoed people's confidence in the Church and did enormous and lasting damage.

These days we have a tendency, all too well developed, to think that it is the duty of the State to undertake all social and remedial activity. In the earlier part of the twentieth century, and subsequently in the closing decades, the view was held, especially by many conservative Catholics in Ireland, that the role of the State should be restricted, that the extension of its power sapped the morale, let alone the morals, of the nation.

But, according to Professor D. Vincent Twomey, in his 2003 book, *The End of Irish Catholicism?*, 'in effect, the referenda on abortion had as their subtext: the elected representatives cannot be trusted. And this must have had serious implications for democracy'[1]. 'It is arguable,' he says, 'that the various campaigns to protect the unborn through constitutional amendment may have, unintentionally, further undermined the trust of the public in Ireland's legislators'[2].

That democracy survived in Ireland is down more to the good sense of the people than the wisdom of some of their leaders.

ENDNOTES

I

[1] Thomas Bokenkotter, *A Concise History of the Catholic Church* (New York, 1990), pp297-309.

[2] H. Daniel-Rops, *A Fight for God. 1870-1939* (London, 1966), p.13.

[3] H. Somerville, *The Catholic Social Movement* (London, 1933), p.13.

[4] Seancus, 'The Question of Catholic Organisation', *Irish Rosary*, Vol.VI (1902), pp210-20.

[5] *The Irish Catholic*, 15 August 1903.

[6] See encyclical *Pascendi Gregis* (1907); decree *Lamentabili Sane* (1907).

[7] Somerville, *op. cit.*, p.8.

[8] M.A.R. Leys, *European Catholics and The Social Question* (Oxford, 1943), p.28.

[9] Pope Leo XIII, *Rerum Novarum* (1891). The encyclicals are available individually in the CCL. See also Claudia Carlen (ed.), *The Papal Encyclicals 1740-1981* (Raleigh, 1990), IV Vols.

[10] Somerville, *op. cit.*, p.16.

[11] Daniel-Rops, *op. cit.*, p.139.

[12] Edward Cahill, *The Catholic Social Movement* (Dublin, 1930), p.4.

[13] *ibid.*, p.5.

[14] *Catholic Social Yearbook, 1932* (Oxford, 1932). See back inside page; Charles Plater, *The Priest and Social* (London, 1914), pp127.

[15] Somerville, *op. cit.*, p.172.

[16] John Fitzsimons and Paul McGuire (eds.), *Restoring All Things: A Guide to Catholic Action* (New York, 1938), pp98-126.

[17] Pope Leo XIII, *Graves de Communi* (1901), par.4.

[18] *ibid.*, par.4, 8.

[19] Pope Pius X, *Fin dalla prima* (1903), par.3.

[20] *ibid.*, *II Fermo Proposito* (1905), par.22, 23, 25, 26.

[21] *ibid.*, par.7, 20.

[22] *ibid.*, par.50, 14, 29, 41, 73.

[23] Eamonn Duffy, *Saints and Sinners: A History of the Popes* (London, 1997), pp245-70.

[24] *Il Fermo Proposito* (1905), par.4.

[25] Rene Bazin, *Pius X* (London, 1928), pp162-69.

[26] Pope Pius X, *Pascendi Gregis* (1907), par.39.

[27] *ibid.*, par.3, 44.

[28] *ibid.*, par.50, 51, 52, 55.

[29] C. Falconi, *Popes of the Twentieth Century* (London, 1967), p.54.

[30] Gabriel Daly, *Transcendence and Immanence. A Study on Catholic Modernism and Integralism* (Oxford, 1980), p.218.

[31] Pope Pius X, *Lamentabili Sane* (1901).

[32] Patrick J. Corish, *The Irish Catholic Experience* (Dublin, 1985), pp226-49; Emmet Larkin, *The Roman Catholic Church and The Creation of the Modern Irish State, 1876-1886* (Dublin, 1975), pp247-87.

[33] *ibid.*

[34] Geraldine Grogan, *Daniel O'Connell and The German Catholic Movement* (Dublin, 1991), pp224.

[35] Emmet Larkin, 'Socialism and Catholicism in Ireland', *Church History, Vol.XXXIII* (Dec. 1964), pp462-83.

[36] Edward Cahill, 'The Catholic Social Movement', *Irish Ecclesiastical Record, 5th Series, Vol. 36* (Dec. 1930), p.585.

[37] J. Kelleher, 'Priests and Social Action in Ireland', *Studies* (Sept. 1915), pp169-79.

[38] Quoted in Charles Plater, *op. cit.*, p.112.

[39] Horace Plunkett, *Ireland in the New Century* (London, 1904), pp492-93.

[40] M.J.F. McCarthy, *Five Years in Ireland 1985-1900* (London, 1901), p.173.

[41] *ibid.*, p. 521.

[42] Patrick McGill, *Children of the Dead End* (London, 1914), p.17.

[43] Gerald O'Donovan, *Father Ralph* (London, 1913), p.34.

[44] Horace Plunkett, *Ireland in the New Century* (London, 1904), pp101-102.

[45] L. Paul-Dubois, *Contemporary Ireland* (Dublin, 1911), pp492-93.

[46] *ibid.*, p.490.

[47] Horace Plunkett, *op. cit.*, p.44.

[48] P. Coffey, *The Church and The Working Classes* (Dublin, 1906).

[49] P. Coffey, *Scholasticism Old and New* (Dublin, 1907), pp1-2.

[50] Denis Carroll, *They have fooled you again: A life of Fr Michael O'Flanagan* (Dublin, 1993).

[51] Lambert McKenna, *James Connolly* (Dublin, 1920).

[52] Reports of the Proceedings of the Maynooth Union, 1895-1905 (Maynooth, 1906).

[53] Seancus, 'The Question of Catholic Organisation', *Irish Rosary*, Vol.VI (1902), pp210-20.

[54] Thomas Morrissey, *Towards a National University William Delaney SJ (1835-1924): An Era of Initiative in Irish Education* (Dublin, 1985), pp210-212.

[55] *The Leader* (1 July 1901).

[56] *ibid.* (3 March 1901).

[57] *ibid.* (8 July 1901).

[58] *ibid.*

[59] Patrick Maume, *D.P. Moran* (Dublin, 1995), p.55; *Handbook of The Catholic Association* (Dublin, 1902), p.2.

[60] David Miller, *Church, State and Nation in Ireland 1898-1921* (Dublin, 1973), pp115-138.

[61] *New Ireland Review*, Vol.XIV (1901), p.373.

[62] D.P. Moran, *The Philosophy of Irish-Ireland* (Dublin, 1907).

[63] *ibid.*, p.81.

[64] L. Paul-Dubois, pp492-93.

[65] *The Leader* (5 May 1906).

[66] *Census of Population of Ireland* (1901), General Report.

[67] See, Paul–Dubois, *op. cit.* Plunkett, *op. cit.*

[68] Catholic Commercial Club (DDA, Walsh Papers. File 381/6, Box 379/11).

[69] *ibid.*

[70] *The Clongownian* (1916), p.5; *The Belvederian* (1919), p.9.

[71] *The Castleknock Chronicle*, Vol.18 (1903), p.44.

[72] Annual Reports of the Catholic Truth Society of Ireland, 1903-10. (Hereafter cited as CTSI).

[73] Douglas Hyde, *The Revival of Irish Literature* (London, 1894).

[74] *ibid.*

[75] D.P. Moran, *The Philosophy of Irish-Ireland* (Dublin, 1907), p.6.

[76] *ibid.*, p.83.

[77] *ibid.*, p.80.

[78] Report of the Proceedings of the Maynooth Union (1898), p.17. The Maynooth Union had been founded in 1895 as a centenary memorial to keep past students in living touch with their Alma Mater.

[79] *ibid.*, p.18.

[80] Prionsias Mac Aonghusa, *Conradh na Gaeilge 1893-1993* (Dublin, 1993).

[81] *Irish Monthly*, Vol.46 (Jan. 1918), p.23.

[82] Report of the Proceedings of the Maynooth Union (1894), pp33-43.

[83] *ibid.*

[84] *The Irish Catholic*, 24 November 1900.

[85] *ibid.*, 15 June 1901

[86] Edward O'Dwyer, *A University for Catholics in Relation to the Material Interests of Ireland* (Dublin, 1900).

[87] CTSI pamphlet No.77/F1 (Dublin, 1901); pamphlet No.1238/SE (Dublin, 1902); pamphlet No.206/SE (Dublin, 1905).

[88] CTSI Annual Report, 1914, p.4.

[89] Walter MacDonald, *Reminiscences of a Maynooth Professor* (London, 1925), pp191, 317, 330-357.

[90] CTSI Annual Report, 1906, p.17.

[91] Michael O'Riordan, *Catholicity and Progress in Ireland* (London, 1906), p.308.

[92] *ibid.*, p.210.

[93] CTSI Annual Report, 1909, p.45.

[94] John Horgan, *Great Catholic Laymen* (Dublin, 1906).

[95] *Irish Rosary* (1903), pp210-20.

[96] *ibid.*, p.279.

[97] Evelyn Bolster, *The Knights of St. Columbanus* (Dublin, 1979), pp7-12.

[98] Denis Gwynn, *Edward Martyn and the Irish Revival* (London, 1930), pp1-7.

[99] *Saint Mary's Pro-Cathedral* (Dublin, 1908).

[100] *Gazeteer of Irish Stained Glass: The Work of Harry Clarke and An Túr Gloine 1903-1963* (Dublin, 1988).

[101] *Handbook of the Catholic Association* (Dublin, 1902), p.42. Summary statement for the reasons for the establishment of The Catholic Association for Ireland, 1902 (DDA, Walsh Papers, Politics Box).

[102] *ibid.*

[103] *ibid.*

104 *The Irish Catholic*, 15 August 1903.

105 *ibid.*

106 Report of the Proceedings of the Maynooth Union (1902–03), p.56, 66.

107 *ibid.*, 1903, p.8.

108 *The Irish Times*, 18 January 1904.

109 *The Irish Catholic*, 25 February 1904.

110 Catholic Association, Minute Book of the National Council and the Executive Committee, 25 January 1904 (N.A.I. Dub. 88/A/1).

111 Geraldine Grogan, *Daniel O'Connell and the German Catholic Movement* (Dublin, 1990), p.18.

112 *Handbook of the Catholic Association*, pp1–2; pp21–28.

113 Report of the Proceedings of the Maynooth Union (1904), p.36.

114 *ibid.*, p.6.

115 *ibid.*, p.47.

116 *Constitution of the Catholic Defence Society* (Dublin, 1905), p.19.

117 *ibid.*, p.20.

118 *ibid.*, p.22.

119 *ibid.*

120 *Irish Rosary* (1907), p.644.

121 *ibid.*, p.825.

122 David Miller, *Church, State and Nation* (Dublin, 1973), pp224-229.

123 *ibid.*

124 *ibid.*, p.230.

125 *ibid.*

126 *Irish Catholic Directory* (hereafter *ICD*), *1908* (Dublin, 1908), pp456-457.

127 *ibid.*, p.473.

128 Pope Pius XI, *Lamentabili Gregis*, On the Doctrine of the Modernists (1907).

129 *ibid.*, par.8.

130 *ICD, 1908* (Dublin, 1908), p.478.

131 *ibid.*

132 *The Irish Catholic*, 25 October 1909; Patrick J. Corish, *Maynooth College 1795-1995* (Dublin, 1995), pp248-50, 292.

133 *ibid.*

134 Walter MacDonald, *Reminiscences of a Maynooth Professor* (London, 1925), Preface, pp7-8.

135 *ibid.*

136 *ibid.*

137 *Irish Theological Quarterly*, Vol.1, No.1 (1907), p.2.

138 *ibid.*

139 *Pascendi Gregis*, Remedies.

140 Karl Rahner (ed.), *Encyclopaedia of Theology* (London, 1985), p.973.

141 Gerald O'Donovan, *Fr Ralph* (London, 1913), p.3.

142 *Irish Times*, 3 April 1943.

143 Gerald O'Donovan, *op. cit.*, pp346-348.

144 *ibid.*, p.248.

145 Correspondence with Gabriel Daly on the subject of modernism, 1992.

146 Hubert Jedin, *History of the Church*, Vol.IX (London, 1981), p.468.

147 *ICD, 1909* (Dublin, 1909), pp459-60.

[148] *Irish Rosary* (1907), p.872.

[149] *ibid.*, (1910), p.960.

[150] *ibid.*, pp68–69.

[151] CTSI pamphlet No.SE/310 (Dublin, 1907).

[152] CTSI pamphlet No.MM/389 (Dublin, 1909).

[153] CTSI pamphlet No.DD/413 (Dublin, 1909).

[154] CTSI Report of the Proceedings of the 1909 Conference, p.16; *ICD, 1909*, p.497.

[155] Patrick J. Corish, *op. cit.*, p.207.

[156] *ICD, 1918*, p.537.

[157] *ibid.*, p.538; *ICD, 1927*, p.588; in conversation with Jim Kemmy, TD, 3 June 1997.

[158] David Miller, *op. cit.*, p.176.

[159] *Irish Monthly*, Vol.XLVI, (Jan. 1918), pp29–30.

[160] *ICD, 1911*, p.458.

[161] *ibid.*, p. 526.

[162] Austin Clarke, *Twice around the Black Church* (Dublin, 1990), p.30.

[163] *Daily Irish Independent*, 11 November 1911.

[164] *Freeman's Journal*, 1 December 1911.

[165] *The Irish Catholic*, 13 April 1912.

[166] *Industrial Journal*, 1 December 1911.

[167] Timothy Hurley, *Legislation of the Catholic Church on the Production and Distribution of Literature* (Dublin, 1911).

[168] Timothy Hurley, *The National Crusade against Evil Literature* (Dublin, 1913).

[169] CYMS Report of the Annual Conference 1907 (Dublin, 1907), p.2.

[170] *Irish Rosary* (1913), p.56.

[171] *Freeman's Journal*, 6 November 1911.

[172] *The Leader*, 12 June 1912.

[173] *ibid.*

[174] Patrick J. Corish, *op. cit.*, p.241.

[175] *ibid.*

[176] *ibid.*, p.240.

[177] Peter Coffey, *The Church and The Working Classes* (Dublin, 1906).

[178] Patrick J. Corish, *op. cit.*, p.241.

[179] *Irish Worker*, May 1911.

[180] James Connolly, *Labour Nationality and Religion* (Dublin, 1910), p.4.

[181] *Irish Worker*, May 1911.

[182] Curran to Archbishop Walsh, 20 July 1911 (DDA, Walsh Papers, Priests' File).

[183] *ICD, 1912*, pp509–11; *The Irish Catholic*, 25 February 1911.

[184] Hughes to Archbishop Walsh, 19 September 1913. Hughes, a member of the Bakers' Trade Union, was both an ardent Catholic and an active Trade Unionist who wrote frequently in the *Irish Worker*. He was bringing to Archbishop Walsh's attention the sermon of Fr Condon, which he felt did not help the situation in Dublin during the Strike (DDA, Walsh Papers, 384/2).

[185] CTSI Report of The Proceedings of the 1913 Conference, pp42–43.

[186] *ibid.*, pp16–21. Address, 'Capital and Labour and The Catholic Church'.

[187] *ibid.*, p.34; p.25.

[188] *ibid.* pp46–47.

[189] Central Catholic Library, The Leo Guild Library collection is still in existence and

is housed in the CCL, 74 Merrion Square, Dublin 2.

190 Charles Plater, *Catholics and Social Action* (Dublin, 1912), p.24; Charles Plater, *The Priest and Social Action* (London, 1914); CTSI Report of The Proceedings of the 1912 Conference, pp41-48.

191 *Freeman's Journal*, 26 November 1912.

192 John B. Hughes, *Poverty in Dublin: A Study* (Dublin, 1914), p.1.

193 *ibid.*, pp11-12.

194 Fr Lambert McKenna was the Spiritual Director of the Leo Guild. The scope of his interest in the application of Catholic social teaching resulted in the 1913-1914 publication of six pamphlets by the *Irish Messenger Office*, some of which ran to two or more editions. They were: *The Church and Labour; The Church and the Working Man; The Church and Working Women; The Church and The Working Guild; The Church and Trade Unions; The Church and Social Work*. In 1920 he published *The Social Teachings of James Connolly*. Most of the members of the Leo Guild were clergy, and Fr McKenna encouraged them to pass on their knowledge and skills to lay groups in their parishes.

195 Fr Lambert McKenna, *The Social Teachings of James Connolly* (Dublin, 1920).

196 CTSI Report of the Proceedings of the 1910 Conference, p.35.

197 *ibid.*

198 Desmond Bowen, *Souperism: Myth or Reality* (Cork, 1970).

199 CYMS, *100 years of the CYMS* (Dublin, 1949), p.2.

200 *ICD, 1914*, p.504.

201 *ibid.*, pp516-17.

202 *The Irish Catholic*, 25 October 1913; *Freeman's Journal*, 20 October 1913.

203 *ICD, 1914*, p.533.

204 *The Irish Catholic*, 25 October 1913.

205 *Irish Worker*, 8 November 1913.

206 P.J. Brady to Archbishop Walsh, 4 May 1906 (Walsh Papers, Laity file 374/8, Box 3781). P.J. Brady was the secretary of the Ancient Order of Hibernians.

207 *Irish Worker*, 8 November 1913; *Freeman's Journal*, 26 October 1913.

208 *ICD, 1914*, p.35.

209 First Report of the Catholic Protection and Rescue Society of Ireland (Dublin, 1914), p.5.

210 *ibid.*

211 CTSI pamphlet No.SE/501 (Dublin, 1914); pamphlet No.FI/518 (Dublin, 1914).

212 CTSI pamphlet No.SE/501 (Dublin, 1914), p.1.

213 Frank Duff television interview, 1974 (Legion of Mary Archives, video recording).

214 *ICD, 1914*, p.532.

215 Irish Transport and General Workers' Union, 1915 Membership Book (Irish Labour History Society Archives).

216 CTSI pamphlet No.SE/488 (Dublin, 1913).

217 CTSI pamphlet No.SE/499 (Dublin, 1913).

218 CTSI pamphlet No.SE/484 (Dublin, 1913).

219 P.J. Connolly, *The Social Question and a Programme of Social Pamphlets* (Dublin, 1914).

220 *ibid.*, p.1.

221 *The Society of St Vincent de Paul in Ireland 1845-1945: A Sketch by an Active Member* (Dublin, 1945).

222 Society of St Vincent de Paul Annual Report 1921, p.5.

223 *Centenary Record of St Vincent's, Glasnevin, 1856-1956* (Dublin, 1956), p.13.

224 *Handbook for Catholic Social Workers in Dublin* (Dublin, 1911).

225 *ibid.*, 1920.

226 Society of St Vincent de Paul Annual Report for Down and Connor, 1914.

227 *ibid.*

228 *ibid.*, 1915. This Annual Report also contains a letter from James Ken to Cardinal Logue, 27 February 1915, which is a reprint of the original.

229 Evelyn Bolster, *The Knights of St Columbanus* (Dublin, 1979), p.6; *The Irish Catholic*, 10 April 1915, contains an article by Canon O'Neill on the developments leading to the founding of The Knights of St Columbanus.

230 *ibid.*

231 CTSI Report of the Proceedings of the 1916 Conference, p.31.

232 *ibid.*, p.35.

233 Alfred O'Rahilly, 'The Catholic Social League', *Irish Monthly* (July, 1917), pp435-442.

234 Alfred O'Rahilly and T. Smiddy (eds), *University and Labour Series* (Cork, 1916).

235 Alfred O'Rahilly, 'The Catholic Social League', *Irish Monthly* (July, 1917), p.435.

236 CTSI Report of the Proceedings of the 1917 Conference, pp29-39. The main theme of this conference was the issue of Social Catholicism.

237 *ibid.*, 1918 Conference: 1919 Conference, p.57, 1920 Conference, pp64-72.

238 CTSI Reorganisation Scheme approved by the Catholic hierarchy, 1920.

239 *ibid.*

II

1 *Ubi Arcano Dei* (London, 1922), par.58, 54, 55, 56; H. Daniel-Rops, *A Fight for God* (London, 1966), p.292.

2 *Ubi Arcano Dei*, par.7, 12, 14, 15. Philip Hughes, *Pope Pius XI* (London, 1937), p.121; R. Anderson, *Between the Wars: Tthe Story of Pius X* (Chicago, 1977), p.71.

3 *Ubi Arcano Dei*, par.9, 35, 58, 59, 61.

4 *ibid.*

5 *ibid.*

6 Hubert Jedin (ed.), *The History of the Church Vol.X: The Church in the Modem World* (London, 1981), p.308.

7 P. Finlay, *The Authority of the Bishops* (Dublin, 1934), p.17.

8 *ICD, 1924* (Dublin, 1924), p.456.

9 *ibid.*, 1925, p.553.

10 *ibid.*, 1926, p.571.

11 *ibid.*, 1925, p.567.

12 *ibid.*, 1925, p.561.

13 Catholic Truth Society of Ireland Annual Report 1921, p.2. Hereafter cited as CTSI Annual Report.

14 CTSI minutes of the Committee of Management, 1920. Report on reorganisation plan.

15 CTSI Annual Report, 1922-23, p.2.

16 *ibid.*, 1928, p.5.

17 *ibid.*, 1929, p.4.

18 *ibid.*, 1922, p.3.

19 *ibid.*

[20] *The Irish Catholic*, 27 October 1922.

[21] CTSI Annual Report, 1923, Introduction.

[22] *ibid.*

[23] *ibid.*, 1922.

[24] *ibid.*, 1923.

[25] CTSI Annual Conference Report, 1923, p.6

[26] Margaret O'Callaghan, 'Religion and Identity', *The Crane Bag*.Vol.7, No.2 (1983), p.74.

[27] Kevin O'Higgins, *The Catholic Layman in Public Life* (Dublin, 1924), p.25.

[28] *ibid.*, p.15.

[29] *ibid.*, p.13.

[30] CTSI minutes of the Publications Subcommittee, October-November, 1923.

[31] CTSI Annual Conference Report, 1928, p.4.

[32] CTSI minutes of the Committee of Management, 30 May 1924, 18 July 1924.

[33] CTSI minutes of the Organisation Subcommittee, January-February, 1924.

[34] CTSI circular, p.2.

[35] *ibid.*

[36] *ibid.*, p.3.

[37] CTSI Annual Report, 1924, p.12.

[38] CTSI Organisation Subcommittee Draft Annual Report, 1925.

[39] CTSI minutes of the Organisation Subcommittee, 20 January 1925-12 February 1925.

[40] *ibid.*, 25 February 1925-10 March 1925.

[41] CTSI Annual Report, 1925, p.16.

[42] CTSI minutes of the Organisation Subcommittee, 30 June 1925.

[43] *ibid.*, July 1925-August 1925.

[44] CTSI Annual Report, 1926-27, p.3

[45] CTSI Annual Reports, 1918-1925.

[46] Patrick Corish, *The Irish Catholic Experience* (Dublin, 1986), pp195-7.

[47] The Synod of Maynooth 1927, 'Pastoral Address issued by Archbishops and Bishops of Ireland to their flocks on the occasion of the Plenary Synod held in Maynooth, 15 August 1927'.

[48] The Synod of Maynooth 1927, 'Decrees which affect the Catholic Laity' (Dublin, 1930), p.2.

[49] *ibid.*, p.11.

[50] *ibid.*, p.12.

[51] *ibid.*, pp13-14.

[52] CTSI Annual Report, 1927, p.3; 1928, p.5.

[53] *ibid.*, 1927, p.6.

[54] *ibid.*, p.7.

[55] *Up and Doing: A Handbook of Catholic Action* (Dublin, 1928), p.80.

[56] *ibid.*, p.4.

[57] *ibid.*, p.3.

[58] Luigi Civardi, *A Manual of Catholic Action* (Dublin, 1933), p.150.

[59] *Catholic Action, Principles and Practice* (Dublin, 1934), p.24.

[60] *The Serried Ranks of Catholic Action* (Dublin, 1934), p.24

[61] *Catholic Action in Ireland* (Dublin, 1932), p.15.

[62] *The Catholic Social Movement* (Dublin, 1931), p.24.

[63] *The Splendid Cause* (Dublin, 1933), p.24.

[64] Lynn Doyle, *The Spirit of Ireland* (London, 1935), p.9.

[65] John Swift, *John Swift: An Irish Dissident* (Dublin, 1991), p.141.

[66] *ibid.*

[67] *Irish Press*, 17 January 1934; *The Irish Catholic*, 17 January 1934.

[68] Swift, *op. cit.*, p.100.

[69] T.J. Kiernan, 'Catholic Action', *The Capuchin Annual* (1934), pp141-3.

[70] Central Catholic Library, *The First Ten Years of an Irish Enterprise* (Dublin, 1932), p.48.

[71] Irish Guild of Catholic Nurses (DDA, Byrne Papers).

[72] A.M.P. Smithson to Revd P. Dunne, 11 July 1933 (DDA, Byrne Papers).

[73] Ruth Nicholls to Archbishop Byrne, 8 August 1933 (DDA, Byrne Papers).

[74] Memorandum (N.D.) circulated by Irish Guild of Catholic Nurses. The Jesuit Motto 'A.M.D.G.' was stamped at bottom signalling Fr Devane's involvement (DDA, Byrne Papers).

[75] Board of Government of the Knights of St Columbanus to Archbishop Byrne, 22 February 1922 (DDA, Byrne Papers).

[76] *Constitution and Laws of the Knights of St Columbanus in Ireland* (Dublin, 1924), (DDA, Byrne Papers).

[77] *ibid.*

[78] *ibid.*

[79] *ibid.*

[80] John J. Sheil (Supreme Knight) and Patrick F. Leydon (Supreme Secretary) to Irish Hierarchy, 17 August 1934 (DDA, Byrne Papers).

[81] *Ritual of Knights of St Columbanus* (Belfast, 1917), (DDA, Byrne Papers).

[82] CTSI Annual Report, 1927, p.12.

[83] *ibid.*, p.13.

[84] Interview with Tony O'Sullivan, Supreme Treasurer of the Knights, October 1991; Evelyn Bolster, *The Knights of St Columbanus* (Dublin, 1979), pp57-8, 68.

[85] *ibid.*, Bolster, p.68.

[86] Fr Edward Cahill to Archbishop Byrne, 20 October 1926, (DDA, Byrne Papers).

[87] Minute Books of An Rioghacht, 1926-1946, in the possession of Patrick Waldron, Ranelagh, Dublin.

[88] *ibid.*

[89] *ibid.*

[90] Waldron, 'An Rioghacht: A Retrospect', *The Irish Monthly* (June, 1951), p.179.

[91] *Programme of a Catholic Social League*, 31 October 1926 (DDA, Byrne Papers).

[92] An Rioghacht pamphlet (DDA, Byrne Papers).

[93] *ibid.*

[94] *ibid.*, Waldron, 'An Rioghacht: A Retrospect', p.179.

[95] *Draft Policy of Weekly Paper* (IJA, Cahill Papers).

[96] *ibid.*

[97] *ibid.* An Rioghacht: Schemes for Social Reconstruction (1928)

[98] Edward Cahill, *The Framework of a Christian State* (Dublin, 1932), p.701.

[99] Claude Cane to Fr Edward Cahill, 13 August 1926 (IJA, Cahill Papers).

[100] Edward Cahill, 'Freemasonry: A Study in Catholic Social Science', *Irish Ecclesiastical Record*, Vol.29, (January-June 1927), 5th Series, pp349-366; Part 2, 'Historical sketch', pp481-99; Part 3, 'False Ideas about Freemasonry', pp616-26, *IER*, Vol.29 (Jan.-June 1929); Part 4, 'What is Freemasonry', *IER*, Vol.30 (July-Dec. 1927), pp15-29; Part 5,

'Masonic Aims and Methods', *IER*, Vol.32, (July–Dec. 1928), pp449-461.

[101] Denis Fahey, 'Freemasonry Exposed', *Catholic Bulletin*, Vol.18 (1928), pp264-271.

[102] 'Freemasonry in Ireland', *Irish Rosary* (October, 1929), pp110-118.

[103] The Central Catholic Library has a large section of books specifically related to the subject of Freemasonry (Section 13, Reference Department).

[104] George Clune, *Freemasonry: Its origins, aims and methods* (Dublin, 1932), p.32; *ICD, 1924*, p.554; *LM*, 1927, p.568.

[105] Edward Cahill, *Freemasonry and the Anti-Christian Movement*, 3rd ed. (Dublin, 1949).

[106] *The Leader*, 2 November 1929, pp318-20.

[107] *Irish Independent*, 2 November 1929; 5 November-24 December (twenty-one letters).

[108] *ICD, 1931*, p.586.

[109] *The Hidden Hand in the Mexican Atrocities* (1925), (DDA, Byrne Papers).

[110] *Have you ever given a thought?*

[111] John Nugent to Archbishop Byrne, 28 January 1938 (DDA, Byrne Papers).

[112] *ibid.*

[113] 'The Need for Organisation', *The Hibernian Journal*, Vol.VII, No.12 (December 1927), p.72.

[114] *ibid.*, p.74.

[115] CTSI Annual Report, 1920. Paper read by P.J. Daniel, pp82-88

[116] *ibid.*, p.86.

[117] *ICD, 1926*, p.569.

[118] Ambrose Crofts, 'Catholic Organisation in Holland', *Irish Monthly*, Vol.XXIX, No.2, (February 1925), p.92.

[119] CYMS, Ambrose Crofts, 'CYMS Arrives' (1927). Notes on his plans for the reorganisation of the Society.

[120] CYMS, John Costelloe to John M. Leech, 1 May 1931.

[121] CYMS, Costelloe to Honorary Secretary, Waterford Branch, 5 February 1929.

[122] *CYMS Federation Constitution and Statutes* (1927) (DDA, Byrne Papers).

[123] R.P. Riordan to Fr Dunne, 26 May 1928 (DDA, Byrne Papers).

[124] *Irish Independent*, 21 April 1928.

[125] Souvenir programme of CYMS Federation Social Week, April 16-22, 1928 (DDA, Byrne Papers).

[126] *ibid.*, p.9.

[127] *ibid.*, p.11.

[128] *ibid.*, p.16.

[129] 'Topics of the Month: The Catholic Social Week', *Irish Rosary* (May 1928), pp390-93.

[130] *Irish Independent*, 13 October 1926.

[131] *ibid.*

[132] *Cork Examiner*, 30 November 1925, 28 February 1927.

[133] 'Films', *Irish Monthly* (March 1925), pp161-2.

[134] The Synod of Maynooth 1927, 'Decrees which affect the Catholic Laity' (Dublin, 1930). In particular see Nos.216-220.

[135] *ibid.*

[136] *ibid.*

[137] CTSI Submission of Evidence, *The Problem of Undesirable Printed Matter: Suggested Remedies* (Dublin, 1926), p.6.

[138] Uta Ranke-Heinemann, *Eunuchs for the Kingdom of Heaven* (New York, 1990), p.292.

139 The Modesty Dress and Deportment Crusade, *Wanted: A New Woman* (1928), p.6. (DDA, Byrne Papers).

140 Mary Butler, 'The Ethics of Dress', *Irish Monthly*, Vol.41 (1917), pp219-20.

141 *ibid.*, p.220.

142 *ibid.*, p.221.

143 *ibid.*, p.223.

144 *ICD, 1928*, p.1 l, p.596, pp605-06.

145 CTSI minutes of the Organisation Subcommittee, March 1927.

146 'Modern Fashions in Ladies' Dress', *Irish Messenger Office* (Dublin, 1927), p.12.

147 File on MDDC, 1928 (DDA, Byrne Papers).

148 *ibid.*

149 *ibid.*

150 *ICD, 1928*, p.609.

151 *ibid.*

152 'The Designs of Women's Dress', *Irish Rosary* (January, 1928), p.4; 'Women's Modesty in Dress' (April 1928), p.26.

153 *Irish Rosary* (October 1928), p.202.

154 *Irish Rosary* (February 1929), pp256-57.

155 'Decency in Feminine Dress', *Irish Rosary* (February 1929), pp61-62.

156 MDDC pamphlets, *Our Lady's League, Summer Modesty*. (DDA, Byrne Papers).

157 *The Irish Catholic*, 3 May 1942. Article on the 'Progress of the Crusade for Modesty'.

158 *CYMS Quarterly Review*, Vol.4, No.4 (December 1942), p.3.

159 Catholic Girl Guides of Ireland, *Catholic Girl Guides of Ireland, A History 1927-1977* (Dublin, 1977), p.6.

160 CTSI minutes of the Committee of Management, 1926.

161 Caitriona Clear, 'The Women cannot be blamed: The Commission on Vocational Organisation, Feminism and Home Makers in Independent Ireland in the 1930s and 1940s', (M. O'Dowd and S. Wickert, eds) *Chattel Servant or Citizen – Women's Status in Church, State and Society* (Dublin, 1995), pp179-186.

162 'Fr Michael O'Carroll, An Interview with', in CCL, Veritas House, June-July 1996.

163 *ibid.*, see also televised interview with Frank Duff, 1978 (CCL Legion of Mary, Duff Papers).

164 Frank Duff to Archbishop Byrne, 24 November 1928 (DDA, Byrne Papers).

165 Archbishop Byrne to Frank Duff, 26 November 1928 (DDA, Byrne Papers).

166 Sir Joseph Glynn to Archbishop Byrne, 3 March 1930 (DDA, Byrne Papers).

167 Fr Michael O'Carroll interview; Leon O'Broin, Frank Duff (Dublin, 1982), p.56.

168 Fr Michael O'Carroll; also in records of Legion of Mary Information Bureau (CCL, Duff Papers).

169 O'Broin, *Frank Duff*, p.61.

170 Frank Duff, *Miracles on Tap* (Dublin, 1961), p.206.

171 O'Broin, p.56.

172 *ibid.*

173 Peter McKevitt, Confidential Report on Catholic Action, 1939 (DDA, McQuaid Papers, Laity File).

174 *ibid.*

175 O'Carroll; O'Broin., *op. cit.*, p.57.

176 CCL, Duff Papers.

177 Legion of Mary Correspondence (DDA, McQuaid Papers, ABS/XXII/A3. Laity File). Also included in the Laity File are material and correspondence related to the Pillar of Fire Society and the Mercier Society.
178 *ibid*.
179 *ibid*.
180 Dermot Keogh, *Jews in Twentieth Century Ireland* (Dublin, 1998).
181 McQuaid to Duff, 6 November 1942; Duff to McQuaid, 10 November 1942; McQuaid to Duff, 12 November 1942; McQuaid to Duff, 16 November 1942 (DDA, McQuaid Papers, Laity File).
182 Leon O'Broin to McQuaid, 4 December 1942; O'Broin to McQuaid, 4 January 1943 (DDA, McQuaid Papers, Laity File).
183 *The Bell*, Autumn 1944, p.16.
184 O'Broin, pp58-68; McQuaid to O'Broin, 5 January 1943, 7 January 1943, 15 February 1943 (DDA, McQuaid Papers, Laity File).
185 O'Broin, p.69; *The Irish Catholic*, 11 August 1983 (Interview with Fr Michael O'Carroll on Frank Duff).
186 McQuaid to Duff, 26 January 1944, 21 February 1944, 6 April 1944, 22 April 1944 (DDA, McQuaid Papers, Laity File).
187 Evelyn Bolster, *The Knights of St Columbanus* (Dublin, 1979), p.70, 95.
188 Hoover to McQuaid, 17 September 1958 (DDA, McQuaid Papers, AB8/B/XVIII).
189 George O'Brien, *The Economic History of Ireland from The Union to The Famine* (London, 1921).
190 Denis Gwynn, *The Irish Free State 1922-1929* (Dublin, 1930), p.235.
191 *Official Handbook of The Irish Free State, 1932* (Dublin, 1932), pp38-9.
192 Mary E. Daly, *Industrial Development and Irish National Identity, 1922-1939* (Dublin, 1992), p.15, 36, 37, 176.
193 *Irish Independent*, 13 October 1923.
194 Donal Nevin (ed.), *Trade Union Century* (Cork, 1994), pp62-63.
195 Joseph Keating, 'Ireland in Transition', *Irish Monthly* (October 1923), pp288-89.
196 *Cork Examiner*, 13 November 1923.
197 *ibid.*, 14 November 1923.
198 *ICM*, 1925, p.593.
199 Thomas Morrissey, *A Man called Hughes* (Dublin, 1993), pp218-19.
200 *ICD, 1925*, p.603.
201 *ibid.*, p.568.
202 Papers of General W.R.E. Murphy, Commissioner of Dublin Metropolitan Policy, 1923-25, in the possession of his grandson Karl Murphy, Dublin.
203 Joseph A. Glynn, *The Catholic Layman* (Dublin, 1924), p.35.
204 CTSI Annual Report 1924, p.17.
205 J. Maguire Esq., 'Pamphlet of Statistical and Social Enquiry Society of Ireland', 30 January 1925 (DDA, Byrne Papers).
206 *ibid*.
207 Byrne/O'Reilly Correspondence, 1925-1927 (DDA, Byrne Papers).
208 CTSI pamphlet No.742/SE. (Dublin, 1923).
209 CTSI pamphlet No.785/SE. (Dublin, 1923).
210 CTSI pamphlet No.826/MM. (Dublin, 1925).
211 CTSI pamphlet No.1054/SE11, (Dublin 1929).

[212] CTSI minutes of the Committee of Management, 19 September 1924.

[213] CTSI pamphlet No.292/SE. (Dublin, 1906).

[214] CTSI pamphlet No.633/SE. (Dublin, 1919).

[215] CTSI pamphlet No.634/SE. (Dublin, 1919).

[216] CTSI minutes of the Committee of Management, 5 April 1922.

[217] CTSI minutes of the Committee of Management, 20 November 1925, 8 January 1926.

[218] *ibid.*, Report of interview with His Grace the Archbishop of Dublin, Dr Edward Byrne.

[219] CTSI minutes of the Committee of Management Correspondence between Frank O'Reilly and Archbishop Harty, August 1927.

[220] *ibid.*

[221] Nevin. *op. cit.*, pp62-3.

[222] *ICD, 1925*, p.595.

[223] Byrne to O'Mahoney, 1 June 1922. (DDA, Byrne Papers, Laity File 3: Catholic Protection and Rescue Society of Ireland).

[224] *ibid.*

[225] *ibid.*

[226] *Proselytism: its operation in Ireland* (Dublin, 1926), p.18 (DDA, Byrne Papers).

[227] *ibid.*

[228] Report to the Lordships the Bishops of Ireland by the Committee appointed at the Maynooth Union to investigate Proselytism in Ireland, October 1926. (DDA, Byrne Papers, Laity File 3, CPRSI).

[229] *ibid.*, p.2.

[230] Annual Reports of the International Catholic Girls Protection Society 1920-1926 (DDA, Byrne Papers, Laity File 4).

[231] *ICD, 1926*. See Section on pastorals.

[232] *ibid.*

[233] *Frank Duff – One of the Best* (Dublin, N.D.), p.18. This pamphlet in praise of Frank Duff was most probably published by The Legion of Mary.

III

[1] J.H. Whyte, *Church and State in Modern Ireland, 1923-1979* (Dublin, 1984), pp24-39; F.S.L. Lyons, *Ireland Since The Famine* (Glasgow, 1971), pp487-88.

[2] F.S.L. Lyons, *op. cit.*, p.488.

[3] Diarmaid Ferriter, *A Nation of Extremes: The Pioneers in Twentieth Century Ireland* (Dublin, 1999), pp86-191.

[4] *ibid.*

[5] Licensing Law Reform, 19 March 1923 (NAI Dept Justice. H.U7A).

[6] CTSI minutes of the Publications Subcommittee, 1923-1924.

[7] CTSI pamphlet No.598/SE; pamphlet No.696/SE; pamphlet No.699/SE; pamphlet No.788/SE; pamphlet No.495/SE.

[8] Catholic Total Abstinence Federation of Ireland, Official Report of The Second Ordinary General Conference (1919).

[9] In conversation with Fr Stephen Redmond SJ, archivist with the Irish Jesuit Archives. Fr James Cullen SJ had founded The Pioneer Movement in 1899.

[10] P. Coffey, *Aids and Obstacles to Ireland's Progress: The enemy within our Gates* (Dublin, 1915), p.14.

[11] CTSI pamphlet No.495/SE, pp3-4.

[12] *ibid.*, 'Bona Fide' Trading refers to the situation where a 'traveller' could obtain alcohol in a Public House other than one within a three-mile radius of where he/she lived. The situation lent itself to facilitating an abuse of the Licensing Laws.

[13] Catholic Total Abstinence Federation of Ireland, *Proceedings of the Third Ordinary General Congress* (1923), p.7 (hereafter cited as CTAFI).

[14] *ibid.*, p.8.

[15] CTAFI, *Proceedings of The Fourth Ordinary General Congress* (1924), p.19.

[16] Licensing Law Reform, 19 March 1923 (NAI Dept Justice H.U47A).

[17] *ICD, 1926*, p.583.

[18] *ibid., 1925*, p.581.

[19] *ibid., 1927*, p.573.

[20] Ferriter, *op. cit*, p.94.

[21] *ICD, 1927*, p.573.

[22] CTSI Annual Report 1924, p.3.

[23] CTSI, *Up and Doing: A Handbook of Catholic Action* (Dublin, 1928), p.6.

[24] CTSI Annual Report 1925, p.4; Annual Report 1929; Report of Michael O'Connor, Hon. Sec., Tralee Branch, 28 June 1927.

[25] CTSI , Roscrea Branch Report of Thomas Tobin, Hon. Sec., 1928.

[26] CTSI , Castlebar Branch Report of J.P. Ryan, Hon. Sec., 1928.

[27] *ibid.* CTSI minutes of Organisation Subcommittee, March-April 1928; CTSI Annual Report 1928; Castlebar Branch Report, 1931.

[28] CTSI minutes of Organisation Subcommittee, June-July 1929; *ibid.*, September 1929.

[29] CTSI minutes of Committee of Management. Letter, 4 October 1929, from Martin J. Doherty, Cooracleere, Co. Clare, to Hon. Sec., CTSI; Letter, 5 October 1929, from Frank O'Reilly to Revd M. Hehir, PP, Cooracleere, Co. Clare.

[30] Brother Craven to Archbishop Byrne, 21 May 1921. Letter includes a circular presented to every newsagent in the country petitioning for their help in his campaign (DDA, Byrne Papers, Laity File).

[31] *ibid.*, Circular with heading, 'The Newsagents of .... Who are to God and Ireland true'.

[32] Richard Devane, 'Indecent Literature: Some Legal Remedies', *Irish Ecclesiastical Record*, 5th Series, No.25 (February 1925), pp182-204.

[33] 'The Crusade for Clean Literature', *Irish Rosary* (June 1924), pp473-75.

[34] Letter to Editor, 3 December 1925, *Irish Rosary* (Jan. 1926).

[35] *The Irish Catholic*, 24 January 1925.

[36] Letter written by James Hart of the Newsagents' Association, to the Editor, reiterating his Association's willingness to co-operate with the movement to suppress evil literature, *Irish Rosary* (April 1926), pp307-09.

[37] *ICD, 1926*, p.558.

[38] *ibid.*, p.560.

[39] CTSI minutes of the Organisation Subcommittee, 1 December 1925.

[40] *ibid.*, Organisation Report, 1925.

[41] *ibid.*

[42] CTSI minutes of the Organisation Subcommittee, January 1926.

[43] CTSI Annual Report, 30 June 1926, p.9.

[44] *ibid.*, pp9-10.

[45] L.M. Cullen, *Eason and Son: A History* (Dublin, 1989), p.263.

[46] *Irish Independent*, 20 October 1926.

[47] Cullen, *op. cit.*, p.267.

[48] *The Irish Times*, 2 May 1927.

[49] *Irish Independent*, 11 October 1927.

[50] *ibid.*, 7 June 1927.

[51] Devane, *op. cit.*

[52] *ibid.*

[53] Richard Devane, *The Imported Press – A National Menace: Some Remedies* (Dublin, 1950), p.1.

[54] Stephen Brown, 'A Catholic Library for Dublin', *Studies* (1 June 1922), pp207-210.

[55] Stephen Brown, *The Central Catholic Library – The First Ten Years of An Irish Enterprise* (Dublin, 1932), p.20. With a foreword by Desmond Fitzgerald TD, Minister in the First Government of the Irish Free State.

[56] *ibid.*, p.21.

[57] Stephen Brown, 'A New Storehouse of Catholic Thought', *The Month* (March 1923), pp57-62.

[58] Stephen Brown, 'The Central Catholic Library: an Apologia', *Irish Ecclesiastical Record*, 5th Series, No.24 (March 1924), pp78-81.

[59] Stephen Brown, 'The Catholic Novelists: A Plea and a List', *Irish Rosary*, (February 1924), p.108.

[60] CTSI minutes of the Organisation Subcommittee, April 1925.

[61] Richard Devane, 'Indecent Literature: Some Legal Remedies', *Irish Ecclesiastical Record*, 5th, No.25 (February 1925), pp473-75.

[62] CTSI minutes of the Organisation Subcommittee, 25 February-10 March 1925.

[63] CTSI minutes of the Organisation Subcommittee, October-November 1924.

[64] Bishop Downey to Frank O'Reilly, 1 August 1925 (CTSI).

[65] Frank O'Reilly to Bishop Downey, 10 August 1925 (CTSI).

[66] *ibid.*

[67] CTSI minutes of the Committee of Management, 21 August 1925.

[68] Senator J.J. O'Farrell to Frank O'Reilly, 25 September 1925 (CTSI).

[69] CTSI minutes of the Organisation Subcommittee, October 1925.

[70] *ibid.*

[71] CTSI Annual Report, 30 June 1926, p.2.

[72] CTSI minutes of the Organisation Subcommittee, October 1925.

[73] *ICD, 1927*, p.567.

[74] J.P. Clare to Representative of Dept of Posts and Telegraphs, 19 April 1926 (NAI Jus. 7/2/17. Dept of Posts and Telegraphs).

[75] CTSI minutes of the Committee of Management, 19 April 1926.

[76] Frank O'Reilly to Archbishop Harty, 26 February 1926; Archbishop Harty to O'Reilly, 13 April 1926 (CTSI).

[77] CTSI minutes of the Committee of Management, 19 March 1926; *ICD*, April 1926, p.581.

[78] Minutes of the Evil Literature Subcommittee, 1926; *The Problem of Undesirable Printed Matter: Suggested Remedies*, evidence of the CTSI presented to the Department Committee of Enquiry 1926 (Dublin, 1926), pp99.

[79] *ibid.*, p.50.

[80] *ibid.*, pp6-17.

[81] *ibid.*, p.9.

[82] *ibid.*, p.10.

[83] *ibid.*, p.12.

[84] *ibid.*, p.13.

[85] *ibid.*, p.50.

[86] *ibid.*, p.5.

[87] Frank O'Reilly to Archbishop Byrne, 27 May 1926 (DDA, Laity File).

[88] CTSI minutes of the Organisation Subcommittee, May 1926.

[89] CTSI Annual Report, 30 June 1926, p.3.

[90] CTSI Circular, 'The Circulation of Undesirable Printed Matter'.

[91] CTSI minutes of the Organisation Subcommittee, 17 May 1926.

[92] CTSI Annual Report, 30 June 1926, p.5.

[93] CTSI Branch Reports, 16 May-16 June 1926. Branches included Tralee, Newbridge, Wexford, Kanturk and Cavan.

[94] James Geoghegan to Frank O'Reilly, 21 June 1927 (CTSI).

[95] Frank O'Reilly to James Geoghegan (N.D.), (CTSI).

[96] CTSI minutes of the Organisation Subcommittee, 2 June 1927.

[97] CTSI Annual Report, 1927, pp6-7.

[98] *ibid.*

[99] CTSI minutes of the Organisation Subcommittee, May-June 1928.

[100] CTSI minutes of the Committee of Management, 22 June 1928.

[101] *ibid.*, 17 August 1928.

[102] *ibid.*, 21 September 1928.

[103] *ibid.*, 26 October 1928.

[104] CTSI Annual Report, 1929, p.17.

[105] *Tuam Herald*, 20 October 1928.

[106] *Cork Examiner*, 15 October 1928.

[107] *Irish Independent*, 16, 20 October 1928.

[108] *The Irish Times*, 16-20 October 1928.

[109] *The Irish Times*, 18 October 1928.

[110] *The Irish Times*, 29 September 1928.

[111] *The Sunday Times*, 28 October 1928.

[112] *ibid.*

[113] *ibid.*

[114] *ibid.*

[115] *Irish Independent*, 26 November 1928.

[116] CTSI minutes of the Committee of Management, 21 November 1928.

[117] *ibid.*

[118] *Irish Independent*, 26 November 1928.

[119] *ibid.*

[120] *ibid.*, CTSI minutes of the Committee of Management, 21 December 1928; *ibid.*, 13 January 1929.

[121] *Irish Independent*, 26 November 1928.

[122] CTSI minutes of the Organisation Subcommittee, June-July 1929; minutes of the Committee of Management, 18 October 1929.

[123] Frank O'Reilly to William Cosgrave, 25 October 1929 (NAI, Dept of Taoiseach File S/2325).

[124] *ibid.*
[125] William Cosgrave to O'Friel, 28 October 1929 (NAI, Dept of Taoiseach File S/2325).
[126] *ibid.*
[127] James Fitzgerald-Kenny to William Cosgrave, 5 November 1929; Murphy to O'Friel, 8 November 1929 (NAI, Dept of Taoiseach File S/5381/2).
[128] Murphy to O'Reilly, Draft Letter, 15 November 1929 (NAI, Dept of Taoiseach File S/5341/2).
[129] Minutes of the Committee of Management, April 1930.
[130] *The Catholic Mind* (May 1930), pp3-17.
[131] 'Ineffective Censorship: Why The Act is not doing its work – Official Remissness', *Catholic Truth Quarterly* (January-March 1940), pp2-9.
[132] CTSI minutes of the Committee of Management, May 1937.
[133] CTSI minutes of the Vigilance Subcommittee (Literature), 1 October 1937. Confidential Report, 'Censorship of Publications Act, 1929 and its workings', 1937.
[134] CTSI minutes of the Vigilance Subcommittee (Literature), November 1938.
[135] *ibid.*, 17 November 1938.
[136] *ibid.*, June 1939.
[137] *ibid.*
[138] *ibid.*
[139] *ibid.*
[140] CTSI minutes of Committee of Management, January 1941.
[141] CTSI minutes of the Publications Subcommittee, 1939-1940; *ibid.*, 1939-1946.
[142] *ICD, 1923*, p.547. Report of a meeting of the Irish Vigilance Association, addressed by Revd J.S. Sheehy, Dean of All Hallows College, Dublin; CTSI Annual Report, 1923, p.62.
[143] F.S.L. Lyons, *Ireland since the Famine* (Glasgow, 1971), p.686.
[144] *ICD, 1923*, p.548.
[145] *Irish Rosary* (June 1922), p.407-08.
[146] William Magennis, 'The Cinema as a Social Factor', *Studies* (March 1944), pp76-84.
[147] *ICD, 1925*, pp547-48; *The Irish Catholic*, 26 February 1924.
[148] *ICD, 1926*, p.563.
[149] CTSI minutes of the Committee of Management, 17 November 1933; minutes of the Vigilance Subcommittee (Cinema), 1933.
[150] *ibid.*
[151] CTSI minutes of the Committee of Management, 8 May 1934, October 1934.
[152] *ibid.*, 16 December 1934.
[153] CTSI minutes of Vigilance Subcommittee (Cinema). Confidential Report on the Censorship of Theatres, 1938; Reports of the CTSI Censors, 1938-1939.
[154] Denis O'Dwyer, 'The Little Theatre Movement', *Irish Rosary* (March 1931), pp185-190.
[155] Editorial, *Irish Rosary* (March 1931), pp165-66.
[156] *ibid.*
[157] *ibid.*, p.327.
[158] Philip Ryan, *Jimmy O'Dea: The Pride of the Coombe* (Dublin, 1990), p.210.
[159] *ibid.*, p.212.
[160] Joseph Dunn, *No Vipers in the Vatican* (Dublin, 1997), p.269.
[161] Philip Ryan, *Noel Purcell: A Biography* (Dublin, 1992), pp85-61.

162 J.H. Whyte, *Church and State in Modern Ireland, 1923-1979* (Dublin, 1980), pp28-29.

163 Seán Ó Faoláin, *A Purse of Coppers* (London, 1937), pp31-34.

164 CTSI minutes of the Committee of Management, 15 June 1934.

165 *The Irish Times*, 11 June 1935.

166 T.W. Curd, 'The Crux of The Cinema', *Irish Rosary* (May 1931), p.339.

167 Kevin Rockett, *Film and Ireland: A Chronicle* (London, 1980), p.7.

168 *Up and Doing* (July 1935), p.7.

169 *The Irish Times*, 23 March 1935.

170 *The Cork Examiner*, 24 April 1935.

171 *The Mayo News*, 30 March 1935.

172 *Today's Cinema*, 2 April 1935.

173 *Waterford News*, 29 March 1935.

174 *Irish Independent*, 12 June 1935.

175 Frank Walsh, *Sin and Censorship: The Catholic Church and The Motion Picture Industry* (Yale, 1996), pp45, 64-65, 111, 147, 169-170. According to Frank Walsh, by the summer of 1934, the Legion Campaign had developed a momentum. It was, in the words of one priest, 'Catholic Action's Big Opportunity', p.111.

176 *Irish Press*, 4 May 1935.

177 In conversation with Fr Stephen Redmond SJ, archivist, Irish Jesuit Archives (IJA).

178 *Irish Press*, 11 June 1935, 12 June 1935; *The Irish Times*, 11 June 1935; *Daily Evening Herald*, 11 June 1935.

179 *The Cinema*, 10 February 1937.

180 Catholic Action Section and Programme of Claude Road Branch, Drumcondra, Dublin 1, May 1937 (CYMS).

181 *CYMS Quarterly Review* Vol.3, No.2 (Summer 1941), p.13.

182 *ibid.*, Vol.4, No.2 (Summer 1942), p.14.

183 J.V. Hallessey to Archbishop Byrne, 18 September 1939 (DDA, Byrne Papers, Laity File, Box 3) J.V. Hallessey was Director of Organisation for the CYMS.

184 *L'Osservatore Romano*, 5 May 1935.

185 James Montgomery to T.J. Hallessey, 3 October 1939 (DDA, Byrne Papers, Catholic Film Society of Ireland).

186 *ibid.*, 29 October 1939.

187 Cardinal Maggliore to Hallessey, 5 December 1939 (DDA, Byrne Papers, Catholic Film Society of Ireland).

188 *Vigilanti Cura*, 1936.

189 *The Irish Times*, 27 August 1994. Review of T.D. Matthews, *Censored: The Story of Film Censorship in Britain* (London, 1994), p.298.

190 Gabriel Fallon, 'The Celluloid Menace', *Capuchin Annual* (1938), pp248-71.

191 The Records of An Rioghacht in Fr Edward Cahill's Papers include clippings from the newspapers of the USA and Britain, and show that the organisation was particularly impressed by the work of the Legion of Decency (IJA, Cahill Papers, An Rioghacht).

192 *Irish Independent*, 9 April 1938.

IV

1 *Quadragesimo Anno*, 1931.

2 *ibid*, par.15, 25, 34, 56, 87, 91.

[3] J.H. Whyte, *Church and State in Modern Ireland, 1923-1979* (Dublin, 1980), pp67-68.

[4] *ibid.*

[5] Documents, *Irish Ecclesiastical Record*, 5th Series, Vol. 38. (July-December, 1931) pp540-42.

[6] *The Irish Catholic Herald*, 31 October 1931.

[7] *ibid*, 21 November 1931.

[8] *Catholic Bulletin*, December 1931, pp907-10.

[9] *ibid.*, November 1931, pp822-23.

[10] T.W.C. Card, 'The Coming Conflict, Capitalism Versus Communism', *Irish Monthly*, Vol. 30 (1932), p.353.

[11] G.M. Godden, 'The Soviet Power at Work in England and Ireland', *Irish Rosary* (September 1931), pp678-684.

[12] Austin Clarke, *Twice Around the Black Church* (Dublin, 1990), p.30.

[13] *Irish Independent*, 19 October 1931.

[14] Dáil Debates Vol. 50 (1934), Col. 2505-10, 1 March 1934.

[15] *The Standard*, 19 November 1932.

[16] CYMS Annual Report, 1932-33, p.4.

[17] Catholic Able-Bodied Men's Association to Archbishop Byrne, 5 March 1933. (DDA, Byrne Papers).

[18] *ICD, 1934*, pp572-74.

[19] Patrick Hogan, *Could Ireland Become Communist?* (Dublin, N.D.).

[20] *The Irish Catholic Herald*, 17 February 1935.

[21] CTSI minutes of the Committee of Management, 15 April 1932.

[22] CTSI minutes of the Committee of Management, 16 March 1934.

[23] *ibid*, 20 April 1934; 15 June 1934; 20 July 1934; 16 April 1937; 14 May 1937.

[24] *ibid*, 14 May 1937.

[25] *ibid*, 18 November 1933.

[26] CTSI Report, 'The Production and Distribution of Anti-Communist Propaganda' (June 1938).

[27] *ibid.*

[28] *ibid.*

[29] *ibid.*

[30] *The Irish Catholic*, 9 July 1932. See 'CYMS Notes'.

[31] *ibid.*, 29 August 1932, 'Our Branches and The Evils of Today'.

[32] *ibid*, 13 August 1932, 'The CYMS: Its Present and Future Development in Ireland'.

[33] *ibid.*

[34] CYMS Annual Report 1934, CYMS Annual Report 1939.

[35] *ICD, 1934*, p.582.

[36] *ibid.*

[37] *Irish Independent*, 22 February 1933, 'Readers' Opinions'.

[38] *ibid.*

[39] *ibid.*, 25 February 1933.

[40] *The Irish Catholic*, 25 March 1933.

[41] *ibid.*, 6 May 1933.

[42] Dublin Branches Correspondence Files, 1933 (CYMS, Costelloe to Dublin Branches Files).

[43] *ibid.*

44 *The Irish Catholic*, 6 May 1933.
45 *Irish Weekly Independent*, 1 April 1933.
46 Mike Milotte, *Communism in Modern Ireland* (Dublin, 1984), pp118-19.
47 *ICD, 1934*, p.595.
48 *Limerick Leader*, 9 April 1932, 16 April 1932.
49 *The Irish Catholic*, 13 August 1932.
50 *ICD, 1933*, p.585; *Irish Catholic*, 8 April 1933.
51 *ibid.*
52 *Irish Press*, 26 May 1933.
53 *The Irish Catholic*, 17 June 1933.
54 *Sunday Independent*, June 1933.
55 *ibid.*
56 *Irish Press*, 7 June 1933.
57 *Fairview CYMS Journal* Vol.1 (August, 1933), p.l.
58 *The Irish Catholic*, 11 February 1933.
59 A.M. Crofts, *Property and Poverty* (Dublin, 1948), pp269. This book was due for publication in 1938; Catholic Social Action (Dublin, 1936), pp327.
60 *The Standard*, 18 March 1933.
61 A.M. Crofts, *Workers of Ireland: Which Way?* (Waterford, 1934), p.42.
62 *ICD, 1933*, p.586.
63 *Connaught Tribune*, 10 June 1933.
64 Mike Milotte, *op. cit.*, p.10.
65 *ibid.*, p.109.
66 Fr O'Donoghue to John Costelloe, 5 June 1934; John Costelloe to O'Donoghue, 6 June 1934. (CYMS, Costelloe Correspondence). Fr O'Donoghue was Spiritual Director of the Galway Branch.
67 *ibid.*
68 *Irish Independent*, 2 June 1934.
69 *ICD, 1934*, pp572-74.
70 *ibid.*
71 Hon. Sec. Kilkenny City Branch to John Costelloe, 1933-1934 (CYMS, Costelloe Correspondence, Kilkenny File, 1933/34)
72 *Irish Independent*, 21 November 1933.
73 Hon. Sec. Ossory Diocesan Council to John Costelloe, 16 July 1936 (CYMS, Costelloe Correspondence, Ossory Diocesan Council).
74 Ann Boran, 'One Miner's Mission', *Resource* (Summer 1984), p.4.
75 *Kilkenny Journal*, 23 March 1931. See also Pat Feeley, 'The Castlecomer Mine and Quarry Union', *The Old Limerick Journal No.6* (Spring 1981); *The Kilkenny People*, 12 November 1971; Anna Nolan and William Brennan, 'Nixie Boran and The Colliery Community of North Kilkenny' in W. Nolan and K. Whelan (eds) *A History of Kilkenny County* (Dublin 1985) pp567-585.
76 *Kilkenny Journal*, 23 March 1931.
77 *Kilkenny People*, 23 October 1933; in conversation with Fr William Purcell, CC, Moneen Roe; Jerry Joyce, *Laity: Help or Hindrance* (Dublin, 1994), p.96. Fr Joyce was Parish Priest of Castlecomer.
78 Jerry Joyce, *op. cit.*, p.7.
79 John Costelloe to Hon. Sec. Galway Branch, 24 June 1933 (CYMS, Costelloe

Correspondence).

[80] John Costelloe to J.J. Hyland, Oughterard Branch, 25 January 1936 (CYMS, Costelloe Correspondence).

[81] *Irish Weekly Independent*, 18 January 1936.

[82] *ibid.*

[83] *Irish Workers' Voice*, 18 January 1936.

[84] *Irish Weekly Independent*, 18 January 1936.

[85] *Evening Mail*, 24 January 1937.

[86] CYMS Annual Report, 1937.

[87] Confidential questionnaire issued by the CYMS Vigilance Department, 1936.

[88] Horan to Hon. Sec. Aughrim Street Dublin Branch, 31 January 1936 (CYMS, Aughrim Street Branch File). Horan was an organising secretary for two organisations.

[89] *CYMS News Bulletin,* January 1936.

[90] *Irish Weekly Independent*, 9 April 1938.

[91] *ibid.*

[92] Raymond J. Raymond, 'De Valera, Lemass and Irish Economic Development, 1933-1945', in John A. Murphy and J.P. O'Connell (eds), *De Valera and His Times* (Cork, 1983), pp115-16.

[93] Mary E. Daly, *Industrial Development and Irish National Identity: 1922-1939* (Dublin, 1992), p.173.

[94] Muintir na Tíre, *Rural Ireland —Handbook of Muintir na Tíre* (1941), p.42.

[95] *Irish Independent*, 1 November 1932.

[96] *The Irish Catholic Herald*, 21 May 1932.

[97] CTSI Annual Report, 1932; *Dublin Book of The Congress* (1932). See also minutes of the 1932 Eucharistic Congress Subcommittee; souvenir brochures of 1932 Eucharistic Congress (CTSI).

[98] G.J. Chesterton, *Christendom in Dublin* (London, 1932), p.15; see also Radharc, *The Year of the Congress* (Dublin, 1932). This is a Radharc-produced film of the 1932 Eucharistic Congress. Radharc was part of the Catholic Communications Institute of Ireland, previously known as the Catholic Truth Society of Ireland.

[99] *Irish Independent*, 'Eucharistic Congress Record' (Dublin, 1932), p.64; *Irish Independent* 'Eucharistic Congress Souvenir Number 1932' (Dublin, 1932), p.96; *The Irish Press* 'Eucharistic Congress Souvenir, 1932' (Dublin, 1932), p.48.

[100] *The Irish Press* 'Eucharistic Congress Souvenir, 1932' (Dublin, 1932), p.36, 'Can Irish Agriculture Stand Alone?'

[101] *ibid.*

[102] *ibid.*, p.32.

[103] *Irish Press*, 11 January 1933.

[104] *ibid.*, 16 January 1933.

[105] *ibid.*, 23 January 1933.

[106] *ibid.*, 2 May 1932.

[107] Maurice Manning, *The Blueshirts* (Dublin, 1970), pp55-9, 74.

[108] *United Ireland,* 15 October 1932.

[109] *ibid.*

[110] *ibid.*, 29 July 1933.

[111] *ibid.*

[112] *Quadragesimo Anno*, 1931.

[113] *The Irish Times*, 21 July 1933.

[114] *ibid.*, 11 August 1933.

[115] *ibid.*, 13 November 1933.

[116] *Irish Independent*, 10 June 1935; *Irish Press*, 10 June 1935.

[117] *United Ireland*, 22 December 1934.

[118] *ibid.*, 14 December 1933; 1 November 1933; 24 March 1934; 31 March 1934; 7 April 1934; 19 May 1934; 26 May 1934; 2 June 1934.

[119] John Murphy, *The College: A History of Queen's/University College Cork* (Cork, 1995), p.283.

[120] *United Ireland*, 6 January 1934.

[121] *ibid.*, 11 August 1934.

[122] *Non Abbiamo Bisogno*, 1931.

[123] *Quadragesimo Anno*, 1931.

[124] Oswald Von Nell-Breunig, *Re-organisation of the Social Economy – The Social Encyclicals Developed and Explained* (New York, 1936), pp258-260.

[125] Edward Coyne, 'Corporative Organisation in Ireland', *Studies*, Vol.25 (1934), pp185-202.

[126] *ibid.*

[127] 'From the Hill-Tops', *Catholic Bulletin*, Vol.27 (1937), pp98-99.

[128] Cornelius Lacey, 'Christian Corporatism', *Irish Ecclesiastical Record* 5th Series Vol. XIV (Jan.-June 1937), pp225-241.

[129] *ibid.*, p.239.

[130] *ibid.*

[131] Denis O'Keeffe, 'The Corporative Organisation of Society', *Studies*, Vol.26 (June 1937) pp176-189.

[132] *ibid.*

[133] Editorial, *Catholic Bulletin*, Vol.23 (1933), pp277-78.

[134] *Outlook*, 2 January 1932, p.3.

[135] CTSI, *First Fifty Years of CTSI, 1899-1949* (Dublin, 1949), see index of publications, pp60-111.

[136] *Irish Messenger Office*, see catalogue for 1930-39, *Social Action Series*.

[137] Charles K. Murphy, *The Spirit of Catholic Action* (London, 1943), p.2.

[138] Edward Cahill, *The Framework of a Christian State* (Dublin, 1932).

[139] George Clune, *Christian Social Reorganisation* (Dublin, 1940).

[140] Denis Fahey, *The Kingship of Christ According To The Principles of Thomas Aquinas* (Dublin, 1931).

[141] A.M. Crofts, *Property and Poverty* (Dublin, 1938).

[142] John J. Webb, *The Guilds of Dublin* (Dublin, 1929).

[143] George Clune, *The Medieval Guild System* (Dublin, 1943).

[144] CTSI pamphlet No.1054/SE 11 (Dublin, 1929); Catholic Social Guild, *The Guild Social Order* (Oxford, 1936), p.59.

[145] Oswald Von Nell-Breunig, *Re-organisation of the Social Economy. The Social Encyclicals Developed and Explained* (New York, 1936).

[146] John Murphy, *op. cit.*, pp282-87; Hilaire Belloc, *The Great Heresies* (London, 1938).

[147] *Quadragesimo Anno*, par.78-97.

[148] Interview with Dr Niall Tierney, 6 March 1996, at Veritas House.

[149] A.M. Crofts, *Catholic Social Action* (Dublin, 1936), p.79.

[150] Edward Cahill, *op. cit.*, p.408, 656.

[151] *CYMS Quarterly Review*, Vol.3, No.1 (Spring 1941), p.35.

[152] *ibid*, p.36; CYMS Catholic Social Reconstruction Papers, see 'Rural Ireland's Part'.

[153] Luigi Civardi, *A Manual of Catholic Action* (London, 1935).

[154] Muintir na Tíre, *Official Handbook, 1941*, p.115.

[155] *ibid*.

[156] Muintir na Tíre, *Official Handbook, 1940*, p.26.

[157] *The Irish Times*, 7 June 1940.

[158] *ibid*.

[159] Fergus O'Higgins, 'The Guilds of Regnum Christi', *Link-up* (February 1989), p.18.

[160] Roland Burke Savage, 'The Church in Dublin, 1940-1965', *Studies* (Winter 1965), p.298.

[161] *Manual of the Guilds of Regnum Christi* (Dublin, 1934), p.5.

[162] *Catholic Mind*, Vol.5, No.2, (February 1934), p.34.

[163] Frank O'Reilly to Fr Patrick Dunne, 17 December 1935 (DDA, Byrne Papers, Laity File). Fr Dunne was Archbishop Byrne's Secretary. The 'Silent Archbishop' as he was known, was particularly reclusive in his later years, suffering from Parkinson's disease. One consequence of this was the neglect of some of his administrative duties.

[164] Memorandum on the League of Social Justice and Charity, December 1935 (DDA, Byrne Papers).

[165] Frank O'Reilly to Fr Patrick Dunne, 20 November 1936 (DDA, Byrne Papers).

[166] *ibid*.

[167] CTSI Annual Report, 1935, pp17-19.

[168] *Catholic Bulletin*, Vol.25 (August 1935), pp586-87.

[169] *The Standard*, 5 July 1935.

[170] *Irish Independent*, 27 June 1935.

[171] *The Irish Times*, 28 June 1935; *Irish Press*, 28 June 1935.

[172] *ibid.*, See also newspaper clippings relating to CTSI 1935 Congress (CTSI).

[173] Muintir na Tíre, *Rural Ireland* (Tipperary, 1940), p.34.

[174] *The Irish Times*, 24 December 1977, Roland Burke Savage, 'Towards the Development of a Social Conscience in the Catholic Church in Ireland, 1891-1939'.

[175] *Irish Monthly*, Vol.65 (1937), p.577.

[176] Edward Coyne, 'The Social Order Summer School', *Irish Monthly*, Vol.65 (1937), pp577-587.

[177] Annual Meeting of the Cork CYMS, October 1934.

[178] T.J. Dolan, Hon. Sec., Glasnevin Branch to John Costelloe, 13 February 1936. (CYMS Dublin Branches File); *CYMS Quarterly Review*, Vol.2, No.4 (Christmas, 1940), p.50; *ibid.*, Vol.1, No.3 (Summer 1939), p.29.

[179] CYMS, Annual Report of the Central Executive Committee, 1939-1940, p.4.

[180] CYMS, Annual Report, 1939, p.6.

[181] Patrick Corish, *Maynooth College, 1795-1995* (Dublin, 1995), p.315.

[182] Evelyn Bolster, *The Knights of St Columbanus* (Dublin, 1979), p.68.

[183] Patrick Corish, *op. cit.*, p.316; Evelyn Bolster, *op. cit.*, p.74.

[184] Evelyn Bolster, *op. cit.*, pp79-80.

[185] CYMS Catholic Social Reconstruction Papers; *CYMS Quarterly Review*, Vol.1, No.2 (Spring 1939), pp7-8.

[186] Evelyn Bolster, *op. cit.*, pp70-71. Other members were Seán Lemass, Seán MacEntee, Dr J. Stafford Johnson, Joseph Walshe and Seán MacEoin.

[187] Dermot Keogh, *The Vatican, The Bishops and Irish Politics* (Cambridge, 1986), p.204.

[188] Edward Cahill to Éamon de Valera, 23 August 1936 (IJA, Cahill Papers).

[189] Edward Cahill, *The Framework of a Christian State* (Dublin, 1932), pp451-503. See also chapters on 'Catholic Social Principles'.

[190] Sean Faughnan, 'The Jesuits and the drafting of the Irish Constitution of 1937', *Irish Historical Studies*, Vol.XXVI, No.101 (May 1988), p.83.

[191] Éamon de Valera to Edward Cahill, 2 August 1932 (IJA, Cahill Papers).

[192] *The Clongownian*, Vol.XIV, No.3 (June 1937), pp9-12.

[193] T.P. O'Neill and P. O'Fiannachta, *Eamonn De Valera* (Dublin, 1970), p.295. P. O'Fiannachta, also known as the Earl of Longford.

[194] Edward Cahill to Éamon de Valera, 4 September 1936 (IJA, Cahill Papers).

[195] Éamon de Valera to Edward Cahill, 29 September 1936 (IJA, Cahill Papers).

[196] Jesuit Subcommittee on the Constitution (IJA, Bartley Papers; Cahill Papers).

[197] Louis McRedmond, *To the Greater Glory: A History of the Irish Jesuits* (Dublin, 1991), pp287-89.

[198] Draft Submission of Jesuit Subcommittee on the Constitution (IJA, Bartley Papers).

[199] Louis McRedmond, *op. cit.*, p.288.

[200] Edward Cahill to Éamon de Valera, 13 November 1936 (IJA, Cahill Papers).

[201] Éamon de Valera to Edward Cahill, 24 May 1937 (IJA, Cahill Papers).

[202] Éamon de Valera to Edward Cahill, 19 September 1936 (IJA, Cahill Papers).

[203] Sean Faughnan, *op. cit.* p.99.

[204] J. Whyte, *op. cit.*, p.377.

[205] Dermot Keogh, *op. cit.*, pp207-220.

[206] Sean P. Farragher, *Dev and his Alma Mater* (Dublin & London, 1984), pp173-74.

[207] *ibid.*

[208] *ibid.*

[209] Sean Faughnan, *op. cit*, p.99.

[210] Francis McManus, *The Years of the Great Test* (Dublin, 1967), p.170.

[211] Edward Cahill to Éamon de Valera, 2 May 1937 (IJA, Cahill Papers).

[212] Brian Farrell, *De Valera's Constitution and Ours* (Dublin, 1983), pp103-122.

[213] Tim Pat Coogan, *De Valera, Long Fellow, Long Shadow* (London, 1993), p.489.

[214] J.H. Whyte, *op. cit.*, pp50-56.

[215] *Irish Press*, 3 May 1937.

[216] Dermot Keogh, *Ireland and the Vatican: The Politics of Diplomacy in Church–State Relations, 1922-1960* (Cork, 1995), pp132-40.

[217] Brian Farrell, *op. cit.*, p.110.

[218] Tim Pat Coogan, *op. cit.*, p.497.

[219] Edward Coyne, 'The Vocational Structure of Ireland', *Irish Monthly*, Vol.66 (1938), pp394-402.

[220] Ita Mallon, 'The Draft Constitution: Work for a Woman's Party', *Hibernia* (June 1937), p.15.

[221] 'Comment', *Hibernia* (May 1937), p.16.

[222] *ibid.*

[223] An Rioghacht, minutes of the Ard Comhairle, May-June 1937 (IJA, Cahill Papers).

[224] Statement from An Rioghacht (IJA, Cahill Papers).

[225] Brian J. McCaffrey to Éamon de Valera, 27 May 1937 (IJA, Cahill Papers). McCaffrey was President of An Rioghacht at this stage.

226 *ibid.*
227 *ibid.*
228 *ibid.*
229 *ibid.*
230 Edward Cahill to Éamon de Valera, 29 May 1937 (IJA, Cahill Papers).
231 Brian J. McCaffrey to Éamon de Valera, 27 May 1937 (IJA, Cahill Papers).
232 *ibid.*
233 Edward Cahill, 'The Irish Constitution (Bunreacht na hÉireann) 1937'. Copy of article written for *Revisita Javeriana* (IJA, Cahill Papers).
234 In conversation with Fr Michael O'Carroll, 3 June 1995.

V

1 Brian Farrell, *Seán Lemass* (Dublin, 1983), p.48.
2 Reports of the Commission of Inquiry into Banking Currency and Credit, 1938 (Dublin, 1938), p.1.
3 Edward Cahill to Éamon de Valera, 2 May 1937 (IJA, Cahill Papers). See also An Rioghacht's, 'Schemes for social reconstruction: I. Catholic Agricultural Colonies' (IJA, Cahill Papers).
4 Draft of speech given by Fr Cahil at a meeting of An Rioghacht, 30 January, 1935 (IJA, Cahill Papers).
5 *Irish Press*, 31 January 1935.
6 Bulmer Hobson to Edward Cahill, 6 June 1936 (IJA, Cahill Papers).
7 *Social Justice*, No.6 (August 1936), p.13.
8 Memorandum of evidence for Commission of Inquiry into Banking, Currency and Credit, March 1935 (IJA, Cahill Papers).
9 *ibid.*, Recommendations, p.2.
10 *ibid.*, p.3.
11 *ibid.*, p.5.
12 Brian J. McCaffrey to Edward Cahill, 14 June 1935 (IJA, Cahill Papers); Cahill to McCaffrey, 16 June 1935 (IJA, Cahill Papers).
13 *Social Justice*, No.14 (December 1936), pp111-121.
14 Mrs B. Waters to Fr John McQuaid, 31 January 1937 (DDA, McQuaid Papers). Mrs Waters refers to this fact in her correspondence with Fr McQuaid. Fr McQuaid was a supporter of the Guilds of Regnum Christi, Headmaster of Blackrock College, and Chairman of the Catholic Headmasters Association.
15 Reports of the Commission of Inquiry into Banking Currency and Credit, 1938 (Dublin, 1938), pp694.
16 *ibid.*, p.510. The other signatory to this appendix was Professor George O'Brien.
17 *ibid.*, p.502.
18 *ibid.*, Minority report No.3, p.668.
19 *ibid.*, pp664-65.
20 *ibid.*, pp659-660.
21 *ibid.*, p.658; Bulmer Hobson, *Ireland Yesterday and Tomorrow* (Tralee, 1968), pp100-13.
22 A.J. Gaughan, *Alfred O'Rahilly, Vol.II Public Figure* (Dublin, 1989), p.313; interview with Fr Michael O'Carroll, CSSP, Blackrock College, a friend of Professor O'Rahilly.
23 *Cork Examiner*, 5 September 1938; *Irish Independent*, 5 September 1938.

[24] Vincent Grogan, 'The Banking Commission Report', *Bonaventura* (Winter 1938), pp92-93. Vincent Grogan was a prominent member of the Knights of St Columbanus.

[25] *ibid.*, pp82-83.

[26] 'Comment', *Hibernia* (January 1938), p.17.

[27] *ibid.*, September 1938, p.16.

[28] *ibid.*

[29] *ibid.*

[30] Memorandum, 17 April 1939 (NAI, Dept of Finance Files, S.10612); Joseph Lee, *Ireland 1912-1985* (Cambridge, 1989), p.564.

[31] ibid., Lee, *Ireland 1912 -1985*, p.564.

[32] *ibid.*

[33] *ibid.*, p.200.

[34] *ibid.*

[35] *ibid.*

[36] Ronan Fanning, *The Irish Department of Finance 1922-1958* (Dublin, 1978), p. 359; interview with John Waldron, 10 July 1996. John Waldron is a son of one of the founders of An Rioghacht.

[37] Ronan Fanning, *op. cit.*, p.363; An Rioghacht, minutes of the Ard Comhairle, 1937-1948, refer only briefly to these 'difficulties'.

[38] Ronan Fanning, *op. cit.*, p.365.

[39] Mary E. Daly, *Industrial Development and Irish National Identity, 1922-1939* (Dublin, 1992), p.153.

[40] *ibid.*

[41] Reports of the Commission of Inquiry into Banking Currency and Credit, 1938 (Dublin, 1938), pp502-10.

[42] *An Rioghacht Bulletin* (Autumn, 1937), p.7. Address by Fr Edward Coyne SJ.

[43] Ronan Fanning, *op. cit.*, p.359; Eithne MacDermott, *Clann Na Poblachta* (Cork, 1998), pp394-406.

[44] *Studies*, No.27 (1938), p.394.

[45] *ibid.*, p.395.

[46] *ibid.*

[47] *ibid.*, p.406.

[48] Edward Coyne, 'The Encyclicals and the Banking Commission', *Irish Monthly* (February 1939), p.76.

[49] *ibid.*

[50] *ibid.*

[51] *ibid.*, p.80.

[52] *ibid.*, p.90.

[53] P.J. O'Loghlen, 'The Encyclicals and the Banking Commission', *Irish Monthly* (March 1939), pp297-304. This article consisted of a reply and a refutation of Fr Coyne's allegations.

[54] *ibid.*, p.298.

[55] *ibid.*, p.304.

[56] Denis Fahey, 'Off Sterling – The Report of our Private Banking Commission, with Comments on the Official one', *Hibernia* (May 1938), pp9-10.

[57] Cardinal MacRory to Edward Cahill, 10 June 1938 (IJA, Cahill Papers). The Cardinal requested that An Rioghacht be established in the North as 'An Arm of Catholic Action'.

[58] Fr Patrick Power to Fr John Fahey, Provincial, 16 October 1933 (IJA, Cahill Papers).

[59] Edward Cahill to Provincial, 16 May 1934 (IJA, Cahill Papers).

[60] CTSI pamphlet No.1383/SE.22 (Dublin, 1936), p.20.

[61] *ibid.*, p.24.

[62] Provincial to Edward Cahill, 6 February 1935 (IJA, Cahill Papers).

[63] Edward Cahill to Provincial, 4 April 1935 (IJA, Cahill Papers).

[64] *Irish Press*, 28 August 1938; *Irish Independent*, 28 August 1938.

[65] *ibid.*

[66] *Irish Independent*, 29 August 1938.

[67] P.J. Connolly to Edward Cahill, 20 August 1938 (IJA, Cahill Papers). Fr P.J. Connolly was the Editor of *Studies*.

[68] Patrick Bartley to Provincial, 31 August 1938 (IJA, Bartley Papers).

[69] Kiernan to Canavan, 29 August 1938 (IJA, Cahill Papers).

[70] Canavan to Provincial, 30 August 1938 (IJA, Cahill Papers).

[71] *ibid.*

[72] *ibid.*

[73] *ibid.*

[74] Jesuit Constitution Committee, 24 September–18 October 1936, Session IV, 15 October 1936 (IJA, Bartley Papers).

[75] Edward Coyne to Provincial, 1 September 1938 (IJA, Coyne Papers).

[76] *ibid.*

[77] Provincial to Edward Cahill, 25 October 1936 (IJA, Cahill Papers).

[78] *ibid.*

[79] James Meenan, *George O'Brien: A Biographical Memoir* (Dublin, 1980), p.138.

[80] *Irish Press*, 19 October 1938.

[81] Alfred O'Rahilly, *Money* (Cork, 1942).

[82] *ibid.*

[83] *The Standard*, 7 March 1941.

[84] *Irish Independent*, 1 April 1941.

[85] *ibid.*

[86] Anthony J. Gaughan, *Alfred O'Rahilly, Vol.III, Controversialist, Part II, Catholic Apologist* (Dublin, 1993), p.82.

[87] *National Student* (May 1941), p.4.

[88] James Beddy, 'Monetary Policy in Eire', *Studies* Vol.XXX (September 1941), p.44.

[89] *The Standard*, 7 November 1941.

[90] *ibid.*, December 1941; January 1942.

[91] Press censorship reviews, *The Standard* (NAI, Dept Justice D14/36).

[92] J.H. Whyte, *op. cit.*, p.71.

[93] Alfred O'Rahilly, *Money* (Cork, 1942), p.ix.

[94] *ibid.*, p.xiv.

[95] *ibid.*, ppxx–xxi.

[96] *ibid.*, p.xvi, 628.

[97] *ibid.*, p.642.

[98] James Meenan, *George O'Brien: A Biographical Memoir* (Dublin, 1980), p.138.

[99] Alfred O'Rahilly, 'Aquinas versus Marx', *Studies*, Vol.32 (1943), p.81.

[100] George O'Brien, 'The Impact of The War on the Irish Economy', *Studies*, Vol.35 (1946), p.217.

[101] George O'Brien, *An Essay on the Economic Effects of the Reformation* (London, 1923), p.121.

[102] George O'Brien, *An Essay on Medieval Economic Teaching* (London, 1920), p.227.

[103] *ibid.*

[104] George O'Brien, *Economic Relativity* (Dublin, 1942), p.26.

[105] *ibid.*, p.26.

[106] *ibid.*, p.29.

[107] *ibid.*, p.32.

[108] George O'Brien, *Economic Effects of the Reformation* (London, 1923), p.175.

[109] George O'Brien, *Economic Relativity*, p.32.

[110] James Meenan, *op. cit.*, p.191.

[111] *Leinster Leader*, 19 July 1941; *Irish Press*, 19 July 1941.

VI

[1] Peter McKevitt, *Proposals for the Initiations of a Scheme of Catholic Action in Ireland* (Vatican, 1939).

[2] *ibid.*, p.5, 15.

[3] J.H. Sheridan to John Costelloe, 18 January 1938 (CYMS, Costelloe Correspondence).

[4] *Programme of Catholic Action*, May 1937 (CYMS, Drumcondra Branch).

[5] J.H. Sheridan to John Costelloe, 17 February 1938 (CYMS, Costelloe Correspondence).

[6] J.P. McPolin, 'The Work of Muintir Na Tíre', *Irish Monthly*, Vol.64 (1936), pp319-325. Dr James McPolin was the Co. Limerick Medical Officer of Health. He was also chairman of the Limerick Branch of the Irish Medical Association. An amateur theologian, he had a long-standing interest in Catholic Action, and was a prominent member of the Knights of St Columbanus and the Irish Guild of Catholic Doctors. In 1934, he had spoken on the importance of the lay apostolate at the Annual CTSI Congress, which was devoted to the subject of Catholic Action. The following year he spoke about vocational organisation at a Muintir Na Tíre Rural Week-end. He had adopted as his guiding principle the motif '*Sentire cum Ecclesia*' ('On Guard with the Church'); Report of inquiry into the housing of the working classes of the city of Dublin 1939-1943 (Dublin, 1944); Professor J.W.T. Dillon 'Slum Clearance: Past and Present', *Studies*, Vol.34 (1945), pp13-20.

[7] J. Waters, 'Diseases of the Social System', *Irish Ecclesiastical Record*, 5th Series, Vol.52 (July-Dec 1938), pp392-93.

[8] *The Irish Times*, 24 December 1977. Article by Roland Burke Savage, 'Towards the Development of a Social Conscience in the Catholic Church in Ireland: 1891-1939'.

[9] Roland Burke Savage, 'A Problem of Catholic Action: The formation of Lay Leaders', *Irish Ecclesiastical Record*, 5th Series, Vol.53 (1939), pp30-46.

[10] Report on the Present Position of Catholic Action in Ireland, 1936 (IJA, Catholic Action Files).

[11] *ibid.*

[12] *ibid.*

[13] *Evening Herald*, 3 March 1942. See also, Mairin Johnston, *Around the Banks of Pimilico* (Dublin, 1985), pp115-225; Ruth Barrington, *Health Medicine and Politics in*

Ireland, 1900-1970 (Dublin, 1987), pp348; Gerald Fee, *The Effects of World War II on Dublin's Low-Income Families, 1939-1945*, PhD Thesis, UCD, 1996.

[14] Eamonn MacThomais, *Me Jewel and Darling Dublin* (Dublin, 1974), pp19-23.

[15] Catholic Social Service Conference, *50 years of the CSSC* (Dublin, 1991), p.4.

[16] Hilda Tweedy, *A Link in the Chain, the Story of the Irish Housewives Association 1942-1992* (Dublin, 1992), p.143.

[17] Mary E. Daly, *The Spirit of Earnest Inquiry: The Statistical and Social Inquiry Society of Ireland, 1847-1997* (Dublin, 1997), p.121.

[18] *ibid.*, p.122

[19] *The Society of St Vincent De Paul in Ireland: A sketch by a member* (Dublin, 1945), p.19.

[20] Society of St Vincent De Paul, minutes of the conference of St Frances Xavier, Synge Street, Dublin, 1939-1943.

[21] Sick and Indigent Roomkeepers' Society to Dublin Corporation, 28 March 1943 (Sick and Indigent Roomkeepers' Society, Palace Street, Dublin 2.) This charity has been in existence since 1790 and has been described as Dublin's 'oldest charity' by Deirdre Lindsay in *Dublin's Oldest Charity: The Sick and Indigent Roomkeepers' Society 1790-1890* (Dublin, 1990).

[22] Society of St Vincent De Paul Annual Reports, 1939-1945.

[23] Gerard Fee, *The effects of World War II on Dublin's Low-Income Families, 1939-1945*, p.238.

[24] Sick and Indigent Roomkeepers' Society, Annual Report, 1943, p.2.

[25] *Journal of the Irish Free State Medical Union* (July 1941), p.12.

[26] Catholic Social Services Conference, *50 years of the CSSC* (Dublin, 1992), p.4.

[27] Dáil Reports, 22 November 1943, Col.28.

[28] Report of the Department of Local Government and Public Health, 1941-1942, p.21.

[29] *The Standard*, 28 March 1941.

[30] *ICD, 1945*, p.672.

[31] Dáil Debates, Vol.XCVIII, 12 December 1945, 14 December 1945.

[32] Leon O'Broin, *Frank Duff* (Dublin, 1982), pp57-70.

[33] Frontispiece of *Christus Rex* Journal, established in 1945.

[34] George Clune, *Christian Social Reorganisation* (Dublin, 1940).

[35] *ibid.*, p.506.

[36] C.B. Daly, 'Christian Rex Society', *Christus Rex*, Vol.1, No.1 (1947), pp29-33. C.B. Daly was later to become Cardinal Cathal Daly.

[37] *Handbook of the Catholic Social Services Conference, 1945* (Dublin, 1945).

[38] The principle of subsidiarity in essence, as recommended by *Quadragesimo Anno*, 1931.

[39] Muintir Na Tíre, *Official Handbook for Parish Guilds and Councils*, 1940-1941.

[40] *The Irish Times*, 11 March 1941.

[41] CTSI minutes of the Committee of Management, 1941. Confidential memorandum, 31 March 1941, written by Frank O'Reilly of the Society.

[42] Eugene Kavanagh to Frank O'Reilly, 8 March 1941 (CTSI, CSSC Correspondence). Kavanagh was the Supreme Secretary of the Knights of St Columbanus. Frank O'Reilly was also a member.

[43] Frank O'Reilly to CTSI Committee of Management, 31 March 1941; CTSI minutes of the Committee of Management, Confidential memorandum.

[44] CTSI minutes of the Committee of Management, March 1941, memorandum, 'Summary of views expressed at Conference'.

[45] CTSI Frank O'Reilly memorandum, 31 March 1941.

⁴⁶ Eugene Kavanagh to Frank O'Reilly, 21 March 1941 (CTSI).

⁴⁷ CTSI minutes of the Committee of Management, March 1941, notes on the committees of the new organisation.

⁴⁸ *ibid.*

⁴⁹ *Handbook of the Catholic Social Services Conference*, 1941-1942, pp13-14.

⁵⁰ *ibid.*, p.11.

⁵¹ *Social Workers' Handbook* (Dublin, 1942).

⁵² *Guide to the Social Services* (Dublin, 1945), Introduction.

⁵³ CTSI pamphlet No.1643/MM.119 (Dublin, 1942); 1718/MM.120; 1919/MM.121; 1720/MM.122.

⁵⁴ CTSI Annual Reports, 1939-45.

⁵⁵ Report of the Commission concerning the Second House of the Oireachtas (Dublin, 1936), p.2.

⁵⁶ *ibid.*

⁵⁷ Anthony J. Gaughan, *Alfred O'Reilly, Vol.II, Public Figure* (Dublin, 1989), p.276.

⁵⁸ Report of the Commission concerning the Second House of the Oireachtas (Dublin, 1936), p.2.

⁵⁹ Anthony J. Gaughan, *Memoirs of Senator Joseph Connolly, 1885-1961, A Founder of Modem Ireland* (Dublin, 1996), p.277, 391.

⁶⁰ *ibid.*

⁶¹ *Irish Independent*, 14 May 1937.

⁶² *ibid.*

⁶³ *ibid.*, *Catholic Herald*, 7 May 1937; Alfred O'Rahilly, *Thoughts on the Constitution* (Dublin, 1937), p.60.

⁶⁴ Anthony J. Gaughan, *Alfred O'Rahilly, Vol.I, Academic* (Dublin, 1986), pp149-50.

⁶⁵ John Murphy, *The College: A History of Queen's/University College, Cork* (Cork, 1995), p.270.

⁶⁶ Dermot Keogh, *Twentieth-Century Ireland* (Dublin, 1994), p.104.

⁶⁷ Report of the Commission on Vocational Organisation, 1943 (Dublin, 1944), par.57-8, 513.

⁶⁸ Joseph Lee, *Ireland 1912-1985* (Cambridge, 1989), pp271-87; Joseph Lee, 'Aspects of Corporatist Thought in Ireland: The Commission on Vocational Organisation, 1939-43' in A. Cosgrove and D. McCarthy (eds), *Studies in Irish History Presented to R. Dudley Edwards* (Dublin, 1979), pp324-42.

⁶⁹ Report of the Commission on Vocational Organisation, 1943, par.317.

⁷⁰ *ibid.*, par.716.

⁷¹ *ibid.*, par.702.

⁷² *ibid.*, par.701.

⁷³ *ibid.*

⁷⁴ *ibid.*, par.706.

⁷⁵ *ibid.*, par.712-715.

⁷⁶ *ibid.*, par.708.

⁷⁷ *ibid.*

⁷⁸ *ibid.*, par.716.

⁷⁹ *ibid.*

⁸⁰ *ibid.*, par.717.

⁸¹ *ibid.*, par.718.

[82] *The Standard*, 15 October 1943.
[83] *ibid.*
[84] Joseph Lee, 'Aspects of Corporatist Thought in Ireland', *op cit.*, p.328.
[85] James Meehan, *The Italian Corporative System* (Cork, 1944).
[86] Report of the Commission on Vocational Organisation, 1943, par.49-58.
[87] DAB, Review of James Meenan's book *The Italian Corporative System, Studies*, Vol.33,(Sept, 1944), p.422.
[88] James Meenan, *op. cit.*, pp335-42.
[89] DAB, Meenan Review, *Studies*, Vol.33 (September 1944), p.424.
[90] Michael Connolly, 'The Italian Experiment', *Irish Monthly*, Vol.72 (1944), p.104.
[91] *ibid.*, p.113.
[92] Notes written on the page margins of James Meenan's *The Italian Corporative System*, by Seán MacEntee.
[93] Ronan Fanning, *The Irish Department of Finance*, p.357.
[94] *ibid.*, p.357. Also RTÉ *Undercover*, 9 November 1997, T.K. Whitaker discussed changes in Department of Finance's economic attitudes and strategies, and the influence of Seán Lemass.
[95] James Meenan, *George O'Brien*, p.191.
[96] John Horgan, *Seán Lemass: The Enigmatic Patriot* (Dublin, 1997), p.110.
[97] George O'Brien, 'Capitalism in Transition', *Studies*, Vol.33 (1944), p.44.
[98] *ibid.*
[99] George O'Brien, 'A Challenge to Planners', *Studies*, Vol.33 (1944), p.217.
[100] *ibid.*
[101] George O'Brien, 'The Impact of War on the Irish Economy', *Studies*, Vol.35 (1946), p.190.
[102] Ronan Fanning, *The Irish Department of Finance*, pp384-85.
[103] RTÉ *Undercover*, 9 November 1997. T.K. Whitaker speaking on Seán Lemass.
[104] *ibid.* On the programme, parallels were drawn between Colbert (King Louis XIV's Economic Advisor) and Lemass.
[105] *The Economist*, 27 April 1946; *The New Statesman*, 27 April 1946.
[106] George O'Brien, 'John Maynard Keynes', *Studies*, Vol.35 (1946), p.198.
[107] *ICD, 1944*, p.668.
[108] *ibid.*, p.667.
[109] Ruth Barrington, *Health, Medicine and Politics in Ireland, 1900-1970* (Dublin, 1987), p.140.
[110] Mary E. Daly, *The Buffer State: The Historical Roots of the Department of the Environment* (Dublin, 1997), p.319.
[111] Ruth Barrington, *op. cit.*, pp141-42.
[112] *ibid.*
[113] John Dignan, *Social Security Outlines of a Scheme of National Health Insurance* (Sligo, 1945), p.36.
[114] *ibid.*, p.33.
[115] *Irish Independent*, 14 May 1945.
[116] *Irish Press*, 14 March 1945; *Irish Independent*, 14 March 1945; *The Irish Times*, 14 March 1945.
[117] *Seanad Debates*, Vol.XXIX 1323-4, 21 February 1945.
[118] *The Irish Times*, 21 August 1944, a series of six articles.
[119] CYMS Annual Report 1944; *ICD, 1944*, p.709; *Hibernia* (November 1944), p.1; *The Standard* 13-20 October 1944.

[120] *The Standard,* 25 August-20 October 1944, 2 March 1945.
[121] Peter McKevitt, 'The Report of the Vocational Commission', *Irish Ecclesiastical Record,* 5th Series, Vol. VXIV (December 1944), p.367; Peter McKevitt, *The Plan of Society,* pp197-98.
[122] Peter McKevitt, *The Plan of Society,* pp197-98.
[123] James Meenan, *Italian Corporative System,* p.342.
[124] Peter McKevitt, *op. cit.,* p.206.
[125] *The Standard,* 2 May 1945.
[126] CYMS, Annual Report of the Central Executive Committee, 1944/45.
[127] *Fairview CYMS Silver Jubilee Souvenir Book, 1919-1944,* p.29.
[128] CYMS, Report of the Provisional Committee to the General Meeting, 25 May 1945, p.1.
[129] Catholic Societies Vocational Organisation Conference (henceforth CSVOC), *A Synopsis of the Recommendations of the Vocational Organisation Commission* (Dublin, 1945), p.67.
[130] CSVOC, *The Diagrammatic Representation* (Dublin, 1945), p.15.
[131] *The Standard,* 1 June 1945.
[132] *ibid.,* 9 March 1945.
[133] *ibid.*
[134] *Irish Independent,* 8 March 1945.
[135] Eugene Goulding, 'Report on the CSVOC', *Christus Rex,* Vol. VIII, No.2 (April 1954), p.117.
[136] J. Gaughan, *Thomas Johnston* (Dublin, 1980), p.380.
[137] *ibid.,* p.394.
[138] Donal Nevin (ed.), *Trade Union Century* (Cork, 1994), pp122-23.
[139] John P. Swift, *John Swift: An Irish Dissident* (Dublin, 1991), p.92.
[140] Interview with Dan Norrison, a leading trade unionist who worked with both Larkins.
[141] Donal Nevin (ed.) of *cit.,* pp398-400.
[142] *ibid.*
[143] *Vocational Organisation Bulletin* No.12, January/February 1954.
[144] *ICD, 1955,* p.623.
[145] *ibid.,* pp636-37.
[146] *CYMS Quarterly Review,* January/February, 1954.
[147] *ibid.*
[148] *The Standard,* 1 June 1945.
[149] CYMS, Report of the 15th Annual Conference, 1946.
[150] *ICD, 1947,* p.692.
[151] *Hibernia* (November 1945), p.15.
[152] *ibid.*
[153] *ibid.,* p.16.
[154] *ibid.,* October 1945, p.18.
[155] George Clune, *The Medieval Gild System* (Dublin, 1943).
[156] Charles K. Murphy, *The Spirit of Catholic Action* (London, 1943), p.197; R.S. Devane, *The Failure of Individualism* (Dublin, 1948), p.342; Denis Fahey, *Money Manipulation and the Social Order* (Dublin, 1944), p.104.
[157] Ruaidhri Roberts, *The Story of the People's College, Dublin* (Dublin, 1986), p.135. A number of other developments illustrate the integralist spirit that was becoming more

pervasive in the mid-to-late 1940s. Fr Denis Fahey was disillusioned with the fact that the 1937 Constitution was not Catholic enough. As a result, he established the Marie Duce organisation in late 1945 to campaign not only for vocationalism but more importantly, that the State should formally recognise the Catholic Church as the one true Church. The organisation seemed to reflect some of the tendencies of the decade. In 1946, a member of An Rioghacht, George Gavan Duffy, was promoted to the Presidency of the High Court. He had a major input into Article 40 of the Constitution (on Fundamental Rights). As with Fr Edward Cahill, the founder of An Rioghacht, Duffy often equated Irish Nationalism with Irish Catholicism (an attitude widely held and expressed in Ireland during those decades), and tended to interpret the Constitution in the light of Catholic teaching, as in the famous Tilson Case of 1951. Reflecting current fears of 'Statism' among Vocationalists, he was a staunch defender of individual rights against the State. In the mid-to-late 1940s, as a result of his rulings, he gave Irish law a more distinctly Catholic cast.

158 Ronan Fanning, *The Irish Department of Finance*, Vol.359, p.408.
159 Eithne MacDermott, *Clann na Poblachta* (Cork, 1998), pp60-61, 188.
160 *ibid.*
161 *ibid.*
162 CSVOC Questionnaire (CYMS). One of the most important expressions and instruments of determined integralism in the post-war years was the Christus Rex organisation, which, although founded in 1941, was not given the necessary full approval by the Irish bishops until 1945. According to Fr Cathal Daly, one of the founders, 'Priests alone can provide authoritative guidance for the interpretation of Catholic social teaching, and effective leadership in its application.' – C.D. Daly 'The Christus Rex Society', *Christus Rex*, Vol.1, No.1 (January 1947), pp27-33.

VII

1 *Handbook of the Legion of Mary* (Dublin, 1954).
2 Whyte, J.H., *Church and State in Modern Ireland*, pp169-71.
3 Bolster, Evelyn, *The Knights of St Columbanus*, pp116-117.
4 Sheehan, Helena, *Irish Television Drama: A Society and Its Stories*, RTÉ, 1987.
5 Bolster, p.108.
6 Bolster, pp138-9.
7 Bolster, p.131.
8 CPRSI, Annual Report, 1950.
9 J. Anthony Gaughan, *Olivia Mary Taafe, 1832-1918 Foundress of St Joseph's Young Priests' Society* (Dublin, 1995), pp197-215.
10 According to James Dillon, Browne's cabinet colleague, he had a quiet word with the moderate Archbishop of Tuam, Dr Walsh, in an attempt to defuse the row. Walsh agreed to try to calm down the controversy and secretly meet Browne. When Dillon told Browne, Browne went to Walsh's residence without first arranging an appointment. Walsh was away on Church business. In what Dillon saw as a disastrous error, Browne travelled to meet the neighbouring bishop, Dr Dignan, a 'lunatic' in Dillon's view and one of Browne's most trenchant critics. They had an argument that inflamed the situation. In revealing that he had originally gone down to see Walsh, Browne compromised the position of the potential go-between, who was

forced to row in reluctantly with his more hard-line colleagues.

[11] Gabriel Kelly *et al* (eds), *Irish Social Policy in Context* (Dublin, 1999), p.29.

[12] Maurice Manning, *James Dillon: A Biography* (Dublin, 2000), p.228.

[13] Dáil Debates, 11 April 1951, Vol.125, Col.641.

[14] *Irish Independent*, 23 May 1997; Noel Browne, *Against the Tide* (Dublin, 1986).

[15] James McPolin, 'Public Health Bill', *Christus Rex*, Vol.1, No.3, (July 1947), pp3–16. See also, Patrick J. Conway, 'The State in Economic Life', *Christus Rex*, Vol.2, No.2, (July 1948), p.16; T.F. MacNamara, 'In Memoriam', *Journal of The Irish Medical Association* (December 1955), p.395. This was a tribute to Dr McPolin.

[16] *ICD, 1952*, pp687–8.

[17] *Irish Weekly Independent*, 18 August 1951.

[18] J.H. Whyte, *Church and State in Modern Ireland*, p.272.

[19] Finola Kennedy, *Cottage to Crèche: Family Change in Ireland* (Dublin, 2003); *The Economic and Social Review*, Vol.33, No.2 (Summer/Autumn 2002), pp259–262.

[20] Whyte, pp317–18.

[21] *Irish Press*, 18 October 1955.

[22] *Irish Press*, 20 October 1955.

[23] Conor McCabe, 'Catholics, Communist and Hat-Tricks: The Ireland v Yugoslavia Soccer International of 1955', *Irish Left Review* (July 2009); *Football Studies* II, I (2008); Whyte, pp317–18; John Cooney, *John Charles McQuaid, Ruler of Catholic Ireland* (Dublin, 2003), p.312.

[24] Mary Kenny, *Goodbye to Catholic Ireland* (UK, 1997), p.284.

[25] Bolster, p.140.

[26] Bolster, p.155.

[27] Mary Kenny *Goodbye to Catholic Ireland*, pp281–282.

[28] *The Irish Times*, 21 August 1976.

[29] Margaret Scanlan, *Culture and Customs in Ireland* (2006), p.41.

[30] Kenny, p.297.

[31] Kenny, pp292–97.

[32] Yvonne Scannell, 'The constitution and the role of women', in Brian Farrell (ed.), *De Valera's constitution and ours* (Dublin, 1988), p.129.

[33] R. Cullen Owens, *Smashing Times* (1984); Hilda Tweedy, *A Link in the Chain: The Story of the Irish Housewives' Association* (1992); Ailbhe Smyth (ed.) *Irish Women's Studies Reader* (1993).

[34] Kenny, pp274–99.

[35] Tom Hesketh, *The Second Partitioning of Ireland: The Abortion Referendum of 1983* (Dublin, 1990).

[36] Mary Kenny, *Goodbye to Catholic Ireland* (London, 1997), pp360–63.

[37] Hesketh, p.32.

[38] *ibid.*, p.4; *Response* (Summer 1982).

[39] Hilary Tovey, Perry Share, *A Sociology of Ireland* (2003), pp463–464.

[40] *ibid.*, p,29.

[41] Emily O'Reilly, *Masterminds of the Right* (Dublin, 1992).

[42] Green Paper on Abortion, Dublin, 2000.

[43] *ibid.* pp4, 12–13, 377–78; Joe Lee, *Ireland: 1912-1985, Politics and Society*, pp653–656; David Quinn, 'Ireland's Pro-Life Civil War', *Human Life Review* (Winter 2002); David Quinn, 'Pro-life extremists are their own worst enemies', *The Sunday Times*,

9 February 2003; Emily O'Reilly, *Masterminds of the Right* (Dublin, 1992); *The Irish Catholic*, 30 July 2009; Terence Brown, *Ireland: A social and cultural history 1922-85* (London, 1981); Diarmaid Ferriter, *The Transformation of Ireland 1900-2000* (London, 2004); Dermot Keogh, *Twentieth-Century Ireland: Nation and State* (Dublin, 1994); Joe Lee, *Ireland 1912-85: Politics and Society* (Cambridge, 1989); Cormac O'Grada, *A Rocky Road: The Irish economy since the 1920s* (Manchester, 1997); Paul Sweeney, *The Celtic Tiger: Ireland's economic miracle explained* (Dublin, 1998); John H. Whyte, *Church and State in Modern Ireland 1923-79* (Dublin, 1984); Jennifer E. Spreng, *Abortion and Divorce Law in Ireland* (USA, 2003); Ruth Barrington, *Health, Medicine, and Politics in Ireland, 1900-1970* (1987), Barry Desmond, *Finally and in Conclusion* (2000); Sandra McAvoy, 'The Regulation of Sexuality in the Irish Free State', in Elizabeth Malcolm and Greta Jones (eds) *Medicine, Disease, and the State in Ireland, 1650-1940* (1999); Michael Solomons, *Pro-Life? The Irish Question* (1992); J.H. White, *Church and State in Modern Ireland, 1923-1970* (1971). Lindsey Earner-Byrne, *Divorce, Contraception and Abortion*, (Thomas Gale, 2004); Finola Kennedy, *Cottage to Crèche: Family Change in Ireland*, (Dublin, 2001), p.302; *The Economic and Social Review*, Vol.33, No.2 (Summer/Autumn 2002), pp259-262; John Cooney, *John Charles McQuaid, Ruler of Catholic Ireland* (Dublin, 2003); Mary Kenny, *Goodbye to Catholic Ireland* (1997).

CONCLUSION

[1] Alec R. Vidler, *A Century of Social Catholicism, 1820-1830* (London, 1964), pp42-50.

[2] e.g. *Il Fermo Proposito*, 1905.

[3] See encyclical *Pascendi Gregis*, 1907, which interpreted modernism as a heresy.

[4] *Handbook of the Catholic Association* (Dublin, 1902), p.2.

[5] *The Leader*, 11 July 1901; D.P. Moran, *The Philosophy of Irish-Ireland* (Dublin, 1905).

[6] Edward Cahill, *The Catholic Social Movement* (Dublin, 1931), p.24.

[7] CTSI Annual Conferences, 1918-1921. The alignment of the Bishops and the majority of priests with the new Free State was a predictable stand for order and moderation. Though the priests abstained from involvement in party politics, distrust of de Valera was expressed from many a pulpit in 1927 when he sought a return to constitutional politics.

[8] *Irish Weekly Independent*, 17 September 1927. When, in advance of the September 1927 General Election, a questionnaire was sent by the CTSI on the Report of the Committee on Evil Literature to all candidates, a greater number of 'satisfactory guarantees' were elicited from Fianna Fáil nominees than from those of any other party or grouping. Séan Lemass, 'on behalf of the Fianna Fáil Party', pointed out that it was 'the declared policy of his party to take all necessary legislative action to prevent the importation of immoral literature and also to deal with the home product, which is frequently as bad, if not worse, than the imported variety'.

[9] CTSI Report of Annual Conference, 1923.

[10] Pius XI, *Ubi Arcano Dei*, 1922, par.58. See also par.54, 55, 56.

[11] The Synod of Maynooth 1927, 'Decrees which affect the Catholic Laity'. Translated with some notes by Revd M.J. Brown; CTSI pamphlet No.1104/MM.504 (Dublin, 1930), pp11-13.

[12] CTSI Annual Report, 20 June 1927, p.27.

[13] CTSI Annual Report, 30 June 1924, p.12.

[14] CTSI minutes of the Committee of Management, 1926-1927. See in particular the

meetings between Frank O'Reilly and Archbishop Byrne. Frank Duff similarly
had difficulties with Archbishop Byrne. When attempts were made between 1927
and 1930 to close down the hostels Duff had established, his reply was, 'Tell the
Archbishop to put it in writing and I'll nail it to the door.' (Leon O'Broin, *Frank
Duff* (Dublin, 1982), p.56.) (DDA, Byrne Papers, Laity File).

[15] Interview with Fr Michael O'Carroll, 15 September 1995 in Veritas House. Chancery
officials were prone to accuse Frank Duff of anti-clericalism because of his initiative
in the area of Catholic Action. According to Professor John Murphy, 'anti-clericalism
of the negative, secular type has of yet put down no roots in Ireland, it has to
contend with the massive weight of historical tradition'; John A. Murphy, 'Priests
and People in Modem Irish History, *Christus Rex*, Vol.23, No.4 (October 1969),
p.258. According to Professor Murphy, 'Gone, or going, are paternalism, autocracy,
the infuriating condescension of the churchman, the social eminence of the priest
buttressed too long by sycophants and clericalists, the social unease of too many
laymen in the presence of the priest, the childish fear that criticism of the clergy will
scandalise that fast-disappearing category, the simple faithful.'

[16] CTSI , *First Fifty Years, 1899-1949* (Dublin, 1949), p.21.

[17] *The Irish Times*, 29 September 1928.

[18] CTSI , *First Fifty Years, 1899-1949*, pp21-22.

[19] Proposed Amendments of Censorship of Publications Act, 1929 (NAI, Dept of An
Taoiseach, S.10241, Proposed Amendments 1938-40).

[20] CTSI Confidential Report on The Censorship of Theatres, 1938; Reports of CTSI
Censors, 1938-39.

[21] *United Ireland*, 22 December 1934.

[22] Report on Catholic Action in Ireland, 1936 (IJA, Catholic Action Files).

[23] *ibid.*, p.3.

[24] CYMS, Confidential questionnaire issued by the CYMS Vigilance Department,
September 1936; *Irish Weekly Independent*, 18 January 1936; *Evening Mail*, 24 January 1937.

[25] *The Irish Catholic*, 28 January 1937.

[26] An Rioghacht Correspondence, 1936-38 (IJA, Cahill Papers).

[27] Alfred O'Rahilly, *Thoughts on the Constitution* (Dublin, 1937), pp3-4.

[28] *Irish Independent*, 11-15 May 1937.

[29] *ibid.*

[30] *Catholic Herald*, 7 May 1937.

[31] Reports of the Commission of Inquiry into Banking, Currency and Credit, 1938, p.571.

[32] *ibid.*, minority report No.3, p.668.

[33] *ibid.*

[34] *Cork Examiner*, 5 September 1938; *Irish Independent*, 5 September 1938.

[35] Edward J. Coyne, 'Report of The Banking Commission', *Studies* (Autumn 1938),
pp394-406.

[36] Connolly to Cahill, 25 October 1938 (LLA, Cahill Papers).

[37] George O'Brien, *Economic Relativities* (Dublin, 1942), p.26.

[38] Peter McKevitt, *Report on Catholic Action, 1939* (Vatican, 1939). This report had been
commissioned by the Irish Catholic hierarchy and was the basis for the discussions.

[39] *The Irish Times*, 3 March 1939. Report of the first meeting of the Commission on
Vocational Organisation, 2 March 1939. The Taoiseach, Éamon de Valera, attended
and explained the task the government was entrusting to the Commission.

[40] *ibid.*

[41] Report of the Commission on Vocational Organisation, 1943 (Dublin, 1944), par.706.

[42] J.P. Carroll and J.A. Murphy (eds), *De Valera and His Times* (Cork, 1983), p.114.

[43] *ibid.*, p.115.

[44] *Seanad Debates*, Vol.21, No.7113, July 1938.

[45] E.J. Coyne, 'Corporative Organisation of Society', *Studies*, Vol.33 (March 1934), p.193. The ambiguities surrounding the interpretation of *Quadragesimo Anno* were further exacerbated by the ambivalent alliance between the clergy and the laity in Catholic Action. That tension also reflected the reality that in the 1920s and 1930s, the social background of the great majority of the clergy made it difficult for them to identify themselves with working people, with working-class organisations, or with political movements operating outside the direct influence of the Church for the reform of the social system. The nineteenth-century ecclesiastical hostility to radical social action was echoed in Professor McKevitt's Report on Catholic Action in 1939.

[46] J. Kelleher to M. Moynihan, 6 February 1938. (NA, Dept of An Taoiseach, S10812A).

[47] CYMS, Annual Report of Central Executive, 1944-45; *Irish Weekly Independent*, 11 August 1945.

[48] James McPolin, 'Public Health Bill', *Christus Rex*, Vol.1, No.3 (July 1947), pp3-16. See also, Patrick J. Conway, 'The State in Economic Life', *Christus Rex*, Vol.2, No.2 (July 1948), p.16. The *Christus Rex* Journal in its early years voiced these fears of 'Statism'. Contributors seemed more anxious to pass moral judgements than to spend time amassing the facts. More pages were devoted to denunciations of excessive state intervention than to any other subject. According to Patrick Conway in the afforementiong article, 'Self-help through Muintir na Tíre is preferable to state assistance and the regulations made through vocational organisations are better than Civil Servant's red tape.' Similarly, McPolin was critical of the 1947 Public Health Bill, claiming that it contravened natural law and the Irish Constitution. He had already written on the importance of the family and similar themes in the *Limerick Leader* on 28 December 1946 in an article, 'The State is a Glutton for Power'. In this hard-hitting article, McPolin warned of the necessity for vigilance against any threat to the family from the state. McPolin lobbied public opinion and Church leaders, successfully, to recognise the dangers ahead. It was the Catholic Action movement and McPolin in particular who drew the Church's attention to the possible dangers in the 1947 Legislation. Under McPolin's influence also, the Limerick Branch of the Irish Medical Association became the 'outspoken antagonists against the proposed changes'.

[49] CTSI Annual Reports, 1939-45.

[50] *Survey of the Organised Lay Apostolate in Ireland* (1966), p.8.

[51] Tom Heskith, *The Second Partitioning of Ireland: The Abortion Referendum of 1983* (Dublin, 1990), pp12-13.

EPILOGUE

[1] Professor D. Vincent Twomey, *The End of Irish Catholicism?* (Dublin, 2003), p.129.

[2] *ibid.*, p.130.

INDEX

A

Abbey Theatre, 97, 183, 206
Abortion, 187-8, 193-4, 196, 198-202, 215
Academy of Christian Art, 86
AIM, 196
Ancient Order of Hibernians, 37, 46, 58-9, 111, 115, 205
Anti-Propaganda Committee, 106
Army Comrades Association, 114

B

Banking Commission, 125, 131, 137-9, 141, 144,
    147-51, 156-7, 179
Belfast Catholic Association, 24
Belvedere Newsboys' Club, 39, 160
Beveridge Report, 160, 172-3
Binchy, William, 201
Blueshirts. See also, Fine Gael, 9, 114, 116, 164
Boran, Nixie, 110
Brennan, Joseph, 138, 149, 169
Browne, Dr Noel, 180, 186-8, 196
Browne, Fr Stephen. see also, Central Catholic Library,
    Censorship, 52, 56, 82, 85-6
Byrne, Alfie, 99-100, 160
Byrne, Archbishop Edward, 42, 45, 53, 55, 61, 65-6, 69,
    72-5, 77, 83, 89, 101 ,123, 156, 205

C

C Case, 201
Cahill, Fr Edward SJ. See also, An Rioghnacht, 16,
    54-8, 113, 120-2, 124-5, 127-33, 135-6, 138-40,
    146-9, 154, 161, 174, 180, 183, 207-9
Casti Connubii, 64, 130, 133, 195
Catholic Able-Bodied Men's Association, 105
Catholic Actionists, 39, 42, 69, 83, 98-9, 102, 108, 111,
    119, 122-3, 127, 133, 136, 138, 141, 143, 145, 154, 165,
    175, 189-90, 192, 195, 204-6, 208, 210, 212-3
Catholic Association, 11, 16, 24-6, 37, 60
Catholic Association for International Relations, 86, 182
Catholic Bulletin, 57, 81, 104, 118-9, 124
Catholic Boy Scouts of Ireland, 65, 107, 184, 192
Catholic Cinema and Theatre Patron's Association, 213
Catholic Commercial Club, 20, 123, 138-9
Catholic Communications Centre, 185
Catholic Defence League, 123, 214
Catholic Defence Society, 11, 25-6, 40, 53, 116, 203, 214
Catholic Emancipation, 42, 54, 62, 81
Catholic Emancipation Centenary, 1929, 43, 46, 77, 81,
    124, 205
Catholic Girl Guides of Ireland, 42, 65, 205
Catholic Laymen's Committee, 25
Catholic Literature Crusade, 21, 214
Catholic Newspaper Campaign, 82
Catholic Protection and Rescue Society of Ireland,
    12, 37, 75, 185
Catholic Social Guild, 13, 36, 122, 125
Catholic Social Week. See also, CYMA, 13, 61, 74,
    123-5, 161, 205, 207
Catholic Social Services Conference (Crosscare). See
    also, CSSC, 164, 183, 210, 212
Catholic Social Welfare Bureau, 185
Catholic Societies Vocational Organisation
    Conference (CSVOC), 174, 211
Catholic Stage Guild, 97
Catholic Truth Society of Ireland, 9, 12, 20-2, 31, 45,
    50, 86, 193, 203
Catholic University Graduates Association, 19
Catholic Women's Federation, 65
Catholic Workers' College, 70, 179, 193
Catholic Writers' Association, 86
Catholic Writers' Guild, 81, 86
Censorship, 9, 15, 29, 33-4, 43, 51, 74, 78-82, 87,
    92-101, 129, 151, 181, 183, 193, 203, 205-6

Censorship Board, 51, 91, 93-5, 98, 206

Censorship of Films Act, 1923, 96

Censorship of Films (Amendment) Act, 1925, 97-8

Censorship of Publications Act, 1929, 93-5, 193, 206

Central Catholic Library, 82, 86, 105

Chains or Change, 192, 196

Chair of Catholic Action and Sociology, 125

Chesterton, G.K., 73, 113

Christus Rex, 189, 196

Christus Rex Society, 161, 196, 212

Civardi, Luigi, 42, 122, 204

Clann na Poblachta, 9, 144, 17980, 187-8, 213

Clongowes Union, 20

Clongowes Wood Summer School, 127

Cóir, 202, 215

Columbian Knights, 53

Commission on Banking, 67

Commission on Emigration, 194, 212

Commission on Vocational Organisation, 39, 65, 142, 151, 160, 162, 164, 166, 170, 173-8, 196, 210-1

Commission on the Status of Women, 197

Committee on Evil Literature, 63

Communism, 9, 49, 58, 103-15, 120, 123, 157, 184, 190-1, 206-7

Constitution of Ireland, 9, 126, 132, 138, 142, 183, 194, 197-9, 202, 207, 214

Contraception, 62-3, 89, 188, 193-200

Conway, Patrick, 189

Cork Angelic Warfare Association, 85, 107, 214

Costello, John, 60-1, 110, 187-8

Coyne, Fr Edward, 39, 113, 118, 121, 137-8, 133, 144-6, 148-51, 154, 169, 179, 209, 211

CPRSI, 38, 75

Criminal Law Amendment Act, 1935, 194, 197

Crofts, Fr Ambrose, 60-1, 108, 120-1, 123

CSSC, 161-4, 172, 210

CSVOC, 174-80, 193, 211

CTAFI, 79-81

CTSI. see also, Catholic Truth Society of Ireland, 9, 12, 17, 22-3, 31-8, 40-54, 57,59-60, 62-5, 68-73, 75-9, 81-98, 104-6, 109, 111, 113, 119-21, 123-4, 127, 138, 146, 162, 164, 174, 181, 185, 194, 204-6, 210-12, 214

Cumann na nGaedhael, 67, 78, 80, 87-8, 105, 114-5, 141, 206

CYMS, 9, 24, 33-4, 37, 43, 46, 59-61, 64-5, 68, 77, 83, 100-1, 104-11, 117, 112-5, 155-7, 161, 172, 174, 178, 181, 200-1, 205, 207, 213-4

D

De Valera, Éamon, 55, 95, 104-5, 112-4, 123, 126-36, 138, 140-8, 154, 158, 163-6, 170-1, 195, 207-8, 210

Deeny, James, 188

Department of Finance, 137-8, 140-1, 143-4, 149, 151, 154, 168, 170-1, 208

Devane, Fr Richard, 41, 52, 72, 823, 85-6, 100, 132

Dignan, Bishop John, 173, 178

Dignan Plan, 173-4, 179-80

Divorce, 49, 87, 96, 129, 134, 193-4, 200-2, 213, 215

Draft Constitution, 126-7, 133, 135-6, 165-6

Dublin Vigilance Association, 96

Dublin Well Woman Centre, 197

Duff, Frank. See also, Legion of Mary, 38, 52, 65-8, 70, 72, 75, 77, 123, 156, 161, 163, 181, 193, 205

Duffy, George Gavan, 55, 134, 183

E

Eason's, 84-5

Eight Amendment of the Constitution of Ireland, 1983, 199, 202, 214

Eucharistic Congress (1932), 46, 77, 113, 124, 126, 205

F

Fahey, Fr Denis, 57, 120, 127, 131-2, 146, 182-3, 213

FAI, 190-2

Family and Media Association, 202-215

Family Solidarity, 200, 202, 214

Fascism, 9-10, 116, 153, 170, 177

Father Mathew Union, 78

Fertility Guidance Company, 197

Fianna Fáil, 9, 49, 69, 91, 112-4, 116-7, 125, 132, 136-9, 141-3, 162, 166, 172, 176, 180, 187, 198, 202, 207-8

Fennell, Nuala, 196

Fine Gael, 9, 99, 114-7, 180, 188, 198, 201, 207

First Minority Report, 143-4, 150, 208

The Framework of a Christian State, 57, 120, 122, 127, 130, 132, 146, 161, 207

Freemasonry and the Anti-Christian Movement, 57

Freemasons, 57-9, 63

G

Glynn, Sir Joseph, 47, 55, 66, 72-3, 75, 105, 123

Good Literature Crusade, 82

Grogan, Vincent, 131, 142

Guilds of Regnum Christi, 119, 122-3, 140, 191, 205

H

Hanafin, Senator Des, 202

Handbook for Catholic Social Workers in Dublin, 39

Handbook for Catholic Action, 50-1, 82

Haughey, Charles, 198

Hayes, Canon, 113, 121-2, 190

Health (Family Planning) Act, 197-8

Hesketh, Tom, 199
Hibernia, 119, 126, 133, 142, 146, 178-9, 207
Hobson, Bulmer, 138-9, 140, 149, 180
Hogan, James, 105, 113, 116-7, 121
Horgan, John, 23, 59-60, 115-6, 171
Human Life Ireland, 201
Humanae Vitae, 192-6

I

Intoxicating Liquor Commissions, 78, 80
Iona Institute, 202, 215
Irish Christian Front, 111-2, 123, 155, 161, 205, 207, 214
Irish Countrywomen's Association, 197
Irish Family League, 195, 200
Irish Guild of Catholic Doctors, 127, 157, 201
Irish Guild of Catholic Nurses, 52, 204
Irish Housewives Association, 159, 196-7
Irish Medical Association, 187, 189
Irish Messenger, 38-9, 41, 54, 64, 105, 120
Irish Pro-Life Amendment, 199
Irish Retail and Newsagents Association, 81, 83, 88
Irish Vigilance Association, 12, 32, 45, 81, 88, 96, 203, 206
Irish Women's Liberation Movement, 193-7
Irish Women Workers' Union, 176-7
Irishwomen United, 197

J

Jesuit Submission, The, 129-30
Joint Committee of Women's Societies and Social
    Workers, 195
John Paul II Society, 202, 215

K

Kenny, Mary, 194-6
Kerr, James B., 39-40
Keynes, John Maynard, 144, 170-2
Knights of St Columbanus, 9, 27, 40, 43, 53-4, 59, 68-9,
    96, 111, 116, 119-20, 125-6, 131, 133, 142, 156, 162-3,
    181, 183, 189, 191, 193-5, 200-1, 204, 209, 211, 213-4

L

Labour Party, 110, 112, 143, 176
Lamentabili Sane, 28
Larkin, Jim, 35, 37, 39, 74, 107, 121, 176-7
The Leader, 19, 34, 58, 81
League for Social Justice, 119, 137-8, 141, 144, 147,
    155, 205, 207
League for Social Justice and Charity, 123
Legion of Decency, 98-9, 101-2, 206
Legion of Mary, 9, 38, 42, 65-6, 68, 70, 72, 77, 96, 106,
    122, 155, 164, 181-2, 185, 192-3, 204-5, 213-4

League of the Kingship of Christ, 55, 191
Lemass, Seán, 10, 69, 113, 138, 160, 169, 171-3, 175-6, 193
Leo Guild, 36, 38
Licensed Vintners Association, 78, 80
Licensing Acts of 1924, 78
Limerick Confraterntiy of the Holy Family, 32, 45
Limerick Leader, 107, 189
Lisbon Treaty, 202, 215
Lucey, Fr Cornelius, 118-9, 126-8, 147, 194

M

MacBride, Seán, 114, 179-80, 187-8
MacDonald, Professor Walter, 22, 25, 29-30, 34
MacEntee, Seán, 69, 137, 158, 160, 166, 170, 172-3, 176
Mallon, Ita, 133
Magennis, William, 86, 96, 98
Manual of Catholic Action, 42, 51, 122, 204
Maria Duce, 182-3, 205, 213-4
Martyn, Edward, 24-5, 203
Maynooth College, 29, 67, 79, 123, 147
McAleese, Mary, 201
McKenna, Fr Lambert, 17-8, 36
McKevitt, Fr Peter, 67, 125, 155-8, 161, 172-4, 210
McKevitt Report, 156-8
McPolin, Dr James, 127, 157, 188-90, 211
McQuaid, Fr (Archbishop) John Charles, 65-9, 77, 97,
    120, 122-3, 127, 130-3, 136, 140, 160-2, 164, 179,
    184, 187-8, 191, 194, 205, 208, 210
Meenan, James, 127, 151, 169-70, 173-4
Mercier Society, 67-8, 161, 205
Modernism, 15, 18, 28-31, 44
Modest Dress and Deportment Crusade (MDDC),
    63-4, 204
Monto, 66-7, 72, 75
Moran, David Patrick, 19-20, 24, 31, 58, 81, 203
Mother and Child Campaign, 202, 215
Muintir na Tíre, 67, 104, 113-5, 121-4, 141, 147, 156-7,
    161-4, 174, 178, 181, 185-90, 193, 201, 205-7, 210, 214
Murphy, William Martin, 25, 36-7
Murphy, Professor Charles K., 120, 179

N

National Council of Women in Ireland, 195
National Guard, 114-5
National Vocational Assembly, 162, 166-9, 174, 178, 210
Nell-Breunig, 117, 121
Non Abbiamo Bisogno, 51, 117, 144, 209
Nugent, John D., 58-9
Nugent, Peter, 115
Nugent, T.P., 37

O

O'Brien, George, 39-70, 145, 149-54, 169-72, 209
O'Broin, Leon, 66-8
O'Carroll, Revd Dr Michael, CSSP, 68
O'Donovan, Fr Gerald, 17-8, 25, 30-1
O'Duffy, General Eoin, 78, 80, 114-6, 170
Ó Faoláin, Seán, 30, 68, 97-8, 205
Offences Against the Person Act (1861), 193, 198
O'Higgins, Kevin, TD, 47-8, 69-70, 78, 80, 85, 90-1, 96
O'Keefe, Denis, 119
O'Keefe, Eoin, 55, 140
O'Kelly, Seán T., 69, 126, 169-70, 188
O'Loghlen, Peadar, TD, 55, 139-43, 145, 149
O'Neill, Canon James, 39
O'Rahilly, Alfred, 40, 70-1, 106, 111, 113-4, 121, 123, 125, 127, 137-45, 149-55, 158, 165-6, 169, 170, 174, 179, 208-9
O'Reilly, Emily, 200
O'Reilly, Frank, 73-5, 83-4, 87, 89-91, 94-5, 111, 123, 127, 138, 155, 162-3, 200

P

Pascendi Gregis, 15, 28-30
Pillar of Fire Society, 67-8, 161, 205
Pioneer Total Abstinence Association, 24, 78-80
Pius X, 12-5, 23, 25, 28, 32-5, 39-42, 61, 203-4
Pius XI, 42-3, 47, 51, 61, 77, 103, 121, 126-7, 204, 206
Pro-Life Amendment Campaign, 198-200
Pro-Life Campaign, 202

Q

Quadragesimo Anno, 103-4, 112-21, 124-6, 130, 133, 144, 152-3, 166, 206-7, 209-11

R

Rape Crisis Centres, 197
Report on the Censorship of Theatres, 97
Report of the Commission on Vocational Organisation, 39, 154, 162, 164, 166, 170, 173-4, 177-8, 210-11
Report of the Evil Literature Committee, 86
Report of the Commission of Inquiry into Banking, Currency and Credit 1938, 208-10
Revolutionary Workers' Group, 105, 107, 109
An Rioghacht, 42, 55-7, 67-8, 70, 77, 96, 98-101, 104, 109, 113, 120, 125-7, 131-9, 141-9, 154-7, 161, 174, 179-80, 183, 191, 193, 204-10
Robinson, Senator Mary, 196-7
Rural Weeks, 124-5

S

Scheme for Social Re-construction, 56
Sick and Indigent Roomkeepers' Society, 159
Society for the Protection of the Unborn Child, 199
Spanish Civil War, 9, 112, 207
The Standard, 106, 150-1, 160, 169, 174-6, 178-9
St John Bosco Society, 185
St Joseph's Young Priests' Society, 66, 186, 213
St Patrick's Anti-Communist League, 107-8
St Vincent de Paul Society, 11, 23, 38-40, 43, 47, 50, 65-7, 72, 75, 106, 120, 123, 159, 163-4, 179, 184-5, 210, 213
Summer Schools, 55, 123, 125, 207
Synod of Maynooth (1927), 37, 49-50, 55, 61-4, 83, 204
Synod of Thurles (1850), 45, 50

T

Taafe, Olivia Mary, 186
Temperance Movement, 35, 79-81
Third Minority Report, 140-1, 143-9, 179-80, 208
Thrift, Professor, 92-3
Tierney, Professor Michael, 86, 93, 113, 116-7, 121-2, 165, 211
Tilson Case, 183, 248

U

Ubi Arcano Dei, 42-4, 47, 61, 72, 204
United Ireland, 115-6
United Ireland Party, 114
Up and Doing, 51, 98, 119

V

Vigilance, 27-9, 31, 38, 43, 52, 68, 77, 81-8, 96, 101, 104-11, 117, 157, 189, 203-7, 212-3

W

Waldron, Patrick, 7, 55, 127
Waters, Mrs Berthon, 55, 138-40, 157, 179-80
Whitaker, T.K., 171, 193
Women's Right to Choose Group, 197

X

X Case, 1992, 199, 201

Y

Youth Defence, 201-2, 214-5
Yugoslavia, 112, 184, 190-2

Z